African Americans in Sports

Volume 2

African Americans in Sports

Volume 2

Edited by David K. Wiggins

SHARPE REFERENCE
an imprint of M.E. Sharpe, Inc.

ST. PHILIP'S COLLEGE LIBRARY

SHARPE REFERENCE

Sharpe Reference is an imprint of M.E. Sharpe INC.

M.E. Sharpe INC.
80 Business Park Drive
Armonk, NY 10504

© 2004 by M.E. Sharpe INC.

All rights reserved.

No part of this publication may be reproduced, stored in a retrieval system or transmitted in any form or by any means, electronic, mechanical, photocopying, recording, or otherwise, without the prior permission of the copyright holders.

Library of Congress Cataloging-in-Publication Data

African Americans in sports / David K. Wiggins, editor.
   p. cm.
   Includes bibliographical references and index.
   ISBN 0-7656-8055-6 (set : alk. paper)
   1. African Americans—Sports—Dictionaries. 2. African American athletes—Biography—Dictionaries. 3. African Americans—Societies, etc.—Dictionaries. 4. Sports—United States—Societies, etc.—Dictionaries. I. Wiggins, David Kenneth, 1951– II. Sharpe Reference (Firm)

GV583.A567 2003
796'.092'2—dc21
[B]

2002042799

Cover photo credits: Satchell Paige, David Robinson, and Serena Williams provided by AP/Wide World Photos; male runner (© ArtToday, Inc.); boxer (© Corbis Images/Picturequest)

Printed and bound in the United States of America

The paper used in this publication meets the minimum requirements of
American National Standard for Information Sciences--Permanence of
Paper for Printed Library Materials,
ANSI Z 39.48.1984.

MV (c) 10 9 8 7 6 5 4 3 2 1

CONTENTS

VOLUME 1

Topic Finder xiii
Acknowledgments xxi
Contributors xxiii
Introduction xxvii
Hank Aaron 1
Cleveland Abbott 2
Kareem Abdul-Jabbar 3
Lucinda Adams 4
Herb Adderley 5
Agents 6
David Albritton 7
Muhammad Ali 8
Marcus Allen 9
American Tennis Association 10
Nate Archibald 11
Henry Armstrong 11
Arthur Ashe, Jr. 12
Emmett Ashford 13
Evelyn Ashford 15
Autobiographies 15
Ernie Banks 19
Charles Barkley 19
Don Barksdale 20
Baseball 21
Basketball 23
Dick Bass 26
Don Baylor 27
Elgin Baylor 28
Bob Beamon 28
Bill Bell 29
Bobby Bell 30
James "Cool Papa" Bell 31
Walter Bellamy 32
Dave Bing 33
Black Coaches Association 33
Black Sports Magazine 35
Black Women in Sports Foundation 35
Black World Championship Rodeo 36
Mel Blount 36
Edward Bolden 37
Barry Bonds 38
Bob Boozer 39
John Borican 40
Joseph Bostic 41
Ralph Boston 41
Bowling 42
Boxing 43
Valerie Brisco-Hooks 46
Louis Brock 48
Vivian Brown Reed 49
Jim Brown 49
Larry Brown 50
Roger Brown 51
Roosevelt Brown 52
Kobe Bryant 52
Matthew Bullock 53
Daniel Burley 54
Sol Butler 55
Lee Calhoun 57
Roy Campanella 57
Earl Campbell 58
Milt Campbell 59
John Carlos 60
Harold Carmichael 61

CONTENTS

J.C. Caroline 61	Wayne Embry 95
Cris Carter 62	Julius Erving 96
Central Intercollegiate Athletic Association 63	Lee Evans 97
Wilt Chamberlain 64	Patrick Ewing 97
John Chaney 65	Mae Faggs 99
Ezzard Charles 66	Fencing 99
Oscar Charleston 67	Films 100
Civil Rights 67	George Flippin 102
Nat "Sweetwater" Clifton 71	Curt Flood 103
Coaches and Managers 71	Tiger Flowers 104
Alice Coachman 72	Charles Follis 105
William Montague Cobb 74	Football 105
Chuck Cooper 75	Phil Ford 108
Ted Corbitt 75	George Foreman 109
Russ Cowans 76	Bob Foster 110
Isabelle Daniels 77	Rube Foster 110
Adrian Dantley 77	Joe Frazier 112
Ernie Davis 78	Walter Frazier, Jr. 112
John Henry Davis 79	Clarence Gaines 115
Dominique Dawes 80	Jake Gaither 115
Anita De Frantz 81	Willie Galimore 116
Gail Devers 82	Joe Gans 117
Eric Dickerson 83	Mike Garrett 117
Harrison Dillard 84	Zina Garrison 118
George Dixon 85	Willie Gault 119
Larry Doby 86	George Gervin 119
Arthur Dorrington 87	Althea Gibson 120
Charles Drew 87	Bob Gibson 121
Howard Drew 88	Josh Gibson 122
Walter Dukes 89	Artis Gilmore 122
Eastern Colored League 91	Golf 123
Harry Edwards 91	Ed Gordon, Jr. 125
Teresa Edwards 92	Ned Gourdin 126
Lee Elder 93	Frank Grant 127
Carl Eller 94	Edward Gray 127
Jimmy Ellis 95	Joe Greene 128
	Gus Greenlee 129

CONTENTS

Hal Greer 130
Ann Gregory 130
George Gregory, Jr. 131
Rosey Grier 132
Ken Griffey, Jr. 132
Florence Griffith-Joyner 133
Tony Gwynn 134
Gymnastics 134
Marvin Hagler 137
Harlem Globetrotters 137
Franco Harris 139
Frank Hart 139
Connie Hawkins 140
Bob Hayes 141
Elvin Hayes 142
Marques Haynes 142
Spencer Haywood 143
Thomas Hearns 144
Edwin Bancroft Henderson 145
Rickey Henderson 146
Stephanie Hightower 146
Calvin Hill 147
Grant Hill 148
Jim Hines 149
Historically Black Colleges and
   Universities 149
Historiography 153
Jerome Brud Holland 157
Steve Holman 157
Larry Holmes 158
Horse Racing 159
William Dehart Hubbard 161
Martha Hudson 161
Eddie Hurt 162
Lula Mae Hymes 162
Ice Hockey 165
International Afro-American Sports
   Hall of Fame and Gallery 167
International League of Baseball
   Clubs in America and Cuba 167
Interscholastic Athletic Association
   of Middle Atlantic States 168
Monte Irvin 169
"Rajo" Jack 171
Bo Jackson 171
Levi Jackson 172
Mannie Jackson 173
Peter Jackson 173
Reggie Jackson 175
Joe Jeannette 176
Bernie Jefferson 176
Cornelius Johnson 177
Jack Johnson 178
John Henry Johnson 179
Magic Johnson 180
Michael Johnson 181
Rafer Johnson 182
Robert L. Johnson 183
William "Judy" Johnson 184
Barbara Jones 185
David "Deacon" Jones 186
Hayes Jones 186
K.C. Jones 187
Marion Jones 188
Sam Jones 188
Wali Jones 189
Michael Jordan 190
Jackie Joyner-Kersee 191
Leroy Kelly 195
Ray Kemp 195
Leroy Keyes 196
Don King 196
William "Dolly" King 197
Lacrosse 199
Sam Lacy 199

CONTENTS

Betty Jean Lane	200
Dick Lane	201
Sam Langford	201
Bob Lanier	202
League of Colored Base Ball Clubs	203
Meadowlark Lemon	203
Buck Leonard	205
Sugar Ray Leonard	206
Lisa Leslie	207
Jerry LeVias	208
Carl Lewis	209
John Henry Lewis	210
Oliver Lewis	211
William Henry Lewis	211
Joe Lillard	212
Gene "Big Daddy" Lipscomb	213
Sonny Liston	213
Floyd Little	214
Earl Lloyd	214
John Henry Lloyd	215
Ronnie Lott	216
Joe Louis	217
James LuValle	218

VOLUME 2

Topic Finder	xiii
Acknowledgments	xxi
Contributors	xxiii
Introduction	xxvii
Biz Mackey	219
John Mackey	220
Karl Malone	221
Moses Malone	222
Effa Manley	223
Danny Manning	224
Madeline Manning-Mims	224
Bob Marshall	225
Jim Marshall	226
Ollie Matson	227
Margaret Matthews	227
William Clarence Matthews	228
Willie Mays	229
Willie McCovey	230
Mildred McDaniel	231
Pam McGee	231
Edith McGuire	232
John McLendon	233
Sam McVey	234
Ralph Metcalfe	235
Rod Milburn	235
Cheryl Miller	236
Bobby Mitchell	237
Tom Molineaux	237
Art Monk	238
Earl Monroe	239
Eleanor Montgomery	240
Warren Moon	240
Archie Moore	241
Lenny Moore	242
Joe Morgan	243
Edwin Moses	244
Marion Motley	245
Calvin Murphy	246
Isaac Murphy	247
Eddie Murray	248
National Association of Colored Base Ball Clubs of the United States and Cuba	251
National Bowling Association	252
Negro American League	252
Negro League Baseball Museum	253
Negro National League	254
Negro Southern League	255
Renaldo Nehemiah	256
New York Pioneer Club	256
New York Renaissance Five	257

CONTENTS

Don Newcombe	258
Ozzie Newsome	259
Ken Norton	260
William Nunn, Jr.	260
William Nunn, Sr.	261
Dan O'Brien	263
Hakeem Olajuwon	263
Olympic Games	264
Shaquille O'Neal	268
Buck O'Neil	269
Willie O'Ree	270
Jesse Owens	271
R.C. Owens	272
Satchel Paige	275
Jim Parker	276
Floyd Patterson	276
Mickey Patterson	277
Walter Payton	278
Drew Pearson	279
Calvin Peete	280
Don Perkins	281
Joe Perry	282
Tidye Pickett	282
George Poage	283
Fritz Pollard	283
Fritz Pollard, Jr.	284
Cum Posey	285
Kirby Puckett	286
Pythian Base Ball Club (Philadelphia)	287
Racial Theories	289
Ted Radcliffe	292
Rainbow Coalition for Fairness in Athletics	293
Ahmad Rashad	293
George Raveling	295
Dwight Reed	296
Willis Reed	297
Mel Renfro	297
Butch Reynolds	298
Ray Rhodes	298
Ted Rhodes	299
Willy T. Ribbs	300
Jerry Rice	301
Nolan Richardson	301
Bill Richmond	302
Ric Roberts	303
Oscar Robertson	303
Paul Robeson	305
David Robinson	306
Eddie Robinson	307
Frank Robinson	308
Jackie Robinson	309
Mack Robinson	310
Sugar Ray Robinson	311
Rodeo	312
Johnny Rodgers	313
Wilbur Rogan	315
George Rogers	315
Mike Rozier	316
Wilma Rudolph	317
Bill Russell	318
Cazzie Russell	319
Ralph Sampson	321
Barry Sanders	321
Deion Sanders	322
Gale Sayers	323
Charlie Scott	324
Wendell Scott	324
Shady Rest Golf and Country Club	325
Art Shell	326
John Shippen, Jr.	327
Wilmeth Sidat-Singh	327
Charlie Sifford	328
Paul Silas	329
Ozzie Simmons	330

CONTENTS

Willie Simms 330
O.J. Simpson 331
Mike Singletary 332
"Duke" Slater 332
Slavery 333
Lucy Diggs Slowe 334
Bruce Smith 335
"Bubba" Smith 336
Emmitt Smith 337
John Smith 338
Ozzie Smith 339
Tommie Smith 340
Wendell Smith 341
Fred Snowden 341
Bill Spiller 342
Leon Spinks 343
Michael Spinks 343
Sportswriters 344
Dave Stallworth 346
Willie Stargell 346
Norman "Turkey" Stearnes 347
Louise Stokes 348
Toni Stone 348
George Stovey 349
Vivian Stringer 350
Woody Strode 351
Lynn Swann 352
Swimming 353
Sheryl Swoopes 354
George Taliaferro 357
Jack Tatum 357
Reece "Goose" Tatum 358
Charley Taylor 359
John Baxter Taylor 359
Lawrence Taylor 360
Marshall "Major" Taylor 361
Ed Temple 362
Tennis 363

Debra Thomas 364
Frank Thomas 365
Isiah Thomas 366
John Thomas 367
David Thompson 367
John Thompson 368
Eddie Tolan 369
Gwen Torrence 370
Track and Field 371
Emlen Tunnell 374
Mike Tyson 374
Wyomia Tyus 375
United Golfers Association 377
Wes Unseld 378
Gene Upshaw 378
Volleyball 381
Wake-Robin Golf Club 383
Joe Walcott 383
Herschel Walker 384
Leroy Walker 385
Mel Walker 386
Moses Fleetwood Walker 386
Charlie Ward 387
Paul Warfield 388
Chester Washington 389
Gene Washington 389
Kenny Washington 390
Ora Washington 391
Quincy Watts 391
Weightlifting and Bodybuilding 392
Reginald Weir 394
Willie Wells 395
Charlie West 396
Howard Wheeler 397
Bill White 397
Jo Jo White 398
Reggie White 399

CONTENTS

Sherman White 400
Sol White 400
Willye White 401
Mal Whitfield 402
Sydney Wicks 403
Archie Williams 403
Doug Williams 404
Ike Williams 404
Joseph "Smokey" Williams 405
Serena Williams 406
Venus Williams 407
Bill Willis 407
Harry Wills 408
Maury Wills 409
Rollo Wilson 410
Dave Winfield 410
Jimmy Winkfield 411
Kellen Winslow 412
Women 413
Lynette Woodard 415
John Woodruff 416
Eldrick "Tiger" Woods 416
James Worthy 418
Wrestling 418
Andrew S. "Doc" Young 421
Buddy Young 421
Fay Young 422
Paul "Tank" Younger 423
Chronology 425
Bibliography 431
General Index I-1
Sports Index I-21

TOPIC FINDER

INDIVIDUALS

Hank Aaron 1
Cleveland Abbott 2
Kareem Abdul-Jabbar 3
Lucinda Adams 4
Herb Adderley 5
David Albritton 7
Muhammad Ali 8
Marcus Allen 9
Nate Archibald 11
Henry Armstrong 11
Arthur Ashe, Jr. 12
Emmett Ashford 13
Evelyn Ashford 15
Ernie Banks 19
Charles Barkley 19
Don Barksdale 20
Dick Bass 26
Don Baylor 27
Elgin Baylor 28
Bob Beamon 28
Bill Bell 29
Bobby Bell 30
James "Cool Papa" Bell 31
Walter Bellamy 32
Dave Bing 33
Mel Blount 36
Edward Bolden 37
Barry Bonds 38
Bob Boozer 39
John Borican 40
Joseph Bostic 41

Ralph Boston 41
Valerie Brisco-Hooks 46
Louis Brock 48
Vivian Brown Reed 49
Jim Brown 49
Larry Brown 50
Roger Brown 51
Roosevelt Brown 52
Kobe Bryant 52
Matthew Bullock 53
Daniel Burley 54
Sol Butler 55
Lee Calhoun 57
Roy Campanella 57
Earl Campbell 58
Milt Campbell 59
John Carlos 60
Harold Carmichael 61
J.C. Caroline 61
Cris Carter 62
Wilt Chamberlain 64
John Chaney 65
Ezzard Charles 66
Oscar Charleston 67
Nat "Sweetwater" Clifton 71
Alice Coachman 72
William Montague Cobb 74
Chuck Cooper 75
Ted Corbitt 75
Russ Cowans 76
Isabelle Daniels 77
Adrian Dantley 77

TOPIC FINDER

Ernie Davis 78
John Henry Davis 79
Dominique Dawes 80
Anita De Frantz 81
Gail Devers 82
Eric Dickerson 83
Harrison Dillard 84
George Dixon 85
Larry Doby 86
Arthur Dorrington 87
Charles Drew 87
Howard Drew 88
Walter Dukes 89
Harry Edwards 91
Teresa Edwards 92
Lee Elder 93
Carl Eller 94
Jimmy Ellis 95
Wayne Embry 95
Julius Erving 96
Lee Evans 97
Patrick Ewing 97
Mae Faggs 99
George Flippin 102
Curt Flood 103
Tiger Flowers 104
Charles Follis 105
Phil Ford 108
George Foreman 109
Bob Foster 110
Rube Foster 110
Joe Frazier 112
Walter Frazier, Jr. 112
Clarence Gaines 115
Jake Gaither 115
Willie Galimore 116
Joe Gans 117

Mike Garrett 117
Zina Garrison 118
Willie Gault 119
George Gervin 119
Althea Gibson 120
Bob Gibson 121
Josh Gibson 122
Artis Gilmore 122
Ed Gordon, Jr. 125
Ned Gourdin 126
Frank Grant 127
Edward Gray 127
Joe Greene 128
Gus Greenlee 129
Hal Greer 130
Ann Gregory 130
George Gregory, Jr. 131
Rosey Grier 132
Ken Griffey, Jr. 132
Florence Griffith-Joyner 133
Tony Gwynn 134
Marvin Hagler 137
Franco Harris 139
Frank Hart 139
Connie Hawkins 140
Bob Hayes 141
Elvin Hayes 142
Marques Haynes 142
Spencer Haywood 143
Thomas Hearns 144
Edwin Bancroft Henderson 145
Rickey Henderson 146
Stephanie Hightower 146
Calvin Hill 147
Grant Hill 148
Jim Hines 149
Jerome Brud Holland 157

Steve Holman 157	Sam Lacy 199
Larry Holmes 158	Betty Jean Lane 200
William Dehart Hubbard 161	Dick Lane 201
Martha Hudson 161	Sam Langford 201
Eddie Hurt 162	Bob Lanier 202
Lula Mae Hymes 162	Meadowlark Lemon 203
Monte Irvin 169	Buck Leonard 205
"Rajo" Jack 171	Sugar Ray Leonard 206
Bo Jackson 171	Lisa Leslie 207
Levi Jackson 172	Jerry LeVias 208
Mannie Jackson 173	Carl Lewis 209
Peter Jackson 173	John Henry Lewis 210
Reggie Jackson 175	Oliver Lewis 211
Joe Jeannette 176	William Henry Lewis 211
Bernie Jefferson 176	Joe Lillard 212
Cornelius Johnson 177	Gene "Big Daddy" Lipscomb 213
Jack Johnson 178	Sonny Liston 213
John Henry Johnson 179	Floyd Little 214
Magic Johnson 180	Earl Lloyd 214
Michael Johnson 181	John Henry Lloyd 215
Rafer Johnson 182	Ronnie Lott 216
Robert L. Johnson 183	Joe Louis 217
William "Judy" Johnson 184	James LuValle 218
Barbara Jones 185	Biz Mackey 219
David "Deacon" Jones 186	John Mackey 220
Hayes Jones 186	Karl Malone 221
K.C. Jones 187	Moses Malone 222
Marion Jones 188	Effa Manley 223
Sam Jones 188	Danny Manning 224
Wali Jones 189	Madeline Manning-Mims 224
Michael Jordan 190	Bob Marshall 225
Jackie Joyner-Kersee 191	Jim Marshall 226
Leroy Kelly 195	Ollie Matson 227
Ray Kemp 195	Margaret Matthews 227
Leroy Keyes 196	William Clarence Matthews 228
Don King 196	Willie Mays 229
William "Dolly" King 197	Willie McCovey 230

TOPIC FINDER

Mildred McDaniel	231
Pam McGee	231
Edith McGuire	232
John McLendon	233
Sam McVey	234
Ralph Metcalfe	235
Rod Milburn	235
Cheryl Miller	236
Bobby Mitchell	237
Tom Molineaux	237
Art Monk	238
Earl Monroe	239
Eleanor Montgomery	240
Warren Moon	240
Archie Moore	241
Lenny Moore	242
Joe Morgan	243
Edwin Moses	244
Marion Motley	245
Calvin Murphy	246
Isaac Murphy	247
Eddie Murray	248
Renaldo Nehemiah	256
Don Newcombe	258
Ozzie Newsome	259
Ken Norton	260
William Nunn, Jr.	260
William Nunn, Sr.	261
Dan O'Brien	263
Hakeem Olajuwon	263
Shaquille O'Neal	268
Buck O'Neil	269
Willie O'Ree	270
Jesse Owens	271
R.C. Owens	272
Satchel Paige	275
Jim Parker	276
Floyd Patterson	276
Mickey Patterson	277
Walter Payton	278
Drew Pearson	279
Calvin Peete	280
Don Perkins	281
Joe Perry	282
Tidye Pickett	282
George Poage	283
Fritz Pollard	283
Fritz Pollard, Jr.	284
Cum Posey	285
Kirby Puckett	286
Ted Radcliffe	292
Ahmad Rashad	293
George Raveling	295
Dwight Reed	296
Willis Reed	297
Mel Renfro	297
Butch Reynolds	298
Ray Rhodes	298
Ted Rhodes	299
Willy T. Ribbs	300
Jerry Rice	301
Nolan Richardson	301
Bill Richmond	302
Ric Roberts	303
Oscar Robertson	303
Paul Robeson	305
David Robinson	306
Eddie Robinson	307
Frank Robinson	308
Jackie Robinson	309
Mack Robinson	310
Sugar Ray Robinson	311
Johnny Rodgers	313
Wilbur Rogan	315
George Rogers	315
Mike Rozier	316

TOPIC FINDER

Wilma Rudolph 317	Vivian Stringer 350
Bill Russell 318	Woody Strode 351
Cazzie Russell 319	Lynn Swann 352
Ralph Sampson 321	Sheryl Swoopes 354
Barry Sanders 321	George Taliaferro 357
Deion Sanders 322	Jack Tatum 357
Gale Sayers 323	Reece "Goose" Tatum 358
Charlie Scott 324	Charley Taylor 359
Wendell Scott 324	John Baxter Taylor 359
Art Shell 326	Lawrence Taylor 360
John Shippen, Jr. 327	Marshall "Major" Taylor 361
Wilmeth Sidat-Singh 327	Ed Temple 362
Charlie Sifford 328	Debra Thomas 364
Paul Silas 329	Frank Thomas 365
Ozzie Simmons 330	Isiah Thomas 366
Willie Simms 330	John Thomas 367
O.J. Simpson 331	David Thompson 367
Mike Singletary 332	John Thompson 368
"Duke" Slater 332	Eddie Tolan 369
Lucy Diggs Slowe 334	Gwen Torrence 370
Bruce Smith 335	Emlen Tunnell 374
"Bubba" Smith 336	Mike Tyson 374
Emmitt Smith 337	Wyomia Tyus 375
John Smith 338	Wes Unseld 378
Ozzie Smith 339	Gene Upshaw 378
Tommie Smith 340	Joe Walcott 383
Wendell Smith 341	Herschel Walker 384
Fred Snowden 341	Leroy Walker 385
Bill Spiller 342	Mel Walker 386
Leon Spinks 343	Moses Fleetwood Walker 386
Michael Spinks 343	Charlie Ward 387
Dave Stallworth 346	Paul Warfield 388
Willie Stargell 346	Chester Washington 389
Norman "Turkey" Stearnes 347	Gene Washington 389
Louise Stokes 348	Kenny Washington 390
Toni Stone 348	Ora Washington 391
George Stovey 349	Quincy Watts 391
	Reginald Weir 394

TOPIC FINDER

Willie Wells 395
Charlie West 396
Howard Wheeler 397
Bill White 397
Jo Jo White 398
Reggie White 399
Sherman White 400
Sol White 400
Willye White 401
Mal Whitfield 402
Sydney Wicks 403
Archie Williams 403
Doug Williams 404
Ike Williams 404
Joseph "Smokey" Williams 405
Serena Williams 406
Venus Williams 407
Bill Willis 407
Harry Wills 408
Maury Wills 409
Rollo Wilson 410
Dave Winfield 410
Jimmy Winkfield 411
Kellen Winslow 412
Lynette Woodard 415
John Woodruff 416
Eldrick "Tiger" Woods 416
James Worthy 418
Andrew S. "Doc" Young 421
Buddy Young 421
Fay Young 422
Paul "Tank" Younger 423

SPORTS

Baseball 21
Basketball 23
Bowling 42
Boxing 43
Fencing 99
Football 105
Golf 123
Gymnastics 134
Horse Racing 159
Ice Hockey 165
Lacrosse 199
Olympic Games 264
Rodeo 312
Swimming 353
Tennis 363
Track and Field 371
Volleyball 381
Weightlifting and Bodybuilding 392
Wrestling 418

TEAMS

Harlem Globetrotters 137
New York Pioneer Club 256
New York Renaissance Five 257
Pythian Base Ball Club
 (Philadelphia) 287

INSTITUTIONS AND ORGANIZATIONS

American Tennis Association 10
Black Coaches Association 33
Black Sports Magazine 35
Black Women in Sports Foundation 35
Black World Championship Rodeo 36
Central Intercollegiate Athletic
 Association 63
Eastern Colored League 91
Historically Black Colleges and
 Universities 149

International Afro-American Sports Hall of Fame and Gallery 167
International League of Baseball Clubs in America and Cuba 167
Interscholastic Athletic Association of Middle Atlantic States 168
League of Colored Base Ball Clubs 203
National Association of Colored Base Ball Clubs of the United States and Cuba 251
National Bowling Association 252
Negro American League 252
Negro League Baseball Museum 253
Negro National League 254
Negro Southern League 255
Rainbow Coalition for Fairness in Athletics 293
Shady Rest Golf and Country Club 325
United Golfers Association 377
Wake-Robin Golf Club 383

KEY PERSONNEL, CULTURAL THEMES, AND SOCIAL ISSUES

Agents 6
Autobiographies 15
Civil Rights 67
Coaches and Managers 71
Films 100
Historiography 153
Racial Theories 289
Slavery 333
Sportswriters 344
Women 413

ACKNOWLEDGMENTS

I would like to express my deepest appreciation to all the contributors for their time, patience, and hard work. Their commitment to this project has been unwavering. Ellen Drogin Rodgers was indispensable during the final days of rewrites and was selfless, as usual. I would also like to thank my wife Brenda and two boys, Jordan and Spencer, for their constant support and understanding. Lastly, I would like to thank Lisa Reeves for her editorial assistance. This project could not have been completed without her help and expertise.

EDITOR
David K. Wiggins
George Mason University

CONTRIBUTORS

Donna Abruzzese
George Mason University

Ronald Althouse
West Virginia University

Logan Bailey-Perkins
University of Miami

C. Robert Barnett
Marshall University

Gai Ingham Berlage
Iona College

Jack W. Berryman
University of Washington

Mary Jo Binker
George Mason University

Gregory Bond
University of Wisconsin, Madison

Larry S. Bonura

Ron Briley
Sandia Preparatory School

Dana D. Brooks
West Virginia University

John M. Carroll
Lamar University

Amy M. Cawley
Salem Academy, Winston-Salem

Nicholas P. Ciotola
Senator John Heinz Pittsburgh Regional History Center

James R. Coates, Jr.
University of Wisconsin, Green Bay

Eddie Comeaux
University of California, Los Angeles

Doris R. Corbett
Howard University

Scott A.G.M. Crawford
Eastern Illinois University

Richard O. Davies
University of Nevada, Reno

Robert Davis
Yale University

Gregory H. Duquette
University of Alberta

Sara A. Elliott

Robert Epling
Reinhardt College

John D. Fair
Georgia College & State University

Albert J. Figone
Humboldt State University

John E. Findling
Indiana University Southeast

Rob Fink
McMurry University

Michael T. Friedman
University of Maryland

Alison M. Gavin
George Mason University

Gerald R. Gems
North Central College

Larry R. Gerlach
University of Utah

Steven P. Gietschier
The Sporting News

Dennis Gildea
Springfield College

Gregory S. Goodale
University of Illinois at Urbana-Champaign

Adolph H. Grundman
Metropolitan State College, Denver

Pamela Grundy

Susan Hamburger
Pennsylvania State University

CONTRIBUTORS

C. Keith Harrison
University of Michigan

Clay E. Harshaw
Guilford College

Billy Hawkins
University of Georgia

Leslie A. Heaphy
Kent State University

Debra A. Henderson
Ohio University

Adam R. Hornbuckle

Trisha M. Hothorn

Cecile Houry
University of Miami

David W. Hunter
Hampton University

J. Thomas Jable
William Paterson University

Rick Knott
St. Bonaventure University

Deane A. Lamont
Saint Mary's College

Rita Liberti
California State University, Hayward

Alar Lipping
Northern Kentucky University

Michael E. Lomax
University of Georgia

Richard D. Loosbrock
Adams State College

Stephen R. Lowe
Olivet Nazarene University

Angela Lumpkin
The University of Kansas

Bill Mallon
Duke University

Michael Marsh
Chicago Reader

Daniel S. Mason
University of Alberta

Keith McClellan

Daniel A. Nathan
Skidmore College

Murry R. Nelson
Pennsylvania State University

James E. Odenkirk
Arizona State University

Michael Oriard
Oregon State University

Steven J. Overman
Jackson State University

Troy D. Paino
Winona State University

Clyde Partin
Emory University

Adam Phillips
George Mason University

Robert Pruter
Lewis University

Danny Rosenberg
Brock University

Gary A. Sailes
Indiana University

Tracey M. Salisbury
University of North Carolina at Greensboro

Sue Scaffidi
Lenoir-Rhyne College

John R. Schleppi
University of Dayton

Raymond Schmidt

Kenneth L. Shropshire
University of Pennsylvania

Calvin H. Sinnette

David C. Skinner

Earl Smith
Wake Forest University

Maureen M. Smith
California State University, Sacramento

Donald Spivey
University of Miami

CONTRIBUTORS

Jim L. Sumner
North Carolina Museum of History

Richard A. Swanson
University of North Carolina at Greensboro

John A. Vernon
National Archives and Records Administration

Sara B. Washington
Michigan State University

John S. Watterson
James Madison University

Danielle A. Mincey White
George Mason University

Audrey A. Wiggins
University of North Carolina at Greensboro

Brenda P. Wiggins
George Mason University

Suzanne Wise
Appalachian State University

Jerry J. Wright
Pennsylvania State University at Altoona

Alison M. Wrynn
California State University, Long Beach

Susan G. Zieff
San Francisco State University

INTRODUCTION

African-American athletes have made extraordinary contributions to sport at both the national and international levels of competition. Since the nineteenth century, African-American athletes have achieved enormous success in interscholastic, college, Olympic, and professional sport. Although experiencing racial injustice and discrimination, such athletes as Tom Molineaux, Jack Johnson, Jesse Owens, Satchel Paige, Jackie Robinson, Althea Gibson, Muhammad Ali, Michael Jordan, Eldrick "Tiger" Woods, and Serena Williams have garnered fame and fortune and mesmerized people of all races for their athletic exploits. Perhaps more than anything else, the great performances of African-American athletes have served as examples of achievement and symbols of possibility for the African-American community and helped in the process of assimilation.

Over the last two decades an increasing number of scholars have recounted the story of African-American involvement in sport. These studies have included examinations of such topics as Negro league baseball, the role of sport in historically black universities, involvement of African-American athletes in predominantly white university sport, and biographies of notable African-American athletes and the racial inequities still existing in sport. Although varying in quality, these studies have all combined to provide a more complete picture of the experiences of African-American athletes and how the racial realities of this country have impacted sport at all levels of competition.

Included among these studies are several biographical encyclopedias that furnish good information on the individual accomplishments of some of this country's most famous African-American athletes. Perhaps the best known of these works are David L. Porter's *Biographical Dictionary of American Sports* (1988) and *African-American Sports Greats* (1995). This encyclopedia complements Porter's fine work and that of others by incorporating biographical entries, but it makes advances by also including topical and organizational entries. In addition, this encyclopedia stands apart from other reference works in that it includes large numbers of entries that deal with various aspects of sport behind segregated walls. Readers will find coverage of such notable all-black institutions as the Negro National League as well as such lesser-known parallel sport organizations as the American Tennis Association, the Central Intercollegiate Athletic Association, the National Bowling Association, the United Golfers Association, and the Black Coaches Association. This encyclopedia is unique, moreover, by virtue of the fact that it includes many entries on African-American coaches, managers, executives, entrepreneurs, and sportswriters. Only by including these individuals in the encyclopedia can a full understanding of sport in the African-American community be realized.

This encyclopedia is certainly not exhaustive in scope. The selection of entries was based on judgments about their significance to the African-American experience in sport and potential appeal to both the lay public and academic audience. Those entries that are included are written in a clear and concise fashion by contrib-

INTRODUCTION

utors who have expertise in some aspect of the African-American experience in sport. All of the contributors have either written about or shown a passion for the study of African-American athletes, race relations, or sport history. In each of the more than four hundred entries a great deal of attention is devoted to essential facts and details as well as to historical context and changes over time. Every effort has been made to provide more than a mere recounting of accomplishments and list of records and career statistics. Each entry also includes biographical references to the most important sources on the particular topic. Readers can turn to these sources as they pursue their own studies and seek additional information.

Biz MACKEY

Born July 27, 1897, Eagle Pass, Texas
Died 1959, Los Angeles, California
Baseball player and manager

His professional career spanned four decades, from 1918 to 1947. Mackey possessed a powerful throwing arm and a quick release. Homestead Grays owner Cumberland Posey ranked Mackey as Negro baseball's all-time greatest catcher. The switch-hitting Mackey led Hilldale to their first title in 1923, batting .364. The next year he hit .325, helping Hilldale earn an invitation to the first black World Series Championship against the Kansas City Monarchs. In 1925, the Hilldale Giants captured the series over the Monarchs. In 1927, Mackey was one of the most popular players on a team of Negro league All-Stars who became the first professional team to play in Japan. He later made two more Japanese trips with the Philadelphia Stars. From 1922 to 1931, Mackey compiled a .327 average, with a high of .365 in 1930. He batted over .300 every season from 1924 to 1931. In the first East-West All-Star game in 1933, he was chosen over Hall of Fame teammates Josh Gibson and Oscar Charleston to bat cleanup. He completed his career as player-manager for the Newark Eagles, guiding the team to the Negro World Championship in 1948. Mackey helped prepare his Newark Eagles Larry Doby, Don Newcombe, and Monte Irvin for the major leagues. Mackey was also responsible for the development of Roy Campanella. *Total Baseball* lists Mackey as one of the 400 greatest baseball players. In 1999, members of the Society for Baseball Research chose Mackey as the seventeenth greatest Negro league player.

Larry S. Bonura

Biz Mackey (second from left) with some of his Hilldale Giants teammates in 1927. *(National Baseball Hall of Fame Library, Cooperstown, NY)*

FURTHER READING

"'Biz'" Mackey: The Jolly Giant." *Negro League Baseball.com* (www.negroleaguebaseball.com/1999/September/biz_mackey.html).

Debono, Paul. "The Indianapolis ABCs: The Pride of the Negro Leagues." *Indiana Historical Society* (www.indianahistory.org/pub/traces/abcs.html).

Enders, Eric. "Timeline of International Baseball, 1847–Present." *EricEnders.com* (www.ericenders.com/internationalbb.htm).

"40 Greatest Negro League Figures by SABR." *Baseball Almanac* (www.baseball-almanac.com/legendary/lisabr40.shtml).

Holway, John B. *Blackball Stars*. Westport, CT: Meckler, 1988.

Holway, John B., and Bob Carroll. "The 400 Greatest." *Baseball Almanac* (www.baseball-almanac.com/legendary/li400gr.shtml).

Lanctot, Neil. *Fair Dealing and Clean Playing: The Hilldale Club and the Development of Black Professional Baseball, 1910–1932*. Jefferson, NC: McFarland, 1994.

National Baseball Hall of Fame (www.baseballhalloffame.org/hofers_and_honorees/hofer_bios/johnson_judy.htm).

John MACKEY

Born September 24, 1941, Queens, New York
Football player

John Mackey, one of six children of Walter and Dora Mackey, attended Hempstead High School in New York and Syracuse University. He joined the Baltimore Colts as a second-round draft pick in 1963. He played tight end for the Colts until 1971; in 1972 he joined the San Diego Chargers. Mackey was inducted into the Professional Football Hall of Fame in 1992.

Mackey was only the second player in the National Football League (NFL) to perform strictly as a tight end. A strong blocker but with breakaway speed, he was a scoring threat on every play. He was the first of this new breed of tight ends to make long runs routine. In 1966 he scored six touchdowns on plays of more than fifty yards. He was also noted for his brute force and willingness to use his forearm to gain space to catch a pass.

In addition to being named All-NFL in 1966 through 1968, Mackey also was a sound businessman. In 1967, for example, he owned a profitable carryout liquor shop in Baltimore. As professional football became more and more popular and TV rights began to top $45 million annually, NFL players began to doubt owners' claims that pro football was not a prudent investment and felt that they deserved a greater share of the league's income. When Mackey became president of the NFL Players Association in 1970, he worked hard to raise player income and was an effective catalyst and bridge between black and white players. Moreover, despite the risks involved (including being harassed, benched, traded, or even cut despite great play), he challenged the accounting figures furnished by the owners to both the U.S. Congress and the Players Association and led a player's strike that won significant gains. In 1972 he filed an antitrust suit that overturned the reserve clause in the NFL contract, opening the way to free agency.

Mackey did not find the road to enshrinement easy. His leading the NFL Players Association to an unprecedented players strike during the 1970 season nearly derailed his election to the Professional Football Hall of Fame. He was passed over fourteen times for induction into the hall, and it was not until the last year of eligibility as a modern player that he was finally elected.

During his professional career, Mackey caught 331 passes for 5,236 yards and thirty-eight touchdowns. Based on average yards per catch and touchdowns per game, he outperformed Mike Ditka, another great Hall of Fame tight end. Mackey was a durable player, missing only one game in his ten years in the NFL.

After pro football, Mackey became a business executive in Long Beach, California. He is a recipient of the NAACP Paul Robeson Award and became chairman of the board of the Community for Education Foundation in Los Angeles in 1993.

Keith McClellan

FURTHER READING

Carroll, Bob, Mike Gershman, David Neft, and John Thorn, eds. *Total Football II: The Official Encyclopedia of the National Football League.* New York: HarperCollins, 1999.

Chicago Tribune, July 29, 1993.

New York Times, January 26, 1992, August 2, 1992, and October 4, 1992.

Phelps, Shirelle, ed. *Who's Who Among Black Americans, 1994/5.* 8th ed. Detroit: Gale Research, 1994.

Karl MALONE

Born July 24, 1963, Summerfield, Louisiana
Basketball player

Karl Malone was raised by his mother, Shirley Ann, and stepfather, Ed Turner, after his father left home. Malone led Summerfield High School to three straight Louisiana state basketball championships. He then attended Louisiana Tech University, where he was three times named All-Conference and earned the nickname "the Mailman" for always delivering points in the clutch. After his junior year, Malone entered the 1985 National Basketball Association (NBA) draft, becoming the Utah Jazz's first round pick.

The six-foot nine-inch, 260 pound Malone, unusually fast and agile for his size, was named to the 1986 NBA All-Rookie team. In sixteen seasons with the Jazz he has become arguably the finest power forward in NBA history. A consistent, multidimensional scorer, going into the 2001–2002 season Malone was the NBA's

Utah Jazz forward Karl Malone grabbing a rebound in a 1992 game against the Miami Heat. *(AP/Wide World Photos)*

second-leading career scorer. Malone has averaged more than twenty points in fifteen consecutive seasons; his 25.9-point season average is the eighth best in league history. He ranks first in the number of seasons scoring more than 2,000 points and is second all-time in free-throw attempts and in field goals made. A complete player, Malone is second on NBA charts for defensive rebounds and fourteenth in total rebounds. During sixteen seasons he has missed only seven games, three from injury, and ranked fourth all-time in minutes played.

Thirteen times an All-Star, he is the only player named first-team All-NBA eleven years in a row (1989–1999). The MVP of the 1989 and 1993 All-Star Games, he was named the league's MVP 1997 and 1999. Malone was a member of the U.S. "Dream Team" that captured the gold medal in basketball in the 1992 and 1996 Olympics. He was named Utahn of the Year in 1997 for his civic and charitable activities.

Larry R. Gerlach

FURTHER READING

Deseret News, October 11, 1994.
Hubbard, Jan, ed. *The Official NBA Encyclopedia*. 3d ed. New York: Doubleday, 2000.
McCallum, Jack. "Big Wheel." *Sports Illustrated*, April 27, 1992, 62–74.
Salt Lake Tribune, March 24, 1996, May 19, 1997, and December 28, 1998.
USA Today, April 3, 1998.
Utah Jazz Media Guide. Salt Lake City: Utah Jazz, 2001.
Wiley, Ralph. "Does He Ever Deliver!" *Sports Illustrated*, November 7, 1988, 72–77.

Moses MALONE

Born March 23, 1955, Chesterfield County, Virginia
Basketball player

A twelve-time NBA All-Star, Malone was raised by his mother in a poor black neighborhood in Petersburg, Virginia. There basketball became the core of his life. Malone is most remembered as the first pro basketball player drafted out of high school. In 1974, he passed up a scholarship to attend the University of Maryland and at age nineteen signed a six-year contract with the ABA Utah Stars. In 1976 he moved to the NBA Houston Rockets. Primarily a center at six feet, ten inches and 255 pounds, Malone played the most games without fouling out (1,207) of any NBA player; he averaged twenty points a game for eleven years.

Malone was a serious and steady player,

Philadelphia 76ers center Moses Malone calling for the ball in a 1982 game against the Cleveland Cavaliers. *(AP/Wide World Photos)*

once called the "world's richest blue-collar worker." In 1979, Malone set the all-time record for offensive rebounds in one season (957) and led the Rockets to the NBA playoffs. In 1983 he led his team, the Philadelphia 76ers, to the championship over the dominant Los Angeles Lakers and was unanimously selected MVP for the series.

Malone retired in 1995 after twenty-one years in professional basketball (nineteen in the NBA). He is the third-leading rebounder (16,212) and fifth-leading scorer (27,409) in NBA history. He is first in offensive rebounds (6,731) as well as made free throws (8,531). Malone was elected to the Basketball Hall of Fame in May 2001.

Malone is married and has two children. He now dedicates much of his time to work with underprivileged children.

Donna Abruzzese

FURTHER READING

Lundgren, Hal. *Moses Malone: Philadelphia's Peerless Center.* Chicago: Regensteiner, 1983.

Mitchell, Fred. "Moses Malone Backs Miles' Jump to Pros." *Chicago Tribune*, June 28, 2000.

Moritz, Charles, ed. *Current Biography Yearbook.* 47th Annual Cumulation. New York: Wilson, 1986.

National Basketball Association (www.nba.com/history/mmalone).

Washington Post, May 31, 2001.

Effa MANLEY

Born March 27, 1900, Philadelphia, Pennsylvania
Died April 18, 1981, Los Angeles, California
Baseball owner

Manley was from 1935 to 1948 co-owner with her husband Abe Manley of the Brooklyn/Newark Eagles, a Negro National League team. Although most people assumed Effa was a light-skinned African American, in her autobiography she stated that actually she was white. She claimed to have been the illegitimate daughter of Bertha Gordon Brooks, a white seamstress, and John M. Bishop, a wealthy white financier who had a seat on the New York Stock Exchange. Throughout her life she culturally identified with African Americans.

During the 1930s and 1940s, Manley was one of the most colorful and influential people in Negro league baseball. In an era when women were second-class citizens and blacks had few, if any, rights, she managed to become a respected force not only in the Negro Baseball Leagues but also in the civil rights movement. When her husband acquired the Brooklyn Eagles franchise in 1935, Manley immediately assumed an active co-owner role by taking over the day-to-day business operations of the club. This allowed Abe to focus on player recruitment. In 1936, when the Brooklyn Eagles had difficulty competing with the Brooklyn Dodgers for fans, Abe Manley purchased the Newark Dodgers, a black semipro team, and moved the Brooklyn Eagles to Newark. The Brooklyn Eagles were now the Newark Eagles. The Manleys were active in the National Negro League organization. When Abe was elected treasurer, Effa managed the finances of the Negro National League, with the approval of its members.

Until her death in 1981 Manley devoted herself to keeping the history of Negro league baseball alive and trying to get the National Baseball Hall of Fame to recognize many of its outstanding players. In 1976 with the help of a professional writer, Leon Hardwick, she wrote a book titled *Negro Baseball . . . Before Integration.*

Gai Ingham Berlage

FURTHER READING

Berlage, Gai Ingham. *Women and Baseball: The Forgotten History.* Westport, CT: Greenwood Press, 1994.

Kirsch, George, Othello Harris, and Clarie Nolte, eds. *Encyclopedia of Ethnicity and Sports in the United States*. Westport, CT: Greenwood Press, 2000.

Manley, Effa, and Leon Hardwick. *Negro Baseball . . . Before Integration*. Chicago: Adam Press, 1976.

Overmyer, James. *Effa Manley and the Newark Eagles*. Metuchen, NJ: Scarecrow Press, 1993.

Danny MANNING

Born May 17, 1966, Hattiesburg, Mississippi
Basketball player

Danny Manning is the son of Edward, a former professional basketball player, and Darnelle, a teacher; he and wife, Julie, have two children of their own, Taylor and Evan. He is a graduate of Page High School (Greensboro, NC) and the University of Kansas, with a degree in public relations. Manning has played basketball for the Los Angeles Clippers, Atlanta Hawks, Phoenix Suns, Milwaukee Bucks, Utah Jazz, and Dallas Mavericks.

One of only two high school players invited to the 1984 Olympic Trials, Manning was a highly recruited All-American. In 1988, he led Kansas to the NCAA Championship, upsetting both favored Duke and Oklahoma. Manning was named tournament MVP with a thirty-one point, eighteen-rebound performance in the championship game. He was named College Basketball Player of the Year and finished his collegiate career as the number-two leading scorer in NCAA tournament history. Drafted first overall in 1988, Manning played in the 1993 and 1994 All-Star Games and won the NBA's 1998 Sixth Man Award.

Manning's near championship performance has been recognized as among the most memorable individual efforts in tournament history, and it has served as a model to young African-American athletes. He almost single-handedly led an injury-depleted and unheralded team to a series of upsets, leading to his remarkable performance in the championship.

Manning has been a member of the USA Board of Basketball Directors (1992–1994) and has served as spokesperson for the National Association of Police Athletic Leagues. He has also participated in the NBA's Reading Is Fundamental literacy program.

Gregory H. Duquette

FURTHER READING

Cravens, Jeff. "Oh Danny Boy." *Olympian*, July/August 1988, 14–17.

Heisler, Mark. "Nice While It Lasted." *Los Angeles Times*, August 25, 1988.

Hoffer, Richard. "Hard-Bitten Clipper." *Sports Illustrated*, February 21, 1994, 58–63.

Moran, Malcolm. "Manning Lifts His Whole Family to No. 1 Status." *New York Times*, April 5, 1988.

Madeline MANNING-MIMS

Born January 11, 1948, Cleveland, Ohio
Runner

One of five children, Manning was raised by her mother and stepfather. A graduate of John Hay High School in Cleveland, Tennessee State University, and Oral Roberts University, Manning overcame childhood spinal meningitis to become an Olympic gold medalist and world-class middle-distance runner.

Manning won her first Girls AAU National Championship at age seventeen, competing in the 440-yard dash as a member of a Cleveland city team. She soon joined the U.S. national team. At Tennessee State, Manning initially ran the 400-meter race but soon shifted to the 800 meters, in

Women's Track and Field All-America Women's Track and Field Team in the 880-yard race. Manning is a 1975 recipient of the Mobil Cup, but her greatest honors came in 1984, when she was inducted into U.S. National Track and Field Hall of Fame, and in 1987, with her induction into the International Women's Sports Hall of Fame. Manning is today an ordained minister within the Faith Christian Fellowship International. She is also a contemporary gospel singer and speaker.

Susan G. Zieff

See also: Ed Temple; Track and Field.

FURTHER READING
Davis, Michael D. *Black American Women in Olympic Track and Field*. Jefferson, NC: McFarland, 1992.
Newman, Steve. "Temple and the Tigerbelles." *Coaching Review* 4 (January/February 1981): 17–21.
Woolum, Janet. *Outstanding Women Athletes*. Phoenix, AZ: Oryx Press, 1998.

★ ★ ★

Madeline Manning-Mims on the podium following her world record breaking performance in the 800-meter final at the 1968 Olympic games in Mexico City. (AP/Wide World Photos)

which she won a gold medal at the 1968 Mexico City Olympics.

A four-time Olympic track team member (1968, 1972, 1976, 1980), Manning captained the U.S teams in the latter three games. She was the first American woman to win an Olympic gold medal in the 800 meters (1968), also setting an Olympic record. At the 1972 Munich Olympics, Manning won a silver medal in the 4 x 400-meter relay; four years later she was the first woman to break 2:00 in the 800 meters. Between 1967 and 1980, Manning won ten national indoor and outdoor titles in the 800 meters and the 880-yard dash. She set three world records and four American records.

A winner of numerous awards and honors, Manning was named to the 1972

Bob MARSHALL

Born March 12, 1880, Milwaukee, Wisconsin
Died August 27, 1958, Minneapolis, Minnesota
Football player

Bob Marshall was a graduate of Central High School in Minneapolis, Minnesota, and the University of Minnesota (1906). Marshall was an All-American football player at Minnesota, played semiprofessional football, and joined the newly organized National Football League. After his football career Marshall was employed by the State Department of Minnesota.

Marshall entered Minnesota in the fall of 1902 and began his college football career under the guidance of coach Dr. Henry L. Williams. He was an offensive and defensive left end; it was his play as offensive end that gained him acclaim. For two years he was a substitute, but in 1904 he became a starting player. In his first year as a starter, Minnesota's football team compiled lopsided victories: 65–0 over Carleton College, 32–0 over Iowa State, and 146–0 over Grinnell College. In the game against Grinnell Marshall scored seventy-two points: four touchdowns and thirteen field goals.

In 1904 Marshall led Minnesota to the Big Ten Championship, with a record of 13–0, and in 1905 and 1906 to second-place finishes in the Big Ten Conference. In 1905 he became the second African American to be selected as an All-American; he was selected again as an All-American in 1906.

After his graduation from Minnesota in 1906, Marshall went on to play semiprofessional football. In 1920 he joined the newly organized National Football League for a season with the Rock Island Independents. He returned to the NFL in 1925 to play his last season in professional football with the Duluth Kelleys. In 1971 Marshall was posthumously inducted to the College Football Hall of Fame.

Alar Lipping

FURTHER READING
Ashe, Arthur R., Jr. *A Hard Road to Glory—Football: The African American Athlete in Football*. New York: Amistad, 1988.
Chalk, Ocania. *Black College Sport*. New York: Dodd, Mead, 1976.
"Gopher History." *Eric Thrall.com* (www.ericthrall.com/gophers/football/).

★ ★ ★

Jim MARSHALL

Born December 30, 1937, Danville, Kentucky
Football player

Marshall was the "iron man" of the National Football League (NFL). During his twenty-year career (1960–1979), spent mostly with the Minnesota Vikings, Marshall, who played defensive tackle, never missed any of his team's 282 games, setting an NFL record that still stands for consecutive games played.

Marshall, who graduated from East High School in Columbus, Ohio, attended Ohio State University (OSU), where he played on two national championship teams and was named an All-American in 1958. OSU inducted Marshall into its Athletic Hall of Fame in 1978 and later named him to its All-Century team.

Marshall started his professional career in 1959 with the Saskatchewan Roughriders of the Canadian Football League and entered the NFL in 1960 with the Cleveland Browns. In 1961, Marshall was traded to the Vikings, where he played nineteen seasons and started in four Super Bowls. For seventeen of those seasons Marshall was the Vikings' defensive captain, including during the 1970s, when Minnesota's defense was known as the "Purple People Eaters."

Marshall set an NFL career record with twenty-nine fumbles recovered, including one in 1966 that he returned sixty-six yards in the wrong direction to set the league record for longest safety. Marshall is one of four Vikings to have his number (seventy) retired and to have played in two NFL Pro Bowl games.

Since retirement, Marshall has been active in Minneapolis, cofounding "Life's Missing Link," a community-based program focused on helping at-risk youth.

Michael T. Friedman

FURTHER READING
Brown, Curt. "Purple People Eaters No More; Now Just People." *Minneapolis Star Tribune*, January 19, 1992.
"Jim Marshall." Dorna Sports Promotions (www.dornausa.com/speaker/nfl/nfl_index/marshall.html).

"Jim Marshall." *Minnesota Vikings* (www.vikings.com/alumni/jimmarshall.htm).

"Legends of The National Football League: Jim Marshall #70 Minnesota Vikings." *Life's Missing Link* (www.lifesmissinglink.com/jim.htm).

★ ★ ★

Ollie MATSON

Born May 1, 1930, Trinity, Texas
Football player

Ollie Matson is the son of Gertrude, a schoolteacher, who moved to San Francisco, where Matson excelled in football and track and field at Washington High School and for the City College of San Francisco. Matriculating at the University of San Francisco, he was selected as a *defensive* All-American in 1951, despite leading the country in rushing with 1,566 yards on 245 attempts, averaging 6.39 yards per attempt, and leading the nation in scoring, with 126 points on twenty-one touchdowns. Playing for an undefeated USF team in 1951, Matson finished his career with a then all-time college rushing record of 3,166 yards on 547 plays in thirty games, averaging 105.5 yards per game while scoring thirty-five touchdowns. He finished third at the 1952 Olympics to win a bronze medal in the 400-meter run and a silver medal as a member of the second place 1,600-meter relay team.

After joining the Chicago Cardinals as a first-round draft choice in 1952, Matson excelled in the National Football League (NFL) for fourteen seasons, also playing for the Los Angeles Rams, Detroit Lions, and Philadelphia Eagles. In 1959, he was traded to the Rams for a stunning nine players; he was All-NFL four consecutive years and played in the Pro Bowl five times. He was elected to the NFL Hall of Fame in 1972 and is a member of the College Football Hall of Fame. His combined net yards on rushing, receiving, and kick returns were 12,844 over his NFL career.

Albert J. Figone

FURTHER READING
Carroll, B., M. Gershman, D. Neft, J. Thorn, and Elias Sports Bureau, eds. *Total Football: The Official Encyclopedia of the National Football League*. New York: HarperCollins, 1999.
Olderman, Murray. *The Running Backs*. Englewood Cliffs, NJ: Prentice Hall, 1969.
Orr, Jack. *The Black Athlete: His Story in American History*. New York: Pyramid Books, 1970.
Porter, David L., ed. *Biographical Dictionary of American Sports: Football*. Westport, CT: Greenwood Press, 1987.
Sullivan, George. *The Great Running Backs*. New York: Putnam, 1972.

★ ★ ★

Margaret MATTHEWS

Born August 5, 1935, Griffin, Georgia
Long jumper

One of the first women to graduate from high school and college in her neighborhood, Margaret Matthews is best known as the first American woman to broad-jump over twenty feet. Matthews's track and field career was full of national and international accomplishments in the broad jump, sprints and team relays. Her father was a construction worker, and her mother was a laundry worker in Georgia, so she had little financial assistance from home.

Her high school physical education teacher, Marion Morgan, especially influenced Matthews. Morgan inspired Matthews to become an honor student and successful athlete, which earned her an athletic scholarship to Tennessee State University for track and field. The 1956 Olympics in Melbourne, Australia, brought Matthews a bronze medal for her contribution to the U.S. 400-meter relay team. Well

Tennessee State's winning team in the 440-relay at the 1958 Women's National A.A.U. Track and Field Championships. Left to right: Isabelle Daniels; Lucinda Williams; Barbara Jones; and Margaret Matthews. *(AP/Wide World Photos)*

known for her use of psychological warfare and for her bouts against her rival Willye White, Matthews was a tough competitor. In 1958, she broke a record that had been held for over seventeen years by becoming the first American woman to broad-jump over twenty feet. She also became the first woman athlete from Tennessee State University to hold a world track and field record. Despite inconsistencies in her training and performance, Matthews was selected to the Amateur Athletic Union All American Team in 1957, 1958, and 1959. Following college, she married college sweetheart and student-athlete Jesse Wilburn. The mother of two sons, Matthews acquired a teaching job at Klondike Elementary School in Memphis.

Sara B. Washington

FURTHER READING
Adkins, Vivian B.L. "The Development of Negro Female Olympic Talent." Ph.D. diss., Indiana University, 1967.
Davis, Michael D. *Black American Women in Olympic Track and Field.* Jefferson, NC: McFarland, 1992.
Hine, Darlene C. *Facts On File Encyclopedia of Black Women in America, Dance, Sport, & Visual Arts.* New York: Facts On File, 1997.
Plowden, Martha W. *Olympic Black Women.* Grenta, LA: Pelican, 1996.

★ ★ ★

William Clarence MATTHEWS

Born January 7, 1877, Selma, Alabama
Died April 9, 1928, Washington, DC
Baseball player, attorney

William Clarence Matthews was the son of William Henry Matthews, a tailor, and Elizabeth Abigail Matthews, a housewife. He attended Harvard University (B.A.) and Boston University Law School (LL.B). Matthews was an outstanding college baseball player and lawyer whom a latter-day sportswriter characterized as "the Jackie Robinson of his time." He served as special assistant to the U.S. attorney in Massachusetts (1913) and as legal counsel to black separatist leader Marcus Garvey (1920–1923). Following his 1924 effort to get out the black vote for President Calvin Coolidge, Matthews was named a special assistant to the U.S. attorney general.

Matthews, who made the varsity squad his freshman year, had a stellar career at Harvard, playing both shortstop and center field at a time when baseball was America's preeminent sport, and colleges provided most of the talent for the major leagues. In 1905, his last Harvard season, Matthews batted .400 and stole twenty-two bases in twenty-five games. He also played football. In addition, Matthews was highly regarded for his refusal to compromise his amateur status by playing semiprofessional baseball as other college players were doing.

Neither talent nor character permitted Matthews to transcend the color line, however. College opponents sometimes refused to play against him. During his one professional season on an all-white team in Vermont's "outlaw" Northern League, his presence caused so much furor that he was unable to sign a major league contract with the Boston Nationals.

Mary Jo Binker

FURTHER READING

Boris, Joseph J., ed. *Who's Who in Colored America: A Biographical Dictionary of Notable Living Persons of Negro Descent in America*. Vol. 1. New York: Who's Who in Colored America, 1927.

"Brief Funeral Rites for W.C. Matthews." *Baltimore Afro American*, April 21, 1928.

Lindholm, Karl. "William Clarence Matthews: 'The Jackie Robinson of His Day.' " *The Cooperstown Symposium on Baseball and American Culture 1997* (Jackie Robinson), ed. Peter M. Rutkoff. Jefferson, NC: McFarland, 1999.

———. "William Clarence Matthews: Brief Life of a Baseball Pioneer 1877–1928." *Harvard Magazine* (September–October 1998): 58.

★ ★ ★

Willie MAYS

Born May 6, 1931, Westfield, Alabama
Baseball player

The son of steel mill worker William and mother, Ann, Mays was called up by the struggling Giants in 1951 after batting .477 in thirty-seven games with Minneapolis (Giants's minor league team). He was voted Rookie of the Year as the Giants stormed back from thirteen games behind the Brooklyn Dodgers to win the pennant.

Offensively, Mays's statistics offer only a hint of his greatness. No one except Babe

Willie Mays at spring training in 1957 in Phoenix, Arizona with the New York Giants. *(AP/Wide World Photos)*

Ruth had hit more home runs when he retired. He played in at least 150 games in a season thirteen times, won a batting title, finished second three times, and third twice. Mays was the National League's (NL) Most Valuable Player (MVP) twice and accumulated 300 or more total bases in thirteen consecutive seasons—a feat equaled only by Lou Gehrig and exceeded only by Hank Aaron.

Defensively, Mays was in a league of his own. The all-time leader in outfield putouts and total chances, in the 1954 World Series Mays made a catch at the Polo Grounds that has been described as simply "the Catch." Sprinting toward the center field fence with his back to home plate, Mays turned at the last second and caught Vic Wertz's shot at a dead run over 440 feet from home plate.

Mays was inducted into the National Baseball Hall of Fame on the basis of his 3,283 hits, a .302 lifetime batting average, and fielding average of .981. His 660 home runs rank third on the all-time list behind

Hank Aaron and Babe Ruth. The *Sporting News* named him Player of the Decade for the 1960s.

Albert J. Figone

See also: Autobiographies.

FURTHER READING
King, Joe. *The San Francisco Giants*. Englewood Cliffs, NJ: Prentice Hall, 1958.
Light, Jonathan F. *The Cultural Encyclopedia of Baseball*. Jefferson, NC: McFarland, 1997.
Reicher, Joseph L. *The Baseball Encyclopedia*. 6th ed. New York: Macmillan, 1985.
Smith, Ron. *The Sporting News Selects Baseball's Greatest Players: A Celebration of the 20th Century's Best*. St. Louis: Sporting News, 1998.
Sports Illustrated. *Baseball: The Biographical Encyclopedia*. Kingston, NY: Total Sports, 2000.

San Francisco Giants' Willie McCovey digging the ball out of the dirt at first base in a 1978 game against the Philadelphia Phillies. (AP/Wide World Photos)

★ ★ ★

Willie McCOVEY

Born January 10, 1938, Mobile, Alabama
Baseball player

Signed as a free agent in 1955, McCovey marked his major league debut with a four-for-four day against future Hall of Famer Robin Roberts. His sophomore season, however, was plagued by a severe slump, and he was reassigned to the minors. Returning to the big leagues that same season, McCovey platooned between left field and first base, because 1958 National League (NL) Rookie of the Year Orlando Cepeda was entrenched at first base.

Cepeda was traded to St. Louis in 1965, and McCovey played almost exclusively at first base until 1973. He was a productive power hitter, earning Most Valuable Player (MVP) honors in 1969 and six National League All-Star selections. McCovey was traded to the San Diego Padres in October 1973, where he played for two and a half seasons. He was then traded to Oakland in 1976 but opted for free agency and played for the Giants in 1977. McCovey's twenty-eight home runs, eighty-six RBIs, and fifteen game-winning hits made him the *Sporting News* and United Press International Comeback Player of the Year. He was inducted into the Baseball Hall of Fame in 1986.

Since retiring as a player, McCovey joined the Giants's public- and community-relations staff. Each season he presents the "Willie Mac" award to the Giants player who best exemplifies the spirit and leadership McCovey manifested during his twenty-two-year major league career.

Albert J. Figone

FURTHER READING
Grieve, Curley. "He Always Wanted to Be a Giant." *Pittsburg Sun-Telegraph,* August 10, 1959.
Peters, Nick. "From Mobile...to Cooperstown." *Sporting News,* January 20, 1986, 42.
Reicher, Joseph L. *The Baseball Encyclopedia*. 6th ed. New York: Macmillan, 1985.
Spander, Art. "Her Son, the Ballplayer." *San Francisco Chronicle,* September 17, 1977.

Sports Illustrated. *Baseball: The Biographical Encyclopedia.* Kingston, NY: Total Sports, 2000.

★ ★ ★

Mildred McDANIEL

Born November 3, 1933, Atlanta, Georgia
High jumper

Mildred McDaniel attended Atlanta's David T. Howard High School, where she dominated basketball and track events, particularly the high jump. She was the only U.S. woman athlete to win a gold medal in the 1956 Olympics in Melbourne, Australia. That victory was even more meaningful, considering McDaniel beat the ten-year high-jump record holder, Romania's Iolanda Balls, in the process.

As a high school student, McDaniel was singled out by Tuskegee University track coach Major Cleveland Abbott, who encouraged her to apply to Tuskegee. She won the AAU outdoor high jump in 1953. Nicknamed "Tex," she perfected her jumping style in time to participate in the 1955 Pan American Games, where she won the high jump.

McDaniel graduated from Tuskegee University in 1957 and was voted woman Athlete of the Year in Atlanta, Georgia. She also won the Sullivan Award for the best amateur athlete, claiming seven national titles during her years at Tuskegee. She retired from competition after graduation and married Louis Singleton in 1958; they moved to California the following year. In 1994 she retired from teaching physical education and coaching track after thirty-four years in the Pasadena Unified School District. A resident of Altadena, California, Singleton is in three halls of fame.

Alison M. Gavin

See also: Track and Field.

FURTHER READING
Ashe, Arthur R., Jr. *A Hard Road to Glory: A History of the African American Athlete Since 1946.* New York: Amistad, 1988.
South Central Bell. Mildred McDaniel Singleton "Spirit of Legends" calendar, 1995–1996.
The Women's Sports Encyclopedia: The Comprehensive Guide to Women's Sports, Women's Athletes, and Their Records. San Diego: Markel Enterprises, 1997.

★ ★ ★

Pam McGEE

Born December 1, 1962, Flint, Michigan
Basketball player

The daughter of Dianne and Jimmy McGee, who both held positions at an auto

University of Southern California twins Paula, left, and Pamela McGee cut down the nets in celebration of the school's 1984 NCAA Women's Basketball Championship. *(AP/Wide World Photos)*

factory in Flint, Michigan, McGee is a graduate of Flint Northern High School and the University of Southern California (USC).

McGee was an all-around high school athlete, excelling in basketball, track and field, and volleyball. She and her twin sister Paula led their high school basketball team to a 60–2 record. Pamela and Paula were recruited to play basketball for USC in 1980. In 1983 and 1984 McGee, a six-foot center forward, led USC to back-to-back National Collegiate Athletic Association (NCAA) titles. In 1984 she was named the tournament's Most Valuable Player. She finished her career at USC with an average of over seventeen points and nearly ten rebounds per game.

McGee was a member of the gold medal-winning women's basketball team in Los Angeles in 1984, and she played eight years of professional basketball in Brazil, Spain, France, and Italy. She was the second overall pick in the Women's National Basketball Association's (WNBA) first draft in 1997. She averaged almost eleven points per game with the Sacramento Monarchs. Traded to the Los Angeles Sparks in 1998, McGee announced her retirement in 1999.

McGee is one of only a small number of women basketball players who began their collegiate careers in the early 1980s and were able to play professionally in the United States. Her accomplishments were acknowledged by her hometown when she was inducted into the Greater Flint Afro-American Hall of Fame in 2000.

Rita Liberti

FURTHER READING
Flint Public Library (www.flint.lib.mi.us/index.html).
Jackson, Roger. "USC Has Doubled Its Fun." *Sports Illustrated*, February 22, 1982, 34–36.
"McGee Retires." *Sports Illustrated* (www.sportsillustrated.cnii.com/basketball/wnba/news/1999/05/21/mcgeeretires).

Women's National Basketball Association (www.playerprofile/Pammcgee.html).

★ ★ ★

Edith McGUIRE

Born June 3, 1944, Atlanta, Georgia
Sprinter

McGuire was the youngest of four children born to Clifford and Albertha. She attended Rockdale Elementary School and Samuel H. Archer High School, both in Atlanta, Georgia, and received a degree in elementary education from Tennessee State University (1966). McGuire was an AAU

Tennessee State's Edith McGuire succeeded Wilma Rudolph as this country's greatest woman sprinter during the early 1960s. *(AP/Wide World Photos)*

All-American and Olympic champion before becoming a teacher in Atlanta and in Detroit, where she worked with underprivileged children in a federal program.

McGuire was one of Coach Edward S. Temple's famed Tigerbelles at Tennessee State University from 1961 to 1965. As part of the 1964 Olympic team, McGuire won a gold medal in the 200 meters, breaking the world record, and silver medals in the 100 meters and as a member of the 4 x 100-meter relay team. Only the second African-American woman to win three medals in one Olympic Games, she set a world-record in the 200 meters of 23.0 seconds that broke former Tennessee State teammate Wilma Rudolph's world record.

In her short career, McGuire held records at the world, Olympic, Canadian, AAU American, and AAU championship levels in the 200 meters and 220-yard dash. She was a four-time AAU All-American (1961, 1963, 1964, 1966) and in 1966 became a USA All-Time Top Ten Indoor Champion in the 220-yard dash.

In 1975 McGuire was inducted into the Tennessee Sports Hall of Fame; four years later she received the highest national level of recognition in her sport when she was inducted into the U.S. National Track and Field Hall of Fame.

Susan G. Zieff

See also: Ed Temple; Track and Field.

FURTHER READING

Page, James A. *Black Olympian Medalists.* Englewood, CO: Libraries Unlimited, 1991.

Plowden, Martha W. *Olympic Black Women.* Gretna, LA: Pelican, 1996.

Tricard, Louise Mead. *American Women's Track and Field: A History, 1895 Through 1980.* Jefferson, NC: McFarland, 1996.

★   ★   ★

John McLENDON

Born April 4, 1915, Hiawatha, Kansas
Died October 8, 1999, Cleveland, Ohio
Basketball coach

Raised by his father John, an architect and postal worker, and stepmother Minnie, a schoolteacher, McLendon became one of the country's most talented and influential basketball coaches, contributing to coaching strategy, the development of African-American athletic institutions, and the use of athletics to promote racial integration and international good will.

McLendon (B.A., University of Kansas, and M.A., University of Iowa) was advised as an undergraduate by the inventor of basketball himself, James Naismith. After taking a job at Durham's North Carolina College for Negroes in 1937, McLendon helped build basketball into a major sport within the Colored (now Central) Intercollegiate Athletic Association, energizing the game with his innovative fast-break strategy, winning multiple CIAA championships and helping to found the celebrated CIAA tournament.

In 1953, after a brief stint at Hampton University, McLendon became head coach at Tennessee A & I State University. In 1954 his team became the first from a historically black college to play in an integrated national tournament, the NAIA. The Tigers won the NAIA tournament in 1958, 1959 and 1960, the first college team to win three straight national championships. McLendon subsequently coached the professional Cleveland Pipers and teams at Kentucky State College and Cleveland State University. In 1978 he was admitted to the Naismith Basketball Hall of Fame, one of countless honors he received in his long career.

McLendon believed strongly in the ability of athletics to foster racial and international understanding. He sought out matches with predominantly white teams and led efforts to convince the NAIA and the NCAA to admit historically black schools. He traveled extensively overseas, taking teams to Europe, Japan, Latin America, the Soviet Union, and elsewhere. He also devoted energy to younger athletes through such organizations as Chicago's Martin Luther King Boy's Club.

A prolific writer and historian, McLendon detailed his coaching techniques in *Fast Break Basketball: Fundamentals and Fine Points* (1965). Near the end of his life, he turned his attention to developing the CIAA Hall of Fame, now the John McLendon CIAA Hall of Fame.

Pamela Grundy

See also: Coaches and Managers.

FURTHER READING

George, Nelson. *Elevating the Game: The History and Aesthetics of Black Men in Basketball*. New York: Simon & Schuster, 1992.

Grundy, Pamela. *Learning to Win: Sports, Education and Social Change in Twentieth-Century North Carolina*. Chapel Hill: University of North Carolina Press, 2001.

Katz, Milton S., and John B. McLendon, Jr. *Breaking Through: The NAIA and the Integration of Intercollegiate Athletics in Post World War II America*. Privately printed, 1988.

★ ★ ★

Sam McVEY

Born May 17, 1885, Oxnard, California
Died December 23, 1921, New York, New York
Boxer

Born Samuel E. MacVea, Sam McVey grew up and began his boxing career in 1902 in Oxnard, California. Twice in 1903 he fought Jack Johnson for what was billed as "The Negro Heavyweight Title"; Johnson won both fights, although the rematch went the full twenty rounds. From there, the "Oxnard Wonder" moved to New York and then to Paris, where opportunities were better for black fighters. Faced with the color barrier in the United States, McVey fought all over the world, compiling a record of sixty-three wins, fifteen losses, twelve draws, and two no-contest bouts. Standing five feet, ten inches and weighing 200 pounds, McVey, like Johnson, is regarded as one of the finest heavyweights of his era. McVey was inducted into the International Boxing Hall of Fame in 1999. He earned a special place in ring history by fighting the longest match of the twentieth century, a forty-nine-round scrap against fellow African-American heavyweight Joe Jeannette. The bout took place on April 17, 1909, in Paris. It featured thirty-eight knockdowns and ended only when McVey was unable to answer the bell for the fiftieth round.

Following his historic match against Jeannette, McVey won twenty-two of his next twenty-four fights, seventeen by knockouts. In Sydney on September 30, 1911, he won the Australian heavyweight championship by beating Jack Lester. He defended that title four times.

McVey's last fight was on August 2, 1921, in Lancaster, Pennsylvania, a no-decision bout. On December 23, 1921, penniless and thirty-seven years old, McVey died of pneumonia. Jack Johnson paid his funeral expenses.

Dennis Gildea

See also: Boxing.

FURTHER READING

Cressy, John. "Boxer Who Endured 49 Rounds to Get His Due." *Los Angeles Times*, April 19, 1999.

Rust, Edna, and Art Rust, Jr. *Art Rust's Illustrated History of the Black Athlete*. New York: Doubleday, 1985.

"Sam McVey." *International Boxing Hall of Fame* (www.ibhof.com).

Sammons, Jeffrey T. *Beyond the Ring: The Role of Boxing in American Society*. Urbana: University of Illinois Press, 1988.

★ ★ ★

Ralph METCALFE

Born May 30, 1910, Atlanta, Georgia
Died October 10, 1978, Chicago, Illinois
Sprinter, track coach, congressman

Born to Clarence and Marie Metcalfe, Ralph grew up in Chicago and attended Tilden Tech High School. He earned a philosophy degree (B.A.) from Marquette and a master's degree in physical education from the University of Southern California. He spent his professional career as a track coach, university instructor, businessman, and member of the U.S. Congress.

In high school, Metcalfe was the national interscholastic sprint champion; between 1932 and 1934, while attending Marquette, he was the only man to win the NCAA 100–200 doubles three consecutive times. At AAU meets during this period he won five straight titles in the 200–220 and was the first athlete to break the twenty-second barrier in the 220. Overall, he held eleven AAU sprint titles. In the 1932 Olympics, Metcalfe medaled in the 100 and 200 meters (silver and bronze respectively). He won a gold medal in the 1936 Olympics in the 400-meter relay, setting an Olympic and world record, and won a silver medal in the 100, coming in second to Jesse Owens.

Throughout his life, Metcalfe was committed to excellence. He was inducted into the USA Track and Field, Black Athletes, National Track and Field, and Wisconsin Halls of Fame. He served on the U.S. Olympic Board of Directors (1969) and the President's Commission on Olympic Sport (1975) when he served in Congress from 1971–1978. He founded the Ralph H. Metcalfe Youth Foundation which aided poor families in the community through youth programs on athletics, health and education.

Debra A. Henderson

See also: Racial Theories; Eddie Tolan; Track and Field.

FURTHER READING

Ashe, Arthur R., Jr. *A Hard Road to Glory: A History of the African-American Athlete, 1919–1945*. New York: Amistad, 1993.

Page, James A. *Black Olympian Medalists*. Englewood, CO: Libraries Unlimited, 1991.

Porter, David L., ed. *The Biographical Dictionary of American Sports*. Westport, CT: Greenwood Press, 1988.

"Ralph Metcalfe." *USA Track and Field Official Site* (www.usatf.org).

★ ★ ★

Rod MILBURN

Born May 18, 1950, Opelousas, Louisiana
Died November 11, 1997, Baton Rouge, Louisiana
Hurdler

Rod Milburn was the son of Rodney Milburn and a graduate of J.S. Clark High School, Opelousas, Louisiana, and Southern University, Baton Rouge, Louisiana. Milburn won world recognition as a national and Olympic champion and world-record holder in the 120-yard and 110-meter high hurdles.

Milburn began running the 120-yard high hurdles as a high school sophomore, winning the event at the prestigious Golden West Invitational as a senior. As a Southern University freshman, he won the NAIA championship and finished fourth in the AAU national championships in the 120-yard high hurdles. In 1971 Milburn won the NAIA, NCAA, AAU, and Pan American Games titles and established a world record of 13.0 seconds in the 120-yard high hurdles. The following year, he defended his NAIA and AAU titles and won the Olympic gold medal in the 110-meter high hurdles in a world record time of 13.24 seconds. In 1973 he won a second NCAA title.

In 1974 Milburn joined the professional International Track Association. The Athletics Congress, which replaced the AAU as the nation's track and field governing body, reinstated Milburn as an amateur in 1980. That year he placed fourth in the TAC national championship and ranked fifth among the world's high hurdlers. Milburn retired from track and field in 1984 and was elected to the National Track and Field Hall of Fame in 1993. His death in 1997 resulted from a fall into a railroad car filled with liquid sodium chlorate at the Georgia Pacific paper plant, where he worked.

Adam R. Hornbuckle

FURTHER READING
Page, James A. *Black Olympian Medalists*. Englewood, CO: Libraries Unlimited, 1991.
Wallechinsky, David. *The Complete Book of the Summer Olympics*. Sydney 2000 ed. Woodstock, NY: Overlook Press, 2000.

★ ★ ★

Cheryl MILLER

Born January 3, 1964, Riverside, California
Basketball player

Cheryl Miller's father, Saul Miller, is a computer systems analyst, and her mother, Carrie Miller, is a nurse. Miller's outstanding career in basketball began in her childhood. Playing against her athletic brothers, she often found the opposition more demanding in her backyard than at the local playground. At Riverside Polytechnic High School she began her domination of women's basketball, averaging thirty-seven points per game in her four-year career. The heavily recruited Miller decided to attend the University of Southern California (USC). She helped lead the team to back-to-back NCAA titles in 1983 and 1984. Her gold medal in the 1984 Los Angeles Olympic Games added to her legendary status in women's basketball, and in 1985 she was named *Sports Illustrated* National Player of the Year. In 1986 she was the first woman nominated for the esteemed Sullivan Award.

Unfortunately, there was no multi-million-dollar contract waiting for a female basketball star in the mid-1980s, so Miller put her USC academic degree to work and entered the world of sports broadcasting. The pull of basketball was strong, however, and in 1993 she returned to USC as the head coach of the women's basketball team. Despite the controversy this move caused—the former USC coach, Marianne Stanley, sued the university over equity issues—Miller persevered and led the team to the NCAA tournament in 1994. She was hired as the first head coach and general manager of the WNBA's Phoenix Mercury and led the team to the WNBA finals in 1998 against the eventual champions, Houston.

Today Miller has returned to sports broadcasting and serves as an analyst for TNT and TBS. Miller's outstanding athletic skills, success as a coach, and work as a sport announcer have made her an outstanding role model for other women in athletics.

Alison M. Wrynn

See also: Olympic Games.

FURTHER READING

Ashe, Arthur R., Jr. *A Hard Road to Glory: A History of the African-American Athlete Since 1946*. Vol. 3. New York: Warner Books, 1988.

Bentley, Ken. *The Story of Black Women in Sports*. Los Angeles: Carnation, 1983.

Porter, David L., ed. *African-American Sports Greats: A Biographical Dictionary*. Westport, CT: Greenwood Press, 1995.

Woolum, Janet. *Outstanding Women Athletes: Who They Are and How They Influenced Sports in America*. Phoenix, AZ: Oryx Press, 1992.

★ ★ ★

Bobby MITCHELL

Born June 6, 1935, Hot Springs, Arkansas
Football player

Bobby Mitchell, a receiver and running back, integrated the previously all-white Washington Redskins.

Mitchell had a standout career at the University of Illinois from 1954 to 1958, setting a Big Ten record of 8.6 yards per rush. He also broke conference records as a hurdler at Illinois before graduating in 1958.

Drafted by the Cleveland Browns, he played in the backfield with fullback Jim Brown, gaining 1,330 yards in four years. At six feet and 196 pounds, however, Mitchell failed to satisfy Coach Paul Brown, who wanted to replace Mitchell with another big back, Jim Brown.

In December 1961, Mitchell was traded to the Washington Redskins for Heisman Trophy winner Ernie Davis, who had been drafted by the Redskins earlier in the month. In 1962, Mitchell became the best-known player among five African Americans who integrated the last all-white team in the NFL. In his first year as a Redskin, he was shifted to wide receiver, where he led the league with seventy-two receptions. In 1967, under Coach Otto Graham, Mitchell returned to running back, where he remained until the end of his playing career in 1969.

An All-Pro from 1962 to 1964, Mitchell also played in the Pro Bowl four times. In eleven seasons, he gained 2,735 yards rushing and scored fourteen touchdowns. In addition to excelling in punt and kickoff returns, he caught 521 passes for 7,953 yards and sixty-five touchdowns. He was inducted into the Pro Football Hall of Fame in 1983.

John S. Watterson

See also: Ernie Davis.

FURTHER READING

Clary, Jack. *Washington Redskins*. New York: Macmillan, 1974.

Lovero, Thom. *Washington Redskins: The Authorized History*. Dallas: Taylor, 1996.

Porter, David L., ed. *Biographical Dictionary of American Sports*. Westport, CT: Greenwood Press, 1987.

Ross, Charles K. *Outside the Lines: African Americans and the Integration of the National Football League*. New York: New York University Press, 1999.

Walsh, Jack. "Redskins Trade Davis to Browns for Mitchell and Rookie Halfback." *Washington Post*, December 15, 1961.

★ ★ ★

Tom MOLINEAUX

Born 1784, Maryland or Virginia
Died August 4, 1818, Galway, Ireland
Boxer

Although most secondary accounts indicate that Molineaux was born in slavery and ultimately received his freedom after winning several boxing matches for his master, there is no primary evidence to substantiate this view. It is just as possible that Molineaux was born a free black. Irrespective of his early background, it is known that Molineaux eventually migrated to New York City, where he became

Tom Molineaux garnered international acclaim for his fights with England champion Tom Crib in 1810 and 1811. (© Bettman/CORBIS)

a porter and dockworker and engaged in informal boxing matches.

In 1809 Molineaux traveled to England and almost immediately began training as a boxer under the tutelage of Bill Richmond, an American-born black who taught pugilism at his Horse and Dolphin Tavern in London. Molineaux's prodigious physical talents and boxing skills soon became evident, and in 1810 he was matched in a championship fight against the famous English boxer Tom Crib. The fight was an extraordinarily bloody and controversial affair, with Crib declared the victor after the forty-fourth round. Molineaux and Crib fought a rematch at Thistleton Gap, outside London, in 1811; Crib once again beat "The Tremendous Man of Colour" in eleven rounds.

Molineaux fought several times following his bouts with Crib, including matches against Jack Carter and William Fuller. He was never the same fighter, however, after his classic encounters with Crib. Heavy drinking, endless partying, and indifference to training combined to diminish Molineaux's once great physical skills and boxing talents. In 1818, just seven years after his second fight with Crib, Molineaux passed away in Galway, Ireland.

David K. Wiggins

See also: Boxing; Bill Richmond.

FURTHER READING
Brailsford, Dennis. *Bare Knuckles: A Social History of Prize Fighting.* Cambridge: Lutterworth Press, 1988.
Cone, Carl B. "The Molineaux-Crib Fight, 1810: Wuz Tom Molineaux Robbed?" *Journal of Sport History* 9 (Winter 1982): 83–91.
Goodman, Michael H. "The Moor vs. Black Diamond." *Virginia Cavalcade* 29 (Spring 1980): 164–73.
Gorn, Elliott J. *The Manly Art: Bare-Knuckle Prize Fighting in America.* Ithaca, NY: Cornell University Press, 1986
Magriel, Paul. "Tom Molineaux." *Phylon* 12 (December 1951): 329–36.

★ ★ ★

Art MONK

Born December 5, 1957, White Plains, New York
Football player

Art Monk played in the National Football League (NFL) for sixteen years and distinguished himself as one of the best and most consistent wide receivers in history.

Born to Arthur Monk, a welder, and Lela Monk, a domestic, James Arthur Monk grew up in White Plains, New York, where he played high school football and was an acclaimed hurdler. After high school Monk attended Syracuse University, where he was a triple threat on the gridiron. During his four-year career, he had 102 receptions for 1,644 yards, rushed for

1,140 yards, and gained 1,105 yards on kick returns.

Selected in the first round by the Washington Redskins in the 1980 NFL draft, the six-foot, three-inch Monk was named to the NFL All-Rookie Team. Quiet, workmanlike, and modest, Monk compiled remarkable career statistics (940 receptions, 12,721 yards, sixty-eight touchdowns) and was a key player on Washington's Super Bowl championship teams. Moreover, in 1984 Monk made an NFL-record 106 receptions in a single season. Eight years later, he set a NFL record for most career receptions, with 820. Named to three Pro Bowls, Monk also set a record by making at least one catch in 183 straight games. All of these records have since been broken.

In addition to his statistical achievements, Monk was noted for his intelligence, decency, and professionalism. "In terms of character, he was one of the best guys I've ever been around," said former Redskins head coach Joe Gibbs. "He was a role model for the youth, he was tough, he was smart and he had more talent than anyone. He made hard things look easy."

Monk played his final two seasons with the New York Jets and Philadelphia Eagles. However, he remains in the Washington area, where he co-owns an advertising agency and is the cofounder of a nonprofit organization, the Good Samaritan Foundation, which provides job skills for inner-city youth.

Daniel A. Nathan

FURTHER READING

Justice, Richard. "Art Monk: The Quiet Hero." In *Redskins: A History of Washington's Team*. Washington, DC: Washington Post Books, 1997.

Nack, William. "A Monk's Existence." *Sports Illustrated*, September 7, 1992, 32–40.

Porter, David L., ed. *African-American Sports Greats: A Biographical Dictionary*. Westport, CT: Greenwood Press, 1995.

Wilbon, Michael. "Art Critics Agree, Monk Is a Masterpiece." *Washington Post*, January 27, 2001.

★ ★ ★

Earl MONROE

Born November 21, 1944, Philadelphia, Pennsylvania
Basketball player

Earl Monroe's father, Vernon Monroe, was a night watchman, and his mother, Rose, was a grocery store manager. He graduated from John Bartram (Philadelphia) High School in 1962. An injury he suffered as a schoolboy soccer player turned him to basketball. He majored in elementary education at Winston-Salem (NC) State College from 1963 to 1967. Monroe averaged 26.7 points per game for his college career, and a 41.5 per average in his senior year in 1967. He led Winston-Salem State to the National Collegiate Athletic Association (NCAA) College Division Championship. He was selected as a *Sporting News* first-team All-American in 1966 and gained other All-American selections in 1967.

Monroe played in the National Basketball Association (NBA) for thirteen years, beginning in Baltimore (1967–1971), where he was selected as NBA Rookie of the Year in 1968. He then played for the New York Knicks from 1972 to 1980; he was a member of New York's 1973 championship team and participated in four NBA All-Star Games (1969, 1971, 1975, 1977). Monroe's exciting style of aggressive one-on-one offensive play contributed to the rising popularity of the NBA in the 1970s.

Monroe's honors include selection to the National Association of Intercollegiate Athletics (NAIA) Basketball Hall of Fame (1975), the Naismith Memorial Basketball Hall of Fame (1989), and the NBA Fiftieth Anniversary Team (1996).

Upon his retirement from professional basketball in 1980, his longtime musical interest led him to build a rehearsal studio in his home. He founded a record company, Pretty Pearl, and aided a number of young singers, rhythm and blues groups, and rappers in the African-American community.

John R. Schleppi

FURTHER READING
Hubbard, Jan, ed. *The Official NBA Encyclopedia.* 3d ed. New York: Doubleday, 2000.
New York Times, April 30, 1990.
Walton, David, and John Hareas, eds. *The Sporting News Official NBA Register.* 2000–2001 ed. St. Louis: Sporting News, 2000.

★ ★ ★

Eleanor MONTGOMERY

Born 1947, Cleveland, Ohio
High jumper

Raised in Cleveland, Ohio, Montgomery established a trend of excellence in high-jump competitions throughout her career. She competed at John Adams High School and at the Cleveland Recreation Department Track Club, where Alex Ferenczy, who trained several Olympic hopefuls, coached her. She set several records in Ohio; hard work and determination ensured her a position on the 1964 All America Women's Track and Field Team at the age of seventeen.

In the fall of 1965, after graduating from high school, Montgomery attended Tennessee State University. Montgomery quickly became a major contributor to the success of the legendary Tiberbelle team. She won high-jump competitions at the Pan American Games in 1963 and 1967. She also won the high jump at the 1964 and 1968 Olympic trials, earning a spot on both U.S. Olympic teams. Throughout her career, Montgomery won six national high-jump titles in indoor and outdoor Amateur Athletic Union track and field meets. Her talent produced several record-setting high jumps at the national level. In honor of many exceptional performances, Montgomery was presented with two prestigious awards in track and field, the Dieges Award and Saettel Award.

Sara B. Washington

FURTHER READING
Davis, Michael D. *Black American Women in Olympic Track and Field.* Jefferson, NC: McFarland, 1992.
Thaxton, Nolan A. "A Documentary Analysis of Competitive Track and Field for Women at Tuskegee Institute and Tennessee State University." Ph.D. diss., Springfield College, 1970.
Tricard, Louise M. *American Women's Track and Field: A History, 1895 Through 1980.* Jefferson, NC: McFarland, 1985.

★ ★ ★

Warren MOON

Born November 18, 1956, Los Angeles, California
Football player

A star quarterback at the University of Washington, Moon played for the Edmonton Eskimos in the Canadian Football League (1978–1983) and for the Houston Oilers and three other teams in the National Football League (1984–2000), retiring as the most prolific passer in NFL history.

Moon was the only boy of seven children born to Harold Warren, Sr. (a laborer), and Pat (a nurse). An All-City player at Hamilton High in Los Angeles, he played his freshman year in college at West Los Angeles Junior College. In 1975, he enrolled at the University of Washington, where he flourished as quarterback, completing 242 passes in 496 attempts for 3,277 yards and nineteen touchdowns. He was selected Conference Player of the Year in 1977 and Most Valuable Player of the 1978 Rose Bowl. He graduated with a B.S. in communications.

Despite his achievements, no NFL team selected him in the draft, and Moon signed as a free agent with the Edmonton Eskimos in the Canadian Football League. In six seasons with Edmonton, he completed 1,369 of 2,832 passes for 21,228 yards. Under Moon's leadership, Edmonton won the Grey Cup five consecutive seasons, 1978 through 1982. In 1983 he set a new season record with 5,648 passing yards, achieved a single-game mark of 555 yards, and was named the CFL's Most Valuable Player.

The NFL finally took notice, and Houston signed Moon as a free agent in 1984; he was named Rookie of the Year. From 1987 through 1993 he led the Oilers to seven straight playoff appearances; from 1988 through 1994 he was selected for the Pro Bowl. Moon subsequently played for Minnesota (1994–1997), Seattle (1997–1998), and Kansas City (1998–2000), retiring at the end of the 2000 season.

Through his extraordinary career Warren Moon overcame racial barriers in the National Football League and demolished stereotypes about black quarterbacks, thereby opening up the position to African-American players who followed him.

Robert Pruter

FURTHER READING
Mabunda, Mpho L., ed. *Contemporary Black Biography.* Vol. 8. Detroit: Gale Research, 1995.
Pierson, Don. "Moon in an Orbit of His Own." *Chicago Tribune*, December 22, 2000.
Porter, David L., ed. *Biographical Dictionary of American Sports: 1992–1995 Supplement for Baseball, Football, Basketball, and Other Sports.* Westport, CT: Greenwood Press, 1992.

★ ★ ★

Archie MOORE

Born December 13, 1913, Benoit, Mississippi
Died December 9, 1998, San Diego, California
Boxer

Born Archibald Lee Wright to Thomas and Lorena Wright, Moore was adopted as an infant by his aunt (Willie Pearl Moore) and uncle (Cleveland Moore, a laborer). Moore attended Dumas elementary school, Lincoln School, and Missouri Training School for Boys, a reform school.

At seventeen Moore joined the Civilian Conservation Corps, where he started a boxing team. His first professional victory was a second-round knockout of "Piano Man" Jones in 1935. He won the California middleweight title in 1943 by beating Jack Chase. Moore captured the world light heavyweight title by beating Joey Maxim on December 17, 1952. He earned $800 for the fight, while Maxim was paid $100,000. Moore fought Rocky Marciano for the heavyweight title on September 21, 1955, losing in the ninth round. In his second attempt at the title, Moore met Floyd Patterson on November 30, 1956, and lost in the fifth round. In his final attempt, Moore faced Muhammad Ali on November 15, 1962, and lost in round four. In each of the title fights, Moore was at least ten years older than his opponent. His last fight was a 1963 exhibition bout against Mike DiBiase, which he won with a knockout in the third round.

After a lengthy career in the ring, Moore trained other fighters. He worked in George Foreman's camp for the famous 1974 "Rumble in the Jungle" versus Ali. Moore also starred in the film *Huckleberry Finn*.

Moore fought in the ring for almost thirty years and is the only boxer to fight both Rocky Marciano and Muhammad Ali. He is believed to have the most career

Archie Moore (right) lands an overhand right to the jaw of Tony Anthony in defense of his light heavyweight championship in 1957 in Los Angeles. *(AP/Wide World Photos)*

knockouts (129). Moore was elected to the Boxing Hall of Fame in 1966 and the International Boxing Hall of Fame in 1990.

Maureen M. Smith

See also: Boxing; Floyd Patterson.

FURTHER READING
Kindred, Dave. "A Celebration of Life." *Sporting News*, December 21, 1998, 62.
Moore, Archie. *The Archie Moore Story*. New York: McGraw-Hill, 1960.
Newsweek, December 21, 1998, 31.
O'Brien, Richard, and Mark Mravic. "A Smiling Champion." *Sports Illustrated*, December 21, 1998, 30–31.

★ ★ ★

Lenny MOORE

Born November 25, 1933, Reading, Pennsylvania
Football player

Moore was the son of George Moore, a steelworker-laborer, and Virginia Talley Moore, a cleaning lady. He attended Penn State from 1952 to 1956, establishing a single-season rushing mark of 1,082 yards. Moore's exceptional speed and ability to control the ball made him the prototypical flanker/running back. A seven-time All-Pro selection and a five-time All-NFL selection, Moore spent his entire professional career with the Baltimore Colts (1956–1967). In that time he played in seven Pro Bowls, gained nearly 12,500 combined yards, and scored 113 career touchdowns.

Named Rookie of the Year in 1956, Moore's speed, allied with the passing skills of quarterback Johnny Unitas, made the Colts the dominant team in the NFL during the late 1950s. Thereafter, Moore's career slumped due to injuries. Beginning in 1963, however, he launched a comeback that included at least one touchdown in eighteen straight games (1963–1965)—an NFL record. In 1964 he was named NFL Player of the Year and Associated Press (AP) Comeback Player of the Year. He was inducted into the Pro Football Hall of Fame in 1975. Upon his retirement, Moore became one of CBS Sports' first African-American sports announcers.

After his broadcasting stint ended, Moore worked at several different jobs before becoming director of promotions for the Baltimore Colts in 1975. He remained in that position until the team moved to Indianapolis in 1984. Since then, Moore has been a program specialist with the Maryland Department of Juvenile Justice.

Mary Jo Binker

FURTHER READING
Ashe, Arthur R., Jr. *A Hard Road to Glory: A History of the African-American Athlete, 1619–1918*. New York: Amistad, 1993.
Barnett, C. Robert. "Lenny Moore." In *Great Athletes of the Twentieth Century*, editors of Salem Press. Pasadena, CA: Salem Press, 1992.
Porter, David L., ed. *African-American Sports Greats: A Biographical Dictionary*. Westport, CT: Greenwood Press, 1995.

Joe MORGAN

Born September 19, 1943, Bonham, Texas
Baseball player

Morgan was born in the segregated community of Bonham, Texas, but when he was five his father Leonard moved the family to Oakland, California. Morgan's hero was Jackie Robinson, and he was to play Robinson's position of second base, leading the Cincinnati Reds to two world championships and earning selection to the Baseball Hall of Fame in 1990.

In his freshman year at Castlemont High School in Oakland, Morgan made the varsity squad. Because of his small size (five feet seven inches, 155 pounds), Morgan initially was little recruited by major league teams. In 1963, the Houston Colt .45s (who would change their name to the Astros in 1965) took a chance and signed Morgan. From 1963 to 1964 he played for Houston farm teams in Modesto (California), Durham (North Carolina), and San Antonio (Texas), with brief stints in Houston at the end of each season. As a rookie second baseman in 1965, he was voted Rookie Player of the Year by the *Sporting News*.

From 1966 to 1971, Morgan started at second base for Houston. Following the 1971 season, however, Morgan was traded to the Cincinnati Reds as part of an eleven-player deal. The trade to Cincinnati proved to be a blessing, and Morgan enjoyed his best major league seasons with the Reds. In Cincinnati, Morgan joined with Tony Perez, Johnny Bench, and Pete Rose to create a dynasty known as the "Big Red Machine." In 1972, the Reds won the National League pennant, losing in the World Series to the Oakland As. The Reds attained a division championship in 1973, and in 1975 and 1976 won consecutive World Series titles. Morgan was the catalyst for these championship teams, earning National League Most Valuable Player honors in 1975 and 1976.

However, the Big Red Machine began to unravel during the late 1970s, and in 1978 Morgan batted only .236. After the 1979 season, Morgan declared free agency and rejoined the Houston Astros. Houston won a divisional title in 1980, but Morgan moved on to the San Francisco Giants for the 1981 and 1982 seasons. Batting .289 with fourteen home runs, Morgan kept the Giants in the 1982 divisional race and was selected by the *Sporting News* as the National League's Comeback Player of the year. He completed his playing career with stints in Philadelphia (1983) and Oakland (1984).

In twenty-two seasons, Morgan hit 268 home runs, drove in 1,133 runs, stole 689 bases, garnered 2,517 hits, walked 1,865 times, and attained a lifetime batting average of .271. Morgan was elected to National League All-Star teams nine times and won five Gold Glove Awards. After his playing days, Morgan returned to college and acquired a business degree, purchasing beer and fast-food franchises.

Morgan has also carved out a career in baseball broadcasting. From 1986 through 1993, he announced for the San Francisco Giants and served as a commentator for the NBC Game of the Week. Since 1994, he has worked for ESPN, forming a lively and informative collaboration with broadcaster John Miller. He also remains an articulate voice for the inclusion of African Americans in baseball management.

Ron Briley

FURTHER READING
Cohen, Joel H. *Joe Morgan: Great Little Big Man*. New York: G.P. Putnam, 1978.
Joe Morgan File. *National Baseball Hall of Fame Museum and Library*. Cooperstown, New York.
Morgan, Joe, and David Falkner. *Joe Morgan: A Life in Baseball*. New York: W.W. Norton, 1993.
Twombly, Wells. "Little Joe of the Astros." *Sport*, January 1967, 46–49.

★ ★ ★

Edwin MOSES

Born August 31, 1955, Dayton, Ohio
Hurdler

Moses Edwin was the second of three sons of Irving Moses, an elementary school principal and science teacher, and Gladys, a curriculum supervisor. They both worked for the Dayton school system.

Moses was an outstanding track athlete at Dayton's Fairview High School and Morehouse College in Atlanta. He ran his first 400-meter hurdle race in 1975. His smooth, striding gait and elegant hurdling technique made Moses a "natural" for the event. In his second run over the distance he clocked fifty-two seconds.

At the 1976 Olympics in Montreal, Canada, Moses won the Gold Medal in the 400-meter hurdles in a world-record 47.64 seconds. A year later, he took the world record to 47.45. In 1980 the United States boycotted the Moscow Olympics; in that Olympic year, however, he set a new world record of 47.13 seconds. His final world record was a 47.02 set in Koblentz, Germany, in 1983.

At the 1984 Los Angeles Olympics, Moses took the Olympic oath on behalf of all athletes during the opening ceremony and triumphed in the 400-meter hurdles. At the 1988 Seoul Olympics he earned a bronze medal. He was unquestionably a brilliant performer in his specialization; track and field historians consider his nearly ten-year winning streak—122 consecutive races (1977–1987)—as one of the sport's defining achievements.

He received the Sullivan Award in 1983 and was the *Sports Illustrated* Sportsman of the Year in 1985. He retired from track in 1988.

Scott A.G.M. Crawford

See also: Track and Field.

FURTHER READING

Greenspan, Bud. *100 Greatest Moments in Olympic History.* Los Angeles: General Publishing Group, 1995.

Kirsch, George B., Othello Harris, and Claire E. Nolte, eds. *Encyclopedia of Ethnicity and Sports in the United States.* Westport, CT: Greenwood Press, 2000.

Porter, David L., ed. *African American Sports Greats: A Biographical Dictionary.* Westport, CT: Greenwood Press, 1995.

Wels, Susan. *The Olympic Spirit: 100 Years of the Games.* Del Mar, CA: Tehabi Books, 1996.

★ ★ ★

Marion MOTLEY

Born June 5, 1920, Leesburg, Georgia
Died June 27, 1999, Leesburg, Georgia
Football player

One of four children of Shakeful and Blanche Motley, Motley spent most of his youth in Canton, Ohio, where his father worked in a steel mill. Motley was among the handful of African-American players who integrated professional football immediately after World War II.

At Canton McKinley High School, Motley played baseball, basketball, and football. At the University of Nevada-Reno, he

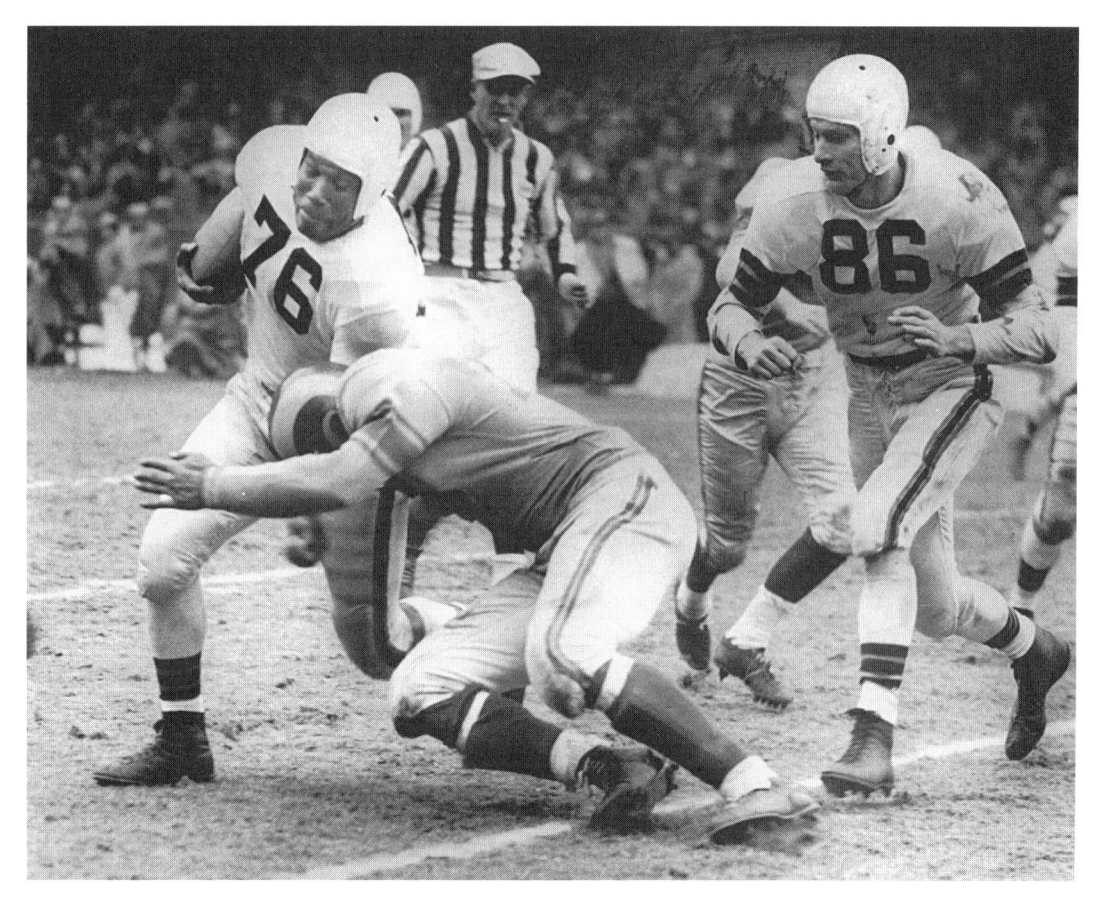

Marion Motley (76) picking up important yardage here for the Cleveland Browns, has the distinction of being the first African American selected to the Pro Football Hall of Fame. *(AP/Wide World Photos)*

was an outstanding running and defensive back as well as punt and kickoff receiver from 1940 to 1943. Joining the Navy in 1944, he played at the Great Lakes Naval Base under Coach Paul Brown. After being discharged, Motley wrote to Paul Brown asking for a tryout with the Cleveland Browns, which had recently entered the newly created All American Football Conference (AAFC). According to Motley, Brown initially refused his request. Soon afterward, however, Brown invited Motley to join the team, perhaps because he was needed as a roommate for African-American guard Bill Willis.

At six feet, two inches and 235 pounds, Motley helped lead the Browns to four AAFC titles between 1946 and 1949. In 1950, when the Browns won the NFL championship, Motley led the league in rushing with 810 yards. In his eight years with the team, Motley racked up 4,712 yards, averaging 6.1 yards per carry. He retired after a year with Pittsburgh, 1955, in which he played linebacker.

Motley was married to Eula Coleman in 1943 and had three sons. He was inducted into the Pro Football Hall of Fame in his native Canton in 1968. In 1968–1969, he returned briefly to pro football as a scout for the Washington Redskins, then coached by his former teammate Otto Graham.

John S. Watterson

FURTHER READING
Clary, Jack. *Cleveland Browns.* New York: Macmillan, 1973.
Porter, David L., ed. *Biographical Dictionary of American Sports, Football.* Westport, CT: Greenwood Press, 1987.
Pluto, Terry. "Marion Motley Was a Giant of Any Time." *Akron Beacon-Journal*, June 28, 1999.
Ross, Charles K. *Outside the Lines: African Americans and the Integration of the National Football League.* New York: New York University Press, 1999.

★ ★ ★

Calvin MURPHY

Born May 9, 1948, Norwalk, Connecticut
Basketball player

At five feet, nine inches tall, Calvin Murphy is one of the smallest men ever to play professional basketball. His mother was a former professional player on a barnstorming team called the Bomberettes. As a basketball player Calvin Murphy was a folk hero before he even played in college. He was a three-year letter winner at Norwalk High School and national high school All-American in 1965–1966. He was also a state champion in baton twirling. He chose to play at Niagara University, in part because that gave him an opportunity to twirl at halftime of Buffalo Bills games.

While at Niagara University Murphy scored 2,548 points in seventy-seven games for a 33.1 points per game scoring average, which ranks fourth best all-time in the NCAA. He scored a career-high sixty-eight points in a single game against Syracuse University, also fourth best of all time. Murphy was a two-time first-team All-American. In spite of his success against top-level competition, NBA teams were reluctant to draft him, because they believed he was too small. He was the only All-American not taken in the first round of the draft.

Once he joined the NBA, however, Murphy became known for his speed and shooting accuracy. He was one of only two players to shoot over 90 percent from the free-throw line for five consecutive seasons. He set an NBA record of seventy-eight consecutive free throws. He scored forty points or more six times in his NBA career. His career-high fifty-seven points came in a playoff game against the New Jersey Nets in 1978. He played thirteen seasons with San Diego then the Houston Rockets. He is the franchise's all-time leading scorer. The legendary coach Red Auerbach once said he was the fastest guard he had ever seen.

Rick Knott

FURTHER READING

Basketball Hall of Fame (www.hoophall.com/halloffamers/MurphyCalvin.htm).
Jares, Joe, and Curry Kirkpatrick. "A Couple of Coming Out Parties." *Sports Illustrated*, December 11, 1967, 30–33.
LaBlanc, Michael L., ed. *Basketball: Professional Sports Team History*. Detroit: Gale Research, 1994.
Porter, David L., ed. *Biographical Dictionary of American Sports: Basketball and Other Indoor Sports*. Westport, CT: Greenwood Press, 1989.
"San Diego's Calvin Murphy, Pro Basketball's Tiny Giant." *Ebony*, February 1971, 38–42.

★ ★ ★

Isaac MURPHY

Born April 16, 1861, Frankfort, Kentucky
Died February 12, 1896, Lexington, Kentucky
Jockey

Born Isaac Burns, Murphy began using his grandfather's last name when he began racing. His father, James Burns, was a free man who served in the Union army and died in a Confederate prison camp. After his father's death, Murphy began a horseracing apprenticeship in Lexington. After two years at the Williams and Owning Racing Stable, Murphy began racing. His first major race was in 1878, and he ultimately received national attention as the lead jockey for the Hunt Reynolds Stable of Lexington.

Murphy's riding style separated him

Isaac Murphy (third from right) with several of his friends and associates at an 1890 clambake. Murphy had already realized international acclaim as a jockey, capturing all the major events aboard many of horseracing's most famous horses. *(Keeneland Library)*

from his peers, in that he rarely used a whip or spur on his mounts. He preferred to urge his horse gently forward and use perfect timing and pace to gain victory. Murphy was the first jockey to win the Kentucky Derby three times. At the height of his career, Murphy was the highest paid athlete in the country, winning every major race except the Futurity. Throughout his career, Murphy battled with weight problems, chronic alcoholism, and racial discrimination. In early 1890, he attempted to branch out as an owner, but he was unsuccessful.

Murphy retired from racing in 1895. His legacy included a career racing record of 628 victories out of 1,412 races (44 percent) and selection as the first jockey inducted into the National Museum of Racing Hall of Fame in 1955. In 1956, he was selected for the Jockey Hall of Fame at Pimlico Race Track in Maryland.

Tracey M. Salisbury

See also: Civil Rights; Horse Racing.

FURTHER READING
Ashe, Arthur R., Jr. *A Hard Road to Glory: A History of the African-American Athlete, 1619–1918.* Vol. 1. New York: Warner Books, 1988.
Hotaling, Edward. *The Great Black Jockeys: The Lives and Times of the Men Who Dominated America's First National Sport.* Rocklin, CA: Forum, 1999.
Wiggins, David K. "Isaac Murphy: Black Hero in Nineteenth-Century American Sport, 1861–1896." In *Glory Bound: Black Athletes in a White America.* Syracuse, NY: Syracuse University Press, 1997.

Eddie MURRAY

Born February 24, 1956, Los Angeles, California
Baseball player

Eddie Murray's father (Chades) was an hourly worker, and his mother (Carrie) was a housewife. One of baseball's greatest hitters, he was one of three major leaguers with 3,000 hits (3255) and 500 home runs (504). He played twenty-one years for five teams, most notably the Baltimore Orioles. The switch-hitting Murray played more games at first base than anyone else in major league history, winning three Gold Gloves, though in his last years he was primarily a designated hitter. An eight-time All-Star, in 1981 he led the American League in home runs (tied) and in runs batted in. His four brothers also played professional baseball, Rich reaching the majors.

Murray played in youth leagues and high school in Los Angeles before being drafted by Baltimore in 1973, where he was American League Rookie of the Year in 1979. He batted cleanup for the Orioles as they reached the World Series in 1979 and won it in 1983. Although he had been well liked, a 1986 injury sparked critical comments from the Orioles' owner; Murray was branded as out of shape, lazy, and responsible for the team's decline. He responded by shunning the media; thereafter, despite his contributions to the community, he was rejected by Baltimore fans.

Traded after the 1988 season, Murray continued his productivity, but his reputation declined further. After appearing for Cleveland in the 1995 World Series, he returned to Baltimore the following season, sparked a return to the playoffs, and regained the affection of the fans. Murray became Baltimore's first-base coach after his 1997 retirement. He was inducted into the National Baseball Hall of Fame in July 2003.

David C. Skinner

FURTHER READING

Allen, Bob. *The 500 Home Run Club. Baseball's 16 Greatest Home Run Hitters from Babe Ruth to Mark McGwire*. Champaign, IL: Sports, 2000.

Boswell, Thomas. *Why Time Begins on Opening Day*. New York: Penguin, 1984.

Honig, Donald. *The Greatest First Basemen of All Time*. Chicago: Follett, 1988.

"Murray Attains 3,000 with Quiet Dignity: Slugger Not Dwelling on Historic Feat." *USA Today Baseball Weekly*, July 5, 1995, 15.

St. John, Allen. "The Quiet Man." *Village Voice*, July 27, 1993, 157.

NATIONAL ASSOCIATION OF COLORED BASE BALL CLUBS OF THE UNITED STATES AND CUBA

The National Association of Colored Base Ball Clubs of the United States and Cuba is the story of Nathaniel "Nat" Colvin Strong, sports promoter and booking agent. By the late 1890s, Strong handled scheduling for the Cuban Giants and Cuban X-Giants baseball clubs, and controlled a number of white semipro ballparks in metropolitan New York. Strong quickly built a lucrative booking empire, arranging games for white, black, and Cuban clubs in New York City. However, his unfair treatment of players depleted talented teams, reduced quality of play, and ultimately lost revenue from gate receipts.

In 1905, to protect his business interest, Strong and several eastern club owners formed the National Association of Colored Base Ball Clubs of the United States and Cuba. Strong served as secretary and business manager and his close friend H. Walter "Slick" Schlichter as president. The association consisted initially of five clubs: the Philadelphia Giants, owned by Schlichter; the Brooklyn Royal Giants, owned by John Connors, the only black owner; Ed Lamar's Cuban X-Giants; John Bright's Original Cuban Giants; and the only Cuban team composed of all Cuban players, the Cuban Stars of Santiago de Cuba, owned by Manuel Campos of Brooklyn, New York.

With the addition of Cuban and American teams, Strong's "league" increased to ten by 1908. Association teams rarely played each other in a league format; instead, to maximize revenues, games were booked against white teams or other top black clubs. An association championship pennant was awarded based on total games won and lost.

Strong expanded his booking empire into the Midwest. But black clubs in Chicago and Detroit ignored his control and threats, and became safe havens for dissatisfied eastern players, gradually eroding Strong's association.

The final blow came with the formation of the New York Lincoln Giants in 1911 by Roderick and Edward McMahon. The McMahons ignored Strong and his association and proceeded to raid its clubs, forcing several to disband. By the close of the 1911 season, with too few teams or games to award a championship pennant, Nat Strong's once-powerful National Association of Colored Base Ball Clubs of the United States and Cuba quietly went out of business.

While the National Association of Colored Base Ball Clubs of the United States and Cuba was not a traditional baseball league, from 1905 to 1911 it contributed to greater recognition, opportunity, and growth of organized black professional baseball.

Jerry J. Wright

FURTHER READING
Lanctot, Neil. *Fair Dealing and Clean Playing: The Hilldale Club and the Development of Black Professional Baseball, 1910–1932.* Jefferson, NC: McFarland, 1994.
Ribowsky, Mark. *A Complete History of the Negro Leagues, 1884–1955.* New York: Birch Lane Press, 1995.
Riley, James A. *The Biographical Encyclopedia of the Negro Baseball Leagues.* New York: Carroll and Graf, 1994.
White, Sol. *Sol White's Official Base Ball Guide.* Philadelphia: H. Walter Schlichter, 1907.

NATIONAL BOWLING ASSOCIATION

The National Bowling Association (NBA) is a nonprofit corporation founded on August 20, 1939, in Detroit, Michigan. The organization was originally titled the National Negro Bowling Association (NNBA); it was renamed in 1944. Primarily the NBA was formed to encourage African Americans to develop recreational and professional skills in bowling. Secondly, the NBA served as a support organization to African-American bowlers who were denied membership in other bowling associations, such as the American Bowling Congress (ABC) and the Women's International Bowling Congress (WIBC), whose constitutions contained "Caucasians only" clauses. The NBA also served as a developmental agency for African Americans interested in becoming professional bowlers.

In 1939, the NBA held its first tournament in Cleveland, Ohio. Only men competed in this first event, but women began competing the following year. The NBA ran regular competitions, suspending play only from 1943 to 1945. In the late 1940s, the NBA actively fought for the integration of African Americans into mainstream bowling organizations and competitions. In 1950, the racial restrictions were removed from the constitutions of the ABC and the WIBC. On May 24, 1951, the first African-American bowlers participated in an ABC-sponsored competition. The NBA is currently in its sixty-fourth year and has over 30,000 members.

Tracey M. Salisbury

See also: Bowling.

FURTHER READING
Ashe, Arthur R., Jr. *A Hard Road to Glory: A History of the African-American Athlete*. New York: Warner Books, 1988.
Dent, David J. *In Search of Black America: Discovering the African-American Dream*. New York: Simon & Schuster, 2000.
"The TNBA Story." National Bowling Association (www.tnbainc.org/history/nbastory.html).

★ ★ ★

NEGRO AMERICAN LEAGUE

The Negro American League (NAL) formed in 1937 and operated through the 1959 season. The structure of the league and its composition did not remain the same through those twenty-two seasons, but most of the teams came from the South and Midwest until 1948, when the second Negro National League folded and a number of eastern clubs joined the NAL.

After the 1942 season, with the creation of a second Negro league in 1937 the World Series, begun back in the 1920s, was revived. In addition, a new tradition began with the creation of an East-West Classic, played at Chicago's Comiskey Park. This All-Star contest became one of the most popular games in Negro league history, as everyone came out to see their favorite stars compete.

A number of teams enjoyed great success in the NAL, especially the Kansas City Monarchs, under the solid leadership of businessman J.L. Wilkinson and his business manager, Tom Baird. The Monarchs won the first NAL pennant in 1937. The Cleveland Buckeyes provided solid competition in the 1940s under owners Wilbur Hayes and Ernie Wright. Birmingham and Indianapolis teams also enjoyed success in the NAL during the 1940s.

Not all the teams in the NAL enjoyed success or even long tenures. Teams came and went fairly quickly when they could not make enough money to meet their obligations. The Cincinnati Tigers, for example, were in the league for only its first season. The Toledo Crawfords and Raleigh Tigers also joined the league for only one season before the players moved on or, in the case of the Raleigh club, the squad went back to playing independently (so as not to have to pay a franchise fee or guarantees for games).

In 1949 the NAL went through a structural change with the formation of East and West Divisions with five clubs in each. This setup lasted until 1952, by then only six teams remained in the league. The league suffered declining attendance and newspaper coverage when Jackie Robinson entered the majors in 1947 and other players quickly followed. The Birmingham Black Barons were the last team to close their doors, in 1960, bringing an end to both the NAL and the tradition of the Negro leagues that had begun in 1920.

Leslie A. Heaphy

See also: Baseball; Negro League Baseball Museum.

FURTHER READING
Clark, Dick, and Larry Lester. *The Negro Leagues Book.* Cleveland: Society for American Baseball Research, 1994.
Heaphy, Leslie. "Shadowed Diamonds: The Growth and Decline of the Negro Leagues." Ph.D. diss., University of Toledo, 1995.
Riley, James A. *The Biographical Encyclopedia of the Negro Baseball Leagues.* New York: Carroll and Graf, 1994.

★ ★ ★

NEGRO LEAGUE BASEBALL MUSEUM

Sports museums are about the production of meaning, and the Negro League Baseball Museum (NLBM) stands as a reminder to African Americans of a cultural heritage about which they are ambivalent. The presence of the first blacks in any twentieth-century white professional sport only slightly predates the nation's watershed 1953–1954 civil rights legislation that awakened the country to the need for full integration, triggering the movement for integration in college and professional athletics. Records from the 1880s indicate that a few African Americans played on major league baseball teams; however, by 1887, major league teams "released" African-American players because Jim Crow laws and the "Gentlemen's Agreement" barred black men from the major leagues.

Andrew "Rube" Foster is credited with leading the formation of the Negro National League at a two-day meeting in Kansas City, Missouri, in February 1920. From 1920 to 1955, more than thirty communities were homes to franchises organized into six leagues: the Negro National League, the Eastern Colored League, the American Negro League, the East-West League, the Negro Southern League, and the Negro American League.

The Negro League Baseball Museum, Incorporated (East 18th Street, Kansas City, Missouri) established in 1990, was founded by Horace M. Peterson III to preserve more than sixty years of history dealing with Negro league baseball. Its officers and directors constitute a body of prominent African-American men and women as well as sports dignitaries and national notables devoted to promoting African-American achievement through educational scholarship and initiatives, minority entrepreneurship, and sport management. *Silhouettes*, official newsletter of the NLBM, is published quarterly.

Dana D. Brooks and Ronald Althouse

FURTHER READING
Peterson, Robert. *Only the Ball Was White: A History of Legendary Black Players and All-Black Professional Teams.* New York: Gramercy Books, 1970.

Ribowsky, Mark. *A Complete History of the Negro Leagues 1884–1955*. New York: Birch Lane Press, 1995.

Riley, James. *The Biographical Encyclopedia of the Negro Baseball Leagues*. New York: Carroll and Graf, 1994.

Silhouettes: The Official Newsletter of the Negro League Baseball Museum, 8 (Spring/Summer 2000) (www.nlbm.com).

★ ★ ★

NEGRO NATIONAL LEAGUE

In 1920 Andrew "Rube" Foster helped found the Negro National League (NNL) in Kansas City. Foster managed to bring together a group of businessmen, reporters, attorneys, and former players to create the first successful Negro league, with eight teams. The centerpiece of the new league became Foster's own Chicago American Giants. The other original entrants included the Indianapolis ABCs, the Dayton Marcos, the Kansas City Monarchs, the St. Louis Giants, the Detroit Stars, the Chicago Giants, and the traveling Cuban Stars.

Foster served as president and booking agent for the league until he became ill in 1926. Foster helped create a league that with franchise fees, official umpires, fines for fighting and jumping contracts, and guarantees for games. Each year the league officials and owners met to discuss issues and set new schedules. After the 1923 season this conference's business also included the newly created Eastern Colored League (ECL) and the creation of a World Series.

Foster's American Giants won the first pennant, while Detroit captured second place. This was the first of the Giants' twelve championships. The other successful NNL team was the Kansas City Monarchs, under the ownership of J.L. Wilkinson. The Monarchs won seventeen championships and two World Series.

The NNL finally folded after the 1931 season as the Great Depression hit the country. Negro league teams had a difficult time finding paying opponents to play and making their rental payments on the stadiums they leased. The NNL teams rented stadiums from local white teams and played when they were out of town. Foster secured these agreements and negotiated the fees.

The NNL gave many players the opportunity to play baseball. Outfielder James "Cool Papa" Bell played in St. Louis, while the great Oscar Charleston played for a number of teams including the Indianapolis ABCs.

After the NNL folded, the 1932 season was played with teams from the Negro Southern League and a new East-West League, formed for just the one season. The NNL had succeeded where earlier league efforts had failed, beginning a series of leagues that lasted until 1960 when the Birmingham Black Barons finally stopped playing.

Leslie A. Heaphy

See also: Baseball; Rube Foster; Negro League Baseball Museum; Negro Southern League.

FURTHER READING

Clark, Dick, and Larry Lester. *The Negro Leagues Book*. Cleveland: Society for American Baseball Research, 1994.

Heaphy, Leslie. "Shadowed Diamonds: The Growth and Decline of the Negro Leagues." Ph.D. diss., University of Toledo, 1995.

Riley, James A. *The Biographical Encyclopedia of the Negro Baseball Leagues*. New York: Carroll and Graf, 1994.

★ ★ ★

NEGRO SOUTHERN LEAGUE

On March 4, 1920, in Birmingham, Alabama, booking agent Monroe Young convened a handful of black and white owners from independent baseball clubs to create a new league. Christened the Southern Negro League, the new circuit began play with seven clubs located in cities across the South: the Atlanta, Georgia, Black Crackers; the Birmingham, Alabama, Black Barons; the Chattanooga, Tennessee, Black Lookouts; the Jacksonville, Florida, Red Caps; the Knoxville, Tennessee, Grays; the Montgomery, Alabama, Gray Sox; the Nashville, Tennessee, Giants; and the New Orleans, Louisiana, Black Pelicans.

This loose grouping of clubs operated as a regional black semipro league on the periphery of the Negro National League. Clubs paid membership dues to the National Association of Colored Professional Base Ball Clubs, but neither any club nor the league was bound by any formal agreement to serve as a farm system for the Negro National League.

Mired in the Jim Crow South, Southern Negro League teams were denied play against white opponents, significantly limiting their financial potential. But it was a strong, competitive league, due to the founder's foresight in locating franchises in close proximity to the main black population centers of the South. In 1924, the league expanded to ten teams, but by 1926 it was forced to reorganize as the Negro Southern League, under the direction of Bert Roody, when the Negro National League dipped into the southern circuit for replacement clubs. By the 1932 season the league boasted sixteen franchises in southern and northern cities, enjoying a brief elevation from its previous "minor league" status. For the first time, the league had a true president, the Nashville Elite Giants' owner, Tome Wilson, and capital from influential northern club owners.

The league's new stature was short-lived. As the Negro National League and the Negro American League reestablished themselves, stronger southern league teams—such as the Atlanta Black Crackers, Birmingham Black Barons, Jacksonville Red Caps, Kansas City Monarchs, and Memphis Red Sox—changed their affiliations to the northern leagues. This action forced the Negro Southern League to establish franchises in smaller, less populous cities and gradually reduced its success.

From 1936 until the eventual demise of black baseball and the Negro Southern League in 1955, some twenty-five teams constituted this black institution. While the league was never affiliated with any Negro major league organization and was never considered a major league, it contributed in an important way to keeping the northern Negro leagues solvent and provided hundreds of young black players the opportunity to play professional baseball.

Jerry J. Wright

See also: Negro National League.

FURTHER READING

Dixon, Phil, and Patrick J. Hannigan. *The Negro Baseball Leagues: A Photographic History.* Mattituck, NY: Ameron, 1992.

Mills, Prentice. "Diamond in the Dell: Time Travel Through Nashville's Past." *Black Ball News: The Journal of Negro League Baseball History* 2 (1993): 2–14.

Peterson, Robert. *Only the Ball Was White: A History of Legendary Black Players and All-Black Professional Teams.* New York: Oxford University Press, 1970.

Rogosin, Donn. *Invisible Men: Life in Baseball's Negro Leagues.* New York: Atheneum, 1983.

Renaldo NEHEMIAH

Born March 24, 1959, Scotch Plains, New Jersey
Hurdler, football player

Nehemiah is a track legend and former National Football League wide receiver. A graduate of the University of Maryland in 1977, he earned a degree in broadcast journalism. Today, Nehemiah is a sports agent who manages world-class track and field athletes.

Nehemiah, a three-sport high school star, received a track and field scholarship to the University of Maryland in 1977. He won four of The Athletic Congress (TAC) titles, three of them outdoors, and in 1979 won the Pan American Games title and the World Cup. He earned National Collegiate Athletic Association All-American honors in his sophomore year. Nehemiah set world records in the fifty-five, sixty, and 110-meter hurdles. The boycott of the 1980 Moscow Olympic Games shattered Nehemiah's dreams for an Olympic gold medal. He was the first man to break the thirteen-second barrier in the 110-meter hurdles, with a world record of 12.93 in 1981. Though he had no experience in football at the collegiate level, his dominance in the ABC "Superstars" Individual Athletic Competition caught the eye of the 49ers Pro Bowl receiver Dwight Clark, who recommended that he try out with the 49ers. He entered the NFL with San Francisco in 1982. In 1984, Nehemiah was invited to play in the Pro Bowl, and in 1985 he earned a Super Bowl championship ring. In 1986, Nehemiah received the Jim Thorpe Award for excellence in two sports.

Nehemiah returned to track in 1986, achieving world rankings four more times from 1988 to 1991 before retiring. Nehemiah challenged the rules of amateurism in court for four years and became the first amateur ever to play professional sports and later be reinstated to compete again as an amateur in track and field. Professional athletes can now participate as amateurs in track and field, because of what is appropriately called the Nehemiah Rule.

A licensed representative in investments and financial planning, Nehemiah worked with Lara, Shull and May Ltd. He also has been involved in broadcasting, served as an assistant track coach at George Mason University, and later joined Octagon, the sports marketing and entertainment division of The Interpublic Group, one of the world's largest advertising and marketing communications groups, as the director of track and field. Nehemiah held a similar position with Gold Medal Management, Boulder, Colorado, for two years.

Doris R. Corbett

FURTHER READING
Annerino, John. *African Americans in Track and Field*. Boston: Evergreen, 1998.
Dandera, Joseph. *If I Were a San Francisco 49er*. Los Angeles: Picture Me Books, 1993.
Pierson, Don. *Renaldo Nehemiah: The Bionic Hurdler*, Sports Stars Series. Chicago: Children's Press, 1980.

★ ★ ★

NEW YORK PIONEER CLUB

The New York Pioneer Club (NYPC) was founded in 1936 by Robert Douglas, William Culbreath, and Joseph J. Yancey. Originally named the New York Olympic Club and intended only as a track club for Harlem men and boys, the NYPC eventually became an integrated track club that strove to improve race relations by fostering excellence in both education and sport. Members of the club, who were expected to practice proper deportment and adhere to a specific speech and dress code, would capture many individual titles in Amateur

Athletic Union–sponsored track meets and garner international acclaim for their victories in Olympic competition.

Like many other all-black or integrated sports teams, the NYPC experienced various forms of racial discrimination, particularly during the middle years of the twentieth century. The club dealt with these forms of racial discrimination in various ways, sometimes actually refusing to participate in athletic meets, and in other instances acquiescing in order to compete. In 1946, for instance, the club refused to participate in the National AAU track and field championships in San Antonio, Texas, because of that city's segregated hotel accommodations. Just four years later the club commuted some three hours from Lincoln University in Oxford, Pennsylvania, to the National AAU track and field championships at the University of Maryland rather than stay in a segregated hotel in Maryland or eat in a segregated restaurant. Fortunately, those more glaring forms of racial discrimination would gradually begin to subside during the second half of the century, allowing the NYPC to engage more openly in athletic competitions and contribute to sport to the present day.

David K. Wiggins

FURTHER READING

Abramson, Jesse. "Democratic Ideal: The Pioneer Club." *Amateur Athlete*, September 1945, 11, 15.

Cooper, Pamela. *The American Marathon*. Syracuse, NY: Syracuse University Press, 1998.

Corbitt, Theodore. "Testimonial to a Pioneer: Joseph J. Yancey." *Road Runners Club*. New York Association Newsletter (1975): 10.

NEW YORK RENAISSANCE FIVE

The New York Renaissance Five, founded in 1922, comprised the first all-black professional basketball team in the United States. They existed before the Harlem Globetrotters and were known for playing a very different style of basketball. Instead of playing for entertainment, the New York Renaissance Five (known as the "Rens") played to win, and they were very successful. Over the history of the organization (1922–1949) they compiled an impressive 2588 wins against only 539 loses. From 1932 to 1936, the Rens posted 473 wins and only lost forty-nine times. Within one eighty-six-day stretch (1932–1933), the Rens won a remarkable eighty-eight games. During the 1939 season the Rens went 112–7 and defeated the NBL champion Oshkosh All-Stars 34–25 to capture the championship at the World Professional Tournament in Chicago.

The Rens were the brainchild of Bob Douglas, who is known as the "father of black basketball." Douglas began his career by organizing two amateur teams of black players from 1919 to 1923. The teams, known as the Spartan Braves and the Spartan Hornets, played both black and white teams in the New York City area. Douglas branched out from amateur basketball when he was not allowed to keep some of his players who had played other sports professionally. The end of his association with amateur basketball marked the beginning of his association with the Rens.

Douglas floated his idea for a professional touring basketball team to the owners of the Harlem Renaissance Casino. The casino was newly opened and was eager to flourish in what was then the epicenter of black culture, Harlem. Douglas met this need by agreeing to name the team the Renaissance (after the casino); in exchange, the team would be able to practice and play on the casino's dance floor. The relationship was a resounding success. John Issacs, who played with the Rens from 1936 to 1941, said, "It was twofold: People came to see the team and came to dance; Once the game was over, People stayed. It was like, 'Let's go back to dancing.'"

The Rens were considered barnstormers. They had a home at the Harlem Renaissance Casino, but they maintained a hectic schedule traveling throughout the country playing semipro, black college, and other professional teams. They even played the premier team of that era, the Original Celtics. The games against the Celtics, featuring Dutch Dehnert, Nat Holman, and Joe Lapchick, were particularly popular, drawing as many as 15,000 fans. While the Rens enjoyed the chance to compete as equals on the basketball court, they did not enjoy that luxury in the broader society. There were race riots in some cities when they played. Victories against all-white teams could be especially tense. The lack of acceptance extended to their professional existence, when the Rens were denied acceptance into the American Basketball League in 1925. In a show of solidarity, the Original Celtics refused to join the league as well. The coming of the Great Depression marked the end of the ABL and the beginning of the greatest professional years for the Rens. The Celtics could safely be considered the dominant team of the 1920s, but the Rens enjoyed that distinction during the 1930s.

The quality of the Rens is evident in both their record and in the reputation they developed over their professional history. They were known as consummate basketball professionals, credits to the "team" aspects of the game. "To this day, I have never seen a team play better team basketball," Hall of Fame coach John Wooden has said.

Adam Phillips

See also: Basketball.

FURTHER READING
Naismith Memorial Hall of Fame, *Official homepage of the Naismith Memorial Basketball Hall of Fame*, June 2001–October 2001 (www.hoophall.com).
NBA.com History Archives. Official homepage of the National Basketball Association (www.nba.com), June 2001–October 2001.
Rayl, Susan J. "The New York Renaissance Professional Black Basketball Team, 1923–1950," Ph. D. diss., Pennsylvania State University, 1996.

★ ★ ★

Don NEWCOMBE

Born June 14, 1926, Madison, New Jersey
Baseball player

Don Newcombe began his baseball career as an eighteen-year-old fastball pitcher for the Newark Eagles of the Negro National League. In 1945, his second year in the Negro leagues, he accumulated a record of eight wins and three losses and attracted the attention of the Brooklyn Dodgers. After signing with the Dodgers in 1946, he played in the minor leagues until he joined the parent club in Brooklyn in 1949.

Newcombe became one of the dominant pitchers in baseball. In 1949, he won seventeen games, struck out 149 batters, and recorded five shutouts, winning the National League Rookie of the Year award. He continued his pitching dominance in 1950 and 1951, winning nineteen and twenty games, respectively. Also in 1951 he led the league in strikeouts, with 164.

He served in the military for the 1952 and 1953 seasons, returning to Brooklyn in 1954. In 1955 Newcombe again won twenty games, helping the Dodgers win the World Series. His best year came in 1956, when he won twenty-seven games, the National League Most Valuable Player award, and the first-ever Cy Young award.

Newcombe moved with the Dodgers to Los Angles in 1958 before bouncing around between several teams. In 1962, he concluded his baseball career as an outfielder and first baseman for the Chunichi Dragons in Japan. During his ten year career, Newcombe won 149 games and lost ninety. He helped Brooklyn win three National League pennants and one World Series.

Rob Fink

FURTHER READING

Baseball Encyclopedia: The Complete and Definitive Record of Major League Baseball. 10th ed. New York: Macmillan, 1996.

Golenbock, Peter. *Bums: An Oral History of the Brooklyn Dodgers.* New York: G.P. Putnam's Sons, 1984.

Kahn, Roger. *The Boys of Summer.* New York: Harper and Row, 1972.

Riley, James A. *The Biographical Encyclopedia of the Negro Baseball Leagues.* New York: Carroll and Graf, 1994.

★ ★ ★

Ozzie NEWSOME

Born March 16, 1956, Muscle Shoals, Alabama
Football player and executive

Born in Muscle Shoals, Alabama, Newsome attended Colbert County High School and the University of Alabama (1974–1977), where he started in forty-eight consecutive games as a wide receiver and was a consensus All-American in his final season.

Newsome was a first-round draft pick by the National Football League's Cleveland Browns in 1978; he missed only six games in thirteen seasons from 1978 to 1900. He was the first rookie in twenty-five years to be named the Browns' Offensive Player of the Year, in 1978. Newsome caught 662 passes for 7,980 yards and forty-seven touchdowns, earning the nickname "Wizard of Oz." He holds the Browns record for career receptions and receiving yardage, was twice named to the All-Pro team (1979 and 1984), and was selected for three Pro Bowls (1981, 1984, 1985) and the ALL-NFL team of the 1980s. In 1986 Newsome won the Ed Block Courage award, for continuing to play in spite of being injured.

Newsome received the NFL Player's Association Whizzer White award for community service in 1990, the year he retired from playing football. In 1994 he was inducted into the College Football Hall of Fame.

Newsome moved to Baltimore with the Browns in 1996 and became a scout for the team, now the Ravens. In 1996, he was named vice president for Ravens player personnel and is credited with designing and recruiting a team that evolved into a Super Bowl contender in 2001. He was inducted into the NFL Hall of Fame in 1999 and named senior vice president for football operations for the Ravens in 2001.

Trisha M. Hothorn

FURTHER READING

Jones, Brent. "A Newsome Given Raise, Bigger Title by Modell." *Baltimore Sun,* August 3, 2001.

George, Thomas. "A Sports of the Times: He's Made It, and Yet More Needs Doing." *New York Times,* August 7, 1999.

"Newsome to Be Fifth Tight End Enshrined in Hall of Fame." *Cable News Network/Sports Illustrated* (www.sportsillustrated.cnn.com).

"An Ozzie Newsome Biography." *Pro Football Hall of Fame* (www.profootballhof.com).

★ ★ ★

Ken NORTON

Born August 9, 1943, Jacksonville, Illinois
Boxer

Born out of wedlock to teenagers, Ken Norton was named Ken Florence until his mother, Ruth, married John Norton in 1947. Unlike most boxers, Ken Norton grew up in a middle-class family. His mother was a hospital administrator and his stepfather was a fire-truck driver and later a police department dispatcher.

A multisport athlete in high school, the six-foot three-inch, 200-pound Norton was heavily recruited to play college football. He attended Northeast Missouri State University but dropped out during his sophomore year. In 1964 he joined the U.S. Marines Corps. Soon thereafter, the rugged Norton began boxing, eventually winning the All-Marine Championship three times.

Following his discharge from the Marines in 1967, Norton began prizefighting professionally. Due to his impressive strength and the tutelage of trainer Eddie Futch, Norton compiled a 30-1 record with twenty-four knockouts over six years.

On March 31, 1973, the relatively unknown Norton earned a split decision and the North American Boxing Federation heavyweight title with a twelve-round decision over the former champ Muhammad Ali. In addition to giving Ali only his second loss, Norton broke his jaw. Though Norton later held the World Boxing Council (WBC) heavyweight belt, his first fight with Ali was the pinnacle of his career. Six months later, Norton lost a split decision in a rematch with Ali. Due to his strong showings against Ali, however, Norton earned a title shot. On March 26, 1974, in Caracas, Venezuela, the intimidating George Foreman knocked out Norton in the second round. Two years later, Norton fought Ali for a third and final time. Ali, who had since regained the heavyweight title, won a unanimous, if controversial, decision.

In 1977, Norton won two WBC title-elimination fights and was eventually awarded the heavyweight championship, after Leon Spinks failed to honor a commitment to defend the title against Norton. His reign as champ was brief, however. In his first defense, Norton lost a fifteen-round bout with Larry Holmes. Norton retired from boxing in 1981. His career record was 42–7–1, with thirty-three KOs.

In February 1986, Norton was involved in a one-car accident in which he suffered massive head injuries. He has since recovered.

Norton was inducted into the International Boxing Hall of Fame in 1992. Six years later, *Ring* magazine ranked him among the fifty greatest heavyweights of all time.

Daniel A. Nathan

See also: Films; Larry Holmes.

FURTHER READING

"Ken Norton." *International Boxing Hall of Fame* (www.ibhof.com/norton.htm).
Magee, Jerry. "Norton Fights Back from Devastation of Car Accident KO." *San Diego Union-Tribune*, February 5, 2001.
Norton, Ken, with Marshall Terrill and Mike Fitzgerald. *Going the Distance*. Champaign, IL: Sports Publishing, 2000.

★ ★ ★

William NUNN, JR.

Born September 30, 1925, Pittsburgh, Pennsylvania
Journalist, football executive

The son of Mabel Stewart Nunn and William G. Nunn, Sr., he starred in basketball while attending Westinghouse High

School. There, he teamed with Charles Cooper, the first black player to sign a National Basketball Association contract. The younger Nunn earned an English degree at West Virginia State College. Like his father, he spent his entire journalism career at the *Pittsburgh Courier*. He became a reporter, sports editor, and managing editor.

After graduating from college, he joined the *Courier*'s sports department and later succeeded Wendell Smith as sports editor. While sports editor, he continued the paper's selections of black college football All-Americans and organized an annual banquet for the honorees. He eventually rose to managing editor of the paper, a post held earlier by his father. He left full-time employment with the paper and joined the Pittsburgh Steelers football team as assistant director of player personnel, scouting college players and running the team's training camp. He became one of the few black men to gain a managerial position in professional football without playing experience. Renowned for his ability to communicate with college players and coaches, Nunn developed strong relationships with black colleges and universities and predominantly white institutions as well. While working with the Steelers he was responsible for scouting or signing many stars, including L.C. Greenwood, Mel Blount, John Stallworth, Joe Gilliam, and Donnie Shell.

Nunn retired from full-time work in 1986 but still occasionally works with the Steelers.

Michael Marsh

FURTHER READING
Cook, Ron. "Nunn Helped Open NFL Door for Black Players." *Pittsburgh Press*, August 24, 1986.
Ruck, Rob. *Sandlot Seasons: Sport in Black Pittsburgh*. Urbana: University of Illinois Press, 1993.
Walker, Jackie. "The Man." *Black Sports*, May 1975, 44–45, 47.

★ ★ ★

William NUNN, SR.

Born January 4, 1900, Pittsburgh, Pennsylvania
Died November 14, 1969, Pittsburgh, Pennsylvania
Journalist, sports executive

The son of Julius Nunn and Mary Hopkins Nunn, he played football while attending Westinghouse High School. After graduation, Nunn worked at the post office. In 1919, he left that "safe" job and joined the *Pittsburgh Courier*, which had been founded only nine years earlier. He spent his entire career in journalism, forty-four years, at the paper. He served the *Courier* as a reporter, columnist, sports editor, managing editor, and board member.

Nunn covered black college sports and helped spearhead the *Courier*'s coverage of Joe Louis. As a *Courier* editor, he helped lead the paper's campaigns for racial justice. Two such campaigns were a fundraiser for the National Association for the Advancement of Colored People (generating $17,000) and a battle to integrate the country's armed forces. He and *Courier* founder Robert L. Vann met with major league baseball's commissioner Kenesaw "Mountain" Landis to discuss the exclusion of black players. He also served as secretary for the Negro National Baseball League. After his death, veteran reporter Eric Roberts called him the "brightest journalistic light" he had encountered.

Nunn was a community leader. A Republican Party activist, he chaired the Western Pennsylvania Republican Council and was an assistant to the party's state chairman. He served as president of the Leondi Club, the largest black social organization in the city. He also was a member of civic and fraternal organizations, including the Omega Psi Phi fraternity.

Michael Marsh

FURTHER READING

Buni, Andrew. *Robert L. Vann of the Pittsburgh Courier.* Pittsburgh: University of Pittsburgh Press, 1974.

"Courier Editor Nunn Truax Election Aide." *Pittsburgh Press*, April 14, 1964.

"Negro Leader Nunn, Ex-*Courier* Editor." *Pittsburgh Post-Gazette*, November 15, 1969.

Walker, Jackie. "The Man." *Black Sports*, May 1975, 44–45, 47.

Wiggins, David K. *Glory Bound: Black Athletes in a White America.* Syracuse, NY: Syracuse University Press, 1997.

"William G. Nunn, Sr., Ex-*Courier* Editor, Buried in Pittsburgh," *Pittsburgh Courier*, November 22, 1969.

Dan O'BRIEN

Born July 18, 1966, Portland, Oregon
Decathlete

The son of a biracial couple and adopted by Jim and Virginia O'Brien at the age of two, O'Brien won The Athletics Congress (TAC) junior decathlon championship as a high school senior in 1984. He qualified for the 1988 Summer Olympic trials but withdrew because of an injury sustained in the long jump. Runner-up in the 1990 TAC decathlon championship, O'Brien established a decathlon world record of 26 feet 3½ inches in the long jump and an American record first day total of 4,656 points.

After winning the 1991 TAC decathlon national championship he captured the 1991 world championship with an American record of 8,812 points, which surpassed Bruce Jenner's 1976 standard by 178 points. O'Brien stunned the athletic world by failing to qualify for the 1992 U.S. Olympic Team; following a first-day world-record performance of 4,698 points, he failed to clear any height in the pole vault. Later that year, O'Brien prevailed with a world record of 8,891 points at Talence, France. In 1993 he won the heptathlon at the indoor World Championships and established a world record of 6,476 points before capturing the decathlon in both the USTAF championships and the outdoor world championships. O'Brien garnered the 1994 and 1995 USTAF decathlon titles and the 1995 world championship. After winning the 1996 Olympic trials, he triumphed at the Olympic Games, winning the decathlon gold medal.

Adam R. Hornbuckle

FURTHER READING
Hendershott, Jon. "Difficult Questions to Ask." *Track and Field News* 45 (August 1991): 26.

Patrick, Dick. "O'Brien Sets Course for 'Greatest' Tag." *USA Today*, August 4, 1992.
Wallechinsky, David. *The Complete Book of the Summer Olympics.* Sydney 2000 ed. Woodstock, NY: Overlook Press, 2000.

★ ★ ★

Hakeem OLAJUWON

Born January 21, 1963, Lagos, Nigeria
Basketball player

Hakeem Olajuwon is the son of Salam and Abike Olajuwon, who were in the cement business. After attending schools in Nigeria, he entered the University of Houston, graduating in 1984. Drafted as the number-one pick by the Houston Rockets, he has remained with them since.

As a boy Olajuwon loved sports but excelled at team handball. He attended boarding schools and a teacher-training high school in Nigeria before accepting a basketball scholarship to Houston, having been noticed by an American recruiter in a tournament in Angola. Olajuwon made an immediate impact at Houston, averaging just over thirteen points per game for his three years but leading the nation in field-goal percentage and rebounding in his senior year (1983–1984). Houston went 88–16 in those years, finishing second in the NCAA tournament in 1984.

In Olajuwon's sixteen years in the NBA he has been named to the first-team All-NBA six times, led his team to back-to-back NBA titles (in 1994 and 1995), was Most Valuable Player (MVP) in the league in 1994 and MVP of the NBA finals in 1994 and 1995. He is the all-time NBA leader in blocked shots.

Hakeem Olajuwon, the outstanding center of the Houston Rockets, drives around the Seattle Super Sonics Ervin Johnson in a 1995 game in Tacoma, Washington. *(AP/Wide World Photos)*

Though not the first foreign-born player to play in the NBA, Olajuwon was the first to come from Africa and among the first to have not attended an American high school. He accelerated a search among college and professional recruiters for basketball players worldwide. Olajuwon is inspirational in the African-American community because he demands that shoes he endorses sell for only thirty-five dollars, and because he has become a devout Muslim. In 1996 he became an American citizen and played on the 1996 U.S. Olympic team. He was named one of the all-time top fifty NBA players in 1996.

Murry R. Nelson

FURTHER READING
Gutman, Bill. *Hakeem Olajuwon: Superstar Center.* Brookfield, CT: Millbrook, 1995.
Olajuwon, Hakeem, with Peter Knobler. *Living the Dream: My Life and Basketball.* Boston: Little, Brown, 1996.

★ ★ ★

OLYMPIC GAMES

The modern Olympic Games began in 1896 at Athens, but no African Americans competed. In 1900, when France won the rugby football championship, one of the French players was Constantin Henriquez de Zubiera; a picture of him in a German sporting magazine makes it fairly certain that Henriquez de Zubiera was the first black man to compete and win a medal in the Olympic Games. He represented France but was most likely Algerian.

In 1904 at St. Louis, George Poage of the University of Wisconsin competed in several sprint and hurdle races, winning two bronze medals. Poage is often considered the first African-American Olympian, but another black American, Joseph Stadler of Cleveland, also competed at St. Louis, winning a silver medal in the standing high jump. The first black Africans (aside from Henriquez de Zubiera) also competed in St. Louis, Len Taunyane and Jan Mashiani, in the marathon footrace. Rather ironically, they were South African members of the Zulu tribe who were in St. Louis as part of an exhibit at the Louisiana Purchase Exposition.

In 1908 at London, John Taylor of the United States won a gold medal in the 1,600-meter medley relay. A student at

Tommie Smith (in middle) and John Carlos (far right) giving their famous black power salute on the victory stand following their first and third place finishes in the 200-meter dash at the 1968 Mexico City Olympics. Smith and Carlos caused such a furor that the U.S. Olympic Committee kicked them out of the Olympic village and sent them home. *(AP/Wide World Photos)*

the University of Pennsylvania, Taylor had earned a degree in veterinary medicine shortly before the Olympics, but he died from typhoid fever within five months of returning from London. It would not be until 1924 that an American black would win an individual gold medal. That came at Paris, when DeHart Hubbard triumphed in the long jump.

The 1936 Olympic Games were held in Berlin, and Adolf Hitler hoped to use them as a showcase for his theories of Aryan supremacy. But the Germans were upstaged by the son of a black Alabaman sharecropper, Jesse Owens. Owens won the 100 meters, 200 meters, and long jump, and ran on the winning 4 x 100-meter relay team, destroying Hitler's theories of a master race. It is often stated that Hitler refused to congratulate Owens, but that is likely not correct. On the first day of the Olympic track and field competition, Hitler congratulated several German champions but refused to congratulate Cornelius Johnson, an African American who had won the high jump. The IOC president, Count Henri de Baillet-Latour, subsequently told Hitler that he was to congratulate all of the champions in public or none of them. Hitler chose to make no further public displays.

Prior to World War II, only a very few African-American women had made U.S. Olympic teams. The only one to compete for the United States was Tidye Pickett, who ran the hurdles at the 1936 Olympic Games. It was not until 1948 that an African-American woman won a medal at the Olympics—in London, when Alice Coachman won the gold medal in the high jump. Since that time, many female African Americans have starred for U.S. track and field teams. Notable among them have been Wilma Rudolph, Evelyn Ashford, Florence Griffith Joyner, and Jackie Joyner-Kersee.

Until the 1950s, most blacks who had competed in the Olympics did so for the United States. There were a few exceptions, arising when Africans from European colonies, notably French ones, competed for the European nations. But beginning in 1956, when Ethiopia competed at the Melbourne Olympics, African Americans were joined by a true influx of black Africans. In 1960 at Rome, the Ethiopian Abebe Bikila won the marathon footrace, a victory he would defend in 1964. He was the first in a long line of great distance runners from African nations, who now dominate distance running at the Olympics.

African Americans have continued to represent the United States at the Olympics in greater and greater numbers and in more and more sports. The first American black to compete in basketball at the Olympics was Donald Barksdale, who won a gold medal in 1948. Since that time, the American basketball team has become more and more composed of African Americans, especially since the NBA and professional players were allowed to compete in 1992. Among the African-American basketball players who have won basketball gold medals for the United States are Michael Jordan, Magic Johnson, Bill Russell, Oscar Robertson, and Charles Barkley.

The first African American to win individual gold medals in a sport besides track and field was John Davis, who won the heavyweight weightlifting championship at the 1948 and 1952 Olympics, and was at the time considered the strongest man in the world.

African Americans have produced most of the great Olympic boxers who have represented the United States since World War II; many of them went on to win world professional championships. Floyd Patterson was the first in this category, winning the Olympic middleweight title in 1952 and becoming heavyweight world champion in 1956. Other African-American Olympic boxing champions who prospered in the pro ranks are Joe Frazier, George Foreman, Sugar Ray Leonard, Pernell Whitaker, and Roy Jones.

But the greatest of them all, and one who called himself "The Greatest," was Muhammad Ali. Born Cassius Marcellus Clay, he won the gold medal in the light-heavyweight division at the 1960 Olympics in Rome. After the Olympics he quickly moved to the top of the professional heavyweight ranks, winning the world title in 1964 in a major upset over Sonny Liston. Shortly thereafter, he embraced the Muslim faith and changed his name to Muhammad Ali. He dominated boxing for the next fifteen years, as an athlete and as a personality.

Racial strife enveloped America in the 1960s, and one would be naive to think that the Olympic Games were immune. Leading up to the 1968 Olympics, Dr. Harry Edwards, a professor of sociology at San Jose State University, called for American blacks to boycott the games in protest of America's racist attitudes. The boycott did not materialize. But after Tommie Smith won the 200-meter race, in which John Carlos came in third, the two African Americans stood on the victory platform with their heads bowed and one arm raised with a black glove while the American flag was raised and the "Star-Spangled Banner" was played. Their action was met with howls of protest from many white Americans, and the IOC banned them from further competition, for making a political statement.

A similar problem occurred in 1972. The 400 meters was won by Vince Matthews, with Wayne Collett second. On the victory platform they stood nonchalantly, barefooted, their warm-up suits unzipped to the waist, and paid no attention while the national anthem played, simply talking casually to each other. Another furor arose, and again the IOC banned them from further Olympic competition.

In 1996 at the Atlanta Olympic Games, Muhammad Ali was given the honor of lighting the Olympic flame at the opening ceremony. Because he was shaking with Parkinson's disease, it was a struggle for him, but he lit all our souls when he raised the torch on high after lighting the flame. Another African American, Rafer Johnson, the 1960 Olympic decathlon champion, had also lit the Olympic flame, at the 1984 opening ceremony.

Like the men, female African Americans have branched out from track and field to other sports. Women's basketball became an Olympic sport in 1976, and many of America's top female hoopsters have been black. These include Cheryl Miller, Theresa Edwards, Sheryl Swoopes, Cynthia Cooper, Chamique Holdsclaw, and Lynette Woodard.

Women's rowing has not seen many African Americans compete, but in 1976 Anita De Frantz earned a bronze medal in the coxed eights. She also made the ill-fated 1980 Olympic team, which did not compete because of President Carter's mandated boycott. De Frantz, a lawyer by training, stridently opposed the boycott. It was to little avail, but she was noticed by the International Olympic Committee, and in 1983 she became the first black woman to be appointed to the IOC. In 2000 she was elevated to first vice president of the IOC. In 2001 she ran for president of the IOC, albeit unsuccessfully.

No African Americans made the U.S. Olympic swimming team until 2000. The first was Anthony Ervin, who tied for first place in the fifty-meter freestyle at Sydney. Through 2000, no black American woman has competed in swimming at the Olympics. Another showcase sport at the Olympics is gymnastics. Several African Americans have starred in gymnastics, most notably Dominique Dawes, who won a gold medal in 1996 as a member of the winning women's team. Dawes also competed in 2000, but with less success.

Few African Americans have competed at the Olympic Winter Games. The first was Tai Babilonia, who competed in pairs figure skating at the 1976 Olympics. Babilonia was of mixed race, having a black mother and a Filipino father. Beginning in 1980, the sport of bobsledding began recruiting track sprinters to help with push starts. This has brought several African Americans to this sport, the most famous ones being Willie Davenport, who won the 1968 Olympic high hurdles title, and Herschel Walker, former Heisman Trophy winner and professional football player, who competed in 1992.

The most decorated African American at the Winter Olympics has been Debi Thomas, a figure skater who was cofavorite for the 1988 women's title with East Germany's Katarina Witt. But Thomas struggled with her free program, and Witt won; Thomas earned a bronze medal.

In certain sports, especially track and field, basketball, and boxing, current American Olympic teams are made up predominately of African Americans. In other sports, such as wrestling, weightlifting, cycling, soccer football, and judo, our teams usually include a few African Americans. But there remain a number of virtual "lily-white" sports, such as equestrian events, fencing (although Peter Westbrook was our top sabreur from 1980–1996), shooting, and sailing. As for administration, few African Americans have moved to the top level of American sports federations.

Bill Mallon

See also: Autobiographies; Civil Rights; Racial Theories; Women.

FURTHER READING
Ashe, Arthur R., Jr. *A Hard Road To Glory: A History of the African-American Athlete.* New York: Amistad, 1993.
Carlson, Lewis H., and John J. Fogarty. *Tales of Gold: An Oral History of the Summer Olympic Games Told by America's Gold Medal Winners.* Chicago: Contemporary Books, 1987.
Page, James A. *Black Olympian Medalists.* Englewood, CO: Libraries Unlimited, 1991.

Shaquille O'NEAL

Born March 6, 1972, Newark, New Jersey
Basketball player

O'Neal was born in Newark, New Jersey, the son of Lucille O'Neal. Two years later she married a career soldier, Sgt. Phillip Harrison, who helped raise the often unruly Shaquille, frequently assuming the role of strong disciplinarian. "Thank goodness I had two parents who loved me and stayed on my case," O'Neal later commented about his childhood.

Despite his enormous size—he stood six feet, seven inches and weighed 225 pounds in the eighth grade—he approached basketball with little enthusiasm until his senior year in high school, when he led a

Shaquille O'Neal meeting with President George Bush at the White House in 1991. *(AP/Wide World Photos)*

small army base high school in San Antonio, Texas, to a 36–0 record and the 1989 Division 2A state championship.

He enrolled in Louisiana State University following an intense recruiting effort by more than 100 colleges. He earned All-Southeast Conference and All-American honors, being named the College Player of the Year in 1991. After his junior season he opted for the NBA draft and was selected by the Orlando Magic. At seven feet, one inch and 300 pounds, "Shaq" made the NBA All-Star team his rookie season. His forte was rebounding and using his bulk to muscle close to the basket for short shots, including "monster" dunks. Conversely, his free-throw inadequacies led teams to foul him repeatedly in what was called a "Hack-a-Shaq" defense. In 1996 he opted for free agency and signed a seven-year, $120 million contract with the Los Angeles Lakers and helped lead the team to the 2000 NBA championship. Through 2000 he averaged twenty-seven points and 12.4 rebounds a game, earning All-League honors each year.

He lives in Orlando during the off season. Popular with fans and the media alike, O'Neal is known for his infectious smile, congenial personality, and exemplary off-court behavior. In 2000 he completed requirements for a baccalaureate degree in general studies, thereby making good on his promise to his parents when he began college eleven years earlier.

Richard O. Davies

FURTHER READING
Baton Rouge Advocate, December 15, 2000.
"Guiding Star." *Sports Illustrated*, June 19, 2000, 42–46.
"Shaq in the Battle Again." *Newsweek*, April 24, 2000, 66–67.
"Shaquille O'Neal Saluted." *Jet*, July 24, 2000, 58–62.

★   ★   ★

Buck O'NEIL

Born November 13, 1911, Carabelle, Florida
Baseball player

Born the son of farm workers in Florida, O'Neil began working in the celery fields at the age of twelve. Encouraged by his family, he pursued his dream of playing baseball while attending Edward Waters College. After graduating in 1930, O'Neil joined the Miami Giants. For the next few years, he played on a number of Negro league teams, including the Memphis Red Sox. In 1938, O'Neil joined the Kansas City Monarchs. He stayed with the team until 1955.

A consistent hitter and knowledgeable player, O'Neil helped the Monarchs win five Negro American League pennants, including four straight from 1939 to 1942. In

Buck O'Neil, one of the more well-known players from the Negro Baseball Leagues. *(Sports Archive)*

1942, O'Neil's Monarchs also won the first Negro World Series between the Negro American League and the Negro National League. O'Neil took a break from baseball in 1943 to join the navy and serve in World War II; he left the military in 1945. The following year, he won the Negro American League batting title with a .353 average.

O'Neil finished his career in the Negro leagues as the Monarchs' manager. In 1956, his baseball career began a new chapter when the Chicago Cubs hired him as a scout. Through this position he signed Ernie Banks and Lou Brock, along with other black players. Then, in 1962, the Cubs made him the first-ever African-American coach in major league baseball. He is still involved in baseball today, serving on the Hall of Fame's Veterans' Committee and as chairman of the board of the Negro Leagues Museum.

Rob Fink

FURTHER READING

"Buck," John. *I Was Right on Time: My Journey from the Negro Leagues to the Majors.* New York: Simon & Schuster, 1996.

Peterson, Robert. *Only the Ball Was White: A History of Legendary Black Players and All-Black Professional Teams.* New York: Oxford University Press, 1970.

Ribowsky, Mark. *A Complete History of the Negro Leagues: 1884 to 1955.* Secaucus, NJ: Citadel, 1995.

Riley, James A. *The Biographical Encyclopedia of the Negro Baseball Leagues.* New York: Carroll and Graf, 1994.

Rogosin, Donn. *Invisible Men: Life in Baseball's Negro Leagues.* New York: Kodansha International, 1983.

★ ★ ★

Willie O'REE

Born October 15, 1935, Fredericton, Nebraska
Hockey player

The youngest of twelve children born to Harry and Rosebud O'Ree, he was the first black hockey player to play in the National Hockey League (NHL). He later became involved in providing opportunities for minority and underprivileged children to play ice hockey.

O'Ree began playing on a backyard rink at the age of three and within two years was playing organized hockey. In 1955, while playing for the Kitchener Canucks junior team, O'Ree was struck by a deflected puck and lost almost all sight in one eye. Told by doctors to stop playing, O'Ree concealed his injury and later switched positions, which allowed him to see the ice surface out of his good eye. He was nicknamed the "king of the near miss," a label that reflected his fast speed and creative stick-handling that, however, only infrequently resulted in goals, likely a result of his impaired vision. A multitalented athlete, O'Ree was invited to the Milwaukee Braves' minor league camp in 1956 and played his first NHL game on January 18, 1958, for the Boston Bruins. However, he was sent to the minor leagues after two games, returning for one more season in 1960–1961. His professional career lasted twenty-one seasons with eleven teams; he eventually settled in San Diego.

In the late 1990s he was named director of youth development for NHL/USA's Hockey Diversity Task Force, which operates twenty-eight developmental programs for minority and disadvantaged youths across the United States. Since 1996, the NHL has hosted the annual Willie O'Ree All-Star Weekend, where minority players aged ten to twelve compete in a game and skills competitions.

Daniel S. Mason

See also: Ice Hockey.

FURTHER READING

Graves, Gary. "Shift Change: More and More Black Players Making Presence Known in NHL." *USA Today,* January 10, 2001, 1C–2C.

Hackel, Stu. "Breaking the Ice: One-eyed Willie O'Ree,

the Man Who Busted the NHL's Color Line." *The Village Voice*, March 2, 1999, 206.

O'Ree, Willie, with Michael McKinley and Cuba Gooding. *The Autobiography of Willie O'Ree: Hockey's Black Pioneer*. Toronto, ON: Somerville House, 2000.

Rhoden, William C. "Hockey Pioneer Takes the Sport to Another Level." *New York Times*, April 28, 1999.

★ ★ ★

Jesse OWENS

Born September 12, 1913, Oakville, Alabama
Died March 31, 1980, Tucson, Arizona
Long jumper, sprinter

Son of Henry Owens, a cotton sharecropper, and his wife Emma, Owens was an outstanding track and field performer who realized lasting fame for his victories in the 1936 Olympic games in Berlin. He first received national attention as a track and field star at Cleveland's East Technical High School. Under the guidance of coach Charles Riley, Owens shattered many records and captured numerous titles as a high school athlete, including tying the world record and garnering two additional victories in the 200-yard dash and broad jump at the 1933 National Interscholastic Track and Field Meet in Chicago.

Following graduation from high school, Owens attended Ohio State University, where he furthered his reputation as one of the world's great track and field stars. His most notable performance as a collegian took place on May 25, 1935, at the Western Conference Track and Field Meet at Ann Arbor, Michigan. In a span of some forty-five minutes, Owens tied the world record in the 100-meter dash with a time of 9.4 seconds and broke world marks in the broad jump with a leap of 26 feet, 8½ inches, the 220-yard dash with a time of 20.3 seconds, and the 220-yard low hurdles with a time of 22.6.

Jesse Owens (center) wearing the traditional Laurel Crown on the podium after capturing the gold medal in the broad jump at the 1936 Olympic games in Berlin. On the right is Lutz Long of Germany who befriended Owens. *(AP/Wide World Photos)*

In 1936 Owens realized international acclaim by capturing four gold medals in the Berlin Olympic Games. In an Olympiad marred by controversy and fraught with great symbolic importance because of Adolf Hitler's Nazi regime and belief in Aryan racial supremacy, Owens garnered victories in the 100 and 200-meter dashes, long jump, and 400-meter relay. Owens returned home to the United States as a hero. He was given a ticker-tape parade in New York City and showered with adulation by people from all walks of life. Unfortunately, the adulation was relatively short-lived, and Owens was soon beset with many of the same problems as his fellow African Americans and frustrated in his efforts to secure meaningful employment. Without a college degree and living in a racially segregated society, Owens failed at several different business ventures, was forced to file for bankruptcy, and raced horses, dogs, and automobiles to make ends meet. He eventually became head of sales for the Leo Rose Sporting Goods Company, served for a time as secretary of the Illinois State Athletic Commission, traveled as a goodwill ambassador for the U.S. State Department, and later in life established a public relations firm and earned a significant amount of money as a public speaker. He spent much time, moreover, raising funds and engendering other forms of support for the U.S. Olympic Committee.

Owens received many honors and awards throughout his lifetime. He was given the NCAA Theodore Roosevelt Award in 1974, the Presidential Medal of Freedom in 1976, and the Living Legacy Award in 1979. He was a charter member of both the National Track and Field Hall of Fame (1974) and U.S. Olympic Hall of Fame (1982). He was also chosen by the Associated Press as the greatest track and field athlete of the first half of the twentieth century, and an *Ebony* magazine poll of 1949 selected him as the greatest of all African-American athletes.

David K. Wiggins

See also: Autobiographies; Films; Olympic Games; Racial Theories; Track and Field.

FURTHER READING

Baker, William J. *Jesse Owens: An American Life*. New York: Free Press, 1986.

Cope, Myron. "The Amazing Jesse Owens." *Sport* (October 1964): 60–63, 98–99.

Mandell, Richard D. *The Nazi Olympics*. New York: Macmillan, 1971.

Owens, Jesse, with Paul Neimark. *The Jesse Owens Story*. New York: Putnam, 1970.

★   ★   ★

R.C. OWENS

Born November 12, 1934, Shreveport, Louisiana
Football player

The son of Climon and Ida Owens and a graduate of Santa Monica High School in Santa Monica, California, and the College of Idaho (B.A.), Owens was a gifted three-sport athlete who played eight years in the National Football League between 1957 and 1965.

Owens's athletic career began at Santa Monica High School, a predominantly white high school in Southern California. By his senior year Owens had earned All-State recognition in football and basketball. Following the example of his mother, a community activist, Owens won a variety of high school leadership offices and was the first African American to attend Boys State in California. After graduating from high school in 1952, Owens turned down scholarship offers from several universities to join eight high school friends and attend the College of Idaho in Caldwell, Idaho, where he played basketball, football, and track. In basketball Owens averaged twenty-one points over four years and in his sophomore year led the nation in rebounding, with 27.6 rebounds per game. In 1955 he also led the nation in receptions and earned NAIA Little-America honors.

After completing his college career, Owens turned down an offer to play football with the San Francisco 49ers to play basketball with the Seattle Buchan Bakers, who had won the 1956 National AAU Tournament in Denver. As a result of its 1956 title, Seattle had won the right to play a series of games against European teams preparing for the Olympics in Melbourne, an opportunity Owens could not pass up. In September 1956 Seattle toured France and Spain, as well as Poland and Czechoslovakia, the first U.S. team to play behind the Cold War's Iron Curtain. Gifted with phenomenal timing and leaping ability, Owens helped the Buchan Bakers to a third-place in the 1957 National AAU Tournament and earned a spot on the AAU All-American team.

In the fall of 1957 Owens signed a free-agent contract with the San Francisco 49ers and began the first of eight years as a wide receiver in the NFL. Almost by accident the 49ers discovered that Owens could outjump NFL defensive backs, and soon Y.A. Tittle and John Brodie were launching high, arching passes to Owens—and the "Alley-Oop" was born. Last-second Alley-Oops for touchdowns gave the 49ers several spectacular victories and helped them to a playoff game with Detroit (which they lost 31–27). Owens was the team's rookie of the year in 1958, but his best year statistically was in 1961, when he caught fifty-five passes for 1,032 yards, the first 49er receiver to surpass 1,000 yards. After the 1961 season Carroll Rosenbloom, owner of the Baltimore Colts, signed Owens as a free agent to a contract that broke a gentleman's agreement among owners not to sign free agents. The signing prompted the controversial "Rozelle Rule," which required compensation for free-agent signings. After two seasons Baltimore traded Owens to the New York Giants, where he played for two seasons before retiring in 1965.

After his retirement Owens worked for the J.C. Penny Company for eight years; one of his assignments was to develop a "stay-in-school" program, which involved speaking to students throughout the nation. Between 1971 and 1977 Owens worked for the federal Department of Housing, Education, and Welfare as an equal employment opportunity specialist. After one year doing marketing and promotions with the Oakland Stompers Soccer Club, Owens returned to the 49ers, where he served as training camp director, administrative assistant, and a public speaker. In developing the 49ers' Summer Reading Program and a variety of other community activities, Owens played a significant role in helping the 49ers serve their community. Owens has received numerous awards for his athletic achievements and contribution to communities across the nation. He is in the NAIA Hall of Fame, the Santa Monica High School Hall of Fame, the College of Idaho Hall of Fame, the Stockton Black Sports Hall of Fame, and Oakland's African-American/Ethnic Sports Hall of Fame.

Adolph H. Grundman

FURTHER READING
Hession, Joseph. *Forty Niners: Collector's Edition.* San Francisco: Foghorn Press.
Phone interviews, July 20, 2001, and August 10, 2001.

Satchel PAIGE

Born July 7, 1906, Mobile, Alabama
Died June 5, 1982, Kansas City, Missouri
Baseball player

Leroy "Satchel" Paige turned his pitching exploits and his character into a great fan attraction during his long playing career. He became the great legend of the Negro leagues and in 1948 added to his stature when he became the oldest rookie in major league history.

Paige grew up in a large household of twelve children and so did not always have a great deal of supervision. His father, John, worked as a gardener, and his mother, Lulu, worked as a washerwoman. He did not attend school regularly but worked at the local train station carrying passengers' satchels and suitcases. Paige finally got a chance to develop his pitching skills when he was sent to Mount Meigs Reform School for stealing jewelry.

Paige started his professional baseball career in 1926 with the Chattanooga Black Lookouts in the Negro Southern League (NSL). During his long career Paige pitched for nearly every Negro league team—sometimes just for one game, because his services were loaned to other teams that needed to boost their attendance. Fans came out in large numbers to see Paige pitch and to watch the show he put on for them. Paige spent the majority of his career with the Pittsburgh Crawfords and the Kansas City Monarchs. He won two World Series and pitched in five East-West Classics. By Paige's own estimate he pitched in 2,600 games, throwing 300 shutouts and fifty-five no-hitters.

Paige's numerous records and winning seasons led to his election to the National Baseball Hall of Fame in 1971. He became

Satchel Paige shown in action during the 1961 Negro American League East-West All-Star Game at Yankee Stadium. *(AP/Wide World Photos)*

the first player from the Negro leagues to receive that honor.

Leslie A. Heaphy

See also: Autobiographies.

FURTHER READING
Clark, Dick, and Larry Lester. *The Negro Leagues Book.* Cleveland: Society for American Baseball Research, 1994.
Donovan, Richard E. "The Fabulous Satchel Paige." *Collier's,* May 30, 1953, 20–24, 54–59, 62.
Fox, William Price, Jr. "A Conversation with Satchel Paige." *Holiday,* August 1965, 18, 24–26, 28.
Paige, Leroy, and David Lipman. *Maybe I'll Pitch Forever.* New York: Doubleday, 1962.
Riley, James A. *The Biographical Encyclopedia of the Negro Baseball Leagues.* New York: Carroll and Graf, 1994.

★ ★ ★

Jim PARKER

Born April 3, 1934, Macon, Georgia
Football player

Parker is considered one of the greatest linemen in National Football League (NFL) history, having played guard and tackle for the Baltimore Colts (1957–1967). Additionally, Parker, who was inducted into both the NFL and College Football Hall of Fames, became the first African American to win the Outland Trophy as college football's outstanding lineman (1956).

Parker is the son of Charles Parker, Sr., a track laborer for the Central Georgia Railroad, and had six siblings. Due to poverty, Parker hitchhiked to Toledo after his junior year of high school to work a summer construction job, while staying with family. He remained in Toledo and graduated from Scott High School. Parker then attended Ohio State University, where he was a two-time All-American (1955, 1956) at offensive guard. During his three seasons, OSU had a 23–5 record and won the 1954 national championship.

In the NFL, Parker displayed dominance and versatility. After four All-NFL seasons as a left tackle, Parker moved to left guard, where he earned another four All-NFL honors. He was the last player to receive All-Pro recognition at both positions. In 1973, Parker became the first full-time offensive lineman to be named to the NFL Hall of Fame. In 1994, he was honored on the NFL's Seventy-Fifth Anniversary All-Time Team at guard.

Since retiring, Parker has remained in the Baltimore area, where he operates Jim Parker Publishing and serves on the Board of Governors for Goodwill Industries.

Michael T. Friedman

FURTHER READING
Henderson, A.N., ed. *Who's Who Among African Americans*. 14th ed. Detroit: Gale Group, 2001.
Porter, David L., ed. *African-American Sports Greats: A Biographical Dictionary*. Westport, CT: Greenwood Press, 1995.
Pro Football Hall of Fame. "Jim Parker" (www.profootballhof.com/players/enshrinees/jparker.cfm).
Smith, Don. "Jim Parker." *The Coffin Corner* 2 (1980) (www.paonline.com/Foo2/1963/Parker-J.htm).

★ ★ ★

Floyd PATTERSON

Born January 4, 1935, Waco, North Carolina
Boxer

Floyd Patterson was the son of Ray and Annabelle Patterson. As a result of delinquent behavior, he was sent at the age of ten to the Wiltwyck School for Boys. Upon returning to Brooklyn, Patterson attended a "600" school (a school for problem youth) in Harlem. In adulthood Patterson held the heavyweight boxing title during a six-year period in a career that spanned three decades.

Patterson won the middleweight Golden Gloves title in 1951 and the U.S. National Amateur Athletic Union middleweight championship in 1952. He was a member of the 1952 U.S. Olympic team and won the middleweight gold medal, knocking out three of his four opponents. Patterson turned pro and was managed by Cus D'Amato. He became the youngest fighter, at age twenty-one, to win the heavyweight title when he beat Archie Moore in 1956. Patterson defended his title against low-quality opponents until he met Sweden's Ingemar Johansson, whom he fought three times. Patterson lost the first fight in the third round but became the first heavyweight to regain the title when he beat Johansson in their second meeting in 1960. In a third meeting, Patterson beat Johansson.

Patterson then faced his toughest challenger, Sonny Liston, in a fight that generated much controversy due to Liston's criminal past. Liston beat Patterson at 2:06 in the first round in 1962. Less than a year later, Liston defended his title against Patterson with another first-round knockout. Patterson was embarrassed by his downfall and wore a disguise after his second loss to Liston. He reappeared in a title fight three years later against Muhammad Ali. Patterson, the sentimental favorite, lost in the twelfth round.

In his retirement, Patterson trained young fighters. He worked with youth groups, served as a boxing commentator for radio and television broadcasts for Madison Square Garden, served Communion to residents in a local nursing home, and even acted in western television movies. He was named chairman of the New York State Athletic Commission and worked to create a pension plan for retired boxers. Patterson resigned the position in 1998, citing memory loss. Patterson was elected to the Boxing Hall of Fame in 1976 and the International Boxing Hall of Fame in 1991.

Maureen M. Smith

See also: Autobiographies; Boxing; Sonny Liston; Olympic Games.

FURTHER READING

Early, Gerald. "The Unquiet Kingdom of Providence: The Patterson-Liston Fight." *Antioch Review* (Winter 90): 44–65.
Hoffer, Richard. "The Souls of the Machine." *Sports Illustrated*, April 13, 1998, 17.
Jackson, George. *Soul Brother Superfighter*. Placerville, CA: Green Valley Graphics, 1985.
Noden, Merrell. "Catching Up with . . . Heavyweight Floyd Patterson." *Sports Illustrated*, November 18, 1996, 4.
Sammons, Jeffrey T. *Beyond the Ring: The Role of Boxing in American Society*. Urbana: University of Illinois Press, 1988.

★ ★ ★

Mickey PATTERSON

Born September 27, 1926, New Orleans, Louisiana
Died August 1996, San Diego, California
Sprinter

Inspired by a speech given by Jesse Owens, Patterson was set on the path from being an accomplished high school student to becoming a legendary track and field athlete. Recruited by famous coach Tom Harris of the Tennessee State University Tigerbelle track and field team, Patterson holds the distinction of being the first African-American woman to win an Olympic medal.

Originally from New Orleans, Patterson fell in love with track and field in elementary school. In 1947, she was named to the All America Women's Track and Field Team. One year later she won a bronze medal in the 220-yard dash at the Olympic Games in London, the first African American woman to do so. Following her athletic career, she graduated from Southern-Baton Rouge. She married Ron Tyler and became the mother of two boys and two girls, making San Diego, CA, her home.

She established a track club, Mickey's Missiles, composed of racially and economically diverse athletes. Throughout her career she coached over 5,000 youths, including two Olympic athletes. Patterson's contributions to the community resulted in several distinctive awards, including San Diego Woman of the Year, Outstanding Contributor to Youth, the Amateur Athletic Union's Woman of the Year, and the NAACP's Outstanding Achievement Award. She died of a heart attack at the age of sixty-nine. In June 2000, Patterson was inducted into the Louisiana Sports Hall of Fame.

Sara B. Washington

FURTHER READING

Ashe, Arthur R., Jr. *A Hard Road to Glory: The African-American Athlete in Track and Field.* New York: Amistad, 1993.

"First Black Female Olympic Medalist Audrey Patterson—Tyler Dies at 69." *Jet,* 1996, 53–4.

Hine, Darlene Clark. *Facts On File Encyclopedia of Black Women in America, Dance, Sport, and Visual Arts.* New York: Facts On File, 1997.

Thaxton, Nolan A. "A Documentary Analysis of Competitive Track and Field for Women at Tuskegee Institute and Tennessee State University." Ph.D. diss., Springfield College, 1970.

★ ★ ★

Walter PAYTON

Born July 25, 1954, Columbus, Mississippi
Died November 1, 1999, Barrington, Illinois
Football player

Walter Payton running around the Washington Redskins' Darrell Green in a 1988 playoff game in Chicago. *(AP/Wide World Photos)*

Walter Payton was the youngest and shyest of three children of a factory worker who played semiprofessional baseball. Both his parents were strict Baptists, and they imbued him with their strong religious faith.

Payton was a good student at Columbus High School, and he was very interested in music. He played in the school band and sang in several jazz-rock combos. Payton played the drums and cymbal in the band and was an excellent dancer, who once made the national finals on the Television show *Soul Train.* He was a broad jumper on his high school track team. His mother was concerned about his getting hurt, so Payton did not play football until his junior year in high school. The first time he carried the ball in a game, he ran sixty-five yards for a touchdown; later in the game he scored on a seventy-five-yard play. When he graduated from high school in 1971, he was heavily recruited to play college football.

Payton chose to enroll at Jackson State University so he could play in the same backfield as his older brother, Edward, who later played professional football for Cleveland, Detroit, Kansas City, and Minnesota. At 5 feet, 10½ inches and 204 pounds, Payton was not big for a running back, yet he could bench-press 390 pounds and do a leg-press series with more than 700 pounds. He could throw a football sixty yards, punt seventy yards, kick a field goal from forty-five yards, and walk across a football field on his hands. While at Jackson State, Payton rushed for 3,563 yards in four seasons and scored a NCAA record 464 points on sixty-six touchdowns, five field goals, and fifty-three extra points. He acquired the nickname "Sweetness" in college because of the smooth way he ran.

In 1975 Payton was the Chicago Bears' first draft choice, and Bears fans, who had not experienced a winning season since 1967, considered Payton the long-awaited savior and the replacement for the great Gale Sayers. He reported to rookie camp, however, with a sore elbow from an injury received in the College All-Star Game and missed the entire pre-season. In the season opener, he was held to no yards rushing on eight carries. Still, he ended the season with 679-yards rushing and led the NFC in kickoff returns. In 1976 he began to breathe fire into the Bears. He wound up the year leading the NFC, with 1,390 yards and thirteen touchdowns. He was an All-Pro choice and appeared in the first of his nine Pro Bowls.

When he retired from professional football, Payton dominated the NFL rushing record book. His records include 16,736 total yards, ten seasons with 1,000 or more yards rushing, and seventy-seven games with more than 100 yards rushing. He led the National Football Conference in rushing in every year from 1976 to 1981, as well as the NFL in 1977. He was the NFL's all-time leading rusher with 16,726 yards, scored 109 career TDs, was All-Pro seven times with the Chicago Bears and the NFL's MVP in 1977, and led the Bears to the Super Bowl title in January 1986. His best season was 1977, when he gained 1,852 yards, led the NFC with ninety-six points scored, and was named the NFL Player of the Year.

Early in his professional football career, Payton showed considerable business acumen. He began investing his money with considerable success in a diversified portfolio under his personal control. With the help of a secretary, an accountant, and a lawyer, Payton ran Walter Payton Enterprises. His company made timberland, invested in real estate, and other business in Mississippi and Tennessee. He also owned restaurants in Chicago and Jackson, Mississippi. He made money from commercial endorsements for shoes, cars, and hotel chains, yet he turned down many endorsements because they did not project the image he wanted or invaded his privacy and his family life. He made numerous free public service announcements for the United Way, the Peace Corps, and charities for deaf and retarded children.

Payton was inducted into the Professional Football Hall of Fame in August 1993. He was named to the NFL's 75th Anniversary All-Time Team in 1994. In late January 1999 Payton was diagnosed with a rare condition known as sclerosing cholangitis, a cancer in which the bile ducts become blocked. He died of the disease at the age of forty-five on November 1, 1999, in Barrington, Illinois.

Keith McClellan

FURTHER READING

Carroll, Bob, Mike Gershman, David Neft, and John Thorn, eds. *Total Football II: The Official Encyclopedia of the National Football League.* New York: HarperCollins, 1999.
Chicago Tribune, July 28, 1993.
New York Times, November 2, 1999; May 13, 2001.
Phelps, Shirelle, ed. *Who's Who Among Black Americans.* 8th ed. Detroit: Gale Group, 1994.
Smith, Don. "Sweetness." *Coffin Corner* (Winter 1995): 15–17.

★ ★ ★

Drew PEARSON

Born January 12, 1951, South River, New Jersey
Football player

Drew Pearson, who played eleven seasons for the Dallas Cowboys (1973–1983), is known for his "Hail Mary" touchdown reception in the 1975 playoffs against the

Dallas Cowboys' wide receiver Drew Pearson who contributed mightily to the team's success and championship seasons. *(AP/Wide World Photos)*

Minnesota Vikings. Following retirement, Pearson formed Drew Pearson Marketing, which has become the largest minority-owned sports licensing firm in the United States.

The son of Samuel and Minnie, Pearson followed Joe Theismann as quarterback for South River (NJ) High School. At the University of Tulsa, Pearson originally played quarterback but shifted to wide receiver as a junior. Though an undrafted free agent, Pearson quickly became a top wide receiver for the Cowboys and was selected to the NFL's All-Decade team for the 1970s. Pearson, whose career was cut short by an automobile accident in 1984, retired with a Cowboy-record (since surpassed) of 489 receptions, 7,822 yards, and forty-eight touchdown catches.

While consistently productive, Pearson was best known for clutch play and game-winning performances. In twenty-two playoff games, he made sixty-seven receptions and scored eight touchdowns. Besides the famous "Hail Mary" pass, Pearson made key playoff plays against the Los Angeles Rams (1973), Atlanta Falcons (1980), and the Green Bay Packers (1982).

Following retirement, Pearson has been a successful entrepreneur. Still living in Dallas, Pearson has used his renown to build Drew Pearson Marketing, which has had sales exceeding $50 million per year. The National Collegiate Athletic Association honored Pearson's success in 1997 with a Silver Anniversary Award, given for distinguished achievements in the twenty-five years since he left college.

Michael T. Friedman

FURTHER READING

Eatman, Nick. "Legends Profile: Drew Pearson, the King of Last-Second Heroics." *Dallas Cowboys.*

Hoovers On-Line. "Drew Pearson Marketing, Inc." (www.hoovers.com/uk/co/capsule/1/0,2163,420 41,00.html).

Moormann, Dave. "Pearson's Life Full of Twists, Turns." *Baton Rouge (LA) Advocate,* January 12, 1998.

National Collegiate Athletic Association. "NCAA Convention: Silver Anniversary Awards." *NCAA News* (www.ncaa.org/news/1998/19980112/active /3502n23.html), January 12, 1998.

Porter, David L., ed. *Biographical Dictionary of American Sports: Football.* Westport, CT: Greenwood Press, 1987.

★ ★ ★

Calvin PEETE

Born July 18, 1943, Detroit, Michigan
Golfer

Peete, the son of Dennis Peete and Irenia (Bridgeford) Peete, was one of this country's most notable African-American golfers. Not introduced to the sport until 1966, at the age of twenty-three, Peete captured twelve titles on the Professional Golfers Association (PGA) tour. Included among these titles was the 1979 Greater Milwaukee Open, the 1982 Anheuser-Busch Classic, the 1983 Atlanta Classic, the 1985 Phoenix Open, and the 1985 and 1986 Tournament Players Championships. In addition to his PGA tournament victories, which earned him over $2 million in prize money, Peete played on both the 1983 and 1985 Ryder Cup teams.

Peete's success has extended to activities beyond the golf course. He has been involved extensively in community service, including years of work with the Sickle Cell Anemia Foundation. For his many accomplishments on and off the golf course, Peete received the 1981 Ben Hogan Award, 1983 Good Guy Award from Gordon's Gin, and 1986 Jackie Robinson Award from *Ebony* magazine.

David K. Wiggins

See also: Golf.

FURTHER READING
McDaniel, Pete. *Uneven Lies: The Heroic Story of African-Americans in Golf*. Greenwich, CT: American Golfer, 2000.
McDermott, Barry. "Long Shot Out of a Trap." *Sports Illustrated*, March 24, 1980, 26–31.
Moore, Kenny. "His Was a Great Act of Faith." *Sports Illustrated*, April 25, 1983, 36–38, 43–45.
Sinnette, Calvin H. *Forbidden Fairways: African Americans and the Game of Golf*. Chelsea, MI: Sleeping Bear, 1998.

★ ★ ★

Don PERKINS

Born March 4, 1938, Waterloo, Iowa
Football player

Perkins was born in Waterloo, Iowa, where his father was a packer in a meat factory. His mother died when he was fifteen. Perkins was an All-State football player at West Waterloo High School. He attended the University of New Mexico where he was named three times an All-Skyline athlete and achieved All-American status in 1960. After graduation, Perkins signed with the Dallas Cowboys, where he played for nine years.

Perkins was the first Cowboy to rush for 100 yards in a game and for more than 6,000 total yards. He was named NFL Rookie of the Year in 1961 and was a Pro Bowl choice in 1962 (and five more times during his career with Dallas). He was also one of the NFL's top ten rushers from 1961 to 1968. Perkins, the last original Cowboy to retire, ended his career in 1969 as the Cowboy's all-time leading rusher. He is one of ten Dallas players named to the acclaimed Ring of Honor (1976).

Perkins has lived in Albuquerque since 1959, where he has worked as a sportscaster and talk-show host for TV and radio. From 1972 to 1985 Perkins worked with the New Mexico Department of Human Services, and from 1987 to 2000 he worked in the City of Albuquerque's Police Department.

Trisha M. Hothorn

FURTHER READING
Carroll, Bob, and Martin Rywell, ed. *Afro-American Encyclopedia*. North Miami, FL: Educational Book Publishers, 1974.
Perkins, Don. "The Fifty Finest." *Albuquerque Tribune*, April 25, 2001.
———. "1961–1968." *Dallas Morning News*, March 12, 1989.
Phone Interview with Don Perkins, October 3, 2001.

★ ★ ★

Joe PERRY

Born January 27, 1927, Steven, Arkansas
Football player

The son of Laura and Fletcher Perry, Perry was a native of Los Angeles. He graduated from Jordan High School, where he excelled in track, football, basketball, and baseball. He then matriculated at Compton Junior College, where he scored twenty-two touchdowns in one season. Before completing his college career he was called into the military and assigned to the Alameda, California, Naval Air Station. Playing on the base's football team, he was spotted by a San Francisco 49er tackle, who alerted the team's administration. Signed as a free agent in 1948, Perry immediately established himself as a premier runner in the All-American Football Conference (AAFC) and later in the National Football League (the 49ers joined the NFL in 1950). Known for his blazing speed, he earned the nickname "The Jet" during his second season.

After leading the AAFC in rushing for two seasons, Perry ranked among the NFL's top rushers, including two seasons (1953, 1954) in which he gained over 1,000 yards. Although Perry was small (six feet, 200 pounds) among NFL fullbacks and suffered numerous injuries during his career, the hallmarks of his sixteen-year career were durability and consistency, as demonstrated by his career 4.8-yard-per-game rushing average. As one of the first African Americans in professional football, Perry received much physical and verbal abuse early in his career, but his outstanding play eventually earned the respect of his teammates and opponents. He was inducted into the Football Hall of Fame in 1969.

Albert J. Figone

FURTHER READING
Carroll, B., M. Gershman, D. Neft, J. Thorn, and Elias Sports Bureau, eds. *Total Football: The Official Encyclopedia of the National Football League*, New York: HarperCollins, 1999.
Olderman, Murray. *The Running Backs*. Englewood Cliffs, NJ: Prentice Hall, 1969.
Porter, David L., ed. *Biographical Dictionary of American Sports: Football*. Westport, CT: Greenwood Press, 1987.
Sullivan, George. *The Great Running Backs*. New York: Putnam, 1972.

★ ★ ★

Tidye PICKETT

Born November 3, 1914, Chicago, Illinois
Died November 1986, Chicago, Illinois
Sprinter, hurdler

Tidye Pickett, the first black woman to be chosen for an American Olympic team, began her running career in the Chicago park and playground system. As a seventeen-year-old student at Chicago's Englewood High School, she was selected as an alternate to the women's 100-meter relay team at the 1932 Los Angeles Olympics. Neither she nor fellow African-American teammate Louise Stokes were selected to run in the relay, despite their top times.

Dedicated training and several victories in U.S. and Canadian track meets led to a place on the 1936 Olympic team. Pickett was a favorite in the 100-meter hurdles. In the second semifinal her foot caught on the top of the hurdle, and she fell. She injured her shoulder, but worse, broke her foot. Pickett's Olympic career was ended—the next two Olympics were canceled because of the Second World War.

Pickett spent the rest of her life working with young people in athletics and education. She taught elementary school, was a principal in the East Chicago Heights School District, and earned her master's degree in educational administration from Northern Illinois University. Upon her retirement, the school where she had been principal was renamed in her honor.

Alison M. Wrynn

See also: Olympic Games; Louise Stokes.

FURTHER READING
Ashe, Arthur R., Jr. *A Hard Road to Glory: A History of the African-American Athlete, 1919–1945.* Vol. 2. New York: Warner Books, 1988.
Bentley, Ken. *The Story of Black Women in Sports.* Los Angeles: Carnation, 1983.
"Berlin Olympics, 1936: Golden Memories." *Northern Illinois University Alumni News* (Summer 1984): 1–2, 5.
Davis, Michael D. *Black American Women in Track and Field: A Complete Illustrated Reference.* Jefferson, NC: McFarland, 1992.
Rubien, Frederick W., ed. *1936 Report of the American Olympic Committee, Games of the XIth Olympiad.* New York: American Olympic Committee, 1936.

★ ★ ★

George POAGE

Born November 6, 1880, Hannibal, Missouri
Died April 11, 1962, Chicago, Illinois
Sprinter

Poage grew up in La Crosse, Wisconsin, where his father (James) worked as a tanner and his mother (Annie) worked as housekeeper. He graduated from La Crosse High School in 1899 and the University of Wisconsin at Madison in 1903. Poage competed in the 1904 Olympic Games and later worked as a teacher, farmer, and post office employee.

An outstanding high school football player and track and field athlete, Poage starred in track and field at the University of Wisconsin. He established Big Ten Conference records in the 440-yard and 220-yard dashes and a school record in the 100-yard dash. As a member of the Milwaukee Athletic Club, the club's first African American, Poage competed in the 1904 Olympic Games in St. Louis, Missouri. His participation in the sixty-meter dash made him the first African American to compete in the Olympics. Poage won two bronze medals, finishing third in both the 200-meter and 400-meter hurdles. Historians disagree as to whether he was the first African American to win an Olympic medal; another African American, Joseph Stadler, won a silver medal in the standing high jump on the same day as the 400-meter hurdles.

After the Olympic Games, Poage taught at East St. Louis High School and Sumner High School. Although his chronology is sketchy after 1915, records indicate that he farmed in Wisconsin or Michigan, taught high school, and worked in the post office in Chicago.

Adam R. Hornbuckle

See also: Olympic Games; Track and Field.

FURTHER READING
Chalk, Ocania. *Black College Sport.* New York: Dodd, Mead, 1976.
Dorn, Pat. "Alumni and the Olympics." *Wisconsin Alumni,* July/August 1988, 22–23.
Mallon, Bill, and Ian Buchanan. *Quest for Gold: The Encyclopedia of American Olympians.* New York: Leisure Press, 1980.
"Poage, George '03." *On Wisconsin,* July/August 1996, 22.
Wallechinsky, David. *The Complete Book of the Summer Olympics.* Sydney 2000 ed. Woodstock, NY: Overlook Press, 2000.

★ ★ ★

Fritz POLLARD

Born January 27, 1894, Chicago, Illinois
Died May 11, 1986, Silver Spring, Maryland
Football player

Fritz Pollard's father (William) was a barber, and his mother (Catherine Amanda) was a seamstress. Pollard graduated from

Lane Tech High School and attended Brown University. He was to be an All-American football player, the first African-American head coach in the National Football League (NFL), a sports promoter, a journalist, and an entertainment agent.

Pollard entered Brown University in 1915 and became a star running back. In January 1916, he became the first African American to play in the Rose Bowl game. The following season Pollard led Brown to victories over both Yale and Harvard. He was the first African-American backfield player selected to Walter Camp's All-American team (1916). During World War I, Pollard served as a Young Men's Christian Association physical director at Camp Meade, Maryland. He was also the head football coach at Lincoln University in 1918–1919.

Pollard played professional football with Akron in 1919 and the following year led the Pros to the NFL championship. He became head coach at Akron in 1921 and later coached NFL teams in Milwaukee and Hammond. Pollard was responsible for bringing a number of African-American players into the NFL, including Paul Robeson. In the early 1920s, Pollard and Jim Thorpe were considered two of the premier running backs in pro football. After retiring as a professional player in 1926, Pollard organized and coached two African-American pro teams (the Chicago Black Hawks and New York Brown Bombers) in order to promote integration. He later became a racial pioneer in journalism and in entertainment. Pollard became the first African American selected to the College Football Hall of Fame (1954).

John M. Carroll

See also: Paul Robeson.

FURTHER READING

Barry, Jay. "Fritz." *Brown Alumni Monthly*, October 1970, 30–33.

Carroll, John M. *Fritz Pollard: Pioneer in Racial Advancement*. Urbana: University of Illinois Press, 1992.

Nesfield, Carl. "Pride Against Prejudice: Fritz Pollard Brown's All-American Pre-World War I Vintage." *Black Sports*, November 1971, 16–20, 31, 53, and December 1971, 60–63, 77, 80–81.

★ ★ ★

Fritz POLLARD, JR.

Born February, 1915, Springfield, Massachusetts
Hurdler

His father (Fritz, Sr.) was a professional football player and businessman, and his mother (Ada) was a housewife. A graduate of Sean High School, the University of North Dakota (B.A.), and John Marshall Law School, Pollard was to become a *Collier's* Little All-American halfback, Olympic medal winner, physical educator, and U.S. State Department official.

Pollard was raised mainly by his paternal grandparents in Chicago. In high school, he was an All-State halfback, city, state, and national interscholastic champion in the high and low hurdles, as well as a first-rate golfer. Pollard attended Brown University in 1933 and showed considerable promise in football and track, equaling a world indoor hurdle record in 1934. He left Brown after one year, however, and transferred to the University of North Dakota in 1936. As a freshman, Pollard was rated the third-fastest hurdler in the world, tying a world record in his first intercollegiate meet. He did this despite training in the spring on the top of railroad boxcars swept clear of snow, because the university had no adequate indoor facilities.

Pollard earned a place on the 1936 U.S. Olympic team and competed in the 110-meter hurdles event in Berlin as one of the "black auxiliaries," as the German press described the African American athletes. Leading most of the way, Pollard hit the final hurdle, stumbled, and finished third for a bronze medal. He returned to North Dakota, where he was a Little All-American in 1938. During World War II, Pollard was a special services officer in the U.S. Army. After the war, he taught physical education in Chicago and worked with the Commission on Youth Welfare. Pollard thereafter worked for the State Department's Overseas Schools program until he retired.

John M. Carroll

FURTHER READING
Ashe, Arthur R., Jr. *A Hard Road to Glory*. Vol. 2. New York: Warner Books, 1988.
Baker, William J. *Jesse Owens: An American Life*. New York: Free Press, 1986.
Carroll, John M. *Fritz Pollard: Pioneer in Racial Advancement*. Urbana: University of Illinois Press, 1992.

Chalk, Ocania. *Black College Sport*. New York: Dodd, Mead, 1976.

★ ★ ★

Cum POSEY

Born June 20, 1880, Homestead, Pennsylvania
Died March 28, 1946, Pittsburgh, Pennsylvania
Basketball, baseball player and owner

Posey grew up with parents who valued education and hard work. His father worked as a riverboat engineer and in banking and real estate, while his mother Anna taught at Ohio State University, where she had graduated. Posey graduated from Homestead High School and went on to three different colleges to study chemistry and pharmacy while playing basket-

Cum Posey (in sweater and knickers, far left) with his Homestead Grays of 1931. *(National Baseball Hall of Fame Library, Cooperstown, NY)*

ball. In 1913 Posey married Ethel Truman; they would have five daughters. After college Posey played professional basketball until 1925 with the Loendi team.

While basketball may have been his first love as an athlete, Posey also played baseball as early as 1911 with the Homestead Grays semipro club. He took over the booking duties for the team in 1912 and quickly made it possible for players to devote all their time to the game. Posey remained the manager or owner of the club through the 1945 season, even occasionally playing a game in the outfield if needed. At times the Grays played as an independent club, and at others they joined the Negro leagues, playing at Forbes Field when the Pirates were out of town. Posey also served as an officer in the Negro leagues and wrote a regular column for the *Pittsburgh Courier*. He kept his team alive for so long by being creative and finding new sources of finances. For example, in the 1930s he brought on board Rufus "Sonnyman" Jackson as co-owner and his brother "See" as the booking agent.

Posey stayed involved in the game until the end. He spent his last year in and out of a sickbed and finally died of lung cancer before the 1946 season.

Leslie A. Heaphy

See also: Basketball.

FURTHER READING
Clark, Dick, and Larry Lester. *The Negro Leagues Book.* Cleveland: Society for American Baseball Research, 1994.
Heaphy, Leslie. "Shadowed Diamonds: The Growth and Decline of the Negro Leagues." Ph.D. diss., University of Toledo, 1995.
Reisler, Jim. *Black Writers/Black Baseball: An Anthology of Articles from Black Sportswriters Who Covered the Negro League.* Jefferson, NC: McFarland, 1994.
Riley, James A. *The Biographical Encyclopedia of the Negro Baseball Leagues.* New York: Carroll and Graf, 1994.

★ ★ ★

Kirby PUCKETT

Born March 14, 1960, Chicago, Illinois
Baseball player

Kirby Puckett's father (William) was a department store and postal worker, and his mother (Catherine) was a housewife. A short, squat center fielder with a winning smile and upbeat personality, Puckett had his career cut short after the 1995 season due to glaucoma in his right eye. His lifetime .318 batting average was the highest by a right-handed hitter since Joe DiMaggio. He led the American League in hits four times, with one batting title and one RBI crown to his credit. His 2,040 hits in his first ten seasons are the most ever in the major leagues. A six-time Gold Glove

Minnesota Twins outfielder Kirby Puckett became one of baseball's most beloved players and a member of the Hall of Fame. *(AP/Wide World Photos)*

winner and an All-Star for ten straight years, he was elected to the Hall of Fame in 2001.

Puckett grew up in the Robert Taylor Homes on the South Side of Chicago. After working on an automobile assembly line, he played ball at Bradley University and Triton College before being drafted by the Minnesota Twins in 1982; he was called up to the majors in May 1984. Puckett played his entire career with the Twins, leading them to World Series titles in 1987 and 1991. His best season was 1988, when he hit .356 with twenty-four home runs, 121 RBI, and 234 hits. He was MVP of the American League Championship Series in 1991 before capping a bravura performance in game six of the World Series with an eleventh-inning home run. Puckett became executive vice president of the Twins in 1996. He has done extensive charitable work.

David C. Skinner

FURTHER READING
Carlson, Chuck. *Puck, Baseball's Last Warrior*. Lenexa, KS: Addax, 1997.
Falkner, David. *Nine Sides of the Diamond. Baseball's Great Glove Men on the Fine Art of Defense*. New York: Times Books, 1990.
Linkugel, Wil A., and Edward J. Pappas. *They Tasted Glory: Among the Missing at the Baseball Hall of Fame*. Jefferson, NC: McFarland, 1998.
Puckett, Kirby, and Mike Bryan. *I Love This Game: My Life and Baseball*. New York: HarperCollins, 1993.
Wendel, Tim. "Curtain Falls on Kirby Era: Puck was the Pastime's Best Ambassador." *USA Today Baseball Weekly*, July 17, 1996.

★ ★ ★

PYTHIAN BASE BALL CLUB (PHILADELPHIA)

The Pythian Base Ball Club was organized in 1866 by political activist Octavius Catto, educator Jacob White, David Knight, and J. Whipper Purnell. It was the second African-American baseball club founded in Philadelphia, just a few months after the Excelsiors. This "association of gentlemen" was somewhat exclusive, as new members were elected by the club's membership, and the annual dues of five dollars made it difficult for most African Americans to join. Skin color, too, was an issue, as 70 percent of the Pythians were mulattoes, who held a disproportionate share of low-white-collar and artisanal positions among Philadelphia's African-American population.

At its height, the Pythian organization fielded four baseball teams. In addition to playing local teams, the Pythians hosted teams from New York, Washington, Harrisburg, and Chicago. As its reputation grew, the Pythian club bolstered its lineup by recruiting out-of-town players. By 1868 the Pythians had become a baseball power, losing only one game in two years. They would have competed favorably with any team (white or black) had they been given the chance. Instead, they competed for the Colored Championship of the United States in 1871 and perhaps on other occasions. Few white teams would play them, even though they sometimes used white teams' facilities and employed white umpires for games against intercity rivals.

The Athletics, Philadelphia's dominant white team, respected the Pythians' baseball prowess and encouraged them to seek admission into the Pennsylvania State Convention of Base Ball Players, which met in Harrisburg in 1867. However, the convention delegates had already drawn the color line, and the Pythians withdrew their application to avoid the embarrassment of public rejection.

Four years later another civil rights issue sounded the death knell for the Pythians. The ratification of the Fifteenth Amendment granted African Americans the right to vote, and founder Octavius Catto openly encouraged them to do so. Election day rioting broke out, and Catto was shot by a rioter. With Catto's death, the Pythians' activities declined. Other than an 1872 newspaper reference to the club, there is no evidence that it continued after that date.

J. Thomas Jable

FURTHER READING

Casway, Jerold. "Philadelphia Pythians." *National Pastime* (Spring 1995): 120–23.

Jable, J. Thomas. "Sport in Philadelphia's African-American Community, 1865–1900." In *Ethnicity and Sport in North American History and Culture*, edited by George Eisen and David K. Wiggins, 157–76. Westport, CT: Praeger, 1995.

Reed, Harry A. "Not by Protest Alone: Afro-American Activists and the Pythian Baseball Club of Philadelphia 1867–1869." *Western Journal of Black Studies* 9 (1985): 144–51.

RACIAL THEORIES

There has been much debate throughout this country's history as to why African Americans have achieved such enormous success in many sports. Although an extremely complex issue, the debate has typically centered around whether the great performances of African-American athletes have resulted from innate physiological gifts or a variety of socio-economic factors. In the late nineteenth century, when black athletes were first making their marks in predominantly white organized sport, many commentators argued that the outstanding performances of such people as Isaac Murphy, Peter Jackson, and Marshall "Major" Taylor resulted from physiological abilities unique to their race. This notion of innate physiological gifts to help explain black athletic performance was merely part of the worldwide discussion taking place at this time on racial differences. Individuals on both sides of the Atlantic were intent on determining the hierarchy of races and differentiating one from another by investigating such factors as human brains, facial angles, skin color, structure of human hair, skull sizes, and different varieties of body lice. These investigations reported that African Americans were physically different from whites and possessed an accompanying character and temperament that was common to their species.

The use of racial theories to explain the great performances of African-American athletes continued into the twentieth century. Many scientists, social commentators, and the like, all speculated that the success of such athletes as University of Pennsylvania runner John B. Taylor and heavyweight boxing champion Jack Johnson could be accounted for by innate physiological abilities characteristic of their race.

Tellingly, however, discussion about the great performances of African-American athletes subsided over the first and second decades of the century. The primary reason for the decline was that the large majority of African-American athletes had been eliminated from predominantly white organized sport because of Jim Crow laws and a number of other societal factors. With the notable exceptions of some outstanding performances of a select number of African-American athletes on predominantly white university campuses, in Olympic competition, and in the sport of boxing, most African-American athletes were forced to compete behind segregated walls on their own amateur and professional teams.

The debate about great black athletic performances resurfaced following the 1932 Olympic Games in Los Angeles and then accelerated around the time of the Berlin games four years later. The record-breaking performances by such famous track stars as Eddie Tolan, Ralph Metcalfe, Eulace Peacock, and Jesse Owens resulted in a plethora of comments from various individuals who argued that the great exploits of these athletes in the sprints and jumping events were due to a longer heel bone, strong Achilles' tendon, or some other unique racial characteristic. Albert McGall, track coach at Yale University, speculated that black sprinters realized better leverage because of the projecting heel bone that was frequently found among their race. Dean Cromwell, the famous University of Southern California and Olympic track coach, believed that African Americans dominated as sprinters and jumpers because they were closer to the primitive then were white men. "His [African Americans'] muscles are pliable," said Cromwell, "and his easy-going disposition is a valuable aid to the mental and physical relaxation that a runner and jumper must have."

These types of comments drew the attention, and sometimes ire, of a number of academicians during the late 1930s and 1940s. Perhaps the most important of these academicians was W. Montague Cobb, a noted physical anthropologist from Howard University who became one of the central figures in the debate over race and athletic performance. Cobb, who had a career-long interest in the physical constitution of African Americans, argued that athletic success was not based on innate racial characteristics. Proper training and incentives combined with physical skills and aptitudes accounted for the making of champions of all shades of color. In a number of publications, most notably a 1936 article "Race and Runners," in *The Journal of Health and Physical Education*, Cobb noted that none of his investigations revealed "Negroid physical characters" that accounted for the dominance of African-American athletes in the sprints and jumping events. Cobb even questioned whether there was such a thing as a racial group, considering the lack of homogeneity within both the white and African-American communities. He noted that Jesse Owens did not even possess what was typically considered the "Negroid type of calf foot and heel bone." In fact, the measurement of Owens's gastrocnemius was more like that of a "Caucasoid rather than the Negroid."

Much of the discussion about black athletic performance during the 1950s revolved around boxing. The overrepresentation of African Americans in the sport led to much speculation. In the following decades the debate over black athletic performance seemed to resurface each Olympic year. This was certainly the case during the decade of the 1960s. The British physician James M. Tanner garnered some attention in 1960 with the publication of *The Physique of the Olympic Athlete*. On the basis of anthropometric measurements of 137 athletes at the Rome Olympics and previously at the British Empire and Commonwealth Games, Tanner and his colleagues surmised that there were significant racial differences among track and field athletes that perhaps enhanced the potential of African Americans in the sprints and jumping events while inhibiting their performances in endurance events. In 1964 the writer Marshall Smith, depending to a great extent on the work of noted anthropologists Carleton S. Coon and Edward E. Hunt, Jr., summarized the various opinions on the question of racial differences and athletic performance. Sportswriter Charles Maher did the same sort of thing with two articles in 1968 for the *Los Angeles Times,* "Blacks Physically Superior? Some say They're Hungrier" and "Do Blacks Have a Physical Advantage? Scientists Differ." By and large, the sport scientists, coaches, and athletes Maher quoted attributed the outstanding performances of African-American athletes to factors other than innate physical superiority. For instance, Tommy Hawkins, the well-known black basketball player for the Los Angeles Lakers, echoed the sentiments of many when he agreed that the black community's seeming preoccupation with sports in this country was a self-perpetuating condition. "From an early age" noted Hawkins, "you identify with people who have been successful from a Negro standpoint. Those people would be in sports and entertainment."

A critical juncture in the debate over race and athletic performance was the publication in 1971 of Martin Kane's *Sports Illustrated* article "An Assessment of Black Is Best." Published during a period of debate over black and white intellectual ability rekindled by such academicians as Arthur R. Jensen and William B Shockley, Kane's article presented evidence supporting the notion that outstanding athletic performances in particular sports were based on racial characteristics inherent in the African-American population. Depending on the opinions of a select number of coaches, athletic researchers, medical doctors, and African-American athletes themselves, Kane suggested that racially linked physical, psychological, and historical factors had resulted in black dominance in sport.

Kane's article drew an angry reaction from a number of people, most notably Harry Edwards, a professor of sociology at the University of California, Berkeley, who had recently led the proposed boycott of the Mexico City Olympic Games. Edwards argued that Kane had failed to establish a link between innate racial characteristics and black athletic performance and that his article suffered from serious methodological problems and erroneous assumptions about the differences between the races. Edwards asserted that a number of societal factors accounted for the high value African-American youth placed on sport and the channeling of a disproportionate number of African Americans into certain sports. In large measure, noted Edwards, sport, and to a lesser extent entertainment, appeared to be the most achievable goals for African Americans; as long as that remained the case, the debate over African-American athletic performance would continue. Unfortunately, concluded Edwards, this circumstance encouraged African Americans to strive for success in a highly selective and competitive profession with only so much room for athletes of any color. While the dream of athletic success became a reality for some African-American youth, the vast majority were left with unfulfilled fantasies of stardom, adulation, and wealth.

The exchange between Kane and Edwards was followed by much debate over the next two decades about African-American athletes and sport performance. Seemingly everyone was weighing in on the question of why African-American athletes were achieving such enormous success in certain sports. Without question, the most publicized comments on the topic came from sportscaster and odds maker Jimmy "The Greek" Snyder. In a 1988 interview with writer Ed Hotaling at a restaurant in Washington, DC, Snyder argued that African-American athletes were superior to their white counterparts because they had been "bred to be that way since the days of slavery." The beginnings of black athletic superiority, said Snyder, had occurred during the Civil War, when "the slave owner would breed his big black with his big woman so that he could have a big black kid." African-American athletes can "jump higher and run faster," continued Snyder, because of their "thigh size and big size."

The fallout from Snyder's infamous interview was immediate, critical, and long-lasting. Individuals from various backgrounds and professions castigated Snyder for his comments, blasting him for "sweeping generalizations on which racial stereotypes and prejudices are built." Just one day after the interview, CBS fired Snyder from *The NFL Today* show after some twelve years on the job. Perhaps most important, the interview would serve as the catalyst a year later for an NBC special devoted to the question of supposed black athletic superiority. Hosted by Tom Brokaw on April 25, 1989, the special included such guests as Harry Edwards, Arthur Ashe, anthropologist Robert Malina, and Richard Lapchick, director of the Center for the Study of Sport and Society at Northeastern University in Boston. Each panelist offered his own spin on the subject; the special drew enormous attention and caused a diversity of reactions.

The question about race, African-American athletes, and sport performance would seemingly decline in intensity over the next decade. This would all change, however, with the publications of John Hoberman's *Darwin's Athletes: How Sport Has Damaged Black America and Preserved the Myth of Race* (1997) and John Entine's *Taboo: Why Black Athletes Dominate Sports and Why We Are Afraid to Talk About It* (2000). Entine's book, in particular, caused much controversy and debate; he claimed that outstanding performances of African-American athletes result from race-based genetic traits. Tellingly, Entine's racialist thinking has been countered by a much more balanced and thoughtful approach to the subject from several noted academicians. Perhaps the two most important of these academicians are Patrick B. Miller and Mark Dyreson. Miller, in his essay "The Anatomy of Scientific Racism: Racialist Responses to Black Athletic Achievement" (1998), and Dyreson in "American Ideas About Race and Olympic Races from the 1890s to the 1950s: Shattering Myths or Reinforcing Scientific Racism?" persuasively discount the claims for innate athletic gifts based on race.

David K. Wiggins

See also: William Montague Cobb; Harry Edwards; Historiography.

FURTHER READING
Dyreson, Mark. "American Ideas About Race and Olympic Races from the 1890s to the 1950s: Shattering Myths or Reinforcing Scientific Racism?" *Journal of Sport History* 28 (Summer 2001): 173–215.
Entine, John. *Taboo: Why Black Athletes Dominate Sports and Why We Are Afraid to Talk About It*. New York: Public Affairs, 2000.
Hoberman, John. *Darwin's Athletes: How Sport Has Damaged Black America and Preserved the Myth of Race*. Boston: Houghton Mifflin, 1997.
Miller, Patrick B. "The Anatomy of Scientific Racism: Racialist Responses to Black Athletic Achievement." *Journal of Sport History* 25 (Spring 1998): 119–51.
Wiggins, David K. "Great Speed but Little Stamina: The Historical Debate over Black Athletic Superiority." *Journal of Sport History* 16 (Summer 1989): 159–85.

★ ★ ★

Ted RADCLIFFE

Born July 7, 1902, Mobile, Alabama
Baseball player

Radcliffe had a white grandfather and a half-Indian grandmother. His father (James) was a bricklayer, and his mother (Mary) was a housewife. Powerful pitcher, hard-hitting catcher, and manager in Negro league, Latin American, and semipro baseball from 1920 to 1952, he earned his nickname "Double Duty" from Damon Runyan after catching and pitching respective games of a Negro league doubleheader at Yankee Stadium in 1932. He was a six-time Negro league All-Star. His brother Alec Radcliff was a star third baseman in the black circuits.

Radcliffe frequently jumped teams during his career. He began in the black big leagues with the Detroit Stars in 1928 and played for the 1931 champion Homestead Grays and 1935 national semipro champion Bismarck. The winning pitcher in the 1941 East-West game, he hit a home run to win the 1944 contest. As player-manager for the Chicago American Giants of the Negro American League (NAL) in 1943, he lost a playoff to Birmingham and then played for the losing Black Barons in the next two Negro World Series. As manager of NAL Chicago in 1950 he signed three white players. After finishing up as player-manager in the 1952 Man-Dak League, he scouted for the Cleveland Indians from 1962 to 1966.

A cigar-chomping character who loved

to tell stories, some of them true, Radcliffe was the oldest living Negro leaguer at the beginning of the twenty-first century, and his colorful personality dominated many card shows, reunions, and interviews.

David C. Skinner

FURTHER READING
Holway, John. *Voices from the Great Black Baseball Leagues*. New York: Dodd, Mead, 1975.
Kelly, Brent. *The Negro Leagues Revisited Conversations with 66 More Baseball Heroes*. Jefferson, NC: McFarland, 2000.
McNary, Kyle P. *Ted "Double Duty" Radcliffe: 36 Years of Pitching & Catching in Baseball's Negro Leagues*. St. Louis Park, MN: McNary, 1994.
Wilson, Nick. *Voices from the Pastime: Oral Histories of Surviving Major Leaguers, Negro Leaguers, Cuban Leaguers and Writers 1920–1934*. Jefferson, NC: McFarland, 2000.

★ ★ ★

RAINBOW COALITION FOR FAIRNESS IN ATHLETICS

Located along the racial fault zones of discrimination and unfairness, Rainbow Coalition for Fairness in Athletes' (RCFA) interests challenge American society to narrow the gap between the ideals and the reality of equality. Inspired by its founder, Reverend Jesse Jackson, RCFA was established in 1992 to make history by forging a national dialogue dealing with issues of racism and sexism in sports. In 1995, RCFA joined with the Black Coaches Association and the Center for the Study of Sport Society in a national summit to identify minority hiring opportunities with National Collegiate Athletic Association (NCAA) member institutions and to submit recommendations for a national debate on discriminatory practices affecting college athletes. RCFA's success during its formative years can be attributed in no small measure to the efforts of Charles Farrell, who was a *Washington Post* editor/writer and served as president of Sports Perspectives.

In 1999, the Rainbow/PUSH Coalition established Rainbow Sports, a division of the Rainbow/PUSH Wall Street Project. Stimulation of a public debate about college athlete's eligibility and academic opportunity remains a focal point in the assault on discrimination in the sport industry. Evoking traditions of the civil rights movement, Rainbow Sports educates, boycotts, and litigates to promote minority opportunities. Its slogan "Sports in the New Millennium" embraces a vision of new opportunities for equal minority participation through dialogues of inclusion, not destructive rhetoric, in a rapidly expanding sports industry. The millennium opens new opportunities in the media for women in sports, in technology and telecommunications, and sports merchandising.

Dana D. Brooks and Ronald Althouse

FURTHER READING
National Rainbow Coalition RCFA News, 1–2 (www.rainbowpush.org), August 1, 1996.

★ ★ ★

Ahmad RASHAD

Born November 19, 1949, Tacoma, Washington
Football player, sportscaster

Ahmad Rashad was born Bobby Moore, the son of Condola (domestic housekeeper) and O.C. Moore (barber, shoe shiner at the Fort Lewis military base). A graduate of Mt. Tacoma High School, which he attended in the years 1964–1968, Rashad graduated from the University of Oregon in 1972 with a degree in education. He was the 1995 recipient of the university's Pioneer Award, the highest honor given to

Minnesota Vikings wide receiver Ahmad Rashad, here catching a pass from quarterback Fran Tarkenton, would become one of the most recognized sports broadcasters and television personalities following his retirement from professional football. *(AP/Wide World Photos)*

alumni; he serves today on the Board of Trustees for the University of Oregon. He holds an honorary doctorate of journalism from the University of Puget Sound. After his conversion to the Muslim faith during his second year in the NFL, he changed his name to Ahmad Rashad. Since 1982, he has been a sportscaster with NBC.

After setting team records in most yards rushing, most receptions, and most points scored at the University of Oregon, Ahmad Rashad became a Heisman Trophy candidate his senior year. He played professional football with the St. Louis Cardinals, 1972–1973; Buffalo Bills, 1974–1976; Seattle Seahawks, 1976; and the Minnesota Vikings, 1976–1982. A four-time All-Pro nominee, Rashad played in the National

Football League's Pro Bowl, 1979, and was named to the National Football Conference (NFC) All-Star team by the *Sporting News* in 1978 and 1979. He was inducted into the University of Oregon Hall of Fame in 1987 and won a Sports Emmy from "InSport" in 1990.

Rashad became a sportscaster with NBC as a pregame analyst on the NBC *NFL Live* show in 1982, and later branched out beyond football to cover the Olympics, tennis tournaments, the NBA finals, and feature interviews. Rashad joined NBC Sports in 1983 as an NFL commentator and reporter for *SportsWorld*. His duties included studio hosting, feature reporting, analysis, and commentary for a variety of sports and events. In 1988, he worked as a studio anchor for NBC during coverage of the Seoul Olympics and won an Emmy for his work. Since 1990, Rashad has been the network's lead courtside reporter throughout the regular season, at the All-Star Game, and through the playoffs and Finals, cohost of *NBA Inside Stuff*, and NBC's Saturday NBA entertainment program. In 1992, Rashad was one of the hosts of NBC's Olympic triplecast from Barcelona. In Atlanta in 1996, he worked as a weekend host and late-night correspondent. In his fourth Olympics for NBC, Rashad was the "Around the Games," reporter during the 2000 Sydney games.

Doris R. Corbett

FURTHER READING
Italia, Bob. *The Minnesota Vikings.* New York: ABDO, 1996.
Klobuchar, Jim. *Purple Hearts and Golden Memories.* New York: Raven Stone, 1999.
Rashad, Ahmad, and Peter Bodo. *Vikes, Mikes and Something on the Backside.* Chicago: New Readers, 1988.

★ ★ ★

George RAVELING

Born June 27, 1937, Washington, DC
Basketball coach

Raveling is married to Vivian James and has one son, Mark. A graduate of St. Michael's (DC) and Villanova University (B.S., 1960), Raveling began coaching basketball at Villanova in 1963. He has also coached at Maryland, Washington State, Iowa, and the University of Southern California (USC). Raveling currently works as a broadcaster, runs basketball clinics, and performs speaking engagements.

At Maryland in 1970, Raveling became the first African-American assistant coach in Atlantic Coast Conference (ACC) history. In 1972, Raveling became the first African-American head coach in the Pacific Coast Conference (PAC Ten) when he was hired at Washington State. Raveling moved on to be the head coach at the University of Iowa from 1983 to 1986. As head coach at USC (1986–1994), Raveling led the Trojans to four consecutive post-season tournaments. In 1992, he was voted Coach of the Year by the National of Association Basketball Coaches (NABC). Raveling was also an assistant coach with the 1984 and 1988 U.S. Olympic teams.

Raveling has been a strong proponent of educational and employment opportunities for African Americans. He protested the National Collegiate Athletic Association's (NCAA) efforts to reduce the number of athletic scholarships and the size of coaching staffs. Throughout his career, he also battled against the NCAA's Propositions 42 and 48, the lack of black executives in the NCAA and USA Basketball, and the shortage of black coaches in men's and women's basketball.

Raveling finished his thirty-one-year collegiate coaching career with an overall record of 336–292. He is also the founder of the "Reading with Raveling" literacy program in Los Angeles area junior high schools.

Gregory H. Duquette

FURTHER READING

Hoffer, Richard. "George Raveling: USC Coach Can Recruit and Tell Jokes, Knows What Schools Are All About." *Los Angeles Times*, May 5, 1986.

Lawlor, Chris. "Un-Raveling." *Scholastic Coach* 61 (April 1992): A18–21.

Lindsay, John. "Black Coaches Plan for Battle: African Americans in Congress Unite on NCAA Issue." *San Francisco Examiner*, October 20, 1993.

Saxon, Lisa Nehus. "Black Coaches Share a View." *Riverside Press-Enterprise*, October 19, 1993.

Spencer, Lyle. "Raveling Has Broader Focus than the Game." *Riverside Press-Enterprise*, January 14, 1994.

★ ★ ★

Dwight REED

Born March 13, 1915, St. Paul, Minnesota
Died May 31, 2000
Football coach

The son of Ora and Dwight T. Reed, Sr., Dwight Reed graduated from Washington High School. One of only three blacks at his school, in one of two black families on the north side of St. Paul, Minnesota, he went on to play football at the University of Minnesota. He achieved All-American honors as an end on the university's national championship teams in 1935, 1936, and 1937. Reed left the university prior to graduation to play three years for a barnstorming basketball team called the Galloping Gophers, made up of former University of Minnesota football players. He later joined the army in 1941 and played one year under legendary Notre Dame player Joe Bach, one of the original Notre Dame "Seven Mules." He went to Italy to join the Ninety-second Infantry Division during World War II.

Reed returned to the University of Minnesota to complete his bachelor's degree and was hired as the football coach for Louisville Municipal College in 1947. The team was so poor financially that it was still practicing in street clothes two days before the first official game of the season. Nonetheless, Louisville Municipal College defeated Lincoln University two consecutive years. After the second loss, Lincoln University offered him its head football coaching job in 1949. Reed assumed the position as director of athletics at Lincoln University in 1957. His accomplishments as Athletics Director included the expansion of Lincoln's athletic program to encompass wrestling, baseball, cross country, golf, gymnastics, soccer, swimming and women's athletics. He assumed the role of track coach himself.

While at Lincoln, Reed served on a number of NCAA and AAU national committees, including the Track and Field Rules Committee for both organizations, as dean of the Missouri Football Coaches Association, on the NCAA Athletic Directors Executive Committee, and as a referee for Big Eight and NCAA track and field national championships. Reed ended his twenty-four-year stint as Lincoln's head football coach in 1973, ranked seventh among college division coaches with a 150–82–7 record. During his tenure at Lincoln University he produced ninety-three All-Americans.

Gary A. Sailes

FURTHER READING

Ashe, Arthur R., Jr. *A Hard Road To Glory: A History of the African-American Athlete*. New York: Amistad, 1988.

Lincoln University Department of Athletics.

Nace, Ed. "Negro Grid Stars Past and Present." *Opportunity* 17 (September 1941): 272–73.

Wilkins, Roy. "Negro Stars on Big Grid Teams." *Crisis* 43 (December 1926): 362–64.

Willis REED

Born June 25, 1942, Hico, Louisiana
Basketball player

Born to a family of farmers, Reed stands out as one of the most recognized and celebrated players in the history of the New York Knickerbockers. He was an integral part of the Knicks only (two) World Championships teams (1969–1970 and 1972–1973), had his number (nineteen) retired by the organization, and even spent some years as coach of the Knicks. Over his career, Reed was a teammate of some of the greatest names in the history of the NBA— with Walt Frazier, Bill Bradley, Cazzie Russell, Dave DeBusschere, and Dick Barnett, among others. Along with his team accomplishments, Reed enjoyed a great deal of individual acclaim and accolades. He was the NBA Rookie of the Year in his first season (1964–1965), led his team in scoring for the first five years of his career, and completed the coveted "MVP trifecta" by becoming the NBA League, All-Star Game, and finals MVP in the 1969–1970 season.

Reed's place in Knick lore was cemented during the team's run to the championship during the 1969–1970 season. He led the Knicks over the Milwaukee Bucks and superstar rookie Lew Alcindor (later called Kareem Abdul-Jabbar) in the Eastern Conference Finals in five games. Then in the NBA finals, Reed and the Knicks met an L.A. Lakers team that included Wilt Chamberlain, Jerry West, and Elgin Baylor. In that series, Reed and the hot-shooting Wilt Chamberlain traded big games all the way to the fifth contest, when Reed went down in the first half with a torn thigh muscle. This allowed the Lakers to win the sixth game and get back in the series. In the decisive seventh game Reed made a dramatic entrance onto the floor of Madison Square Garden just moments before tip-off to rouse his team and the crowd, in what was one of the most memorable moments in NBA history. Still hobbled from his injury, Reed practically ensured the Knicks victory by starting the game and making the first basket. The emotional lift was enough, and the Knicks finished the Lakers off 113–99 and clinched the championship. Reed is now an executive with the NBA's New Jersey Nets organization.

Adam Phillips

FURTHER READING
Berger, Phil. *Miracle on 33rd Street: The New York Knick's Championship Season.* New York: Four Walls Eight Windows, reprint February 1994.
NBA.com (www.nba.com), June 2001–October 2001.
WillisReed.com (www.willisreed.com), June 2001–October 2001.

Mel RENFRO

Born December 30, 1941, Houston, Texas
Football player

Mel Renfro was born in Houston, Texas. His family moved to Portland, Oregon, where he attended Jefferson High School, excelling in track and football. The son of a furniture factory worker, Renfro attended the University of Oregon, where he won numerous awards for his sprinting and hurdling and achieved All-American status as a running back in 1962 and 1963. Renfro was a second-round NFL draft pick by Dallas in 1963, with which he played for fourteen seasons.

He was selected to play in ten successive Pro Bowls, four Super Bowls, and eight NFL/NFC championship games. He led the NFL in receptions in 1969 and is the Cowboys' all-time interception leader (fifty-two) and he averaged 26.4 yards per kickoff return. He was enshrined in the Cowboys' Ring of Honor in 1981 and was elected to the Pro Football Hall of Fame in 1996. Renfro retired in 1977.

Renfro was inducted into the National High School Sports Hall of Fame in 1995; he deems this honor his most memorable, because it recognizes his beginnings. Today he lives in the Portland neighborhood where he grew up and works with Bridge Developments, a Christian organization focusing on inner-city youths.

Trisha M. Hothorn

FURTHER READING
Morgan, David Lee, Jr. "Gary Cartwright. The Coach: Writers Remember." *Dallas Morning News*, March 12, 1989.
Quick, Jason. "An Induction into Prep Hall of Fame a Special Honor for Mel Renfro." *Oregonian*, July 6, 1995.
Rywell, Martin, ed. *Afro-American Encyclopedia*. North Miami, FL: Educational Book Publishers, 1974.

★ ★ ★

Butch REYNOLDS

Born June 8, 1964, Akron, Ohio
Sprinter

The son of Harry, Sr., a maintenance technician, and Catherine, a child-care worker, Butch Reynolds graduated from Hoban High School in Akron, Ohio, in 1983, Butler County Junior College in El Dorado, Kansas, in 1984 and Ohio State University in 1987.

He emerged as a world-class 400-meter sprinter in 1987, setting a low-altitude world record of 44.10 seconds. In 1988, Reynolds set a world record with a time of 43.29. At the 1988 Olympics, Reynolds won silver in the 400 meters and gold in the 4 x 400 meters. In 1990, Reynolds tested positive for steroids and was banned by the International Amateur Athletic Federation (IAAF) for two years, preventing him from qualifying for the 1992 Olympics. In 1993, Reynolds returned to competition and won 400-meter gold at the World Indoor Championships. He later won silver (400 meters) and gold (4 x 400 meters) at both the 1993 and 1995 World Championships. He was injured during the 1996 Atlanta Olympics, and persistent injuries prompted Reynolds to retire in 2000.

Reynolds is recognized for his determined challenge of the IAAF's drug-testing procedures. He unequivocally proclaimed his innocence. Reynolds sued the IAAF, and an Ohio court awarded him $27.4 million in punitive damages; however, the suit was dismissed by a U.S. Court of Appeals.

Banned from competing at the peak of his career, Reynolds' challenge exposed many of the IAAF's bureaucratic flaws and violations of constitutional rights. His fight brought to prominence the issue of athlete's rights in challenging international sport organizations.

Gregory H. Duquette

FURTHER READING
Ferstle, Jim. "'I Want to Clear My Name.'" *Runner's World*, July 1992, 104–107.
Kuehls, David. "Back on Track." *Runner's World*, June 1993, 86–87.
Moore, Kenny. "Preparing a Big Move." *Sports Illustrated*, September 7, 1987, 36–43.

★ ★ ★

Ray RHODES

Born October 20, 1950, Mexia, Texas
Football player and coach

Rhodes was the third African-American head coach (Philadelphia Eagles, 1995–

1998) in the National Football League (NFL). He also was the first African American to receive a second job as an NFL head coach (Green Bay Packers, 1999).

Rhodes helped to integrate Mexia (TX) High School, where he was an All-State football player. He was among the first class of African-American football recruits at Texas Christian University but transferred to Tulsa University after his sophomore year. He played seven years in the NFL (1974–1980) for the New York Giants and San Francisco 49ers as a wide receiver and defensive back.

Between 1981 and 1991 Rhodes coached defensive backs for the 49ers. In 1992, he was hired as defensive coordinator for the Packers. Rhodes left Green Bay in 1994 to become defensive coordinator for the 49ers.

Hired as head coach by the Eagles in 1995, Rhodes earned the 1995 NFL Coach of the Year Award during his first season, as Philadelphia advanced to the playoffs with a 10–6 record. The Eagles made the postseason again in 1996, but Rhodes was fired following losing records in 1997 and 1998. In four seasons, Rhodes's Eagles posted a 37–41–1 record.

Rhodes was hired by the Packers for the 1999 season but was fired after the team posted an 8-8 record. That year the Packers were the first NFL team to have African Americans simultaneously as coach, offensive coordinator, and defensive coordinator.

Michael T. Friedman

FURTHER READING
Armstrong, Jim. "Rhodes Pays Toll for Success." *Denver Post*, October 17, 1999.
Denver Broncos. "Ray Rhodes" (www.denverbroncos.com/lockerroom/coaches_bios/rhodes_ray.php3).
Donnellon, Sam. "NFL Needs to Erase Its Color Line." *Austin American-Statesman*, January 19, 2000.
Saunders, Patrick. "Rhodes' Career Trip Tough as Texas." *Denver Post*, January 21, 2001.

★ ★ ★

Ted RHODES

Born November 9, 1913, Nashville, Tennessee
Died July 4, 1969, Nashville, Tennessee
Golfer

Born to Frank and Della (Anderson) Rhodes, Ted Rhodes is recognized as the first professional African-American golfer. Rhodes had over 150 victories in the United Golfers Association in the 1940s and won the prestigious National Negro Open four times. Rhodes served as golf pro to heavyweight champion Joe Louis from 1945 to 1954. Educated in Nashville public schools, Rhodes aspired to play golf at a time when race restrictions on municipal courts forced blacks to caddie for whites and practice in public parks. Rhodes's years of legal action against the PGA resulted in its dropping the "Caucasian clause" in 1961. Such legal recourse was significant in the black sports community. On August 13, 1969, the Nashville Metropolitan Board renamed Cumberland Golf Course in his honor. Burke Golf of Newark, New Jersey, signed him as the first black to endorse golf equipment. He was inducted into the Tennessee Golf Hall of Fame in 1998.

Alison M. Gavin

See also: Golf.

FURTHER READING
Ashe, Arthur R., Jr. *A Hard Road To Glory: A History of the African-American Athlete, 1919–1945*. New York: Amistad, 1988.
Dawkins, Marvin P., and Graham C. Kinloch. *American Golfers During the Jim Crow Era*. Westport, CT: Praeger Press, 2000.
Elder, Mrs. Rose. Telephone interview, October 22, 2001.
"Leaders of Afro-American Nashville: Theodore 'Ted'

Rhodes 1913–1969," *Nashville Room*, Nashville Library clippings.
Nashville Banner, November 25, 1997.
New York Times, Obituaries, July 6, 1969.
Sports Nashville, November 19, 1998.

★ ★ ★

Willy T. RIBBS

Born January 3, 1956, San Jose, California
Auto racer

The son of Geraldine Henderson-Ribbs and William T. "Bunny" Ribbs, Sr., who owned a plumbing business, Willy Ribbs, best known as Willy T., has competed successfully in many types of automobile racing.

Ribbs followed in his father's footsteps as an amateur road racer. He learned to race in England and won the 1977 Dunlop Tire "Star of Tomorrow" Formula Ford European championship. He debuted in the United States at the 1978 Long Beach Grand Prix. The same year he had an opportunity to drive in a NASCAR race, but his cockiness offended many, and offers evaporated. For the next few years Ribbs was informally blacklisted. He returned to racing in the early 1980s and took Rookie of the Year honors in the Sports Car Club of America Trans-Am Series in 1983. Between 1983 and 1985 he won seventeen races, more than any other Trans-Am driver. Ribbs agreed to drive for independent owner Sherman Armstrong in the 1985 Indianapolis 500 but withdrew when his practice lap times fell far short of the speeds necessary to qualify. In 1986 he competed in three NASCAR Winston Cup races for DiGard before the team folded due to lack of sponsorship. He was named Driver of the Year in 1987 and 1988 in the IMSA (International Motor Sports Association) GTO series. He also received the largest fine ever assessed by the organization, $2,000 for reckless driving, and was the first driver ever suspended by IMSA after he punched fellow competitor Scott Pruett.

With financial support from entertainer Bill Cosby, Ribbs competed in CART (Championship Auto Racing Teams) events in 1990. He qualified for the 1991 Indianapolis 500, the first black driver to do so, but was able to complete only five laps of the race before retiring with mechanical problems. Ribbs finished twenty-first in the 1993 Indianapolis 500 and placed in the top ten five times during the 1994 CART season. In 1999 he became the first African American to drive in the IRL (Indy Racing League) series, and in 2001 he was the first black driver since Wendell Scott in the early 1970s to compete full-time in a major NASCAR series. As the centerpiece of Dodge Motorsports's racing diversity program, Ribbs drove a Dodge truck for Bobby Hamilton in the NASCAR Craftsman Truck series. Disappointing results led to his release at the end of the season.

Ribbs's career has been punctuated by altercations with fellow competitors and the racing establishment, and his early flamboyance and braggadocio alienated the media and potential sponsors. More recently he has emerged as a more mature competitor who argues that while racing needs more diversity, the sport is not racist. Ribbs was the recipient of the first annual Sports Image Award presented by the Sports Image Foundation, which honors sports figures who have given their time and money to improve their communities.

Suzanne Wise

FURTHER READING
Bianco, David. "Willy T. Ribbs, 1956–; Race Car Driver." In *Contemporary Black Biography: Profiles from the Black Community*. Vol. 2, 196–199. Detroit: Gale Group, 1992.
Garrett, Jerry. "Tell 'Em Willy T. Is Back!" *Car and Driver* 45 (February 2000): 123–29.

Kay, Virginia. "Ribbs, Willy T." In *Current Biography Yearbook 2000*. New York: H.W. Wilson, 2000.

McAlevey, Peter. "The Hard Ride of Willy T." *New York Times Magazine*, October 9, 1988.

Moses, Sam. "Racing Suits Willy to a T." *Sports Illustrated*, October 17, 1983, 83–86.

★ ★ ★

Jerry RICE

Born October 13, 1962, Starkville, Mississippi
Football player

Jerry Rice is the son of Joe Rice (a brick mason) and Edie B. Rice. At Moor High School in Crawford, MS, Rice competed in basketball, football, and track and field. Rice attended Mississippi Valley State University, where he set numerous National Collegiate Athletic Association football records. Among other honors, Rice was voted the Most Valuable Player of the Blue-Gray Game and selected as a NCAA Division IAA All-American in 1983 and 1984.

In the 1985 National Football League draft, the six foot two inch, 200-pound Rice was the first-round draft choice of both the United States Football League's Birmingham Stallions (Birmingham had the USFL's first pick) and the National Football League's San Francisco 49ers (San Francisco owned the NFL's sixteenth selection). His career with the 49ers lasted sixteen years. During his time with San Francisco, as a wide receiver, Rice was a part of three Super Bowl-winning teams (1989, 1990, and 1995). He was selected as the National Football Conference's Rookie of the Year in 1985 and the *Sports Illustrated* National Football League Player of the Year in 1986, 1987, 1990, and 1993. He was the NFL MVP in 1987 and Super Bowl XXIII MVP in 1989. He has appeared in multiple Pro Bowls. He holds numerous 49er, NFC, NFL, and Super Bowl records. Perhaps most important of these records is the NFL's career touchdown reception title. In 2001, Rice signed to play with the Oakland Raiders.

Rice and his wife, Jackie, have three children: Jaqui Bonet, Jerry Junior, and Jada Symone. They reside in Atherton, California. Rice is active in numerous charitable activities, including the United Negro College Fund and the Omega Boys Club.

Deane A. Lamont

FURTHER READING

Henderson, Ashyia N., ed. *Who's Who Among African Americans*. Detroit: Gale Group, 2000.

Porter, David L., ed. *Biographical Dictionary of American Sports: 1992–1995 Supplement for Baseball, Football, Basketball and Other Sports*. Westport, CT: Greenwood Press, 1995.

Who's Who in America, 2001. New Providence, NJ: Marquis Who's Who, 2001.

★ ★ ★

Nolan RICHARDSON

Born December 27, 1941, El Paso, Texas
Basketball coach

Richardson was in the initial vanguard of African Americans seeking to break down the walls of racial discrimination in the college coaching profession. In the process he amassed one of the best career won-lost records during the last quarter of the twentieth century.

Orphaned at age three, he was raised by his grandmother, a strict disciplinarian, who encouraged Nolan to be a diligent student. In 1955 he was the first African American to play for Bowie High School in El Paso, where he was a standout in basketball, baseball, and football. He was drafted by the Houston Astros but opted to play basketball for the legendary coach Don Haskins at the University of Texas El Paso, where he earned a degree in secondary education. During a ten-year stint coaching basketball at Bowie High School his teams had a 190–80 record, and he was named the Texas High School Coach of the year three times. In his first season at West Texas Junior College in 1979 his team lost in the national finals, but it won the championship the following year. In 1981 he was named the first African-American head coach at Tulsa University, where his teams had a 119–37 record, won the National Invitational Tournament in 1981, and were invited four times to the NCAA tournament.

In 1985 he was named head coach at the University of Arkansas—at the time considered a major breakthrough for black coaches. There he implemented his system of full-court pressure and match-up zone defenses coupled with a fast break offense that Razorback fans dubbed "forty minutes of hell." His initial season was tragically marred by the slow and painful death of his daughter Yvonne due to leukemia, but he persevered and built one of the most consistently strong programs in major college basketball. In 1990 his team made the Final Four of the NCAA tournament; in 1994 the Razorbacks won the national championship with a close victory over Duke. The following year they lost in the finals to UCLA. At one point they had appeared in fourteen straight NCAA tournaments. He received the Naismith Coach of the Year award in 1994 and during the late 1990s became a leading spokesman for the Black Coaches Association. He agreed to termination on March 2, 2002, after the first year of a lucrative new seven-year contract.

Richard O. Davies

See also: Coaches and Managers.

FURTHER READING
Contemporary Black Biography, 1997, 197–200.
Memphis Commercial Appeal, December 18, 2000.
Sports Illustrated, March 7, 1988, 94–98.
"Thin Skin but Great Heart." *Newsweek*, April 18, 1994, 42.
University of Arkansas (www.uark.edu).

★ ★ ★

Bill RICHMOND

Born August 5, 1763, Staten Island, New York
Died December 28, 1829, London, United Kingdom
Boxer, trainer

During the historical period when most African Americans were legally enslaved, Bill Richmond was born free. His mother was a former slave, set free by her master, the Rev. George E. Charlton. As a young boy, Richmond frequently got into fights along the docks of New York Harbor. On those docks, his fighting skills were greatly admired by the British commander in Manhattan, Lord Percy. In 1777, Richmond agreed to travel with Percy to England.

In London, Richmond worked as a cabinetmaker and trained as a boxer. While fighting as a semiprofessional boxer, Richmond attracted a loyal and substantial following among the various classes of British society. His stature as a highly respected athlete in London society was extremely unusual for any African-American man of the period. In 1800, his wealthy patrons helped him open a successful tavern called the Horse and Dolphin. Richmond became the first African American to make a profitable living as a professional boxer and businessman.

In 1805, Richmond's success as a boxer earned him an opportunity to fight for the title. He became the first African-American athlete to compete for a national or world title in any sport. The champion, Tom Cribb, soundly beat Richmond in a relatively short bout. Richmond fought his last professional fight in 1815. After his retirement from boxing, Richmond served as mentor and trainer to several African-American boxers, including the great Tom Molineaux.

Tracey M. Salisbury

See also: Boxing; Tom Molineaux.

FURTHER READING
Ashe, Arthur R., Jr. *A Hard Road to Glory: A History of the African-American Athlete, 1619–1918*. New York: Warner Books, 1988.
Brailsford, Dennis. *Bareknuckles: A Social History of Prizefighting*. Cambridge, MA: Lutterworth Press, 1988.
Henderson, Edwin Bancroft. *The Black Athlete: Emergence and Arrival*. Cornwell Heights, PA: Publishers Agency, 1976.

★ ★ ★

Ric ROBERTS

Born May 26, 1905, Gainesville, Florida
Died September 12, 1985, Washington, DC
Journalist

As a sophomore at Clark College, Ric Roberts became the first sports editor for the *Atlanta Daily World*. He graduated in 1930 and continued to work at the paper. While there, he and assistant sports editor Lucious Jones received permission to start the 100 Percent Wrong Club. Members of the group participated in a weekly contest of guessing scores of upcoming sports events. It evolved into an annual banquet that honored sports figures and fans.

Roberts left Atlanta for a job at the *Baltimore Afro-American*. He covered sports there and at the *Pittsburgh Courier*. While at the *Courier*, he participated in an interview with baseball commissioner Happy Chandler, who said that if blacks could fight in wars, they could play in the major leagues. The interview was a pivotal point in the campaign to integrate baseball. After working for the aforementioned newspapers, Roberts became sports information director at Howard University. The *Daily World* honored him at a celebration of the fiftieth anniversary of the 100 Percent Wrong Club.

Michael Marsh

FURTHER READING
"Eric B. 'Ric' Roberts Dies at Age 80." *Atlanta Daily World*, September 17, 1985.
Holway, John. *Voices from the Great Black Baseball Leagues*. New York: Da Capo Press, 1992.
Renfroe, Chico. "The Final Whistle Has Blown for Sportsman Ric Roberts." *Atlanta Daily World*, September 17, 1985.
Young, A.S., "Doc." "Black Athlete in Golden Age of Sports: Part IX—The Black Sportswriter." *Ebony*, October 1970, 56–58, 60–62, 64.
———. *Negro Firsts in Sports*. Chicago: Johnson, 1963.

★ ★ ★

Oscar ROBERTSON

Born November 24, 1938, Bellsburg, Tennessee
Basketball player

Oscar Robertson was the second son of Bailey and Mazell Bell Robertson. His father moved to Indianapolis, Indiana, in search of economic opportunity during World War II. After graduating from Crispus Attucks High School in 1956 and the University of Cincinnati in 1960, Robertson pursued an impressive fourteen-year professional basketball career that has earned him recognition as one of the greatest players of all time. At six feet, five inches the "Big O" played as a big point guard who could shoot, pass, and rebound in a style many now associate with Earvin "Magic" Johnson.

Robertson began his climb to basketball immortality when he led the all-black Crispus High team to consecutive state titles in 1955 and 1956. Because of the racism he experienced in Indiana during those two suc-

Oscar Robertson achieved enormous success and led his teams to several championships at the high school, college, and professional levels of competition. (AP/Wide World Photos)

cessful seasons, however, Robertson decided to play his collegiate ball at the University of Cincinnati (1957–1960). While at Cincinnati he became a three-time National Player of the Year and three-time national scoring champion, leading his team to two appearances in the NCAA Final Four (1959 and 1960). In 1960 he was the co-captain with Jerry West of the U.S. Olympic basketball team that easily won the gold medal in Rome and is considered by many to be one of the most talented teams ever assembled. Drafted that year by the Cincinnati Royals, Robertson earned both NBA Rookie of the Year and All-Star Game Most Valuable Player (his first of three) in 1961. The following season he accomplished the unthinkable when he averaged a triple double for the season (30.8 points, 11.4 assists, and 12.5 rebounds per game). During his first five years as a professional he averaged 30.3 points, 10.4 rebounds, and 10.6 assists per game. Robertson earned the league MVP in 1964 but was traded to the Milwaukee Bucks by the financially strapped Royals after the 1969–1970 season. The following season he teamed with young Lew Alcindor (Kareem Abdul-Jabbar) to win the 1971 NBA championship. After making it to the finals in 1974, Robertson retired from the NBA as the highest-scoring guard of all time (26,710 points). At the time of his retirement he was also the all-time career assists leader. Robertson was inducted into the Basketball Hall of Fame in 1979.

Besides his amazing performance on the court, Robertson contributed to professional basketball by helping bring free agency to the league in the 1970s, through his active involvement in the NBA Players Association. After his playing career he became both a civic and business leader in the Cincinnati area, primarily through his land development company that works to reinvigorate economically depressed areas through the construction of low-income housing. In 1996 Robertson once again made headlines by donating a kidney to his daughter, who was suffering from kidney failure.

Troy D. Paino

See also: Basketball.

FURTHER READING
Dickey, Glenn. *The History of Professional Basketball*. Briarcliff Manor, NY: Stein and Day, 1982.
Marchall, A. *Legend in High School Basketball*. Indianapolis, IN: High School Basketball Cards of America, 1992.
Roberts, Randy. *"But They Can't Beat Us": Oscar Robertson and the Crispus Attucks Tigers*. Champaign: Sports Publishing, 1999.
Sachare, Alex. *100 Greatest Basketball Players of All Time*. New York: Pocket Books, 1997.

Paul ROBESON

Born April 9, 1898, Princeton, New Jersey
Died January 23, 1976, Philadelphia, Pennsylvania
Actor, singer, athlete, activist

The youngest of five children sired by William Drew Robeson, a clergyman, and Maria Louisa Bustill, a schoolteacher, Robeson experienced tragedy at age six when his mother perished in a kitchen fire. Raised chiefly by his father, who emphasized education, Robeson graduated from James L. Jamison Colored School, the Somerville, N.J. High School, Rutgers University (A.B.), and Columbia University (LL.B.) He was to be known as a singer, actor, civil rights activist, scholar, lawyer, author, and athlete.

Robeson was the consummate scholar-athlete. At Rutgers he earned fourteen varsity letters in four sports and took first place in the college's oratory contest four successive years. He was elected to Phi Beta Kappa and the Cap and Skull Honor Society. He was the valedictorian for his graduating class and the first Rutgers football player named to Walter Camp's All-American team. He supported himself through law school by playing professional football for the Hammond (Indiana) Pros, the Akron Pros, and the Milwaukee Badgers, as well as by assisting football coaches Fritz Pollard at Lincoln University and G. Foster Sanford at Rutgers.

Robeson's career as an attorney was short-lived. When a stenographer refused to take dictation from him because he was black, Robeson jettisoned the legal profession for the theater. His reputation climbed with lead roles in Eugene O'Neill's *All God's Chillun Got Wings* and *The Emperor Jones*; his performances in *Othello* and *Show Boat*, with his signature song, "Ol' Man River," brought him international acclaim. He appeared in eleven motion pictures and recorded numerous spirituals and folk songs.

Paul Robeson, shown here in his Rutgers University football uniform, was an outstanding all-around athlete, scholar, singer and actor, and civil rights activist. *(AP/Wide World Photos)*

A relentless advocate of civil rights, Robeson campaigned for freedom and equality of the oppressed at home and abroad. In 1943 he met with Commissioner Judge Kenesaw Mountain Landis, and other leaders about desegregating the game. He traveled widely, meeting prominent socialists and African nationalists; to facilitate communication, he mastered twenty languages, five of which were African. He found solace without racial prejudice in the Soviet Union, but his defense of its system reduced his popularity at home and prompted federal investigations of his suspected communism. Stripped of his passport and blacklisted from auditoriums and concert halls across America during the 1950s, Robeson found his livelihood undermined. His name was removed from All-American football teams and omitted from the roster of Rutgers's sixty-five greatest football players. During the closing decades of his life, he suffered from depression and emotional stress. He died from a stroke in 1976.

Just a few of Robeson's prolific honors and awards are the Abraham Lincoln Medal (1943), the NAACP's Spingarn Award (1945), the Champion of African Freedom Award, an award of the Nigerian National Church (1950), the Stalin Peace Prize (1952), and Civil Liberties Memorial Award (1970). He was elected to the Black Sports Hall of Fame in 1973 and posthumously to the College Football Hall of Fame in 1995.

J. Thomas Jable

See also: Films; Football; Fritz Pollard.

FURTHER READING

Duberman, Martin. *Paul Robeson: A Biography*. New York: New Press, 1996.

Robeson, Paul. *Here I Stand*. New York: Othello Associates, 1958.

———. *The Undiscovered Paul Robeson: An Artist's Journey, 1898–1939*. New York: John Wiley and Sons, 2001.

Smith, Ronald A. "The Paul Robeson–Jackie Robinson Saga and a Political Collision." *Journal of Sport History* 6 (Summer 1979): 5–27.

Stewart, Jeffrey C., ed. *Paul Robeson, Artist and Citizen*. New Brunswick: Rutgers University Press, 1998.

★ ★ ★

David ROBINSON

Born August 6, 1965, Key West, Florida
Basketball player

David Robinson was the second of three children of Ambrose, a chief petty officer in the U.S. Navy, and Freda, a nurse. The family later moved to Virginia, and Robinson attended high school in the Norfolk region before receiving an appointment to the U.S. Naval Academy, from which he graduated with a commission as a lieutenant (junior grade) in 1987.

Robinson belied a lot of stereotypes; he was a top student more interested in science than sports, did not play basketball until eighth grade, and did not play competitive basketball seriously until his senior year at Osbourn Park High in Manassas, Virginia. He was a "late bloomer" physically, growing from five feet, nine inches in eighth grade to six feet, seven inches as a senior in high school and seven feet as a senior in college. In his sophomore year at Navy he was the East Coast Athletic Conference (ECAC) Player of the Year. In his junior year he was conference Player of the Year, and in his senior year he was College Player of the Year. Following graduation Robinson entered the navy for a two-year stint, which had been reduced by the secretary of the navy from the normal five-year commitment.

In 1988, 1992, and 1996 he was a member of the U.S. Olympic basketball teams. In 1989 he signed with the NBA's San Antonio Spurs, which had drafted him in 1987. He won the Rookie of the Year award in the NBA in 1990 and the Most Valuable Player Award in 1995. In 1999 the Spurs, led by Robinson and Tim Duncan, won the NBA championship in a strike-shortened season. Robinson and his wife, Valerie, have three sons; they have created the David Robinson Foundation, a Christian organization whose mission is to support families.

Murry R. Nelson

FURTHER READING

Hickok, Ralph. *A Who's Who of Sports Champions: Their Stories and Records*. New York: Houghton Mifflin, 1995.

Eddie ROBINSON

Born February 13, 1919, Jackson, Louisiana
Football player and coach

Eddie Robinson was the only child of Frank, a sharecropper. At the age of six the Robinson family moved from an agrarian setting to the urban pace and bustle of life in the state capital, Baton Rouge. Robinson attended Baton Rouge McKinley High School and early on displayed a passion for anything to do with football. He parked cars in order to gain entry to football games at Southern University or Louisiana State University.

At McKinley, Robinson played quarterback. He graduated in 1937 and then attended a small Baptist college (Leland) in Baker, Louisiana, where he also played quarterback. Not only was Robinson a successful athlete at Leland (Leland won eighteen out of nineteen games in Robinson's junior and senior years), but he also launched his coaching career there. He worked as an assistant coach, designed the offense, and did some recruiting.

In 1941, the president of Grambling State University hired Robinson in a multiple capacity—athletic director, head of physical education, and head football coach. This started what was to be a singular commitment and contribution to not just African-American college football but football in general. Robinson's achievements are monumental. Before he retired, Robinson had far outstripped Bear Bryant's 323 wins and the records of such other legendary figures as George Halas (326), Amos Alonzo Stagg (314), and Pop Warner. As of 1994 Robinson had amassed 397 wins, all at Grambling.

Equally impressive was the placement of more than 200 of his players in the ranks of professional football. In James Harris, Robinson had a pioneering quarterback (played for the Buffalo Bills in 1969); many years later another Grambling product, quarterback Doug Williams, won a January 1988 Super Bowl ring (Williams was the first black quarterback to lead a team to an NFL championship). Williams also succeeded Robinson as coach at Grambling in 1997.

Robinson and Doris Mott have three children. In 1986, the governor of Louisiana proclaimed a special Eddie Robinson Day. Three years earlier Grambling's new athletic arena had been named Robinson Stadium. At his retirement Robinson's record was 408 wins, 165 losses, and fifteen ties. Robinson has since divided his time between speaking engagements and attending Grambling athletic events.

Scott A.G.M. Crawford

See also: Coaches and Managers; Historically Black Colleges and Universities.

Grambling State's legendary coach Eddie Robinson discussing strategy with two of his players at the 1997 Cramton Bowl in Montgomery, Alabama. *(AP/Wide World Photos)*

FURTHER READING

Porter, David L., ed. *African-American Sports Greats: A Biographical Dictionary.* Westport, CT: Greenwood Press, 1995.

Robinson, Eddie, with Richard Lapchick. *Robinson, Never Before, Never Again: The Stirring Autobiography of Eddie Robinson.* New York: St. Martin's Press, 1999.

Smith, Ron. *The Sporting News.* New York: Mallard Press, 1992.

Sports Information, Grambling State University. Telephone interview, April 20, 2001.

★ ★ ★

Frank ROBINSON

Born August 31, 1935, Beaumont, Texas
Baseball player, manager, and coach

Robinson was the youngest of ten children born to Ruth Shaw. She was divorced from Frank Robinson when Frank was an infant. Robinson was to become an outstanding hitter for power and average, a star in both the American and National Leagues, and in 1975 named major league baseball's first African-American manager.

When Robinson was four years old, his mother moved the family to Oakland, California. An acclaimed athlete at McClymonds High School, Robinson was influenced by Oakland coach and talent scout George Powels. After graduating from high school in 1953, Robinson was signed by the Cincinnati Reds. In 1954 and 1955 he enjoyed successful minor league seasons in Columbia, South Carolina (South Atlantic League), but Robinson was the target of bigotry in the South. Called up to the major leagues by the Reds in 1956, he batted .290, hit thirty-eight home runs, and was named National League Rookie of the Year. In 1961, Robinson led Cincinnati to the pennant and was selected as the league's Most Valuable Player.

After ten successful seasons in Cincinnati, Robinson was traded to Baltimore in December 1965. In his first season as an Oriole, Robinson won baseball's triple crown (hitting .316, slugging forty-nine home runs, and driving in 122 runs) and was chosen the American League's Most Valuable Player. Robinson led the Orioles to four American League pennants (1966, 1969, 1970, 1971) and two world championships (1966, 1970). Robinson finished his playing career with the Los Angeles Dodgers (1972), California Angels (1973), and Cleveland Indians (1974–1975).

In 1975, Robinson served as a player-manager for the Indians, becoming major league baseball's first African-American

Frank Robinson, the great Cincinnati Reds and Baltimore Orioles star who became the first African American to manage in Major League Baseball. *(National Baseball Hall of Fame Library, Cooperstown, NY)*

manager, almost thirty years after Jackie Robinson had broken the sport's color line. Dismissed from the Indians in 1977, Robinson returned to major league managing in 1981 with the San Francisco Giants, and, after a third-place finish in 1982, was named National League Manager of the Year. Released by the Giants during the 1984 season, Robinson coached for the Orioles (1985–1987) and managed the team from 1988 through 1991. From 1992 to 1995, he served as assistant to the general manager of the Orioles. Robinson has also worked as an analyst for Fox-TV Sports, and he currently serves in the commissioner's office.

Robinson broke baseball's racial barrier as a manager, but his teams had more losses than victories. But as a player, Robinson attained a .294 lifetime batting average and stands fourth on the all-time home run list with 586. In 1992, he was elected to the Baseball Hall of Fame.

Ron Briley

Jackie Robinson during his last spring training in 1956 at Vero Beach, Florida. *(AP/Wide World Photos)*

FURTHER READING
Fimrite, Ron. "Jaunty Stride into History." *Sports Illustrated*, March 4, 1975, 18–19.
Frank Robinson file. *National Baseball Hall of Fame Museum and Library*. Cooperstown, New York.
Robinson, Frank. "Fighting the Baseball Blackout." *Sport*, July 1988, 66–67.
Robinson, Frank, with Barry Stainback. *Extra Innings*. New York: McGraw-Hill, 1988.

★ ★ ★

Jackie ROBINSON

Born January 31, 1919, Cairo, Georgia
Died October 24, 1972, Stamford, Connecticut
Baseball player

Robinson is a sports figure whose significance transcends sports. By breaking major league baseball's long-standing color line in 1947, he helped usher in a new era of increased general opportunity for African Americans.

Robinson grew up in poverty in Pasadena, California, but developed into a superb athlete. When his senior year at UCLA ended, he was an acclaimed four-sport star in track and field, football, basketball, and baseball. Later, because jobs were few, he played semipro football before being drafted into the army. There he was subjected to a court-martial but exonerated; leaving the army in 1945, he joined the Negro leagues. That October, Branch Rickey, the Brooklyn Dodgers' general manager, convinced the muscular young infielder that he was the man to integrate organized baseball. Two years later, he was the major leagues' Rookie of the Year; two years after that, in 1949, he became an All-Star, won league batting and stolen base crowns, and led his team into the World Series. He was also presented with the Most Valuable Player award and was cast to play himself in the feature film *The Jackie Robinson Story.*

He became a six-time All-Star who batted over .300 six times, established a .311 lifetime batting average, set numerous fielding and stolen base records, and ranked fourth in stolen bases for both the 1940s and 1950s—despite playing only three years in one decade and seven in the other. Further, the Dodgers reached the World Series six times during the ten years he played. Retiring in 1956, he was inducted into the Baseball Hall of Fame five years later.

Thereafter, Robinson sought to use baseball-derived prestige elsewhere. He became an informal civil rights leader until his death in 1972, urging each successive presidential administration to support expanded political rights and economic opportunities for all Americans. Himself a beneficiary of democracy, Jack Roosevelt Robinson endeavored to prod his country into fuller realization of its ideals so that all Americans—of whatever ethnic background or skin color—would be able to compete fairly.

John A. Vernon

See also: Autobiographies; Baseball; Basketball; Civil Rights; Films; Mack Robinson; Wendell Smith.

FURTHER READING
Allen, Maury. *Jackie Robinson: A Life Remembered.* New York: Franklin Watts, 1987.
Faulkner, David. *Great Day Coming: The Life of Jackie Robinson from Baseball to Birmingham.* New York: Simon & Schuster, 1996.
Frommer, Harvey. *Rickey and Robinson: The Men Who Broke Baseball's Color Barrier.* New York: Macmillan, 1982.
Kahn, Roger. "The Ten Years of Jackie Robinson." *Sport,* October 1995, 12, 76–82.
Rampersad, Arnold. *Jackie Robinson, A Biography.* New York: Alfred A. Knopf, 1997.
Stout, Glenn, and Dick Johnson. *Jackie Robinson: Between the Baselines.* San Francisco: Woodford, 1997.
Tygiel, Jules. *The Great Experiment: Jackie Robinson and His Legacy.* New York: Oxford University Press, 1983.

★ ★ ★

Mack ROBINSON

Born July 18, 1914, Cairo, Georgia
Died March 12, 2000, Pasadena, California
Sprinter, Long jumper

Born of sharecroppers, the third of five children, Mack Robinson grew up in poverty in Pasadena, California. Although a younger brother, Jackie, eventually became better known, it was Mack who first demonstrated unusual athletic prowess. In junior high school he established a long-standing high hurdles mark. At Pasadena Junior College he set a national AAU long-jump record and ran the 220-yard and the 200-meter dashes so well that he qualified for the 1936 U.S. Olympic Team.

In Berlin Robinson ran a strong second to Jesse Owens, who set a new Olympic 200-meter record. After European competition, he returned home. That Pasadena extended no hero's welcome embittered the Robinson family. He subsequently attended the University of Oregon, where he won the 1938 AAU 200-meter title but thereafter was unable to cash in financially on either his education or his running skill.

The Depression and prevailing racial circumstances reduced a resentful Robinson to menial jobs for most of his working years. Instead of giving up, he remained in Pasadena, campaigning for recognition of Jackie's feats. He helped secure statues of his brother outside UCLA's baseball field, a post office, a senior citizen center, and a memorial—all bearing the Robinson name. He was elected to the Oregon Hall of Fame, the University of Oregon's Webfoot Society, and was featured in a track and field videotape. Robinson lived to be eighty-five before succumbing to a stroke. Jackie rarely chose to come to Pasadena after he became famous, irked by the earlier snubbing of Mack Robinson. Mack was equally perturbed with the city's racial climate but chose to remain there nonetheless. He possessed comparable tenacity and toughness, but like so many other capable African American athletes, did not enjoy Jackie's opportunities to succeed.

John A. Vernon

See also: Track and Field.

FURTHER READING
Ashe, Arthur R., Jr. *A History of the African-American Athlete, 1919–1945*. New York: Warner Books, 1988.
Baker, William J. *Jesse Owens: An American Life*. New York: Free Press, 1986.
CBS Sports Line. "Jackie Robinson's Olympian Brother, Mack, Dead at 85" (www.cbs.sportsline.com), March 13, 2000.
Robinson, Mack. "My Brother Jackie." *Ebony*, July 1957, 75–82.

★ ★ ★

Sugar Ray ROBINSON

Born May 3, 1921, Detroit, Michigan
Died April 12, 1989, Culver City, California
Boxer

Sugar Ray Robinson was born Walker Smith, Jr. Like most prizefighters, he was born into an impoverished family and community. His father Walker Smith, Sr., a construction worker, and his mother Leila Hurst, a seamstress, were both from rural Georgia and had moved to Detroit. They

Sugar Ray Robinson, the stylish and enormously talented boxing champion, in 1949 at his training camp at Pompton Lakes, New Jersey. *(AP/Wide World Photos)*

later divorced, and Smith moved with his mother and sisters to New York City.

In 1936, Smith borrowed the amateur fight card of a boxer named Ray Robinson for his first official fight and kept the name. A sportswriter apparently said to Smith's manager: "That's a sweet fighter you got there." He replied, "Sweet as sugar." The name stuck. In 1940, after a remarkable amateur career—he was 85–0 and won New York City Golden Gloves titles as a featherweight (1939) and a lightweight (1940)—Robinson turned professional.

Robinson was undefeated as a welterweight. In 1951, when he relinquished the 147-pound title to challenge Jake LaMotta for the middleweight championship, his record was 121–1–2, with the loss (to LaMotta) and both draws coming in nontitle fights against middleweights. Much has been made of the six ferocious

Robinson-LaMotta bouts; Robinson won five of them.

Despite his phenomenal success as a welterweight, Robinson earned more notoriety in the 1950s as a middleweight, holding the middleweight championship five times between 1951 and 1958. Compelled by financial woes and competitive desire, Robinson boxed until 1965, when he was well past his prime.

In his twenty-five-year professional career, Robinson fought 201 times, won 174 fights (109 by knockout), and was a world champion six times. He lost just nineteen decisions—five of which occurred in 1965, when he was forty-four years old. Conventional wisdom has it that Robinson was the greatest combination of brains, brawn, and boxing skill in history.

Yet, Robinson was more than the sum of his boxing accomplishments. According to journalist Richard Lacayo: "He was a hero to a generation of young black men, who adopted his pomaded hairstyle and admired his trademark pink Cadillac. Muhammad Ali called him 'my idol' and borrowed his dancing style. Sugar Ray Leonard borrowed his name." In an era when African Americans were supposed to be humble, docile, and restrained, Robinson embodied black pride and success.

Consistently described as "pound for pound, the greatest boxer in history," Robinson was inducted into the International Boxing Hall of Fame in 1990. In 1999, the Associated Press selected him as the greatest boxer of the twentieth century.

Daniel A. Nathan

See also: Autobiographies; Boxing; Films; Sugar Ray Leonard.

FURTHER READING
International Boxing Hall of Fame. "Sugar Ray Robinson" (www.ibhof.com/robinson.htm).
Lacayo, Richard. "Pound for Pound, the Best Ever." *Time*, April 24, 1989, 89.
Nathan, Daniel A. "Sugar Ray Robinson, the Sweet Science, and the Politics of Meaning." *Journal of Sport History* 26 (Spring 1999): 163–74.
Robinson, Sugar Ray, with Dave Anderson. *Sugar Ray: The Sugar Ray Robinson Story.* New York: De Capo Press, 1970, 1994.

★ ★ ★

RODEO

African Americans have had a long, if not extensive, history in rodeo. Nat Love, a frontiersman, cowboy, and former slave, claimed to be the first African-American rodeo champion. There is some question, however, about the accuracy of this claim, since much of the information provided by Love in his autobiography is unreliable and full of hyperbole. It is known with far more certainty that Pinto Jim and Bronco Jim Davis were the first African Americans to participate in a rodeo, in 1887 in Denver, Colorado.

The most famous African-American rodeo champion of the first half of the twentieth century was Bill Pickett. An outstanding bull rider who once was presented to King George V and Queen Mary

Rodeo rider Jess Stahl atop a bucking horse at the Harney County Roundup in Burns, Oregon. *(Hulton/Archive by Getty Images)*

after a special performance, Pickett was elected to the National Rodeo Cowboy Hall of Fame in 1971, the first African American to receive that honor. Unfortunately, Pickett was similar to other riders of his color and African American athletes in other sports during the period in that he competed behind segregated walls because of racial discrimination in this country. These discriminatory practices resulted in the creation of parallel institutions in the sport, including the Southwestern Colored Cowboys Association.

The 1960s witnessed the desegregation of the sport, with more African Americans finding their way into rodeo than ever before. One of these individuals was Myrtis Dightman, an enormously talented and highly competitive bull rider. Sometimes referred to as the "Jackie Robinson of rodeo," Dightman became the first African American to participate in the National Finals Rodeo. In 1981, some fifteen years after Dightman appeared in the National Finals Rodeo, Charles Sampson of Los Angeles won the world championship in bull riding. The following year he captured the Winston Rodeo Series and awarded the world title. In both 1991 and 1995 Fred Whitfield captured world titles in calf roping. The very recent past has witnessed outstanding performances by other African Americans in the sport, many of them taking place under the sponsorship of the well-known organization Black World Championship Rodeo.

David K. Wiggins

FURTHER READING
Durham, Philip, and Everette L. Jones. *The Negro Cowboys*. New York: Dodd, Mead, 1965.
Katz, William Loren. *The Black West*. New York: Doubleday, 1971.
Kirsch, George B., Othello Harris, and Claire E. Nolte, eds. *Encyclopedia of Ethnicity and Sports in the United States*. Westport, CT: Greenwood Press, 2000.
Smith, Jessie Carney. *Black Firsts: 2,000 Years of Extraordinary Achievement*. Detroit, MI: Visible Ink, 1994.

★ ★ ★

Johnny RODGERS

Born July 5, 1951, Omaha, Nebraska
Football player

Abandoned by his natural father at birth, Rodgers was raised by his stepfather, Eddie Jones, a construction worker, and his mother (name unknown), a nurse's aide. Using sports to escape a troubled youth, he starred in football, basketball, and baseball at Technical High School in Omaha; he was twice named an All-American in football and the Nebraska High School Athlete of the Year in 1969.

At the University of Nebraska, the five-foot nine-inch, 173-pound Rodgers, a wingback, was one of the greatest all-purpose offensive performers in college football history, displaying blazing speed and agility as a receiver, runner, and returner of punts and kickoffs. Leading the University of Nebraska to consecutive national championships (1970–1971), he was named All Big Eight three years and All-American in 1971 and 1972. In 1972 he returned a punt seventy-two yards for a touchdown, leading the Cornhuskers to victory over Oklahoma in "the Game of the Century." In the 1973 Sugar Bowl, playing I-back for the first time, Rodgers sparked a 40-6 rout of Notre Dame by scoring four touchdowns and passing for a fifth, though playing less than three quarters. Rodgers ended his college career setting or tying nineteen school, seven conference, and four NCCA records and winning the 1972 Heisman Trophy.

Rodgers signed in 1973 with the Montreal Alouettes as the highest-paid player in Canadian Football League history. He won Rookie of the Year honors in 1973 and in four CFL seasons was named All-

Johnny Rodgers (right), the 1972 Heisman Trophy winner from Nebraska, with Oklahoma running back Greg Pruitt (left) and Nebraska guard Rich Glover (middle) at a taping for Bob Hope's television show in New York City. *(AP/Wide World Photos)*

Conference four times and All-CFL three times. He led the Alouettes to two Grey Cup finals and the CFL championship in 1974. Rodgers joined the San Diego Chargers in 1977, but a knee injury ended his NFL career in 1978.

Rodgers returned to Nebraska and in 1997 completed undergraduate degrees in advertising and broadcasting. He was elected to the College Football Hall of Fame in 2001.

Larry R. Gerlach

FURTHER READING

Axthelm, Pete. "A Prize for Johnny." *Newsweek*, December 18, 1972, 64.

Balzer, Howard M., ed. *Football Register*. St. Louis: Sporting News, 1979.

Canadian Football League Facts, Figures and Records. Toronto: CFL, 2000.

Devany, Bob. *Devany*. Lincoln, NE: Privately published, 1981.

Jenkins, Dan. "Try to Catch a Bolt of Lightning." *Sports Illustrated*, November 13, 1972, 70, 75–76.

Newhouse, Dave. *Heisman: After the Glory*. St. Louis: Sporting News, 1985.

Reid, Ron. "All That's Been Fractured Is His French." *Sports Illustrated*, October 22, 1973, 90–92.

University of Nebraska Football Media Guides, 1970–1973. Lincoln: University of Nebraska.

USA Today, August 10, 2001.

★ ★ ★

Wilbur ROGAN

Born July 28, 1889, Oklahoma City, Oklahoma
Died March 4, 1964, Kansas City, Missouri
Baseball player

An Oklahoman by birth, Wilbur Rogan was reared in Kansas City and began his baseball career as a catcher with Fred Palace's Colts in 1908. He had a trim, military bearing that made him appear bigger than his actual size. Jocko Conlan declared that he pitched faster than Satchel Paige. After leaving the Fred Palace's Colts, he played with the Kansas City Giants and was credited with fifty-four consecutive wins before joining the army in 1917. He also was chosen to play on the All Nations Team.

In 1926, Rogan became manager of the Kansas City Monarchs, retaining that role until his retirement in 1938. He was variously described as easygoing, jolly, quiet, and gentlemanly but somewhat arrogant. In exhibitions against major leaguers, he was credited with a .329 batting average. After closing out his managerial career, Rogan became an umpire. Rogan also had the distinction of playing in the first black World Series in 1924, when the Kansas City Monarchs defeated the Hilldales of Philadelphia five games to four. The 1924 season was Rogan's best season. He played in fifty games as a pitcher, outfielder, and second baseman, hit .411, and led all pitchers in victories with a 15-5 record, as the Monarchs won their first pennant. While still active as a player, Rogan invested in a pool hall in Kansas City; the *Kansas City Call* reported that the "establishment seemed to do well." After leaving baseball, he worked for the post office, living quietly with his wife on a farm outside Kansas City, where he died in 1964.

Clyde Partin

FURTHER READING
Holway, John B. *Blackball Stars: Negro League Pioneers*. Westport, CT: Meckler Books, 1988.

Ribowsky, Mark. *A Complete History of the Negro Leagues, 1884 to 1955*. New York: Birch Lane Press, 1995.
Riley, James A. *The Biographical Encyclopedia of the Negro Baseball Leagues*. New York: Carroll and Graf, 1994.
Shatzkin, Mike, and Jim Charlton. *The Ball Players*. New York: Arbor House, 1990.

★ ★ ★

George ROGERS

Born December 8, 1958, Duluth, Georgia
Football player

Rogers rose from poverty to graduate from college and win the Heisman Trophy. He became one of the National Football League's premier running backs during an abbreviated career.

After Rogers's father left his mother, Grady Ann, young George and his siblings lived in a succession of low-income housing projects, including in Atlanta, where street life competed with sports. During his sophomore year, he returned to Duluth to live with his aunt, a domestic worker. There he met influential high school coach Cecil Morris, under whose mentoring the young running back gained over 4,000 yards in three years.

Highly recruited, Rogers chose the University of South Carolina. There he gained 5,204 yards, a school record, and played in four bowl games. In his senior year he lead the NCAA in rushing, made first-team All-American, and won the 1980 Heisman Trophy.

Rogers was the first player chosen in the NFL draft by the New Orleans Saints. In his first season, the durable 220-pound running back was the league's leading ground gainer and was voted Rookie of the Year. His admitted cocaine use in 1982, however, placed him before a New Orleans grand jury. After a "falling out" with Coach Bum Phillips, Rogers was used sparingly by the Saints until they traded him to Washington. He led the Redskins in rushing in 1985 and 1986 and played in the 1988 Super Bowl. Haunted by continuing rumors of drug use, plagued with injuries and arthritis, Rogers was waived by the Redskins in 1988. He returned to South Carolina to complete his degree and to work for the university. He was arrested in Columbia in 1990 for cocaine trafficking and sentenced to community service.

Rogers was inducted into the University of South Carolina Hall of Fame and College Hall of Fame in 1997. He endowed a scholarship fund at his alma mater. In retirement, Rogers plays in charity golf tournaments and gives motivational talks with students. He established a foundation that raises money to benefit local hospitals and to provide scholarships. He lives in Columbia with his wife, Lynn, two sons, and a daughter.

Steven J. Overman

FURTHER READING
Brennan, Christine. "Rogers' New Road." *Washington Post*, May 5, 1985, D1.
Gillespie, Bob. "Heisman Winner's Best Awards Are His Kids." *State*, December 9, 1997, 1A.
The Heisman Memorial Trophy (www.heisman memorialtrophy.com/years/1980).
Hunt, Mike. "A Dynamic Success Story." *Sporting News*, September 20, 1980, 55.
Noie, Tom. "George Rogers Knows Heisman Highs, Lows." *South Bend Tribune*, August 14, 1998.

★ ★ ★

Mike ROZIER

Born March 1, 1961, Camden, New Jersey
Football player

A high school football All-American, Mike Rozier, the son of Garrison and Beatrice Rozier, attended Coffeyville (Kansas) Community College before enrolling in the University of Nebraska in 1981. A powerful blocker and runner, the five-foot eleven-inch, 210-pound I-back, who was also a sprinter on the NU indoor track team, posted numerous rushing records. Part of Nebraska's fabled 1983 "Scoring Explosion" backfield with Turner Gill and Irving Fryar, Rozier rushed for more than 100 yards in eleven games, led the nation in rushing with 2,148 yards, and set a NCAA records by scoring twenty-nine rushing touchdowns and averaging 7.81 yards per carry. As of 2001 he still holds the NCAA records for average season and career carry (7.16 yards) and all seven Nebraska career rushing records.

The three-time All Big Eight selection earned All-American honors twice (1982–1983) and won the Heisman Trophy in 1983. The Heisman award was later tarnished when it was revealed that he had signed a pro contract prior to the 1984 Orange Bowl game.

The first selection in the 1984 National Football League (NFL) draft, Rozier played with the Pittsburgh Maulers in 1984 and, when the team folded, joined the Jacksonville Bulls in 1985; there he was the league's second-leading rusher with 1,361 yards. After the USFL season, Rozier signed with the Houston Oilers of the NFL and led the team in rushing for four years (1985–1988). He was third in the American Conference and fourth in the NFL in rushing in 1987 and played in the Pro Bowl in 1987–1988. Released by Houston during the 1990 season, Rozier signed with Atlanta and remained with the Falcons until retiring after the 1991 season.

Larry R. Gerlach

FURTHER READING
Balzer, Howard M., ed. *Football Register*. St. Louis: Sporting News, 1991.

———. *Official USFL Guide and Register*. St. Louis: Sporting News, 1985.

Brady, John T. *The Heisman: A Symbol of Excellence*. New York: Atheneum, 1984.

Kirshenbaum, Jerry. "The Year the Heisman Trophy Went to a Pro." *Sports Illustrated*, October 22, 1984, 21–22.

Newhouse, Dave. *Heisman: After the Glory*. St. Louis: Sporting News, 1985.

Porter, David L., ed. *Biographical Dictionary of American Sports: Football*. Westport, CT: Greenwood Press, 1987.

University of Nebraska Football Media Guide. Lincoln: University of Nebraska, 1981–1983, 2001.

★ ★ ★

Wilma RUDOLPH

Born June 23, 1940, Bethlehem, Tennessee
Died November 12, 1994, Nashville, Tennessee
Sprinter

Wilma Rudolph running in a heat for the 200-meters at the 1960 Rome Olympics. *(AP/Wide World Photos)*

At birth, there was little indication of Wilma Rudolph's great athletic future. The daughter of Ed Rudolph, a porter and handyman, and Blanche Rudolph, a homemaker, she weighed just four and half pounds and was diagnosed with polio. In her first two years she suffered from scarlet fever and two bouts of pneumonia, and as a child she could not use her left leg. Rudolph wore a brace on the limb; however, therapy combined with care from her family allowed her to shed the brace when she was twelve.

Thereafter Rudolph quickly excelled in athletics, particularly basketball. She did not begin to run track until high school, but her speed made her an instant standout. At age sixteen, she qualified for the 1956 Olympic team and won a bronze medal in Melbourne as part of a relay team. Rudolph became pregnant in her senior year of high school; she left the child in the care of her grandmother when she entered Tennessee State University in 1958. At the Olympic trials in 1960, she set a world record in the 200 meters that stood for eight years. At the games in Rome, Rudolph won the 100 meters, 200 meters, and the 4 x 100 relay and became the first American woman to win three gold medals.

After her stunning performance in Rome, Rudolph won the 1961 Sullivan award as the nation's top amateur athlete. After graduation from Tennessee State in 1963, she married her high school sweetheart, the father of her child, and became a high school track coach. For the rest of her life, Rudolph worked in a variety of community-building positions and ran her own foundation. For many, Rudolph, raised in segregated Tennessee, represented the rise of African Americans during the civil rights era. Her dominance at the Rome Olympics coupled with her grace and style made her an icon. She published an autobiography in 1977, and her story was made into a Hollywood movie. She died of brain cancer in Nashville on November 12, 1994.

Richard D. Loosbrock

See also: Autobiographies; Films; Historically Black Colleges and Universities; Olympic Games; Ed Temple; Track and Field; Women.

FURTHER READING
Ashe, Arthur R., Jr. *A Hard Road to Glory: A History of the African-American Athlete Since 1946.* New York: Warner Books, 1988.
Glass Ceiling Website (www.theglassceiling.com/biographies/bio29.htm).
Krull, Kathleen. *Wilma Unlimited: How Wilma Rudolph Became the World's Fastest Woman.* San Diego: Harcourt Brace, 1996.
"Olympian Quintessence: Wilma Rudolph." *Life*, September 10, 1960, 115.
"Others Worthy of Honor, Sports 1960: Wilma Rudolph." *Sports Illustrated*, January 9, 1961, 34.
Rudolph, Wilma. *Wilma: The Story of Wilma Rudolph.* New York: New American Library, 1977.

★ ★ ★

Bill RUSSELL

Born February 12, 1934, Monroe, Louisiana
Basketball player, coach

Bill Russell donning his Boston Celtics uniform for the first time. *(AP/Wide World Photos)*

Bill Russell was the second son of Charles and Katie Russell, who moved to Oakland, California, when he was five years old. After graduating from Oakland's McClymonds High School, Russell led the University of San Francisco (USF) to two consecutive number-one rankings, two NCAA championships, and a fifty-five-game consecutive winning streak during the 1954–1955 and 1955–1956 seasons.

Joining the Celtics in 1956 after playing for the U.S. Olympic basketball team, which won a gold medal, Russell was the ingredient the Celtics needed to become one of the most dominant teams in the history of professional sports. The team's offensive talents were formidable, with Bob Cousy, Bill Sharman, and Ed McCauley; Russell's awesome timing in blocking shots and rebounding allowed the team to exploit its offensive talents fully. Winning the NBA championship during Russell's first year, the Celtics won the Eastern Division nine times, through the 1965–1966 season, and the NBA championship eight consecutive years. After legendary coach Red Auerbach was named the franchise's general manager in 1966 he immediately named Russell as the team's coach—the first African American to serve in that capacity in the NBA. During his three-year tenure as head coach, the team garnered two NBA championships.

Always sensitive to the racism he experienced as a youngster, collegian, and professional, Russell refused to accept induction into the Naismith Memorial Basketball Hall of Fame in 1974. Russell's only explanation was, "I have private and personal reasons." In 1980 the Professional

Basketball Writers Association (PBWA) named him the Greatest Player in the History of the NBA. Russell has also parlayed his intellectual talents into co-authoring three books: "Go Up for Glory" (1966), "Second Wind: The Memoirs of an Opinionated Man" (1979), and "Russell Rules: 11 Lessons on Leadership from the Twentieth Century's Greatest Winner" (2001). Russell has also served as a radio talk-show host, worked as an NBA analyst, has been a speaker, highly sought-after by corporations, and has coached the NBA's Seattle and Sacramento teams.

Albert J. Figone

See also: Autobiographies; Basketball; Civil Rights; K.C. Jones; Olympic Games.

FURTHER READING
Auerbach, Red. *Winning the Hard Way.* Boston: Little, Brown, 1966.
Cousy, Bob, and Bob Ryan. *Cousy on the Celtic Mystique.* New York: McGraw-Hill, 1988.
Hollander, Zander, ed. *Modern Encyclopedia of Basketball.* Rev. ed. Garden City, NY: Dolphin Books, 1981.
Kenyon, Michael J. "Who Is This Man They Call Bill Russell?" *Boston Herald American*, March 6, 1977.
Russell, Bill, and Taylor Branch. *Second Wind: The Memoirs of an Opinionated Man.* New York: Random House, 1979.
Russell, Bill, as told to William McSweeney. *Go Up for Glory.* New York: Conrad-McCann, 1966.

★   ★   ★

Cazzie RUSSELL

Born June 7, 1944, Chicago, Illinois
Basketball player

Russell was the first great African-American basketball player to come from the inner city of Chicago and to attend the University of Michigan. After graduation he was the number-one draft pick in the NBA in 1966.

University of Michigan's Cazzie Russell after being named to the 1966 College Basketball All-American Team. This was the second consecutive year Russell had been named to the team. *(AP/Wide World Photos)*

Russell led his Carver High School team to the Illinois State Championship finals in 1962 and was the top player in the state. By agreeing to attend the University of Michigan, Russell became a model for African-American basketball players in cities like Chicago to consider attending the campus in Ann Arbor. Russell was an unstoppable scorer at Michigan; in his three years there he averaged more than twenty-seven points per game, capped by an average of 30.8 his senior season. This led to his being named College Player of the Year in 1966 by the AP, UPI, and the Basketball Writers Association. He was a first-team

All-American in 1965 and 1966 and second team in 1964. In the NCAA tournament he averaged nearly twenty-five points per game, in nine games over three years.

The New York Knicks drafted Russell first in 1966, but he had difficulty adjusting to being a guard in the NBA, despite being named to the All Rookie team in 1967. He was converted to a small (six-foot, five-inch) forward, and his play improved dramatically. Russell later played with Golden State, Los Angeles, and Chicago before retiring after eleven seasons. He averaged just over fifteen points a game as a professional. He later became an assistant coach with Atlanta and a head coach in the Continental Basketball Association. In 1997 he became the head coach at Savannah College of Art and Design and was still in that position in 2001–2002.

Murry R. Nelson

FURTHER READING
Behee, John. *Hail to the Victors! Black Athletes at the University of Michigan*. Ann Arbor, MI: Swink-Tuttle Press, 1974.
Russell, Cazzie. *Me, Cazzie Russell*. Westwood, NJ: F.H. Revell, 1967.

Ralph SAMPSON

Born July 7, 1960, Harrisonburg, Virginia
Basketball player

The son of Ralph, Sr., a foreman at a window manufacturing plant and Sarah Sampson, was College Basketball Player of the Year for three straight years, 1981–1983.

Sampson was born and raised in Harrisonburg, Virginia, and led his team to the state high school basketball championship twice before enrolling at the University of Virginia in 1979. In his four years at Virginia his team went 112–23, and he was voted first-team All-American and College Player of the Year in 1981, 1982, and 1983. His 1981 team won the National Invitational Tournament, but Virginia failed to win an NCAA title.

Sampson was the first pick in the NBA draft by the Houston Rockets in 1983 and was named Rookie of the Year in 1984. The following year he was voted Most Valuable Player in the NBA All-Star game. He and teammate Hakeem Olajuwon were the first "twin towers" in the NBA, but despite winning the Western Conference finals in 1986, the Rockets were beaten in the NBA finals by the Boston Celtics. Sampson later was traded to Golden State and Sacramento. His agility redefined the center position, as he roamed outside to take jump shots and even dribbled the ball upcourt. His knees, after many surgeries, forced him to retire after the 1990–1991 season. After a season as an assistant coach for James Madison he resigned and later started his own company, which includes licensing and marketing, and a nonprofit foundation. He and his wife, Aleize, have three children.

Murry R. Nelson

FURTHER READING
Henderson, Ashyia N., ed. *Who's Who Among African Americans*. Detroit: Gale Group, 2000.
Hickok, Ralph. *A Who's Who of Sport Champions: Their Stories and Records*. New York: Houghton Mifflin, 1995.
Porter, David L., ed. *Biographical Dictionary of American Sports: Basketball and other Indoor Sports*. New York: Greenwood Press, 1989.
Rosenthal, Bert. *Ralph Sampson, the Center for the 1980s*. Chicago: Children's, 1984.

★ ★ ★

Barry SANDERS

Born July 16, 1968, Wichita, Kansas
Football player

Sanders, the son of William Sanders, a carpenter and roofer, and Shirley Sanders, was one of football's all-time great running backs. He first starred at North High School in Wichita, Kansas, and then took his talents to Oklahoma State University, where he broke numerous National Collegiate Athletic Association (NCAA) records and captured the Heisman Trophy as college football's greatest player. He left Oklahoma State after his junior year and was drafted by the Detroit Lions in the first round of the National Football League (NFL) draft.

Sanders experienced enormous success with the Lions over a ten-year career. During his rookie year he broke a team record of Billy Sims by rushing for 1,470 yards. He remained remarkably consistent over the next nine years, capturing multiple rushing titles, being selected to several Pro Bowls, and garnering numerous All-NFL first-team honors. When he retired after the 1998 season, his career totals included 15,269 rushing yards, 2,921 yards receiving, and 109 touchdowns.

David K. Wiggins

FURTHER READING

Carroll, Bob, et al. *Total Football: The Official Encyclopedia of the National Football League.* New York: HarperCollins, 1999.

Hersom, Bob. "Mr. Touchdown and Mr. Nice Guy." *Sporting News*, October 24, 1988, 34.

Porter, David L., ed. *African American Sports Greats: A Biographical Dictionary.* Westport, CT: Greenwood Press, 1995.

Telander, Rick. "Big Hand for a Quiet Man." *Sports Illustrated*, December 12, 1988, 46–48.

★ ★ ★

Deion SANDERS

Born August 9, 1967, Fort Myers, Florida
Football player, baseball player

Deion Sanders enjoyed a brilliant career with several NFL teams and also played professional baseball; he was the only athlete to appear in both the Super Bowl and the World Series. His highly flamboyant style on and off the field led to a mutually exploitive relationship with the media.

He is the son of Connie, a maid, and Mims ("Daddy Buck"), a recreation director who left when Sanders was six. Encouraged by his mother and stepfather to play youth sports, Sanders earned All-State honors in three sports at North Fort Myers High School, where he played both quarterback and cornerback on the football squad.

At Florida State University, the six-foot one-inch, 195-pound two-time All-American set school records for career interceptions and punt return yards; he was dubbed "Neon Deion" by the college's public relations staff. Sanders also starred on the Seminoles' baseball and track teams, and he played professional baseball during his junior year. As a senior, he received the Jim Thorpe Award as the outstanding defensive back in college football.

Chosen by Atlanta in the first round of the 1989 NFL draft, Sanders became the first two-way starter in the NFL since the early 1960s. He played pro baseball and football simultaneously in Atlanta and for the San Francisco Giants before joining the Dallas Cowboys. Sanders was released by the Cowboys and signed by the Washington Redskins. At age thirty-three he returned to baseball, playing briefly with the Cincinnati Reds and in the minor leagues before retiring from professional sports in July 2001. Sanders had his best baseball season with the Giants in 1995, batting over .300. He was a seven-time Pro Bowl selection, was voted NFL Defensive Player of the Year in 1994, and holds the NFL record for career touchdowns scored on returns.

Sanders pursued a brief career in rap music. In 1997, he underwent a religious conversion and changed his persona. He now speaks to students about setting life goals and recently made a million-dollar donation to a Dallas youth center. Sanders enjoys fishing. He has two children by a first wife and a son with his current wife, Pilar.

Steven J. Overman

FURTHER READING

Flatter, Ron. "Where Sanders Goes, Teams Win." *ESPN.com* (msn.espn.go.com/main.html), 2001.

NFL Players.com (www.nflplayers.com).

Pompei, Dan. "Don't Assume Sanders, Smith Have Nothing Left." *Sporting News* (www.sportingnews.com), August 21, 2000.

Sanders, Deion, with Kevin Cook. "Interview." *Playboy*, August 1994 (www.playboy.com).

Sanders, Deion, and Jim Nelson Black. *Power, Money and Sex: How Success Almost Ruined My Life.* Nashville: Word, 1998.

★ ★ ★

Gale SAYERS

Born May 30, 1943, Wichita, Kansas
Football player

A star college football player who established himself as one of professional football's outstanding halfbacks, Gale Sayers later became a successful athletic and business executive. A brilliant football and track athlete at Omaha (Nebraska) Central High School, Sayers attended the University of Kansas and in 1962 rushed for 1,125 yards—including a 283-yard game against Oklahoma State. He was named a consensus first-team All-American halfback for the 1963 and 1964 seasons, finishing his collegiate career with a total of 2,675 rushing yards.

Sayers was selected in the first round of the 1965 draft by the Chicago Bears and the Kansas City Chiefs of the AFL. Signing with the Bears, Sayers tallied twenty-two touchdowns in 1965, including an NFL-record six in one game against San Francisco, and was named Rookie of the Year. Sayers had a brilliant pro career that included twice winning the league rushing title (1966 and 1969) along with being named to the All-Pro team on five occasions (1965–1969). Serious knee injuries in 1968 and 1970 prematurely ended his football career in 1971 after seven NFL seasons.

Sayers became assistant athletic director at Kansas in 1972, moving to Southern Illinois University as athletic director from 1976 through 1981. In 1982 he entered private business in the Chicago area and in 1984 formed the successful Crest Computer Company, later renamed Sayers Computer Source.

Sayers was named to both the College and Pro Football Halls of Fame in 1977. Despite his injury-shortened career, he is considered one of the greatest open-field runners in football history, as evidenced by his selection for the NFL's fiftieth anniversary All-Time team.

Raymond Schmidt

Gale Sayers, the Chicago Bears' Hall of Fame running back, whose warm friendship with white teammate Brian Piccolo would be immortalized in the book and movie of the same name, *Brian's Song*. (AP/Wide World Photos)

See also: Films.

FURTHER READING
Berger, Phil. *Great Moments in Pro Football*. New York: Julian Messner, 1969.
Sayers, Gale, and Al Silverman. *I Am Third*. New York: Viking Press, 1970.
Silverman, Al. "Professional Team Rookie: Gale Sayers." *Sport*, December 1971, 58–59.
Whittingham, Richard. *Bears, in Their Own Words*. Chicago: Contemporary Books, 1991.

★ ★ ★

Charlie SCOTT

Born December 15, 1948, New York, New York
Basketball player

In the late 1960s, Charlie Scott became the first African-American basketball star in the basketball-obsessed Atlantic Coast Conference. He filled his pioneering role with style, logging accomplishments both on and off the court and winning the loyalty of a wide range of fans.

The New York native first came south to attend Laurinburg Institute in Laurinburg, North Carolina, where he was class valedictorian. He entered the University of North Carolina in the fall of 1966 and became one of the nation's top players, helping lead the Tar Heels to the NCAA championship game in 1968 and the Final Four in 1969. He collected numerous ACC honors, and in 1970, his senior year, he was named a first-team All-American selection, an Academic All-American, and co-ACC Athlete of the Year.

Scott faced many obstacles in his North Carolina career, ranging from the loneliness of being one of only a few black students on campus to the taunts and threats that sometimes greeted him at games away from home. Still, he later explained, he drew strength from the support of coaches and teammates, as well as from the significance his accomplishments held for African Americans around the state and nation.

Like many black college athletes, Scott avoided the radical racial politics of the late 1960s. Although some black athletes boycotted the 1968 Olympics, Scott chose to play, helping the United States to win the basketball gold medal. He rarely displayed public anger over racial slights, and he spoke of coaches and teammates with affection. He became a much-beloved figure in North Carolina, and his story figures prominently in accounts of Tar Heel basketball history, as well as of Carolina coach Dean Smith.

In 1970, Scott signed with the Virginia Squires of the American Basketball Association and shared Rookie of the Year honors before moving to the NBA. He was a three-time NBA All-Star and started for the Boston Celtics team that captured the NBA title in 1976. He retired from basketball in 1980 to pursue a successful career in sports marketing.

Pamela Grundy

FURTHER READING

Briggs, Mark D. "A Tale of Two Pioneers: The Integration of College Athletics in the South During the 1960s in the Age of the Civil Rights Movement." Master's thesis, University of North Carolina, Chapel Hill, 2000.

Chansky, Art. *The Dean's List: A Celebration of Tar Heel Basketball and Dean Smith*. New York: Warner Books, 1996.

Grundy, Pamela. *Learning to Win: Sports, Education and Social Change in Twentieth-Century North Carolina*. Chapel Hill: University of North Carolina Press, 2001.

Martin, Charles. "The Rise and Fall of Jim Crow in Southern College Sports: The Case of the Atlantic Coast Conference." *North Carolina Historical Review* (July 1999): 253–84.

Smith, Dean, with John Kilgo and Sally Jenkins. *A Coach's Life*. New York: Random House, 1999.

★ ★ ★

Wendell SCOTT

Born August 29, 1921, Danville, Virginia
Died December 23, 1990, Danville, Virginia
Auto racer

Scott was the only black driver to win a top level NASCAR (National Association for Stock Car Auto Racing) event. The son of William I. Scott and Martha Motley Scott, he quit school in the eleventh grade to help his mother support the family. After serving in a U.S. Army airborne division during World War II, he returned to his native

Danville and opened a garage. He also began transporting moonshine. When a local race promoter seeking to increase attendance at his track asked the police which black motorists had speeding records, Scott was recommended as someone who could drive fast cars. He first raced in 1949, at the Danville Fairgrounds Speedway and for the next few years competed on the Dixie Circuit. In 1952 he began driving in the NASCAR Modified and Sportsman Divisions, where he won 128 times, including the 1959 Virginia State Sportsman Championship. He moved to NASCAR's top level in 1961, competing on the Grand National Circuit (now Winston Cup).

Scott's only Grand National victory came at Jacksonville (FL) Speedway Park on December 1, 1963. Fearing retribution by the fans if the black driver was kissed by a white beauty queen, officials declared Buck Baker the winner of the "Jake 200" and presented him with the trophy and winner's check. Scott vehemently protested, and an examination of the scoring showed that his number thirty-four Chevrolet was two laps ahead. He eventually received the $1,000 winner's purse but never the right trophy, getting instead a crude wooden one. Injuries received in a wreck at Talladega in 1973 ended Scott's career, although he occasionally entered races after his official retirement. He competed in 495 Grand National races between 1961 and 1973, finishing in the top ten 147 times and winning just over $180,000. His best year was 1969, when he won $27,542. Scott died in 1990 at age sixty-nine from spinal cancer. At the funeral, driver Ned Jarrett noted that Scott had opened not only doors in racing but also hearts and minds.

Scott had battled racism throughout his career. In the early years some tracks would not let him race, some drivers intentionally bumped his car off the track, and the primarily white fans jeered. He was often penalized in pre-race inspections for small things, such as chipped paint. Scott never had the corporate backing that most of his competitors enjoyed and had to make do with second-hand, inferior equipment. He did his own repair work, and his mechanical and driving skills made him much more competitive than his equipment would seem to have warranted.

Scott was the recipient of many awards and honors, including being the first African American elected to the International Motorsports Hall of Fame in Talladega, Alabama (1999). He received the first Curtis Turner Achievement Award for promoting NASCAR racing and was inducted into the National Black Athletic Hall of Fame. In 1997 the street he had lived on in Danville was renamed Wendell Scott Drive. Scott's career was brought to the screen in the 1977 movie *Greased Lightning*, starring Richard Pryor.

Suzanne Wise

FURTHER READING

Contemporary Black Biography: Profiles from the International Black Community. Vol. 19. Detroit: Gale, 1999.

Myers, Bob. "Turn Back in Anger." *Stock Car Racing* (July 1973): 19–23, 71, 75–76.

Smith, Jessie Carney, ed. *Notable Black American Men*. Detroit: Gale, 1999.

Smith, Mike. "Wendell Oliver Scott." *American Racing Classics 2000*. Charlotte, NC: Street and Smith's Sports Group, 2000.

Wilkinson, Sylvia. "Wendell Scott: Rags to Rags." In *Dirt Tracks to Glory: The Early Days of Stock Car Racing as Told by the Participants*, edited by Sylvia Wilkinson. Chapel Hill, NC: Algonquin Books, 1983.

★ ★ ★

SHADY REST GOLF AND COUNTRY CLUB

The Shady Rest Golf and Country Club is considered the first African-American golf and country club in the United States. Established in 1921 in Scotch Plains, New Jersey, Shady Rest was an extremely important institution in the African-American community and larger New York area. It combined, like so many country clubs of the era, a myriad of social activities along with golf, horseback riding, tennis courts, croquet, skeet shooting, restaurant, and clubhouse facilities. Its membership included prominent middle-class African American men and women who found comfort in the company of one another while marking themselves off as a special and privileged group. Frequent visitors to Shady Rest included the likes of Ella Fitzgerald, W.E.B. Du Bois, and Althea Gibson. For a time, the golf professional at the club was John Shippin, usually considered the first golf professional born in the United States.

The most visible and publicized events held at the club were local and national golf tournaments. In 1925 the first championship of the United Golfers Association was held at Shady Rest. This tournament was followed by many others until the club ceased operation in 1963. In that year the club was sold and became the Scotch Hills Country Club, open to the public.

David K. Wiggins

See also: Golf.

FURTHER READING

Dawkins, Marvin P., and Graham C. Kinloch. *African American Golfers During the Jim Crow Era*. Westport, CT: Greenwood Press, 2000.

Kennedy, John H. *A Course of Their Own: A History of African American Golfers*. Kansas City, MO: Andrews McMeel, 2000.

Sinnette, Calvin H. *Forbidden Fairways: African Americans and the Game of Golf*. Chelsea, MI: Sleeping Bear, 1998.

Art SHELL

Born November 26, 1946, Charleston, South Carolina
Football player, coach

A graduate of Maryland State Eastern Shore College in 1968, Shell was drafted that year by the Oakland Raiders of the American Football League and would team up on the left side of the offensive line with guard Gene Upshaw to make one of the strongest offensive line pairings in NFL history. He played in 207 league games over fifteen years (1968–1982). A knee injury during the preseason resulted in his missing the beginning of league play in 1979. He was back, however, in early October. Shell, a six-foot five-inch, 285-pound offensive tackle, made All-AFC six times, was selected to eight NFL Pro Bowl Teams, and was All-Pro in 1973, 1974, and 1977. He played a near-perfect game in the 1976 Super Bowl victory of the Raiders over the San Francisco 49ers.

Shell later served as an assistant coach with the Raiders organization under coaches Tom Flores and Mike Shanahan. In 1989 owner Al Davis appointed Shell as

Art Shell in his first game as head coach of the Oakland Raiders against the New York Jets in 1989 at Giants Stadium in Rutherford, New Jersey. *(AP/Wide World Photos)*

head coach of the Oakland Raiders, making him the NFL's first African-American head coach. Shell guided the Raiders to the AFC Championship game in 1990; the United Press International named him AFC Coach of the year. During his head-coaching stint, from 1989 to 1994, he had a .587 winning percentage. Nevertheless, owner Davis fired Shell in 1994, a decision he would later say was one of the "greatest mistakes I ever made." Shell was inducted into the Pro Football Hall of Fame in 1989.

Donald Spivey and Robert Davis

FURTHER READING
Korch, Rick. *The Truly Great: The 200 Best Pro Football Players of All Time.* Dallas: Taylor, 1993.
Simmons, Ira. *Black Knight: Al Davis and His Raiders.* Ricklin, CA: Prima, 1990.
Sloan, Dave. *Best Sports Stories.* St. Louis: Sporting News, 1990.

★ ★ ★

John SHIPPEN, JR.

Born December 5, 1879, Washington, DC
Died July 15, 1968, Newark, New Jersey
Golfer

John Shippen was the son of well educated, middle-class parents; his father (John Matthew, Sr.) was an ordained minister in the Presbyterian Church, and his mother (Eliza Spotswood) was a housewife. Shippen left high school early to enter professional golf. He competed irregularly and held positions ranging from caddie master to swing instructor.

Shippen's introduction to golf occurred after his father was assigned to the Presbyterian mission on the Shinnecock Indian reservation at Southhampton, Long Island. In 1894 local elites financed one of America's first golf courses, Shinnecock Hills. The teenaged Shippen took a job as a caddie, became acquainted with the club's professional, Willie Dunn, and even received some informal swing lessons. Two years later Shinnecock Hills hosted its first U.S. Open, and by then Shippen was skilled enough to enter the tournament. Theodore F. Havemeyer, president of the U.S. Golf Association, accepted and defended Shippen's entry in spite of a threatened walkout by white professionals. After tying for the first-round lead, Shippen struggled to a fifth-place finish. He entered four more U.S. Opens (1899, 1900, 1902, and 1913), never finishing better than fifth.

Aside from being the first African American to compete in the U.S. Open and thereby the first to collect prize money in golf, Shippen was also one of America's earliest native-born club professionals and a pioneer for African Americans in the elite, white world of early twentieth-century golf.

Stephen R. Lowe

See also: Golf.

FURTHER READING
Kennedy, John H. *A Course of Their Own: A History of African American Golfers.* Kansas City, MO: Andrews McMeel, 2000.
McDaniel, Pete. *Uneven Lies: The Heroic Story of African Americans in Golf.* Greenwich, CT: American Golfer, 2000.
Sinnette, Calvin. *Forbidden Fairways: African Americans and the Game of Golf.* Chelsea, MI: Sleeping Bear, 1998.

★ ★ ★

Wilmeth SIDAT-SINGH

Born 1918, Washington, DC
Died May 9, 1943, Selfridge Field, Michigan
Football and basketball player

Son of Pauline and Elias Webb, a pharmacist from Washington, DC, Sidat-Singh was raised by his mother and stepfather, Dr. Samuel Sidat-Singh, in New York City, where he starred in basketball at DeWitt Clinton High School. He led Clinton High to the public school athletic league title in 1934 and the following year garnered All-City honors for his exploits on the hardwood. He earned a basketball scholarship to Syracuse University and starred for the Orangemen for three years. Sidat-Singh also starred in football at Syracuse, playing halfback alongside Marty Glickman, the internationally known sprinter (and a member of the 1936 U.S. Olympic team). Sidat-Singh was similar to other African-American athletes of the interwar period in that he suffered from various forms of racial discrimination. The most publicized form of racial discrimination confronted by Sidat-Singh took place in 1937 when the University of Maryland insisted that he be kept out of its football game against Syracuse because of his color.

Following graduation from Syracuse, Sidat-Singh wanted to play professional football, but the fledgling National Football League had an unofficial ban on black players from 1934 to 1946. He decided, instead, to turn to basketball, playing for a time with the famous Renaissance Five and later with the Washington Bruins (later Bears). When World War II broke out Sidat-Singh joined the Tuskegee Airmen, the celebrated all-black flying squadron. Unfortunately, he died, along with a C.I. Williams, in a plane crash on May 9, 1943, while flying a routine training mission over Lake Huron.

David K. Wiggins

See also: Basketball.

FURTHER READING
Chalk, Ocania. *Black College Sport.* New York: Dodd, Mead, 1976.
Coates, James R. "Gentlemen's Agreement: The 1937 Maryland/Syracuse Football Controversy." Master's thesis, *University of Maryland,* 1982.
Cyphers, Luke. "Syracuse's Lost Hero: Wilmeth Sidat-Singh." *Post-Standard,* Syracuse, New York, April 25, 2001.
Glickman, Marty, with Stan Isaacs. *The Fastest Kid on the Block: The Marty Glickman Story.* Syracuse, NY: Syracuse University Press, 1996.
Miller, Patrick B. "Slouching Toward a New Expediency: College Football and the Color Line During the Depression Decade." *American Studies* 40 (Fall 1999): 5–30.

★ ★ ★

Charlie SIFFORD

Born June 2, 1922, Charlotte, North Carolina
Golfer

Sifford, the son of Roscoe Sifford, a laborer, and Eliza Sifford, was one of golf's racial pioneers. Like many others who gained fame in the sport, Sifford began his career as a caddie, carrying "sticks" by the age of ten for members of the Carolina Country Club in Charlotte, North Carolina. He eventually began to play the game himself, honing his skills first at a public course in Philadelphia, where he had gone to live with his uncle. His skills were so prodigious that by 1946 he was entering tournaments sponsored by the United Golf Association (UGA), the African-American community's version of the Professional Golfers Association (PGA).

Sifford won his first tournament on the UGA sponsored tour at the 1951 Southern Open in Atlanta, Georgia. This victory was the first of many for Sifford, who came to dominate the competition on the black tour, including the likes of Howard Wheeler, Bill Spiller, and Ted Rhodes. He captured every National Negro Open from 1952 through 1956. He was almost as successful against whites, in non-PGA tournaments, winning, for example, the 1956

Rhode Island Open and 1959 Gardena Valley Open.

Sifford garnered national attention by capturing the PGA-sponsored Long Beach Open in 1957. His next great triumph on the PGA tour did not come until 1967, when at age forty-five he captured the Hartford Open. In 1969 Sifford won the Los Angeles Open, a triumph that garnered him more media exposure than ever before or since. Just five years after winning the Los Angeles Open, Sifford retired from the PGA Tour and became golf professional at Sleepy Hollow Country Club in Bricksville, Ohio. He remained the professional at Sleepy Hollow for thirteen years, satisfying his competitive urges by playing senior tournaments. He won the 1975 PGA Seniors Championship and made some $800,000 in prize money on the Seniors and Super Seniors tour.

David K. Wiggins

See also: Golf; United Golfers Association.

FURTHER READING

Dawkins, Marvin P., and Graham C. Kinloch. *African American Golfers During the Jim Crow Era*. Westport, CT: Greenwood Press, 2000.

Jenkins, Dan. "Old Charlie Jolts the New Tour." *Sports Illustrated*, January 20, 1969, 16–17.

Johnson, William O. "Call Back the Years." *Sports Illustrated*, March 31, 1969, 56–69.

Sifford, Charlie, with James Gallo. *Just Let Me Play: The Story of Charlie Sifford, the First Black PGA Golfer*. Latham, NY: British American, 1992.

Sinnette, Calvin H. *Forbidden Fairways: African Americans and the Game of Golf*. Chelsea, MI: Sleeping Bear, 1998.

★ ★ ★

Paul SILAS

Born July 12, 1943, Prescott, Arizona
Basketball player

Silas was a college and professional basketball star known for his inside scoring and determined rebounding. He became a successful professional coach in 1988 and, as of 2003, was the head coach of the New Orleans Hornets.

Silas, the son of Leon and Clara Silas, attended McClymonds High in Oakland, California, and in the fall of 1960 enrolled at Creighton University. Through hard work and determination he not only led the nation in rebounding one year (1963) but was named an Academic All-American in 1964. Silas, a powerful forward at six feet, seven inches and 230 pounds, averaged 20.5 points per game in his three years at Creighton. More amazing, however, were his rebounding statistics—he averaged 21.6 rebounds per game in his career.

Silas was drafted by the St. Louis Hawks in the second round in 1964 and spent sixteen years in the NBA with St. Louis (Atlanta), Phoenix, Boston, Denver and Seattle, averaging just under ten points per game and just over ten rebounds a game. The figures belie his relentless play and his leadership. He played on three NBA champion teams (Boston twice and Seattle once) and was voted either first or second-team All-Defensive five times (1971, 1972, 1973, 1975, and 1976).

After his retirement as a player in 1980 Silas became the head coach of the San Diego Clippers, remaining until 1983. He was an assistant coach of the New Jersey Nets, the New York Knicks, the Phoenix Suns, and the Charlotte Hornets before becoming the Hornets head coach midway through the 1998–1999 season, a position he retained for 2001–2002. Silas has hosted for many years in New York a corporate basketball tournament that features former NBA players and raises funds for the Boys and Girls Club of Northern Westchester, New York.

Murry R. Nelson

See also: Coaches and Managers.

FURTHER READING
Ashe, Arthur R., Jr. *A Hard Road to Glory: A History of the African-American Athlete.* New York: Ballantine Books, 1976.
Hubbard, Jan, ed. *The Official NBA Encyclopedia.* 3rd ed. New York: Doubleday, 2000.
NBA Global (global.nba.com/history/silas_bio.html).

★ ★ ★

Ozzie SIMMONS

Born June 22, 1914, Gainesville, Texas
Died September 26, 2001, Chicago, Illinois
Football player

Simmons, the son of Bennie Jones and his wife, Frances Jones Simmons, was a graduate of the University of Iowa (B.S.) and earned a graduate-level teaching certificate from Chicago Teachers College. A star halfback and defensive back at Iowa in the mid-1930s, Simmons was one of the first black All-American college football players. Dubbed the "Ebony Eel" for his ability to outwit and outrun his opponents, Simmons rushed for 1,544 yards and scored fourteen touchdowns in his three-year collegiate career (1934–1936). However, his success and his race made Simmons a target on and off the field. Opposing players sometimes teamed up to injure him intentionally.

Simmons's quick getaway, fast pickup, and stop-and-go tactics made him an All-American and All Big Ten honoree in 1934 and 1935. In 1935 and 1936 he was Iowa's top rusher, and he led the team in scoring in 1936. His other honors include induction into the Bob Douglas Black Sports Hall of Fame (1984) and the National Iowa Varsity Club Hall of Fame (1989).

Denied a professional football career because of racial segregation, Simmons played two years with the minor league Paterson, NJ, Panthers before becoming a physical education teacher in Chicago, Illinois.

Mary Jo Binker

FURTHER READING
Author telephone interviews with Eutopia Morsell Simmons, October 1, 15, 2001.
Silag, Bill, ed. *Outside-In: African-American History in Iowa, 1838–2000.* Des Moines: State Historical Society of Iowa, 2001.
Stein, Letitia. "Ozzie Simmons, 87, Early Black All-American Football Player." *Chicago Tribune,* October 4, 2001.
Trowbridge, Matt. "The Man Behind Floyd of Rosedale." *Iowa City Press-Citizen,* November 25, 1989.

★ ★ ★

Willie SIMMS

Born January 16, 1870, Augusta, Georgia
Died February 26, 1927, Asbury Park, New Jersey
Jockey

The son of former slaves, Simms ran away from home as a teenager to become a jockey. He worked in New York for C.H. Pettingill for two years, until Congressman William L. Scott's trainer discovered him in 1887–1888 riding at a small track in Clifton, New Jersey. In 1891, he rode successfully at Saratoga Springs, New York, as a freelancer. Simms rode for Philip J. Dwyer in 1892 before moving to the Rancocas Stable, staying from 1892 through 1894.

Michael F. Dwyer signed Simms in 1895 and sent him to England for four months. One of the earliest Americans to ride in England, Simms pioneered the American style of racing, crouched down low over the horse's withers. Not until two years later, when the white American jockey Tod Sloan copied Simms's style and consistently bested English riders, did they adopt his more efficient riding style. In 1893 and 1894, Simms won five of his six races at Sheepshead Bay, New York, won the Belmont Stakes, and was named the national riding champion. Simms won many other major stakes races, including the Kentucky Derby in 1896 and 1898 and the Preakness in 1898. He earned $20,000 a year in 1895 and, with wise investments in real estate, became one of the wealthiest jockeys in America, with career earnings of $300,000. After retiring as a jockey in 1902 Simms trained racehorses until 1924. Simms never married. He died of pneumonia at his mother's home.

Susan Hamburger

FURTHER READING
Hotaling, Edward. *The Great Black Jockeys: The Lives and Times of the Men Who Dominated America's First National Sport.* Rocklin, CA: Forum, 1999.
New York Times, March 1, 1927.
Porter, David L., ed. *African-American Sports Greats: A Biographical Dictionary.* Westport, CT: Greenwood Press, 1995.

★ ★ ★

O.J. SIMPSON

Born July 7, 1947, San Francisco, California
Football player

The son of Eunice Simpson, Orenthal James ("OJ") Simpson graduated from Galileo High School and the University of Southern California (USC). A professional football player who retired in 1979, he later worked as a sports commentator and actor.

Simpson was considered one of the greatest running backs in the history of professional football. At USC, Simpson had earned All-American honors and had been selected as the nation's top college football player and a Heisman Trophy winner. As the number-one draft pick in the NFL in 1969, Simpson joined the Buffalo Bills. He topped 1,000 yards rushing five consecutive years (1972–1976) and led the National Football League four times in rushing titles, with a career record of 11,236 yards rushing, 203 receptions, 990 yards in kickoff returns, and 14,368 combined, net yards. In 1973 he became the first player to rush for over 2,000 yards, and was the 1973 Pro Bowl Most Valuable Player. He retired from professional football in 1979 to pursue a career in television commercials and work as a sportscaster.

Simpson's entertainment career ended in 1994 when his estranged second wife was murdered. Simpson was charged with the murder but was acquitted after a lengthy trial.

Simpson was inducted into the NFL Hall of Fame in 1985 and the Galileo High School Hall of Fame; Galileo High's football field is named in his honor.

Doris R. Corbett

See also: Films.

FURTHER READING
Ashe, Arthur R., Jr., *A Hard Road to Glory.* New York: Warner Books, 1988.
Biography.com (www.biography.com).
Deford, Frank. "What Price Heroes?" *Sports Illustrated* (June 9, 1969): 33–34, 37, 40.
Henderson, Edwin B. *The Black Athlete: Emergence and Arrival.* Washington, DC: Publishers, 1968.
Porter, David L., ed. *African American Sports Greats: A Biographical Dictionary.* Westport, CT: Greenwood Press, 1995.

★ ★ ★

Mike SINGLETARY

Born October 9, 1958, Houston, Texas
Football player

Singletary became a hometown hero as a standout football player at Evan E. Worthington High School. Singletary's skills both in the classroom and on the football field landed him a scholarship to Baylor University.

While attending Baylor University, Singletary balanced his academic and athletic pursuits, majoring in business administration and minoring in communication, ultimately earning his degree. He was a great linebacker for Baylor, being voted Southwest Conference defensive player of the decade for the 1980s, a consensus all-Southwest Conference selection from 1978 to 1980, and the only junior selected to the All-Southwest Conference team of the 1970s. Singletary also set Baylor school records for career tackles (662), tackles in a season (232), and most tackles in a game (thirty-three). Furthermore, he was the last person to win the Davey O'Brien Award (1979 and 1980) other than a quarterback.

Following Singletary's outstanding football career at Baylor, he was selected by the Chicago Bears in the 1981 National Football League (NFL) draft. During his twelve-year career, Singletary had 172 starts and amassed 1,488 tackles, nineteen sacks, and seven interceptions. He earned NFL Defensive Rookie of the Year honors, was named to ten straight Pro Bowls, was named the 1990 NFL Man of the Year, and was selected to the NFL Team of the 1980s.

Singletary's accomplishments earned him an induction into the Baylor Athletic Hall of Fame in 1990, College Football Hall of Fame in 1995, and the NFL Football Hall of Fame in 1998. Since Singletary's retirement from football in 1993, he continues to utilize his intellectual abilities, as a motivational speaker on the Fortune 500-company lecture circuit.

Eddie Comeaux and C. Keith Harrison

FURTHER READING
Buchholz, Brad. *Seasons of Glory: Grant Teaff and the Baylor Bears*. Texas: Summit Group, 1993.
Singletary, Mike, with Armen Keteyainen. *Calling the Shots: Inside the Chicago Bears*. Chicago: Contemporary Books, 1986.
Singletary, Mike, with Jerry Jenkins. *Singletary on Singletary*. Nashville, TN: Thomas Nelson, 1991.
Telander, Rick. "Just a Bear of a Bear." *Sports Illustrated*, January 27, 1986, 38–40.

★ ★ ★

"Duke" SLATER

Born December 9, 1898, Normal, Illinois
Died August 14, 1966, Chicago, Illinois
Football player

One of six children born to the Rev. George W. Slater and his wife, Frederick W. Slater earned his nickname "Duke" on the sandlot football fields of Chicago's South Side. The family removed to Iowa, and Slater graduated from Clinton High School in 1916. He entered the University of Iowa in 1918 and, at six feet, one inch and 215 pounds, soon starred on its football team as a big, strong, and quick tackle. Often double and triple teamed, Slater earned All-Western Conference Honors and All-America mention from 1919 to 1921. In 1921, Iowa went undefeated, capturing the Western Conference (Big Ten) championship and a share of the national title.

Slater embarked on a ten-year career in professional football in 1922, playing for the Rock Island (IL), Milwaukee, and Chicago Cardinals teams. He gained All-Pro honors from 1923 to 1926.

Slater graduated from the University of Iowa Law School in 1928 and pursued a legal career in Chicago as a corporation counsel and Illinois commerce commissioner. He also found time to coach the Douglass High School football team in Oklahoma City during the 1930s.

In 1948, Slater was elected to the municipal court, one of the first African Americans to hold a judge's position in Chicago. In 1960 he became a Cook County Superior Court judge, and in 1964 a circuit court judge in the divorce division.

His wife, Etta Searcy, died in 1962. They had no children, but Slater involved himself in youth and civic affairs in Chicago with the Boy Scouts, Boys Club, and the Mayor's Commission on Human Relations. He succumbed to stomach cancer in 1966.

Gerald R. Gems

FURTHER READING
Ashe, Arthur R., Jr. *A Hard Road to Glory: Football.* New York: Amistad, 1993.
Chicago Tribune, August 16, 1966.
Maher, Tod, and Bob Gill, eds. *The Pro Football Encyclopedia.* New York: Macmillan, 1997.
Porter, David L., ed. *Biographical Dictionary of American Sports: Football.* Westport, CT: Greenwood Press, 1987.

★ ★ ★

SLAVERY

The institution of slavery was very cruel, inhumane, and oppressive. Members of the slave-quarter community, however, realized some periods of leisure and used it to participate in various popular pastimes and recreational activities. It was customary for slaves, whether living on small farms, larger plantations, or in cities, to be given some time off on Saturdays and Sundays, for marriages and other special occasions, for holidays like Christmas and Easter, and following cotton pickings, tobacco harvesting, and other major bouts of labor.

Slaves spent this time, plus any other they could steal away from their daily labors, in an assortment of ways. Some slaves visited friends and family on neighboring farms or plantations. Many members of the slave-quarter community chose to stay closer to home to recuperate from work, or to party with friends or take care of unfinished household chores. Other slaves, particularly the men, hunted and fished to supplement their monotonous diets. Still other slaves played games, participated in such informal athletic activities as running and jumping contests, and engaged in a variety of different dances. These activities were extremely important because they allowed slaves to realize a degree of individual autonomy and self-respect, and to attain a much-needed sense of community. The chance to socialize with other slaves, opportunities to dance in their own particular style, freedom to roam fields and woods in search of game, and the privilege of testing their physical strength were not only sources of great fun and enjoyment to slaves but ways for them to recognize their uniqueness and separate identity as a group.

The more talented and physically gifted slaves were sometimes obliged to compete for their owners in various recreational and sporting activities. It was common for slave owners to organize parties and conduct dance competitions between their slaves and those from other plantations. To encourage slaves to perform at their best, slaveholders would distribute prizes to the winning dancers and provide liberal amounts of food and drink to all the participants after the contest. Slaves were also used as rowers in boat races between southern planters. Although not the formal regattas engaged in by organized boat clubs of the South, these races were highly competitive and afforded slaveholders perfect opportunities to get together with their counterparts from other plantations and place bets on their slave crews. In addition, slave runners were entered in races against neighboring slaves or local pedestrian racers from southern towns. There is some evidence that slaveholders actually trained and held preliminary races among their slaves to ensure that only their best runners would be entered in these competitions.

Perhaps most important, slaves were used as both boxers and jockeys by their owners. Southern slaveholders enjoyed placing bets on their slave boxers against others from local towns or plantations. Legend has it that outstanding slave boxers, after earning their masters fortunes in bets, were given their freedom and allowed to earn money as professional pugilists. The most famous of these boxers was Tom Molineaux. Born as a slave in either Maryland or Virginia, Molineaux somehow gained his freedom and eventually traveled to England, where he fought Tom Crib twice for the heavyweight championship. Unfortunately, he lost both times.

Slaves proved to be just as valuable as jockeys as they did as boxers. Southern slaveholders, while similar to others in the racing business during this period in that they attached far more importance to their horses than their jockeys, constantly used their more diminutive and talented slaves who could secure victories on the track. Like many of the other talented slaves involved in the sporting lives of their owners, slave jockeys often held privileged positions in the plantation community. In many ways, they were slaves who were almost free. Many of them were allowed a degree of independence that permitted them to leave the plantation occasionally, were not constantly under the supervision of whites, and in some cases had opportunities to earn money. They were admired by their fellow slaves for their physical skills and because they generally had more control over their own destinies than did the majority of slaves. They sometimes were accorded the elevated status in the slave quarter that was usually reserved for conjurors, preachers, storytellers, entertainers, teachers, rebels, and confidence men.

David K. Wiggins

See also: Tom Molineaux.

FURTHER READING
Brailsford, Dennis. *Bare Knuckles: A Social History of Prize Fighting.* Cambridge, MA: Lutterworth Press, 1988.
Hotaling, Edward. *The Great Black Jockeys: The Lives and Times of the Men Who Dominated America's First National Sport.* Rocklin, CA: Forum, 1999.
King, Wilma. *Stolen Childhood: Slave Youth in Nineteenth-Century America.* Bloomington: Indiana University Press, 1995.
Wiggins, David K. "The Play of Slave Children in the Plantation Communities of the Old South, 1820–1860." *Journal of Sport History* 7 (Summer 1980): 21–39.
———. "Sport and Popular Pastimes: Shadow of the Slavequarter." *Canadian Journal of the History of Sport and Physical Education* 11 (May 1980): 61–88.

★ ★ ★

Lucy Diggs SLOWE

Born 1885, Berryville, Virginia
Died 1936, Washington, DC
Tennis player, educator

Lucy Slowe was the youngest child of Henry Slowe, a hotel proprietor, and Fannie Porter Slowe. A graduate of Howard University in 1908 with a bachelor of arts degree, she taught for seven years at Douglass High School in Baltimore. She received a master's degree in 1915 from Columbia University. During the years 1915–1919, Slowe taught at Armstrong High School and was the first dean of women at Howard University, 1922–1937.

Slowe was president of the Women's Tennis Club at Howard University. In 1917, she became the first African American Tennis Association (ATA) women's singles champion. The win constituted the first time a female African American had been a national champion in any sport.

Active in many aspects of her undergraduate life, she sang contralto with the university choir, was vice president and secretary of the Alpha Phi Literary society, was a member of the founding group of the Alpha Kappa Alpha Sorority, Incorporated, served as a counselor to the Race Relations Group of the North American Home Missions of the National Student Council, and served on committees of the national board of the YMCA.

Slowe's successes did not go unacknowledged. A nationally known educator, lecturer, and administrator, she was selected by the District of Columbia Board of Education to organize the first junior high school in the district. She was appointed principal of Shaw Junior High School and served in that capacity until June 1922. Two buildings in Washington, DC have been named in her honor: the Lucy Diggs Slowe Hall of Howard University and the Lucy Diggs Slowe Elementary school.

Doris R. Corbett

See also: Tennis.

FURTHER READING

Alpha Kappa Alpha Sorority, Incorporated. "History: Founders Slowe, Hedgeman" (www.aka1908.com/slowe.htm), April 2, 2001.
American Tennis Association. "Slowe, Lucy Diggs, 1883–1937." (www.atanational.com), April 2.
Moorland-Spingarn Manuscript collections S–Z, Howard University. Slowe, Lucy Diggs, 1883–1937 (www.Founders.howard.edu/moorland-spingarn).
Women's Sports Foundation. "Slowe, Lucy Diggs, 1883–1937" (www.womensportsfoundation.com).

★ ★ ★

Bruce SMITH

Born June 18, 1963, Norfolk, Virginia
Football player

The son of Annie Lee and G.W. Smith, Bruce Smith is regarded as one of the dominant defensive players in the history of the National Football League.

Judged too overweight for football as a youth, Smith did not start playing until the tenth grade, at Booker T. Washington High School, where he was voted high school All-American. As a defensive tackle at Virginia Tech University, Smith was twice chosen the top collegiate athlete in Virginia. He was the 1985 Outland Trophy winner and consensus first-team All-American as a senior. Smith was the top football prospect in the nation upon graduation and the first player chosen by Buffalo in the 1985 NFL draft. Also drafted by the United States Football League, Smith signed with the NFL's Bills.

During his fifteen-year career at Buffalo, the six-foot four-inch, 280-pound defensive end was known for his quickness and ability to shed blockers, and became the sack leader among active NFL players. As one of Buffalo's "Big Three"—along with Thurman Thomas and Andre Reed, Smith contributed to the Bills' outstanding success in the late 1980s and 1990s, including four Super Bowl appearances. His career was interrupted by a substance abuse problem in 1988, and he was on the injured reserve for much of 1991. Smith's outspokenness contributed to an often stormy relationship with the fans and media in Buffalo. He found himself on the Washington Redskin's roster for the 2001 season.

Smith's honors include eleven invitations to the Pro Bowl and being named

Outstanding Player of the 1987 Pro Bowl. He was voted NFL Defensive Player of the Year three times and was a recipient of the George Halas Trophy. He donated $50,000 to the Virginia Tech scholarship fund and was inducted into the university's Hall of Fame in 1995. In February of 2000, Smith became one of the owners of the Norfolk Nighthawks in the Arena Football League. He is married (Carmen) and has a son, Alston.

Steven J. Overman

FURTHER READING
Bechtel, Mark. "Hokies History." *Sports Illustrated*, January 13, 2000, 4ff.
Buffalo News, 1985–2000.
George, Thomas. "For Bruce Smith, Things Happen for a Reason." *New York Times*, February 27, 2000.
NFL.com (sports.nfl.com/players).
Pompei, Dan. "Don't Assume Sanders, Smith Have Nothing Left." *Sporting News* (www.sportingnews.com), August 21, 2000.
Sports Illustrated (sportsillustrated.cnn.com/football/nfl/players).

"Bubba" Smith, the great Michigan State and Baltimore Colts defensive end, who would pursue a successful movie career after his retirement from football. *(AP/Wide World Photos)*

★ ★ ★

"Bubba" SMITH

Born February 28, 1945, Beaumont, Texas
Football player

Charles Smith was born in Beaumont, Texas. His father, Willie Ray Smith, was a high school coach, and "Bubba," as Charles was known, was the third of his sons to become an All-State football player. Smith attended Pollard High School, which his father had made a perennial football powerhouse. During his senior year in high school his team was undefeated. Highly recruited, Smith chose to attend Michigan State University (class of 1967). In Smith's sophomore year, MSU yielded just seventy-six points in eleven games. Spartan fans were so impressed by Smith's defensive prowess that when MSU was on defense they would chant "Kill, Bubba, Kill" to encourage him to shut down the opponents. In 1966 Michigan State won its first nine games. The day before MSU was to play undefeated Notre Dame for the national championship, Smith roared past the Irish practice in a car. As a consequence, he was jailed on the eve of the big game. He was released in time to play in a 10-10 tie.

Smith earned All-American honors in 1965 and 1966. He was the MVP in both the Senior Bowl and the College All-Star Game in 1967. He was the first player picked in the 1967 NFL draft. He played professional football for the Baltimore Colts, 1967–1971. He played in the 1969 Super Bowl and was an AFC All-Star in 1970 and 1971. In 1972, however, he ran into a yard marker during exhibition play and missed the entire season. He was traded to the Oakland Raiders, where he played in the 1973–1974 AFC championship games; he played his final season with the Houston Oilers, in 1975. Smith was elected to the College Football Hall of Fame and was named to the *Detroit News* All-AFC team as a defensive end in 1970 and 1971. After retiring from the NFL, he was a Miller Lite Beer spokesman for six years, then was in the movies, in the popular *Police Academy* series and a variety of other class-B films.

Keith McClellan

FURTHER READING
Gershman, Michael. "Bubba Smith." *Coffin Corner* 19 (Spring 1996): 23.
Phelps, Shirelle, ed. *Who's Who Among Black Americans, 1994/5*. 8th ed. Detroit: Gale Research, 1994.

★ ★ ★

Emmitt SMITH

Born May 15, 1969, Pensacola, Florida
Football player

Born into a large working-class family, Emmitt Smith obtained a college degree and went on to become the leading rusher in NFL history.

He was one of six children of Mary and Emmitt Smith II. His father, a city bus driver, steered his early-maturing son into Pop Warner football. Later, at Escambia High School, Smith was a consensus All-American running back. He posted the third-highest career rushing and scoring totals in national high school history and was voted prep Player of the Year as a senior. In 1986, he represented the nation's prep football players at the White House as part of the "Just Say No" antidrug campaign. One of the top-recruited high school running backs in the country, Smith signed with the University of Florida, where in three seasons he established fifty-eight school records, including a career rushing mark. He was a college All-American and finished in the top ten in the Heisman Trophy balloting.

Selected in the first round of the 1990 NFL draft (the initial year underclassmen were drafted), Smith forewent his senior year and signed with the Dallas Cowboys (he later returned to Florida to complete his degree, earning it in 1996). In eleven seasons with Dallas, the five-foot nine-inch, 210-pound running back made an extraordinary impact on NFL records, becoming the top rusher on the NFL's all-time list. He became the Cowboys' all-time leading scorer and led them to seven Super Bowl appearances. He was voted Super Bowl MVP in 1994. Smith's career was noted for frequent contract negotiations. Although plagued with bone spurs in 1996 and knee problems during the 1998 season, he continued to play with effectiveness.

Smith founded "Emmitt Inc." to market his name and went into partnership with the marketing concern "Emmitt Zone" to sell personalized collectibles. He has demonstrated unusual generosity with his money and time, supporting several charities and conducting football camps for youngsters. Smith is married to the former Miss Virginia, Patricia Lawrence. He has a daughter by a previous relationship.

Steven J. Overman

FURTHER READING
Bradley, John Ed. "Emmitt Unplugged." *Sports Illustrated*, July 1, 1996, 62ff.
King, Peter. "Bottomed Out? . . . Are Emmitt Smith's Best Days Behind Him? *Sports Illustrated* (sportsillustrated.cnn.com), October 8, 1997.
NFL Players.com (www.nflplayers.com).
Smith, Emmitt, with Steve Delsohn. *The Emmitt Zone*. Dallas: Taylor, 1995.

Dallas Cowboys running back Emmitt Smith in a 1992 game against arch-rival Washington Redskins. *(AP/Wide World Photos)*

Sports Illustrated (sportsillustrated.cnn.com/football/nfl/players).

★ ★ ★

John SMITH

Born August 5, 1950, Los Angeles, California
Sprinter, coach

John Smith first burst into track prominence as a sprinter at Fremont High School in Los Angeles. He then attended UCLA, moving up to the 400 meters, and winning the 440-yard event at the 1970 AAU Championships. In 1971, Smith had one of the great years for any quarter-miler, winning the NCAA's, the AAU's, and the Pan-American Games gold medal.

At the 1971 AAU meet he set a world record, running 440 yards in 44.5. His career seemed without limits, but then medical problems slowed him. In the winter of 1972 he became ill with mononucleosis and hepatitis, but he recovered to repeat as NCAA champion. Smith finished second (to Wayne Collett) in the 1972 Olympic Trials to earn a trip to Munich. At Munich, he qualified for the finals, but with a strained hamstring, and he pulled up in the finals at 80 meters, failing to finish. After the

Olympics, Smith turned professional and ran for several years with the International Track Association. He eventually became head coach at his alma mater, UCLA. In 1988, Smith achieved some measure of vicarious satisfaction over his Olympic frustrations when two of his athletes, Steve Lewis and Danny Everett, won gold and bronze at the Olympics in the 400. He coached Quincy Watts (400 meters) and Kevin Young (400-meter hurdles) to gold medals in 1992 and has since become one of the top sprint coaches in the world.

Bill Mallon

FURTHER READING
Ashe, Arthur R., Jr. *A Hard Road To Glory: A History of the African-American Athlete.* New York: Ballantine, 1976.
Wallechinsky, David. *The Complete Book of the Olympics.* New York: Viking, 1984.

★ ★ ★

Ozzie SMITH

Born December 26, 1954, Mobile, Alabama
Baseball player

St. Louis Cardinals Ozzie Smith completing a double play in a 1982 game against the Philadelphia Phillies. *(AP/Wide World Photos)*

For nineteen years Ozzie Smith defined the position of shortstop for major league baseball. Nicknamed "the Wizard," Smith exhibited speed and athleticism both in the field and on the base paths. Throughout his career he stole over 500 bases and won thirteen consecutive gold gloves.

After attending Cal Poly University, Smith began his professional baseball career in 1978 as a member of the San Diego Padres. In 1982, he left the Padres and signed as a free agent with the St. Louis Cardinals. The same year, the Cardinals defeated the Milwaukee Brewers in the World Series.

For the next fourteen years, Smith served as the nucleus of a St. Louis team built around defense and speed. From 1983 through 1992, he averaged over thirty stolen bases a year, recording a career high of fifty-five in 1988. The Cardinals won the National League pennant in 1985 and 1987. Smith's game-winning home run in the ninth inning of game five of the 1985 National League Championship against the Los Angles Dodgers earned Smith the Most Valuable Player award for the series.

By his retirement in 1996, Smith had accumulated a .978 fielding percentage, one of the best ever. He had played in twelve consecutive All-Star Games. His 8,375 assists is the all-time record for shortstops.

Rob Fink

FURTHER READING

Baseball Encyclopedia: The Complete and Definitive Record of Major League Baseball. 10th ed. New York: Macmillan, 1996.

Golenbock, Peter. *The Spirit of St. Louis: A History of the St. Louis Cardinals and Browns.* New York: Harper Entertainment, 2001.

Smith, Ozzie, and Rob Rains. *Wizard.* Chicago: Contemporary Books, 1988.

★ ★ ★

Tommie SMITH

Born June 5, 1944, Acworth, Texas
Sprinter

Tommie Smith was an Olympic gold medalist and one of the greatest sprinters of all time. He is best known, however, for his protest at the 1968 Olympic Games in Mexico City. Born in Acworth, Texas, in 1944, Smith was one of eight children of a migrant farm worker. In 1966 he set four world records in the 200 meters and 220-yard sprints. The next year he captured the world record in the 400 meters and the 440-yard events. He missed the world 100-meter record by only one-tenth of a second. Smith ran track for San Jose State University, where he became associated with Harry Edwards, a sociology professor who organized the Olympic Project for Human Rights to bring attention to racial injustice in the United States.

Despite his athletic accomplishments, Smith's legacy is defined by two minutes in Mexico City. After winning the gold in the 200 meters in world-record time, Smith took the podium for the medal ceremony along with silver medalist Peter Norman from Australia and bronze medalist John Carlos, Smith's teammate. To protest treatment of blacks in the United States, Smith and Carlos refused to stand with their hands over their hearts as the American flag was raised. Instead, each wearing one black glove, they raised their clinched fists and bowed their heads during the national anthem. That scene became one of the most enduring images of the 1960s. The U.S. Olympic Committee suspended Smith and Carlos from the team and expelled them from the Olympic Village, a largely symbolic act since they were staying in hotels with their wives. For the last several years Smith has been the track and field coach at Santa Monica Junior College.

Richard D. Loosbrock

San Jose State's Tommie Smith training for the 1968 Olympic games in Mexico City. *(AP/Wide World Photos)*

See also: John Carlos; Civil Rights; Olympic Games; Track and Field.

FURTHER READING

Ashe, Arthur R., Jr. *A Hard Road to Glory: A History of the African-American Athlete Since 1946.* New York: Warner Books, 1988.

Edwards, Harry. *The Revolt of the Black Athlete.* New York: Free Press, 1969.

Larner, Jeremy, and David Wolf. "Amid Gold Medals, Raised Black Fists." *Life,* November 1, 1968, 64–65.

Smith, Tommie. "Why I Raised My Fist at Uncle Sam." *Sepia,* July 1973, 24–32.

Tommie Smith.com (www.tommiesmith.com/tommie.html).

Wiggins, David K. "'The Year of Awakening': Black Athletes, Racial Unrest, and the Civil Rights Movement of 1968." *International Journal of the History of Sport* 9 (August 1992): 188–208.

★ ★ ★

Wendell SMITH

Born June 27, 1914, Detroit, Michigan
Died November 26, 1972, Chicago, Illinois
Sportswriter

An outstanding basketball and baseball player in high school and college, Smith became one of the best-known and most influential black sportswriters in twentieth-century America. Upon graduation from West Virginia State College in 1937, Smith took a position as sportswriter and columnist for the *Pittsburgh Courier-Journal,* where he worked for ten years before assuming a similar position with the *Chicago Herald-American.* Smith used his position as sportswriter not only to recount the great exploits of African American athletes but to fight the racial injustice in sport. He became particularly well known for his campaigns to include African Americans in major league baseball and to desegregate spring training housing facilities. He had an especially close relationship with Jackie Robinson, and coauthored Robinson's first autobiography, *Jackie Robinson: My Own Story* (1948).

Smith was honored in numerous ways for his many accomplishments. He earned three William Randolph Hearst national awards for outstanding sportswriting, had a Chicago public school named in his honor, and was elected to the Chicago Journalism Hall of Fame, the West Virginia State College Hall of Fame, and the National Baseball Hall of Fame in Cooperstown, New York.

David K. Wiggins

See also: Civil Rights; Sportswriters.

FURTHER READING

Marsh, Michael. "Writer Helped Robinson Along." *Chicago Sun-Times,* March 30, 1997.

Tygiel, Jules. *Baseball's Great Experiment: Jackie Robinson and His Legacy.* New York: Oxford University Press, 1983.

Wiggins, David K. "Wendell Smith, the *Pittsburgh Courier-Journal,* and the Campaign to Include Blacks in Organized Baseball, 1933–1945." *Journal of Sport History* 10 (Summer 1983): 5–29.

★ ★ ★

Fred SNOWDEN

Born April 3, 1936, Brewton, Alabama
Died January 17, 1994, Washington, DC
Basketball coach

Fred Snowden, the son of sharecropper parents, became a high school and university basketball coach and business executive. At age six, Snowden moved with his family to Detroit, MI, where he later attended Northwestern High School. After graduating from Wayne State University, he returned to the high school to coach the basketball team to an outstanding 207–6 record and the Detroit Public League championship seven consecutive times. In 1971 he became an assistant coach for the University of Michigan. Snowden became the second African American to coach at a NCAA Division I university and the first to coach at a major university when he accepted the head coaching position at the University of Arizona in 1972.

Snowden was an outstanding coach for the Wildcats. Under his leadership, the team won the 1976 Western Athletic Conference title, its first in twenty-five years. The championship was the first won by an African-American head coach. Snowden's success at Arizona is credited with opening coaching opportunities for other African Americans. In 1982, he resigned the position amid allegations of financial improprieties. He denied the allegations, and an NCAA investigation exonerated him of any wrongdoing.

After coaching, Snowden started a consulting firm, which he ran for three years. He then became an executive with Baskin-Robbins as the vice president for urban affairs. In 1990 he became the vice president of urban affairs with Food 4 Less Supermarkets in Los Angeles and later was named the executive director of the Food 4 Less Foundation. He died of a heart attack in Washington, DC, after a meeting with Vice President Al Gore.

Clay E. Harshaw

FURTHER READING

Harris, Ron. "Ron Harris: 'Coach' Left Behind a Long List of Winners." *Los Angeles Times*, January 28, 1994.

Renwick, Lucille. "Fred Snowden Dies at 57; Ex-Coach, Entrepreneur; College Basketball: At Arizona, He Became the First Black to Head a Division I Program." *Los Angeles Times*, January 18, 1994.

Thomas, Robert, Jr. "Fred Snowden, Basketball Coach and Black Pioneer, Is Dead at 57." *New York Times*, January 19, 1994.

Tosches, Rich. "Smooth Move: Ex-Arizona Basketball Coach Is Happy in Ice Cream Business, but Misses Thrills." *Los Angeles Times*, August 9, 1989.

★   ★   ★

Bill SPILLER

Born April 9, 1913, Tishomingo, Oklahoma
Died 1988, Los Angeles, California
Golfer

Although his parents separated when he was a youth, Bill Spiller finished high school, then graduated from Wiley College with a degree in education. He spent his professional career in golf, mostly on the black circuit. Spiller also played in a few white tournaments, becoming a pioneer in the desegregation of professional tour golf.

Spiller discovered golf late in life, playing for the first time in 1942 at the age of twenty-nine. He proved to have a latent talent, which emerged quickly. Having mastered the black tour by 1946, Spiller determined to try his skill on the Professional Golfers Association (PGA) Tour. After finishing in the top sixty at the 1948 Los Angeles Open, one of three PGA tour events that admitted blacks, Spiller and fellow black professional Ted Rhodes attempted to enter the Richmond Open. The pair was refused, however, because they were not official PGA members. Spiller and Rhodes immediately brought suit against the PGA on the grounds that its "Caucasian only" membership clause violated their civil rights. In late 1948, the pair dropped the case when the PGA adjusted its tournament policies, allowing event sponsors to admit blacks by special invitation. It seemed only a minor victory, but was actually an important step to desegregating professional tour golf. In January 1960, Spiller sent a letter to California's attorney general detailing his travails with the PGA. The document lent credibility to a California state action that ultimately resulted in the PGA's abolishing its "Caucasian only" membership clause in November 1961.

Stephen R. Lowe

FURTHER READING

Barkow, Al. *Gettin' to the Dance Floor: An Oral History of American Golf*. New York: Atheneum Press, 1986.

Kennedy, John H. *A Course of Their Own: A History of African American Golfers*. Kansas City, MO: Andrews McMeel, 2000.

McDaniel, Pete. *Uneven Lies: The Heroic Story of African Americans in Golf*. Greenwich, CT: American Golfer, 2000.

Sinnette, Calvin. *Forbidden Fairways: African Americans and the Game of Golf*. Chelsea, MI: Sleeping Bear, 1998.

★ ★ ★

Leon SPINKS

Born July 11, 1953, St. Louis, Missouri
Boxer

Leon Spinks, the son of Leon and Kay Spinks, spent his professional career as a boxer. Spinks learned boxing very early as a means to defend himself while growing up in the inner city of St. Louis. Spinks enlisted in the Marines, where he refined his boxing skills in armed forces boxing competition. In 1976, along with his brother Michael, Spinks earned a spot on the Olympic team. During the 1976 Montreal Summer Olympic Games Spinks defeated Sixto Soria of Cuba to win the light heavyweight gold medal. His brother Michael defeated Rufat Riskiev of the Soviet Union to win the middleweight gold medal. The Spinkses became the first brothers ever to win gold medals at the same Olympics in boxing.

Following his Olympic success, in January 1977, Spinks turned pro. He went on to win his first seven bouts. On February 15, 1978, in Las Vegas, Spinks scored one of the biggest upsets in boxing when he outpointed Muhammad Ali for the undisputed heavyweight championship of the world. This was his eighth professional fight; nobody had won the heavyweight title more quickly.

On September 15, 1978, at the Superdome in New Orleans, Ali regained the heavyweight title from Spinks. Spinks's next bout was against Gerrie Coetzee, and it ended in a first-round knockout victory for Coetzee. After four victories following the Coetzee loss, Spinks was back in contention for the World Boxing Commission heavyweight title against Larry Holmes in 1981. Holmes stopped Spinks after three rounds.

In 1986, Spinks filed for bankruptcy despite having earned over $4.5 million as a boxer. He retired from boxing in 1995, ending a career of twenty-six wins, seventeen losses, and three draws.

Alar Lipping

See also: Boxing; Michael Spinks.

FURTHER READING

Ashe, Arthur R., Jr. *A Hard Road to Glory: The African-American Athlete in Boxing*. New York: Amistad, 1988.

Mallon, Bill, and Ian Buchanan. *Quest for Gold: The Encyclopedia of American Olympians*. New York: Leisure Press, 1984.

Porter, David L., ed. *Biographical Dictionary of American Sports: Basketball and Other Indoor Sports*. New York: Greenwood Press, 1989.

Roberts, James B., and Alexander G. Skutt. *The Boxing Register: International Boxing Hall of Fame Official Record Book*. Ithaca, NY: McBooks Press, 1997.

★ ★ ★

Michael SPINKS

Born July 13, 1956, St. Louis, Missouri
Boxer

Michael Spinks, the son of Leon and Kay Spinks, spent his professional career as a boxer and boxing promoter. Spinks became interested in boxing as a teenager, emulating his older brother, Leon, who was a boxer. In 1976, along with Leon, Spinks earned a spot on the Olympic team. During the 1976 Montreal Summer Olympic Games Spinks defeated Rufat Riskiev of the Soviet Union to win the middleweight gold medal; Leon defeated Sixto Soria of Cuba to win the light heavyweight gold medal. The Spinkses became the first boxing brothers ever to win gold medals at the same Olympics.

Following his Olympic success, in April 1977, Spinks turned pro, in the light heavyweight class. Spinks won his first sixteen pro fights. On July 18, 1981 he was given a chance to win the World Boxing Association light heavyweight title against champion Eddie Mustaffa Muhammad in Las Vegas. Spinks outpointed his opponent. On March 19, 1983 Spinks took on the World Boxing Council champion, Dwight Muhammad Qawi. He outpointed Qawi to become undisputed light heavyweight champion of the world.

After successfully defending his light heavyweight crown, Spinks decided to box in the more lucrative heavyweight class. On September 21, 1985 he challenged Larry Holmes for the International Boxing Federation heavyweight crown. Spinks won a unanimous decision over Holmes, becoming the first light heavyweight champion to win the heavyweight title. On April 19, 1986 Spinks defeated Holmes in a rematch.

On June 27, 1988 a lucrative boxing match was fought between Spinks and Mike Tyson for the world heavyweight title. Tyson knocked out Spinks after ninety seconds, but Spinks had earned $13 million from the fight. This was the last match in Spinks's professional boxing career. He retired with an impressive record of thirty-one wins and one loss. Spinks stayed in boxing as a boxing promoter with the Butch Lewis organization.

Alar Lipping

See also: Boxing; Leon Spinks.

FURTHER READING
Arnold, Peter. *All-Time Greats of Boxing.* Secaucus, NJ: Chartwell Books, 1993.
Ashe, Arthur R., Jr. *A Hard Road to Glory: The African-American Athlete in Boxing.* New York: Amistad, 1988.
Blewett, Bert. *The A-Z of World Boxing.* London: Robson, 1996.
Mallon, Bill, and Ian Buchanan. *Quest for Gold: The Encyclopedia of American Olympians.* New York: Leisure Press.

★ ★ ★

SPORTSWRITERS

Black sportswriters have generally received little attention from academicians. They have, however, been a very important and influential group, in that they have recounted the exploits of African-American athletes and actively fought for the elimination of racial discrimination in both sport and the larger American society. An extremely talented group of individuals who for many years were unable to work for the major white press because of their color, black sportswriters provided information on separate black sporting institutions and led campaigns to integrate predominantly white organized sport through notable black periodicals and newspapers. Ironically, during the age of racial segregation black sportswriters could hammer away at the exclusionary policies of organized sport without fear of constant reprisals, since they were not dependent on the white establishment for their success or financial well-being. This is not to say that black sportswriters did not suffer from various forms of racial discrimination. As Jules Tygiel and other scholars have noted, black sportswriters were analogous to the athletes they covered, to the extent that they too were victims of Jim Crow, restricted to segregated hotels, segregated restaurants, and segregated transportation facilities.

Perhaps the first full-time black sportswriter was Frank A. Young, who spent most of his fifty-year career with the *Chicago Defender,* one of the great black newspapers during the interwar period. Following Young into the profession were such talented journalists as Wendell Smith of the *Pittsburgh Courier,* Joe Bostic of the *People's Voice,* Sam Lacy of the *Baltimore Afro-American,* Dan Burly of the *Amsterdam News* and other black newspapers, Ed Harris of the *Philadelphia Tribune,* and Romeo Dougherty of the *Amsterdam News.* Although it would be inappropriate to make broad generalizations about these men, there were certain similarities that marked their careers as journalists. For instance, all of them were constrained to some extent by the limited budgets common to black newspapers. Unlike their white counterparts, they had little office space, limited travel money, and meager staffs. All of them had other responsibilities in addition to their coverage of sports; some of them served as city editors, others were responsible for entertainment columns, and others followed political events. Lastly, nearly all of them devoted much of their writings to baseball. Although sport in historically black colleges, professional basketball, and other athletic activities received coverage in the black press, it was baseball that consumed the bulk of the time of black sportswriters. Hardly a weekly issue went by in any of the black newspapers during the spring and summer without some mention of the Negro baseball leagues or the need to integrate the major leagues. This stands to reason, considering the symbolic importance of baseball as America's "national pastime" and supposedly this country's most democratic of all sports.

The integration of baseball and other sports following World War II did not immediately translate into a better life or working conditions for black sportswriters. In fact, black sportswriters were slow to find their way onto the staffs of major white newspapers across the country. Like coaching and sports administrative positions, continuing racial discrimination made it extremely difficult for black sportswriters to integrate the journalism profession. Only in the last two decades have a significant number of black sportswriters taken positions on the staffs of major white newspapers. Among these journalists are such talented and influential chroniclers of sport as William Rhoden of the *New York Times,* Bryan Burwell of *USA Today,* and Michael Wilbon of the *Washington Post.* These sportswriters, like many others of different colors across the country, have realized national followings and become media personalities through their work on television as well as on the printed page. Examples of this would be Wilbon's regular television appearance and Wilbon's new ESPN production *Pardon the Interruption.*

David K. Wiggins

FURTHER READING

Mansfield, Stephanie. "Revenge of the Words." *Sports Illustrated,* August 5, 2002, 52–56.

Reisler, Jim. *Black Writers/Black Baseball: An Anthology of Articles from Black Sportswriters Who Covered the Negro Leagues.* Jefferson, NC: McFarland, 1994.

Wolseley, Roland E. *The Black Press, U.S.A.* Ames: Iowa State University Press, 1990.

Young, Andrew S. "Doc." "The Black Sportswriter." *Ebony,* October, 1970, 56–58, 60–62, 64.

Dave STALLWORTH

Born December 20, 1941, Dallas, Texas
Basketball player

In 1960, Stallworth was one of the first African-American men recruited to play basketball at predominantly white Wichita State University (WSU). He played at WSU from 1961 to 1964. He is considered the greatest player in the school's history. Stallworth led the team to the 1962 and 1963 National Invitational Tournaments, where he averaged seventeen points a game. In the 1964 NCAA Tournament, he averaged 29.5 points and 19.5 rebounds. He was awarded first-team All-American honors by unanimous decision in 1964. His eligibility ended after the first half of the 1964–1965 season. In his last two games for WSU, he scored a total of ninety-five points. Despite missing half of the season, he received second-team All-American honors in 1965.

The New York Knicks selected Stallworth in the 1965 NBA draft. He played seven seasons with the Knicks, including the 1970 championship season. He played with the Baltimore Bullets and Capital Bullets before retiring in 1975.

Stallworth has been inducted into the Missouri Valley Conference Hall of Fame, the Kansas Sports Hall of Fame, and the WSU Shockers Hall of Fame. He was the first WSU player to have his uniform retired. He resides in the Wichita, Kansas, area.

Clay E. Harshaw

FURTHER READING

Douchart, Mike. *Encyclopedia of College Basketball*. New York: Gale Research, 1995.
Kansas Sports Hall of Fame. "Dave Stallworth" (www.kshof.org/inductees/stallworth.html).
LaBlanc, Michael, ed. *Professional Sports Team Histories: Basketball*. Detroit: Gale Research, 1994.
Lutz, Bob. "Ralph Miller Was Tough Until the End." *Wichita Eagle*, May 16, 2001.
Missouri Valley Conference. "Dave Stallworth" (www.mvc-sports.com/genrel/hofstallworth.html).

★ ★ ★

Willie STARGELL

Born March 6, 1940, Earlsboro, Oklahoma
Died April 9, 2001, Wilmington, North Carolina
Baseball player

The son of an itinerant laborer of mixed African-American and Seminole heritage (William) and a housewife (Gladys), Willie Stargell became a professional baseball player whose demeanor endeared him to fans everywhere and whose achievements earned him election to the Baseball Hall of Fame.

An aunt in Orlando, Florida, raised Stargell before he was reunited with his mother in Oakland, California. He played baseball and basketball and ran track at Encinal High School and briefly attended Santa Rose Junior College. Signed by baseball

Pittsburgh Pirates first baseman Willie Stargell avoiding the slide of the New York Mets John Stearns in a 1979 game at New York's Shea Stadium. *(AP/Wide World Photos)*

scout Bob Zuk in 1958, he played four seasons in the minor leagues before being called up to the Pittsburgh Pirates late in 1962. He remained with the club for twenty-one years, his entire career, retiring after the 1982 season.

Stargell hit twenty or more home runs fifteen times, leading the National League twice, and drove in more than 100 runs five times. One of the game's prolific sluggers, he finished his career with 475 homers and 1,540 runs batted in, both team records and high on the all-time lists. He also helped the Pirates win six NL East division titles and a pair of World Series championships, in 1971 and 1979. An enthusiastic team leader known as "Pops," he awarded his teammates small gold stars for outstanding play.

After retiring, Stargell served as a coach for the Pirates and the Atlanta Braves and participated in many charitable activities, especially the campaign to eradicate sickle cell anemia.

Steven P. Gietschier

FURTHER READING
Adelman, Bob, and Susan Hall. *Out of Left Field: Willie Stargell's Turning Point Season*. New York: Two Continents, 1976.
Angell, Roger. "The Sporting Scene: Wilver's Way." *New Yorker*, November, 26, 1979.
Stargell, Willie, and Tom Bird. *Willie Stargell: An Autobiography*. New York: Harper and Row, 1984.

★ ★ ★

Norman "Turkey" STEARNES

Born May 8, 1901, Nashville, Tennessee
Died September 4, 1979, Detroit, Michigan
Baseball player

Before becoming a slugging outfielder, Stearnes was a schoolboy pitcher at Pearl High School in his hometown of Nashville, Tennessee. After his father died when Stearnes was fifteen years old, he left school for the workplace. However, he continued playing baseball for the Nashville Elite Giants and the Montgomery Grey Sox, until he was discovered by Detroit Stars manager Bruce Petway in 1923. Stearnes then went to Detroit, working for the Briggs Manufacturing Company and playing for the Stars. Stearnes was nicknamed "Turkey" because he had a potbelly and ran with his arms flapping.

Stearnes was a left-handed hitting threat and played "long ball" for twenty years in the black major leagues. Stearnes was a natural hitter with powerful shoulders; he had a unique batting stance, with the front foot turned heel down and toe pointed straight up. He hit thirty-five home runs in 1923 and fifty in 1924 with the Stars in the Negro National League. He was a great outfielder, with good speed and range. He closed out his career as one of the most prolific long-ball hitters in the Negro leagues, with 185 home runs in league play, seven home run titles, and a .359 league batting average. When he retired in 1945, he was one of three leading home run hitters in Negro league history. In addition, he was credited with a .351 batting average in exhibitions against white major leaguers.

Stearnes spent his post-baseball years working at the Ford Rouge Foundry in his adopted hometown of Detroit. He was inducted into the Baseball Hall of Fame in 2000.

Clyde Partin

FURTHER READING
Holway, John B. *Blackball Stars: Negro League Pioneers*. Westport, CT: Meckler Books, 1988.
Ribowsky, Mark. *A Complete History of the Negro Leagues, 1884 to 1955*. New York: Birch Lane Press, 1995.
Riley, James A. *The Biographical Encyclopedia of the Negro Baseball Leagues*. New York: Carroll and Graf, 1994.

Shatzkin, Mike, and Jim Chariton. *The Ball Players.* New York: Arbor House, 1990.

★ ★ ★

Louise STOKES

Born October 27, 1913, Malden, Massachusetts
Died March 25, 1978, Boston, Massachusetts
Sprinter and jumper

The eldest of six children born to William Stokes, a gardener, and Mary W. Stokes, a domestic, Louise Stokes was to be a member of the 1932 and 1936 U.S. Olympic teams. Following her track career Stokes became a professional bowler, worked as a clerk for the Massachusetts Department of Corporations and Taxation, and played an active role in her community.

Stokes was a member of the Onteora Athletic Club while enrolled at Malden High School in Massachusetts. In 1931 she won the James Michael Curley Cup at the Boston Mayor's Day Races, where she broke the New England record in the 100 meters, finishing second in the fifty-meter race and third in the high jump. Later that year she tied the world record in the standing broad jump with a mark of 8 feet 5¾ inches. At the 1932 Olympic trials Stokes's third-place finish in the 100 meters earned her a place on the 400-meter relay team.

Stokes and teammate Tidye Pickett became the first two African-American women to earn places on a U.S. Olympic squad. However, despite their qualifying times both Stokes and Pickett were barred from running in the 400-meter event and were replaced by white athletes. As a member of the 1936 U.S. team Stokes, once again, was not selected to run in the 400-meter relay.

Her achievements were recognized by the New England Amateur Athletic Union, which honored her in 1974 with "Louise Fraser Day" at Boston University.

Rita Liberti

FURTHER READING
Bridgewater State College. "Hall of Black Achievement" (www.bridgew.edu/HOBALtLra_ir.htm).
Chandler Howell, Ann. *In The Blocks: An Olympian's Story.* Chicago: Chandler/White, 1996.
Davis, Michael D. *Black American Women in Olympic Track and Field.* Jefferson, NC: McFarland, 1992.
Himes Gissendanner, Cindy. "African American Women Olympians: The Impact of Race, Gender, and Class Ideologies, 1932–1968." *Research Quarterly for Exercise and Sport* 67 (June 1996): 172–82.
Pieroth, Doris H. *Their Day in the Sun: Women of the 1932 Olympics.* Seattle: University of Washington Press, 1996.

★ ★ ★

Toni STONE

Born July 17, 1921, West Virginia
Died November 2, 1996, Alameda, California
Baseball player

Toni Stone (born Marcenia Lyle) was an African-American female baseball "phenom" in the 1940s and 1950s. Her parents were Boykin Free Lyle, a barber, and Willie Maynard Lyle, a beautician; Marcenia was one of four children. The family moved to St. Paul, Minnesota, when she was six; there she grew up playing baseball with the boys in her neighborhood.

Her professional baseball career began in 1947 when she barnstormed with the San Francisco Lions, an integrated white and black semipro team. She then played for a number of semipro teams. In 1953 she became the first woman to play Negro league baseball, when the Indianapolis Clowns hired her to play second base. Syd Pollack, the Clowns owner, claimed to have signed Stone to a $12,000 contract. (The

Toni Stone, well-known African American baseball player, greets heavyweight boxing champion Joe Louis in this 1949 photograph. (© Minnesota Historical Society/CORBIS)

amount was probably exaggerated for the media; if it were true, she would have gotten more than Jackie Robinson did when he first signed with the Dodgers. One writer has estimated that her actual salary was around $350 a month.) Pollack claimed she was twenty-two, but she was actually thirty-two. That year with the Clowns she played in fifty of the team's 175 games and had a batting average of .243. The highlight of the season came when she got a hit off the legendary pitcher Satchel Paige. The following season the Clowns traded her to the Kansas City Monarchs, where she played for one season.

After Stone's professional playing days, she played recreational baseball with the California American Legion until age sixty-two. She was inducted into the Women's Sports Foundations International Women's Sports Hall of Fame in 1985. She died in 1996 at age seventy-five, predeceased by her husband, Aurelious "A.P." Alberga.

Gai Ingham Berlage

FURTHER READING
Berlage, Gai Ingham. *Women and Baseball: The Forgotten History*. Westport, CT: Greenwood Press, 1994.
DuBay, Diane. "From St. Paul Playgrounds to Big Leagues, Stone Always Loved Baseball." *Minnesota Women's Press*, February 16, 1988.
Grow, Doug. "League of Her Own Tomboy Stone Dead at Age 75." *St. Paul Star-Tribune*, November 5, 1996.
Kirsch, George, Othello Harris, and Clarie Nolte, eds. *Encyclopedia of Ethnicity and Sports in the United States*. Westport, CT: Greenwood Press, 2000.
Thomas, Robert, Jr. "Toni Stone, 75, First Woman to Play Big-League Baseball." *New York Times*, November 10, 1996.

★ ★ ★

George STOVEY

Born 1866, Williamsport, Pennsylvania
Died March 22, 1936, Williamsport, Pennsylvania
Baseball player

George Stovey was a light-complexioned Canadian and a phenomenal left-handed pitcher who was generally regarded as the best black pitcher of his era. He exhibited a trait not often seen in pitchers of that primordial era of baseball, habitually vaulting from the pitcher's box to cover first base on slow rollers up the first base line. *Sporting Life* called Stovey's innovation "wonderful."

After one of Stovey's games, the *Binghamton Leader's* baseball reporter filed this metaphor-happy take on Stovey: "Well, Stovey was in the box again yesterday with the sinister fin and demonic delivery, where he teased the Brooklyn Bridegrooms. He has such a knack of tossing up balls that appear very large but you cannot hit them with a cellar door. . . . [W]hat's the use of bucking against a fellow that can throw at the flagstaff and make it curve into the water bucket?" Stovey played for the Cuban Giants, (1886, 1888–1890, 1893; and the New York Gorhams (1891) as a pitcher and outfielder. He was the first black professional player in New Jersey, playing with Jersey City and Newark in the International Leagues. He and Moses Fleetwood Walker formed the first black battery on an integrated team. Stovey won thirty-five games for Newark in 1887, a record that still stands. In the only six seasons for which he was credited in organized baseball, he registered a lifetime record of 60-40 with a 2.17 earned-run average.

Clyde Partin

FURTHER READING
Holway, John B. *Blackball Stars: Negro League Pioneers.* Westport, CT: Meckler Books, 1988.
Ribowsky, Mark. *A Complete History of the Negro Leagues, 1884–1955.* New York: Birch Lane Press, 1995.
Shatzkin, Mike, and Jim Charlton. *The Ball Players.* New York: Arbor House, 1990.

Rutgers coach Vivian Stringer instructs her players on the way to her 600th career victory in a 1999 game against the University of Texas in Piscataway, New Jersey. *(AP/Wide World Photos)*

★ ★ ★

Vivian STRINGER

Born March 16, 1948, Edenborn, Pennsylvania
Basketball coach

Vivian Stringer was one of seven children of Charles H. Stoner, a coal miner and musician, and Thelma, a homemaker. A graduate of German Township Senior High School and Slippery Rock State College (B.S., M.S.), Stringer is a highly regarded collegiate basketball coach and advocate of women's sports.

Stringer's sport career began as a student at Slippery Rock State College (1966–1970). As assistant professor of recreation, health, and physical education at Cheyney State College from 1971 to 1983, Stringer transformed a recreational-level basketball team into a nationally ranked team compiling a 251–51 (.831) record and a second-place finish in the first NCAA Women's Basketball Championship, in 1982.

Stringer became head coach of the underachieving University of Iowa Hawkeyes in 1982. In her twelve seasons at Iowa, Stringer's team earned nine consecutive NCAA Tournament appearances, one visit to the Final Four, and six Big Ten Conference titles. Stringer's Hawkeye win-loss record of 269–84 (.760) establishes her as the winningest coach in Iowa's history. At Rutgers since 1995, Stringer has become the first coach to take three different college teams to the NCAA Tournament Final Four and the third women's college basketball coach to achieve over six hundred wins, with a career record of 640–197 (.765). She was inducted into the Women's Basketball Hall of Fame in 2000.

Among several international coaching assignments, in 1991 Stringer became the first African-American head coach of a U.S. national woman's basketball team leading, her squad to a bronze medal at the Pan American Games in Havana, Cuba.

Stringer is a three-time winner of the National Coach of the Year award (1982, 1988, 1993) and a winner of *Sports Illustrated*'s National Women's Coach of the Year (1993). She received the Carol Eckman Award in 1993, an honor given to the women's basketball coach demonstrating spirit, courage, commitment, leadership, and service to women's basketball. She is listed in *Who's Who Among Black Americans*. A noted administrator, Stringer was elected to the Women's Sports Foundation Advisory Board and was a key figure in the development of the Women's Basketball Coaches Association.

Susan G. Zieff

See also: Coaches and Managers.

FURTHER READING
Hawkes, Nena Rey, and John F. Seggar. *Celebrating Women Coaches: A Biographical Dictionary*. Westport, CT: Greenwood Press, 2000.
Hult, Joan, "Stringer, C. Vivian (1948–)." In *Black Women in America: An Historical Encyclopedia*, edited by Darlene C. Hine, Elsa B. Brown, and Rosalyn Terborg-Penn. Vol. 2. Bloomington: Indiana University Press, 1994.
Hunt, Donald. *Great Names in Black College Sports*. Indianapolis, IN: Masters Press, 1996.
Porter, David L., ed. *African American Sports Greats: A Biographical Dictionary*. Westport, CT: Greenwood Press, 1995.
Wikgren, Scott. "Vivian Stringer: Big Dreams and the Determination to Make Them Come True." *Coaching Women's Basketball*, March/April 1988, 8–11.
Woolum, Janet. *Outstanding Women Athletes: Who They Are and How They Influenced Sports in America*. Phoenix, AZ: Oryx, 1998.

★ ★ ★

Woody STRODE

Born July 25, 1914, Los Angeles, California
Died December 31, 1994, Glendora, California
Football player, actor

One of the African-American players who reintegrated professional football in 1946, Strode is better known as an actor. A graduate of Jefferson High School in Los Angeles, he entered UCLA, where he played end on the football team and threw the discus for the track team. In 1938, he won football honors as a selectee to the All-Pacific Coast team and consideration for the All-American team.

Strode began his acting career in 1941 and also engaged in professional wrestling. In 1946, the Cleveland Rams of the National Football League moved to Los Angeles, where use of the Coliseum required them to integrate their team. Strode and UCLA teammate Kenny Washington were chosen for the task. Strode played in ten games as an end that season and continued for another year in the Canadian professional football league before becoming a full-time actor.

At six feet, three inches and 205 pounds, Strode presented an imposing figure on the screen, playing both heroes and villains, often typecast as a musicman. He appeared in numerous westerns. Among his most memorable films were *Pork Chop Hill, Spartacus, Sergeant Rutledge, The Ten Commandments*, and *The Man Who Shot Liberty Valance*. Diagnosed with lung cancer, Woody Strode died in his sleep.

Gerald R. Gems

See also: Films; Kenny Washington.

FURTHER READING
Chicago Tribune, January 4, 1995.
Kirsch, George B., Othello Harris, and Claire E. Nolte,

eds. *Encyclopedia of Ethnicity and Sports in the United States*. Westport, CT: Greenwood Press, 2000.

Maher, Tod, and Bob Gill, eds. *The Pro Football Encyclopedia*. New York: Macmillan, 1997.

Strode, Woody, and Sam Young. *Goal Dust: The Warm and Candid Memoirs of a Pioneer Black Athlete and Actor*. New York: Madison Books, 1990.

Time, January 16, 1995.

★ ★ ★

Lynn SWANN

Born March 7, 1952, Alcoa, Tennessee
Long jumper, football player, sports announcer

The son of Willie and Mildred (McGaity) Swann, Lynn Swann attended Serra High School in Foster City, CA. At Serra, Swann was a standout in football and track and field. As a high school student he was named All-American in football and won the state long-jump championship. As a

Pittsburgh Steelers wide receiver Lynn Swann (right) enjoying the company of O.J. Simpson (left) and Steelers teammate Franco Harris during practice for the 1976 Pro Bowl in New Orleans, Louisiana. *(AP/Wide World Photos)*

football player, Swann was a superior receiver; as a senior, he also played quarterback and kicked extra points.

Swann entered the University of Southern California in 1970. He lettered in track and field for the Trojans. In his sophomore year he recorded a twenty-four-foot, ten-inch long jump. While he was a skilled long jumper, Swann's most notable athletic feats at USC occurred on the football field. He was a member of USC's 1972 national champion team and played in two Rose Bowls. Among other honors, Swann was an All-American as a senior wide receiver in 1973. He graduated from USC with a B.A. in public relations.

In the 1974 National Football League draft, Swann was the first-round choice of the Pittsburgh Steelers (twenty-first player selected overall). His career with the Steelers lasted nine seasons. During his time with Pittsburgh as a wide receiver (1974–1982), Swann was a part of four Super Bowl-winning teams (IX, X, XIII, XIV). In Super Bowl X (against the Dallas Cowboys), he was selected Most Valuable Player. His graceful, sometimes acrobatic, moves on the football field were frequently attributed to his years (from fourth grade through high school) of dance training. He appeared in the NFL's Pro Bowl (in 1976, 1977, and 1978) and was inducted into the Professional Football Hall of Fame in 2001.

Swann retired from football in 1982. Since that time he has worked for ABC Television as a sports announcer. He is a member of the Screen Actors Guild and the American Federation of Television and Radio Artists. Swann lives in Pittsburgh, PA, with his wife and two children.

Deane A. Lamont

FURTHER READING

Henderson, Ashyia N., ed. *Who's Who Among African Americans*. Detroit: Gale Group, 2000.

Porter, David L., ed. *Biographical Dictionary of American Sports: Football*. New York: Greenwood Press, 1987.

Professional Football Hall of Fame (www.profootballhof.com).

Tri-Valley Herald, August 3, 2001.

Who's Who in America, 2001. New Providence, NJ: Marquis Who's Who, 2001.

★ ★ ★

SWIMMING

African Americans have not been highly represented in swimming at any level of competition. The sport has seemingly held little appeal for African Americans. Few role models, lack of college scholarships, and no professional competition have certainly played parts in limiting the involvement of African Americans in swimming. At the same time, the sport has resisted integration because of long-held social taboos and deep-seated racial stereotypes. For much of this country's history, African Americans were forced to use separate swimming facilities because of white fears of black bodies and the belief that communicable diseases could be transmitted if the races swam together.

In spite of these restrictions, a number of African-American men and women found their way into the sport and, in some cases, realized national acclaim for their swimming exploits. The first swimmer to receive universal attention for her exploits in the pool was Inez Patterson, the great all-around athlete from Philadelphia who would letter in five sports at Temple University. Patterson won many honors for swimming during the 1920s. Few African-American swimmers followed Patterson into the sport, with the notable exception of Morris Jackson and Emily Jeter, who would qualify for the National Amateur Athletic Union Swim Meet in 1935.

A significantly larger number of African-American swimmers would find their way into the sport during the post–World War II period. Increased enrollment of African Americans in schools and colleges, filing of lawsuits to eliminate racial segregation in public swimming facilities, and a host of other societal factors all combined to bring more African Americans into the sport. The most noticeable increase in African-American swimmers took place on historically black college campuses, especially Morgan State, Tennessee State, and Howard University, which dominated the sport among the race during the 1950s and 1960s. These three schools had the best African-American swimmers during this period, including John Swann and Clyde James from Tennessee State, the first national champions from historically black colleges.

By the 1960s the quality of swimming at historically black colleges had begun to decline. One of the primary reasons was that the best African-American swimmers were beginning to be recruited by predominantly white universities. Similar to what happened in football, basketball, and other sports, predominantly white universities were now recruiting the best African American swimmers, a fact that finally gave these swimmers a chance at national recognition but lessened the quality of the sport at historically black colleges.

The first African-American swimmer to garner national recognition was Nathan Clark of Ohio State, an All-American in the butterfly in 1963. Clark would be followed into predominantly white universities by such swimmers as Fred Evans of the University of Illinois at Chicago, Chris Silva of the University of California at Los Angeles (UCLA), Bob Murray of the University of Michigan, and Trent Lyght of Arizona State University. Of these swimmers, Silva probably realized the most national recognition and publicity. In 1982 Silva was a member of UCLA's national winning 400-meter relay team. The following year, he was a silver medalist in the 400-meter freestyle at the World University Games. In both 1982 and 1983 Silva was named All-American in the fifty-meter freestyle, 400-meter freestyle, and the 400-meter relay.

David K. Wiggins

FURTHER READING
Ashe, Arthur R., Jr. *A Hard Road to Glory*. New York: Amistad, 1993.
Henderson, Edwin B. "Physical Education and Athletics Among Negroes" In *Proceedings. Big Ten Symposium on the History of Physical Education and Sport, Ohio University State University, 1971*, edited by Bruce L. Bennett. Chicago: Athletic Institute, 1972.
Young, Andrew S. "Doc." *Negro Firsts in Sports*. Chicago: Johnson, 1963.

★ ★ ★

Sheryl SWOOPES

Born March 25, 1971, Brownfield, Texas
Basketball player

Swoopes is one of four children of African-American parents. Her mother, Louise, a single parent, often worked two or three jobs to support the family.

Swoopes talent for basketball first received public recognition in 1989, when she was named Texas's inaugural female High School Athlete of the Year. In 1991, playing for South Plains Junior College, she won the Junior College Player of the Year award. At Texas Tech she led the Lady Raiders to two Southwest Conference Championships (1992, 1993) and the NCAA National Championship in 1993. In the NCAA championship game Swoopes scored forty-seven points. She was named MVP of the Final Four and player of the year by *Sports Illustrated* and *USA Today*. The Women's Sports Foundation named her Sportswoman of the Year.

Swoopes international career began in 1993, when she played ten games for an Italian League. She was a member of the U.S. teams that won gold medals at the

Sheryl Swoopes (far right) during medal ceremonies with four other members of the 1996 United States women's basketball team, which took gold by defeating Brazil. In addition to Swoopes are from left: Jennifer Azzi; Lisa Leslie; Carla McGhee; and Katy Steding. (AP/Wide World Photos)

1994 Goodwill Games and the 1996 Olympics. The 1996 U.S. women's Olympic team was named U.S. Olympic Committee and USA Basketball Team of the Year. She was also a member of the U.S. bronze-medal team at the 1994 World Championships.

She was the first woman to have a Nike shoe named after her, "Air Swoopes."

In 1997 she was one of three marquee players signed by the Women's National Basketball Association (WNBA). A picture of a very pregnant Swoopes appeared on the cover of the inaugural issue of *Sports Illustrated Women/Sport*. Swoopes began play with the WNBA Houston Comets six weeks after the birth of her son. She helped the Comets win four consecutive WNBA championships, 1997, 1998, 1999 and 2000. In 2000, she was named MVP and Defensive Player of the Year.

Gai Ingham Berlage

See also: Olympic Games.

FURTHER READING
"100 Greatest Female Athletes: 87. Sheryl Swoopes, Basketball." *Sports Illustrated for Women* (www.CNNSI.com), November 30, 1999.

Ponti, James. *WNBA: Stars of Women's Basketball*. New York: Pocket Books, 1999.

USA Basketball.com. "USA Basketball Bio: Sheryl Swoopes" (www.usabasketball.com/usab/Women/swoopes-bio.html).

George TALIAFERRO

Born January 8, 1927, Gates, Tennessee
Football player

Taliaferro was the son of Robert Taliaferro, a laborer, and his wife, Virnater Eisom Taliaferro, a housewife. A graduate of Indiana University (B.S.) and Howard University (M.S.), Taliaferro was an outstanding college halfback and the first black quarterback in the National Football League (NFL). In 1949 he also became the first black football player drafted by an NFL team, the Chicago Bears, although he did not play for the Bears because of a previous agreement with another team.

In 1945, Taliaferro, then a freshman, led the Hoosiers to their first Big Ten championship, a feat for which the United Press, the Associated Press, and the International News Service (INS) named him to their respective All-American second teams. Following a stint in the army, he was a third-team All-American for the three news services in 1947, and in 1948 he was named to INS's first team. During this period, Taliaferro used his athletic celebrity to integrate public facilities in Bloomington, Indiana.

Professionally, Taliaferro played for the Los Angeles Dons (1949), the New York Yanks (1950–1951), the Dallas Texans (1952), the Baltimore Colts (1953–1954), and the Philadelphia Eagles (1955). His professional honors include 1949 Rookie of the Year (All-American football conference) and Pro Bowl selections for 1951, 1952, and 1953. In 1981 he was named to the National Football Foundation's College Hall of Fame.

After retiring from football, Taliaferro pursued careers in social work, business, and higher education administration in Baltimore, Maryland, Washington, D.C., and Bloomington, Indiana.

Mary Jo Binker

FURTHER READING
Author telephone interview with George Taliaferro, August 15, 2001.
Gilliam, Frances V. Halsell. *A Time to Speak: A Brief History of the Afro-Americans of Bloomington, Indiana.* Bloomington, IN: Pinus Stobus Press, 1985.
Hammel, Bob. "Taliaferro Joins College Football Hall of Fame." *Herald-Telephone* (Bloomington, IN), December 8, 1981.
Kirts, Rex. "Taliaferro, Butler Overcame Obstacles." *Herald-Times* (Bloomington, IN), June 15, 1997.

★ ★ ★

Jack TATUM

Born November 18, 1948, Cherryville, North Carolina
Football player

Tatum was a standout defensive player who early in his career earned a reputation as one of the fiercest hitters in football. The five-foot eleven-inch, two hundred–pound Tatum began attracting national attention as a high school All-American fullback in New Jersey, where he was touted for his hard running and aggressive style of play. He was heavily recruited by most major college athletic programs. He decided upon Ohio State, where assistant coach Lou Holtz promptly moved him to defensive back. Tatum twice made the All-American team. He helped the Buckeyes capture two Big Ten Conference titles and the National Championship in 1968; he was chosen National Defensive Player of the Year his senior year.

Tatum was the Oakland Raiders' first pick in the 1971 NFL draft. He started for the Raiders and made the NFL All-Rookie team. During his years in Oakland (1971–1979) he earned a reputation throughout the league as one of the most devastating tacklers in football. Dubbed "The Assassin," Tatum wrote in his best-selling book of the same title that a "good hit is when the victim wakes up on the sidelines with train whistles blowing in his head and wondering who he is and what ran over him." He delivered just such a blow, and more, to New England Patriots wide receiver Darryl Stingley in a preseason game on August 12, 1978. The blow left Stingley permanently paralyzed and Tatum forever suspect as a sportsman. Tatum was traded to Houston in 1980 and retired from pro ball the following year. Despite a Super Bowl victory in 1976, selection three times to the Pro Bowl, and outstanding defensive play for ten years, Tatum has yet to be inducted into the Pro Football Hall of Fame.

Donald Spivey and Robert Davis

FURTHER READING
Simmons, Ira. *Black Knight: Al Davis and His Raiders.* Ricklin, CA: Prima, 1990.
Stingley, Darryl, with Mulvoy, Mark. *Darryl Stingley: Happy to Be Alive.* New York: Beaufort Books, 1983.
Tatum, Jack, and Joseph Kushner. *Final Confessions of NFL Assassin Jack Tatum.* Coal Valley, IL: Quality Sports Publications, 1996.

★ ★ ★

Reece "Goose" TATUM

Born May 3, 1921, Calion, Arkansas
Died January 18, 1967, El Paso, Texas
Basketball player

The son of a Methodist minister, Tatum is best known as a professional basketball player for the Harlem Globetrotters. Tatum originally played professional baseball in the Negro leagues for Abe Saperstein's team, from 1941 to 1949. Tatum enjoyed a terrific rapport with the fans. Originally, he played in the outfield but was moved to first base so that he would be closer to the fans. His career batting average was .250. In 1947, Tatum started in the All-Star Game. The Philadelphia Phillies sought Tatum's baseball talent in 1949, but he declined the team's offer when he learned of its plans to place him in the minor leagues.

In 1942, Tatum joined Saperstein's Globetrotters basketball team. Tatum played both basketball and baseball until 1949. He is credited with the creation of many of the Globetrotters' comic routines. His on-court comedy earned him the title of "Clown Prince of Basketball." His comedic antics and unique style of play made him the team's top attraction. In 1955, he formed the Harlem Magicians with teammate Marques Haynes. Tatum played with the team until the mid-1960s, when his health deteriorated. He succumbed to a heart attack in 1967.

Clay E. Harshaw

See also: Harlem Globetrotters.

FURTHER READING
Anderson, Dave. *The Story of Basketball.* New York: William Morrow, 1997.
Ashe, Arthur R., Jr. *A Hard Road to Glory: A History of the African-American Athlete Since 1946.* New York: Warner Books, 1988.
Porter, David L., ed. *Biographical Dictionary of American Sports: 1989–1992 Supplement for Baseball, Football, Basketball, and Other Sports.* Westport, CT: Greenwood Press, 1992.
Riley, James A. *The Biographical Encyclopedia of the Negro Baseball Leagues.* New York: Carroll and Graf, 1994.
Rust, Edna, and Art Rust, Jr. *Art Rust's Illustrated History of the Black Athlete.* Garden City, NY: Doubleday, 1985.

★ ★ ★

Charley TAYLOR

Born September 28, 1942, Grand Prairies, Texas
Football player

Taylor was one of seven children of Tyree and Myrtle Taylor. In a thirteen-year career, from 1964 to 1976, he was to be chiefly a pass receiver for the Washington Redskins, consistently receiving postseason honors.

At Dalworth High in Grand Prairie, Taylor was named to the All-State team in football and also won All-State honors in basketball and track. In his freshman year at Arizona State University in 1960, Taylor suffered a near-fatal broken neck. Miraculously, he was able to play halfback as a sophomore, and in his senior year he made the All–Western Athletic Conference first team.

As the Washington Redskins' first draft choice in 1964, Taylor was Rookie of the Year, rushing for 755 yards and catching fifty-three passes, a record for a running back. In 1966, he was switched to end in midseason and ended up leading the NFL with seventy-two catches, for 1,119 yards and twelve touchdowns. In a single game against the Dallas Cowboys, he caught eleven passes for 199 yards and two touchdowns. He led the NFL in pass receptions again in 1967 but for the next two years was hampered by injuries, including a broken ankle. Nevertheless, he caught nearly fifty or more passes a season from 1972 to 1975. When he retired in 1976, he ranked as the NFL's second all-time pass receiver. He played in eight Pro Bowls and one Super Bowl.

His career statistics—649 receptions and seventy-nine touchdowns, as well as 1,488 rushing yards—earned him numerous honors. In 1984, he was inducted into the Pro Football Hall of Fame and the Texas Sports Hall of Fame.

Among the second wave of African Americans to play for the Washington Redskins, the highly professional Taylor was as responsible as any single player for making the once-forlorn NFL team a championship contender.

John S. Watterson

FURTHER READING
Clary, Jack. *Washington Redskins.* New York: Macmillan, 1974.
Loverro, Thom. *Washington Redskins: The Authorized History.* Dallas: Taylor, 1996.
Porter, David L., ed. *Biographical Dictionary of American Sports: Football.* Westport, CT: Greenwood Press, 1987.

★ ★ ★

John Baxter TAYLOR

Born November 3, 1882, Washington, DC
Died December 12, 1908, Philadelphia, Pennsylvania
Sprinter

The son of John and Sarah Thomas Taylor, John Taylor attended racially mixed Central High School in Philadelphia, PA, the Brown Preparatory School (1902), and University of Pennsylvania (1904 and 1907–1908), earning a doctorate in veterinary medicine.

Taylor was the first African American to break intercollegiate running records and was the intercollegiate champion quarter-miler in 1904, 1907, and 1908. He set the 440-yard record in 1904 and lowered it in 1907 (48.35). Taylor competed in the 1908 Olympic Games in the 400 meters and won a gold medal as a member of the 1,600-meter relay team. Taylor was the first African American to win an Olympic gold medal. Additionally, during a preliminary heat, his 1,600-meter team set a world and Olympic record.

During the 1908 Olympic Games, Taylor became embroiled in a controversy during the 400-meter final run between three Americans (John Carpenter, William Robbins, and Taylor) and one British runner (Wyndham Halswelle). A judge ruled that a foul had been committed and disqualified Carpenter. The race was rescheduled; however, Robbins decided to withdraw in protest. Taylor had to decide whether to run, in hopes of achieving success for himself and the African-American community (and risk being perceived as disloyal), or withdraw. He withdrew from the competition and won the gold medal in the 1,600-meter relay.

While competing in the London games, Taylor's health suffered. He became gravely ill after returning home and died of typhoid pneumonia five months later.

Sara A. Elliott

See also: Historically Black Colleges and Universities; Olympic Games; Racial Theories.

FURTHER READING
Ashe, Arthur, R., Jr. *A Hard Road to Glory: A History of the African-American Athlete, 1619–1918.* New York: Warner Books, 1988.
Brawley, Benjamin. *Black Biographical Dictionaries 1790–1950: Negro Builders and Heroes.* Chapel Hill: University of North Carolina Press, 1937.
Chase, Henry. "Racing Towards Higher Ground." *American Visions* 11 (June/July 1996): 20–24.
Henderson, Edwin B. *The Department of Health and Physical Education: Public Schools of the District of Columbia.* Washington, DC: Associated, 1939.
Robinson, Maisah B. *John Baxter Taylor: 1st African-American Olympic Gold Medalist* (www.suite101.com/article.cfm/7389/487900), September 23, 2000.

★ ★ ★

Lawrence TAYLOR

Born February 4, 1959, Williamsburg, Virginia
Football player

The son of Clarence Taylor, a dispatcher for a Newport News, Virginia, shipyard, and Iris Taylor, a schoolteacher, Lawrence Taylor was reared in Williamsburg, Virginia. He graduated from Lafayette High School in 1977. The six-foot three-inch, 240 pound Taylor was a college and professional football standout.

Taylor played football for the University

New York Giants linebacker Lawrence Taylor rushing the passer in a 1986 game at Giants Stadium. *(AP/Wide World Photos)*

of North Carolina. Used at first as a defensive lineman, he saw his career blossom when he was moved to linebacker in 1979. In 1980, his senior year, Taylor led UNC to an 11–1 mark and the Atlantic Coast Conference title. He was named ACC Player of the Year and was a consensus All-American in 1980.

The New York Giants made Taylor the first pick of the 1981 NFL draft. A standout linebacker, Taylor was named NFL defensive Rookie of the Year and defensive Player of the Year in 1981. He continued to dominate throughout the 1980s. He was named All-NFC and to the Pro Bowl roster from 1981 through 1990. He was NFC defensive Player of the Year in 1983 and 1986.

Taylor's best season was 1986, when he led the Giants to a Super Bowl victory. He led the NFL with 20.5 sacks that season and anchored a standout defense. Taylor also led the Giants to a Super Bowl triumph after the 1990 season. In spite of his great on-field performances, Taylor was a controversial player. He had several contract disputes, crossed the NFL Players Association picket lines in 1987, and entered a drug rehabilitation program after the 1988 season. Injuries curtailed his effectiveness in the early 1990s, and he retired following the 1993 season.

Jim L. Sumner

FURTHER READING
Bradley, J.E. "L.T. and the Home Team." *Esquire*, December 1985, 306–308.
Perrin, Tom. *Atlantic Coast Conference Football. A History Through 1991*. Jefferson, NC: McFarland, 1992.
Taylor, Lawrence, with David Falkner. *L.T.: Living on the Edge*. New York: Times Books, 1987.
Zimmerman, Paul. "Terrific Tayloring." *Sports Illustrated*, September 17, 1990, 30–37.

Marshall "Major" TAYLOR

Born November 26, 1878, Indianapolis, Indiana
Died June 21, 1932, Chicago, Illinois
Cyclist

Gilbert and Saphonia Taylor raised their family of eight children in Indianapolis, Indiana. Marshall quit school after completing the eighth grade and went to work at a local bicycle firm. In addition to janitorial duties the owner began to have Marshall perform bicycle tricks in front of the store to attract passersby. While performing Taylor wore an old military uniform, thus earning the nickname "Major."

Taylor joined a local African-American cycling club called the See-Saw Circle after winning his first race in 1892. He won a number of local races and set the mile record on the Indianapolis track. As a result of his wins Taylor earned the disfavor of white racers and officials, who effectively barred him from their races.

Taylor eventually moved to Worcester, Massachusetts, as the personal valet to George Munger, a racer and manufacturer of bicycles. While living in Massachusetts Taylor became a professional rider, winning his first professional race in 1896 at Madison Square Garden in the half-mile.

Taylor earned a national and international reputation by winning the one-mile sprint championship in 1899 in Montreal, Canada. He set seven world records between 1898 and 1900 at distances from a third-of-a-mile sprint through the one-mile race. In 1899 Taylor received recognition as League of American Wheelmen champion and in 1900 was named the National Cycling Association Champion.

During the 1901 season Taylor accumulated forty-two victories racing in sixteen European cities. The 1902 season found Taylor with another forty victories and a new wife, Daisy Morris. Their only daughter, Sydney, was born while Taylor was racing in Australia. Taylor suffered a nervous breakdown in 1904 and did not return to the racing circuit until 1907; he retired in 1910. After retiring Taylor worked in manufacturing for a short time and wrote his autobiography, *The Fastest Bicycle Rider in the World*, published in 1928. He died of a heart attack in Chicago in 1932. His hometown, Indianapolis, named a new velodrome in his honor in 1982.

Leslie A. Heaphy

See also: Autobiographies; Civil Rights.

FURTHER READING
Palmer, Arthur Judson. "The Fastest Man on Wheels." *Sports Illustrated*, March 14, 1960, 7–11.
Ritchie, Andrew. *Major Taylor: The Extraordinary Career of a Champion Bicycle Racer*. San Francisco: Bicycle Books, 1988.
Taylor, Marshall. *The Fastest Bicycle Rider in the World*. Battleboro, VT: Green-Stephen Press, 1971.
Williams, Grant G. "Marshall Walter Taylor: The World Famous Bicycle Rider." *Colored American Magazine*, September 1902, 336–45.

★ ★ ★

Ed TEMPLE

Born September 20, 1927, Harrisburg, Pennsylvania
Track and field coach

Ed Temple's father (Christopher) worked for a time with the U.S. government in Middletown, Pennsylvania. His mother (Ruth) was a housewife. Temple was an only child. In elementary and high school, he took part in football, baseball, and track and field.

Temple graduated from Tennessee State College in 1950. At that time the president of the college desperately needed an assistant coach to help with women's track and field. Although Temple had always dreamed of coaching, his passions were football and basketball. However, he accepted a package deal that was to alter his career path forever. In a biographical interview carried out by Louis Mead Tricard, Temple recalls the words of the university president: "I'll let you [Temple] go to graduate school, give you one hundred and fifty dollars a month, and let you run the post office" (as an additional source of income). This initiated the most successful college program in the history of women's track and field.

Temple's most famous athlete was Wilma Rudolph, who won three gold medals at the 1960 Rome Olympics. Other Olympic champions coached by Temple were Mae Faggs, Wyomia Tyus, Edith McGuire, and Madeline Manning Mims. Altogether, Temple's athletes won twenty-three Olympic medals, thirteen of them gold. His Tigerbelles won thirty-four team titles, and Temple was twice head coach of the U.S. Olympic women's team and the Pan American Games women's team.

While understandably proud of his record of coaching forty Olympians, Temple's real satisfaction was seeing his athletes become successful in their postathletic careers. "Out of forty [Olympians], thirty-nine graduated with their degrees and out of the thirty-nine we had twenty-five with masters and three with their Ph.D. and one M.D." Temple was inducted into the National Track and Field Hall of Fame in 1989. He retired in 1994 and is an active member of both the Nashville Sports Council and the Nashville Sports Authority.

Scott A.G.M. Crawford

See also: Coaches and Managers; Edith McGuire; Wyomia Tyus; Women.

FURTHER READING
Bateman, Hal. "Ed Temple Coach." *USA Track and Field* (www.usatf.org/athletes/hof/temple.shtml).

Rader, Benjamin G. *American Sports: From the Age of Folk Games to the Age of Televised Sport.* Upper Saddle River, NJ: Prentice Hall, 1996.

Sports Information, Tennessee State University—communication/conversation, April 24, 2001.

Temple, Edward. Telephone interview, April 25, 2001.

Temple, Edward, with B'Lou Carter. *Only the Pure in Heart Survive: Glimpses into the Life of a World-Famous Olympic Coach.* Nashville, TN: Broadman Press, 1980.

Tricard, Louise Mead. *American Women's Track and Field: A History, 1895 Through 1980.* Jefferson, NC: McFarland, 1996.

★ ★ ★

TENNIS

Although a segregated sport for decades, tennis was a popular sport for African Americans as early as the 1890s. Institutions like Howard University, Lincoln University, and Tuskegee Institute offered their students the opportunity to compete, albeit against individuals of their own race. In cities on the East Coast, the children of professionals were encouraged to pursue this sport, using the wooden racquets of the times and mostly on the few available clay courts. Edwin B. Henderson, respected teacher and coach in Washington, DC, is credited with introducing this sport to his students as well as to youth in the city.

In 1916, African-American tennis enthusiasts, excluded from all-white events, formed the American Tennis Association (ATA) in order to promote their sport and encourage individuals of all ages to play and compete through local clubs. The ATA sponsored its first national singles championship events in 1917 in Baltimore; Talley Holmes won the men's title and Lucy Slowe the women's title. The first player to dominate on the women's side was Isadore Channels, who won four ATA national crowns in 1922–1924 and 1926. Many wished to see a match between Ora Washington, who won eight ATA singles titles in 1929–1935 and 1937, and the number-one-ranked female player of the time, Helen Wills (Moody), but this match between two of the best women players ever never occurred. Sisters Roumania and Margaret Peters won the ATA Women's Doubles Championships fourteen times between 1938 and 1953.

Reginald Weir and his partner Gerald Norton, Jr., attempted to play in the United States National Lawn Tennis Association's Junior Indoor event in 1929, but when the white establishment learned of their race, they were not allowed to play. Weir won ATA singles titles in 1931–1933, 1937, and 1942; Jimmy McDaniel also won four ATA titles, including 1939, when he defeated Weir in the finals. McDaniel, a Californian, played at Xavier University and later worked for an engineering firm. As the first African American accepted in play in a USLTA event, in 1948, Weir helped open tennis to players of his race; most notable among those who followed were Althea Gibson and Arthur Ashe. Weir, who played tennis at the City College of New York and later became a physician, won the National Senior 45s Indoor Singles Championships in 1956–1957 and 1959. Oscar Johnson was the first African American to win a USLTA-affiliated event, the National Junior Public Parks title in 1948.

Althea Gibson learned tennis from Fred Johnson at the Cosmopolitan Tennis Club in Harlem. Her game was greatly enhanced through play and lessons on Hubert Eaton's court in Wilmington, North Carolina, and through summer competitions under the guidance of Walter Johnson. Beginning in 1947, Gibson won ten consecutive ATA singles championships. Walking through the door opened by Weir and supported by former USLTA women's champion Alice Marble, Gibson was allowed to play in her first USLTA event in 1950. After struggling in the amateur sport of tennis, Gibson forever changed it in 1957 and 1958, when she won the All-England Ladies Singles Championship at Wimbledon and the USLTA Women's Singles Championships, thus becoming the first African American to win these two "Grand Slam" events. Many future champions adopted Gibson's powerful, all-court style of play.

Arthur Ashe won three consecutive ATA men's titles in 1960–1962 after learning the sport under the watchful eyes of his father in Richmond, Virginia. In 1961 he won the National Interscholastic Championship, and in 1965 he captured the National Collegiate Athletic Association singles title. In 1968, he won the United States Tennis Association Men's Singles Championship. In 1969, Ashe helped found the National Junior Tennis League in public parks to promote tennis for minorities. This program, which the USTA supported, grew to over 650 leagues nationally. Ashe died as a victim of the AIDS virus, which infected him during a blood transfusion associated with his heart surgery. His many contributions as a tennis ambassador were recognized by the USTA, which named its championship stadium in his honor.

In addition to Gibson and Ashe, professional tennis players Zina Garrison, Lori McNeil, MaliVai Washington, and Bryan Shelton played in ATA events before achieving various degrees of success in the sport. Garrison, who began her professional career in 1981 achieved the number-four USTA ranking and won a gold medal in doubles in the 1988 Olympic Games. She eventually returned to her hometown of Houston, where she shares her love of tennis with aspiring minority players at MacGregor Park. Sisters Venus and Serena Williams, who developed their powerful games on public courts in an urban setting and played in some ATA events, have demonstrated in an emphatic manner that African Americans can lead and even dominate in this historically elitist sport.

Angela Lumpkin

See also: American Tennis Association.

FURTHER READING
Ashe, Arthur R., Jr. *A Hard Road to Glory-A History of the African-American Athlete.* New York: Warner Books, 1988.
Henderson, Edwin B. *The Negro in Sports.* Washington, DC: Associated Publishers, 1939.
Spradling, Mary Mace Ed. *In Black and White.* Vols. I and II. Detroit: Gale, 1980.

★ ★ ★

Debra THOMAS

Born March 25, 1967, Poughkeepsie, New York
Figure skater

Thomas, the daughter of McKinley Thomas, a computer industry worker, and Janice Thomas, was the first prominent African-American figure skater. An outstanding student at San Mateo (California) High School, Stanford University, and the University of Colorado, Thomas began skating at the age of five and soon thereafter started taking figure skating lessons. At age ten she began a physically taxing training regimen under coach Alex McGowan and entered skating competitions.

Thomas's prodigious talents became nationally known during her freshman year at Stanford in 1985, when she garnered victories at the St. Ivel Skate International in England, the National Sports Festival in Baton Rouge, and the Skate America International in Minneapolis. Her performances were so outstanding that year that she was named Amateur Athlete of the Year by the U.S. Olympic Committee. The following year was even a better one for Thomas, as she captured both the U.S. Senior Ladies National and World Championships at Geneva, Switzerland. In 1988, Thomas finished her amateur skating career by placing a disappointing third to Katarina Witt of East Germany at the Winter Olympics in Calgary, Canada. Following the Olympics, Thomas participated for several years on the professional ice skating circuit. She is currently working on her medical degree.

David K. Wiggins

See also: Olympic Games.

FURTHER READING
Axthelm, Pete. "Cool as Ice, Witt Hits Gold." *Newsweek*, March 7, 1988, 62–64.
Norment, Lynn. "Debi Thomas." *Ebony*, May 1986, 147–48.
Porter, David L., ed. *African American Sports Greats: A Biographical Dictionary*. Westport, CT: Greenwood Press, 1995.
Swift, E.M. "Another Miracle on Ice." *Sports Illustrated*, March 17, 1986, 54–56, 58, 61.

★ ★ ★

Frank THOMAS

Born May 27, 1968, Columbus, Georgia
Baseball player

The son of a textile worker and bail bondsman (Frank, Sr.) and a housewife (Charlie Mae), Frank Thomas graduated from Columbus High School and attended Auburn University. Nicknamed "The Big Hurt," he was to be one of major league baseball's outstanding hitters in the 1990s, winning the American League Most Valuable Player award in 1993 and 1994.

Thomas played football, basketball, and baseball in high school and hoped to attend college on a baseball scholarship. Instead, he accepted a football scholarship to

Chicago White Sox slugger Frank Thomas strokes a single in a 1993 game against the Cleveland Indians. *(AP/Wide World Photos)*

Auburn and played tight end. He made the baseball team too and achieved All-American honors in 1989, his junior year. The Chicago White Sox drafted him, and a year later he was in the major leagues.

Thomas hit .330 in 1990 and soon was recognized as one of the most skillful batters in the American League. He was the first player to bat at least .300 and record more than twenty home runs, 100 runs batted in, 100 walks, and 100 runs scored in seven straight seasons (1991–1997). He won the league batting championship in 1997 and showed remarkable discipline at the plate, striking out seldom for a power hitter. After a contract dispute during spring training of 2001, he played only twenty games before having surgery to repair a torn tricep. He returned for the 2002 season and hit for a .252 batting average with 28 home runs and 92 runs batted in.

Steven P. Gietschier

FURTHER READING

Staff of Beckett Publications. *Beckett Great Sports Heroes: Frank Thomas.* New York: House of Collectibles, 1996.

★ ★ ★

Isiah THOMAS

Born April 30, 1961, Chicago, Illinois
Basketball player

Isiah Thomas was the ninth and last child of Mary and Isiah Thomas II, who separated when he was very young. Left to raise nine children alone, Mary moved the family to a West Side suburb to escape the drugs, gangs, and violence of the city. Thomas graduated from St. Joseph High School (1979) and from Indiana University (1988) with a degree in criminal justice (B.S.). Thomas played his entire professional basketball career with the Detroit Pistons.

Thomas's older brother Larry convinced him to concentrate on basketball to avoid the temptation of drugs and gangs. Gene Pingatore of St. Joseph High School in Westchester, Illinois discovered Thomas playing in an eighth-grade game and offered him a scholarship to his private school. After an outstanding high school career, Thomas left the Chicago area to play college basketball for Bob Knight at Indiana University. He starred for the Hoosiers for two years, leading the team to the NCAA (National Collegiate Athletic Association) title in 1981 while earning the tournament's Most Valuable Player (MVP) award. Thomas chose to leave school after his sophomore year and enter the NBA (National Basketball Association) draft. He was drafted in the first round by the Detroit Pistons and went on to play thirteen seasons for the team. Although considered

Detroit Pistons Isiah Thomas accepts congratulations after recording his 9,000th career assist in a 1994 game against the Los Angeles Clippers. *(AP/Wide World Photos)*

small by professional basketball standards, the six-foot one-inch, 185-pound point guard made a reputation as a rugged competitor. He led a very physical Detroit team to the 1989 and 1990 NBA titles, earning the Most Valuable Player award for the 1990 finals. After his retirement in 1994 Thomas claimed the Pistons' all-time records in points scored (18,822), assists (9,061), steals (1,861), and games played (979). He played in twelve successive NBA All-Star Games, earning selection as the game's MVP in 1984 and 1986, and was named one of the fifty greatest players in NBA history in 1996.

Thomas has remained involved in professional basketball since the end of his playing career. Thomas first became a part owner and vice president of the NBA expansion Toronto Raptors. He hoped to take over the team eventually, but the deal with majority owner Allan Slaight fell through. Thomas left the Raptors organization to work for the National Broadcasting Company as a professional basketball analyst. He later became primary owner of the now-defunct CBA (Continental Basketball Association), before reentering the NBA as coach of the Indiana Pacers in 2000. Thomas has also been involved in banking, land development, and other business ventures in the Detroit area.

Troy D. Paino

FURTHER READING
Challen, Paul C. *The Book of Isiah: The Rise of a Basketball Legend*. Chicago: Login Publishers Consortium, 1996.
Knapp, Ron. *Sports Great Isiah Thomas*. Hillside, NJ: Enslow, 1992.
Sachare, Alex. *100 Greatest Basketball Players of All Time*. New York: Pocket Books, 1997.

★ ★ ★

John THOMAS

Born March 3, 1941, Boston, Massachusetts
High jumper

John Thomas began his track career at Rindge Technical High School, in Boston. As a seventeen-year-old freshman at Boston University, Thomas set a world indoor high-jump record of seven feet, 1¼ inches in 1959. He missed the rest of the 1959 season due to injury but came back to show the best form of his life in 1960. In February 1960 he set indoor world records of seven feet, 1½ inches at the Millrose Games and of seven feet, 2 inches at the AAU Indoor Championships. At the 1960 Penn Relays he set an outdoor world record of seven feet, 1½ inches and thereafter broke the mark several more times that season. He increased the world record to seven feet, 1¾ inches at the New England AAU Meet, to seven feet, two inches at the AAU Championships, and finally to seven feet, 3¾ inches at the final Olympic trials. At the Rome Olympics, Thomas was the heavy favorite, but he finished behind two members of the Soviet team—Robert Shavlakadze, who won the gold, and Valery Brumel. Before the 1964 Olympics, Brumel had taken Thomas's title as the world's premier high jumper; Brumel again defeated Thomas at Tokyo.

Although Thomas did not succeed in winning an Olympic title, he had a fine competitive record. He won two AAU championships outdoors and five indoors, was twice NCAA champion, and for three years he won both the indoor and outdoor high jump at the Intercollegiate American Amateur Athletic Association (IC4A) meet. After retiring from active competition, he took up a coaching appointment at Boston University, but he later became a regional sales manager for a major telephone company.

Bill Mallon

FURTHER READING
Ashe, Arthur R., Jr. *A Hard Road To Glory: A History of the African-American Athlete*. New York: Ballantine, 1976.
Wallechinsky, David. *The Complete Book of the Olympics*. New York: Viking, 1984.

★ ★ ★

David THOMPSON

Born July 13, 1954, Shelby, North Carolina
Basketball player

The son of textile worker Vellie Thompson and Ida Thompson, David Thompson attended Shelby's Crest High School from 1968 to 1971 and North Carolina State University from 1971 to 1975. He became a top college and professional basketball star.

The six-foot, four-inch Thompson was

an exceptional athlete, best known for his leaping ability. He augmented this innate ability with superior basketball skills to become one of the top college basketball players in the history of the sport. He led NC State to a 27–0 mark in 1973 and a 30–1 record in 1974. The 1974 team captured the NCAA title by defeating UCLA and Marquette in the Final Four. Thompson was the Final Four's Most Valuable Player.

Thompson was consensus first-team All-American and Atlantic Coast Conference Player of the Year in 1973, 1974, and 1975. He was Associated Press Player of the Year in 1974 and 1975. He ended his varsity career with 2,309 points and a 26.8-points-per-game average. He became one of the first African Americans to become a sports hero at a predominantly white southern school.

Thompson signed with the ABA's Denver Nuggets after college. He was 1976 ABA Rookie of the Year. The following season, Denver joined the NBA, where Thompson was named first-team All-League in 1977 and 1978. He scored seventy-three points against Detroit on April 9, 1978, and finished that season with a 27.15-point-per-game average, second in the league. He played in four NBA All-Star Games, winning Most Valuable Player selection in 1979.

Injuries and substance abuse began to erode Thompson's game in the early 1980s. Denver traded him to the Seattle Supersonics in 1982. He underwent several drug rehabilitation stints and served four months in prison for a probation violation stemming from a domestic violence conviction. On March 10, 1984, Thompson suffered a career-ending knee injury in a New York nightclub altercation.

Thompson had scored 11,264 points in the NBA and 2,158 in the ABA, with respective scoring averages of 22.1 and twenty-six points per game. He was selected to the Basketball Hall of Fame in 1996.

Jim L. Sumner

FURTHER READING
Bjarkman, Peter. *ACC: Atlantic Coast Conference Basketball*. Indianapolis, IN: Masters Press, 1996.
Green, Ted. "The Man Who Fell to Earth." *National Sports Daily*, May 13, 1990.
Herakovich, Douglas. *Pack Pride: The History of NC State Basketball*. Cary, NC: Yesterday's Future, 1994.
Lupica, Mike. "David Thompson, Back to Earth." *Esquire*, March 1990, 73–74.
Morris, Ron. *ACC Basketball: An Illustrated History*. Chapel Hill, NC: Four Corners Press, 1988.
Sloan, Norm. *Confessions of a Coach*. Nashville: Rutledge Hill Press, 1991.

★ ★ ★

John THOMPSON

Born September 2, 1941, Washington, DC
Basketball player and coach

John Thompson was a graduate of Archbishop Carroll High School. There he led his team to 103 wins and only eight losses. In his last two years in high school, Thompson was awarded All-Conference and All-District honors and led his team to two city championships. He attended Providence University from 1960 to 1964. Captain of the team in his last two years there, he led it to the National Invitational Tournament (NIT) championship. He was awarded All-State honors for two years, 1962–1964. In his senior year he was awarded All-District, All-Conference, All-American, and Team Most Valuable Player honors. He graduated in 1964 with a degree in economics. Thompson played for the Boston Celtics for two years, 1964–1966, serving as a backup center to NBA great Bill Russell. As a member of the Celtics, Thompson won two NBA championship rings.

Thompson began his coaching career in 1966 at Saint Anthony's High School in Washington, DC. He coached there until 1972, compiling a won/loss record of 122-28 and one city championship. He began his coaching career at Georgetown University in 1972, taking over a program that had won only three games against twenty-three losses the previous season. He assumed the position at Georgetown University at a time when there were few black coaches at major universities in the United States. It was labeled at the time "the worst job in college basketball" by Arkansas basketball coach Nolan Richardson.

By 1979, Thompson had turned Georgetown University into a winning program. He led the Hoyas to its first Big East Conference Championship in a road victory against the Syracuse Orangemen. In 1982, he recruited Patrick Ewing. That year, the Georgetown University Hoyas made it to the National Collegiate Athletic Association (NCAA) Final Four before losing to North Carolina in the semifinal. Two years later, in 1984, Georgetown defeated the University of Houston Cougars at the Kingdome in Seattle to win its first and only NCAA National championship. During his legendary career at Georgetown, Thompson and his Hoyas appeared in three Final Fours, played in fourteen consecutive NCAA postseason tournaments (1979–1992), made twenty-four postseason tournament appearances (twenty NCAA, four NIT) and won seven Big East Tournament championships. He holds conference records for most overall Big East wins at 231, most regular-season Big East wins at 198, most conference championships (seven regular season, six tournaments), and won seven Coach of the Year Awards. Thompson coached the U.S. Olympic basketball team to a bronze medal in 1988. Thompson retired from college basketball coaching on January 8, 1999. He currently works as a television basketball analyst.

Gary A. Sailes

FURTHER READING
Hodges, A. Hunter, and James Lawrence. "The Bigger They Are, the Harder They Fall." *Georgetown Voice*, January 14, 1999; April 5, 2001.
Naismith Memorial Basketball Hall of Fame (www.hoophall.com).

★ ★ ★

Eddie TOLAN

Born September 29, 1909, Denver, Colorado
Died January 30, 1967, Detroit, Michigan
Sprinter

Tolan attended Detroit's Cass Technical High School, where he starred as quarterback on the football team. He began his student athlete career at the University of Michigan in 1927. While he dreamed of being a Wolverine football player, his slight build—five feet seven inches, 140 pounds—directed him eventually toward track and field. He enjoyed considerable success as a collegiate sprinter. He won the Amateur Athletic Union outdoor 100-yard dash in back-to-back years (1929–1930) and was the furlong champion in 1929 and 1931. He was also victorious in the National Collegiate Athletic Association 220 in 1931.

Tolan's banner year was 1929, when he twice equaled the world 100-meter record of 10.4 seconds and set a world record in the 100 yards with a time of 9.5 seconds. In 1932, however, American Ralph Metcalfe of Marquette University dominated sprinting on the world and American stages. He beat Tolan in the 100 and 200 meters at the Olympic trials and was the odds-on heavy favorite to win both of the sprints. Nevertheless, Tolan ran the race of his life in the finals and at the finish line he and Metcalfe seemed to be in a dead heat.

Seven judges viewed a film of the race and determined that Tolan had crossed the line two inches ahead of Metcalfe. Tolan was the third University of Michigan athlete to win the Olympic 100-meters gold medal. Tolan and Metcalfe were the first black Americans to win Olympic medals in the sprints. Tolan's time of 10.3 seconds was an Olympic record. He received a second gold medal in the 200 meters, and his time of 21.2 seconds was accepted as the official world record for a curved 200-meter distance.

Tolan's mother, Alice, while thrilled with his Olympic medals, hoped that means would be found to allow her son to complete his education and realize his dream of becoming a physician. This never came to pass. By January 1933 the only job that Tolan could secure was that of a county office filing clerk. Later Tolan joined the world of vaudeville and toured with the maestro of tap dancing, Bill A. "Bojangles" Robinson. He then competed in professional track and field and enjoyed some success in Australia. Later in life he taught physical education. He was inducted into the National Track and Field Hall of Fame in 1982. He never married.

Scott A.G.M. Crawford

See also: Racial Theories; Track and Field.

FURTHER READING
Ashe, Arthur R., Jr. *A Hard Road To Glory: A History of the African-American Athlete, 1919–1945.* New York: Amistad, 1988.
Baker, William J. *Jesse Owens: An American Life.* New York: Free Press, 1986.
Daley, Arthur J. "Tolan US, Equals the World Record in Olympic Victory." *New York Times,* August 2, 1932.
Hickok, Ralph. *A Who's Who of Sport Champions.* New York: Houghton Mifflin, 1995.
Obituary, *New York Times,* February 1, 1967.
Wallechinsky, David. *The Complete Book of the Olympics.* New York: Viking Press, 1984.

★ ★ ★

Gwen TORRENCE

Born June 12, 1965, Atlanta, Georgia
Sprinter

Gwen Torrence was raised by her mother, Dorothy, who worked as a nanny and housekeeper. A graduate of Columbia High School in Decatur, Georgia, and the University of Georgia, she is considered to be one of the best female sprinters in track and field history.

While in high school Torrence was an All-American, three time Georgia state champion, and winner of the 100 and 200-meter titles at the Athletic Congress Junior Olympics. At the University of Georgia she earned twelve All-American honors and was a four-time National Collegiate Athletic Association champion.

Torrence's accomplishments on an international level are also stellar. At the World University Games in 1987 she won the 100 and 200-meter races. She also anchored the winning relay team in the 4 x 100. Torrence competed in the 1988 Olympics in Seoul, finishing fifth in the 100 meters and sixth in the 200. At the 1992 Olympics in Barcelona she captured gold medals in the 200 meters and the 400-meter relays, as well as a silver medal in the 1,600-meter relay. In 1995 she won a gold medal in the 100-meters at the World Track and Field Championships in Tokyo. She returned to her hometown of Atlanta in 1996 to win a gold medal in the 400-meter relay and a bronze medal in the 100 meters.

Some observers criticized Torrence for her fierce individuality. But those same critics were quick to acknowledge her dedication, hard work, and commitment to becoming one of the great track athletes in history.

Rita Liberti

FURTHER READING

Boxer, Sarah. "Taking Her Sweet Time." *Sports Illustrated*, May 23, 1988, 60–62, 64.

Reilly, Rick. "She Stands Alone." *Sports Illustrated*, June 10, 1996, 92–96, 98–100.

Stewart, Mark. *Gwen Torrence*. New York: Grolier, 1996.

University of Georgia Athletic Association (georgiadogs.ocsn.com).

★ ★ ★

TRACK AND FIELD

Of all of mankind's sports, track and field ranks among the oldest. Footraces and throwing contests described in Homer's *Iliad* date back to the twelfth century B.C.E. Modern track and field, however, consists of three general categories—running contests on a flat track or over barriers (hurdles, water obstacles), field events involving throwing or jumping, and competition that combines running and field events (decathlon, heptathlon).

Track and field in America took its cues from England, as students at Oxford and Cambridge Universities raced against each other during the 1860s. Soon afterward, the London Athletic Club sponsored track and field competitions. In the United States the nascent New York Athletic Club, molded after its London counterpart, held the first amateur meet in America in 1868 and initiated a movement that spread among other athletic clubs. To coordinate and administer athletic competitions, the clubs in 1879 formed the National Association of Amateur Athletes of America (NAAAA). Internal strife destroyed the NAAAA in 1888, when its most powerful members withdrew and formed the Amateur Athletic Union. This new organization took control of amateur track and field in America, held regional and national championships, and sent numerous athletes to the Olympic Games following their revival in 1896. The emergence of the National Collegiate Athletic Association in 1906 created a running feud that lasted for more than a half-century with the AAU over the governance of amateur athletics. The principal sticking point was the selection of athletes for international competitions. The Amateur Sports Act of 1978, which provided some support for Olympic athletes and the adoption of an "open" Olympics during the 1980s, ended this dispute. Today, USA Track and Field (USATF) is the national governing body for track and field, long-distance running, and race walking.

African-American athletes made their Olympic debut at the 1904 games in St. Louis, where George Poage won a bronze medal in the 400-meter hurdles and finished fourth in the 400 meters. Howard P. Drew, the next great black sprinter, won national 100-yard dash titles in 1912 and 1913 and the 220-yard dash title in 1913. At the 1912 Olympics, he won his heat in the 100 meters, but a leg injury kept him out of the finals. Twelve years later, in Paris, DeHart Hubbard won the long jump and became the first African-American athlete to win an Olympic gold medal in an individual event. From 1922 to 1927 Hubbard won six straight AAU long-jump championships and two collegiate titles.

African-American sprinters took center stage at the 1932 Los Angeles Olympics. Eddie Tolan and Ralph Metcalfe took gold and silver in the 100 meters, and gold and bronze in the 200 meters, respectively. Then, at the 1936 games in Berlin, Jesse Owens captured the spotlight with gold medals in the 100, 200, 4 x 100 relay, and long jump. Ralph Metcalfe, winner of three straight 100–220 double national collegiate titles 1932–1934 and five consecutive AAU 200–220 national championships 1932–1936, was Owens's teammate for the relay and finished second to him in the 100. John

Woodruff won the 800 meters. Archie Williams and James LaValle took gold and bronze in the 400. Mack Robinson was the silver medalist in the 200. Cornelius Johnson and David Albritton finished first and second in the high jump. The dominant performances of African-American athletes at the 1936 Olympics made a mockery of Hitler's doctrine of Aryan supremacy.

Following World War II, African-American females made their marks in Olympic competition as well. Alice Coachman, high-jump winner at London in 1948, was the first black female to win a gold medal. Wilma Rudolph emerged in 1960 as America's preeminent female track star, winning three gold medals at Rome. She was followed by Wyomia Tyus, who won gold medals in 1964 and 1968.

The London Olympics also brought new African-American male faces to the international stage. Harrison Dillard, national 110-meters hurdles champion in 1946 and 1947, won the 100 meters in 1948 and returned in 1952 to win a gold medal in the 110-meter high hurdles. Also at the 1952 Helsinki games, another national hurdles champion, eighteen-year-old Milt Campbell, displayed his talent in the decathlon with a second-place finish to two-time gold medalist Bob Mathias. Four years later, at the Melbourne Games, Campbell became the first African American to win the decathlon. Rafer Johnson, the 1956 runner-up, won the decathlon at the 1960 games in Rome, where Ralph Boston broke Jesse Owens's twenty-four-year-old long-jump record. Boston won six consecutive U.S. national AAU long jump titles in 1961–1966 but finished second at the 1964 Olympics in Tokyo and third at the 1968 games. In winning the 100 meters in Tokyo, Bob Hayes earned the moniker "World's Fastest Human."

Mexico City, host of the 1968 Olympic Games, served as a global platform upon which African Americans protested social conditions in the United States. The famed "black power" salute of Tommie Smith and John Carlos, gold and bronze medalists in the 200 meters, emanated from a proposed boycott of the games by black athletes. Both runners were dismissed from the team and sent home. The next day, Bob Beamon set a new world record in the long jump. Later in the competition, Lee Evans set a world record in the 400, Jimmie Hines set a new record in the 100, and the men's 4 x 400 and 4 x 100 relay teams raced to new Olympic records. In winning the 100 meters, Wyomia Tyus became the first athlete to win that event at two successive Olympics.

Emerging during the 1970s and 1980s were such superb athletes as Evelyn Ashford, Valerie Brisco-Hooks, Florence Griffith-Joyner, Jackie Joyner-Kersee, Edwin Moses, and Carl Lewis. Ashford competed but did not medal at Montreal in 1976; however, she came back to win gold in the 100 and 4 x 100 relay at Los Angeles in 1984. At the 1988 games, she finished second to Griffith-Joyner in the 100. Flo-Jo sparkled at Seoul with victories in the 100, 200, and 4 x 100 relay, and a second-place finish in the 4 x 400 relay. Her three gold medals equaled the feats of Wilma Rudolph in 1960 and of Valerie Brisco-Hooks in 1984. Joyner-Kersee won gold medals in the long jump and the seven-event heptathlon in 1988, and repeated as the heptathlon gold medalist in 1992. Joyner-Kersee, an all-round athlete, won a total of six Olympic medals, two long-jump world championships, and two heptathlon world titles. Edwin Moses won the 400-meter hurdles in Montreal and duplicated his victories at Los Angeles. He won 107 straight races and was named "Sportsman of the Year" in 1985. Carl Lewis duplicated Jesse Owens's feat of winning four Olympic gold medals (100, 200, 4 x 100, long jump) at the Los Angeles Olympic games. He won two more in 1988, another two in 1992, and one in 1996, giving him a record-tying nine Olympic gold medals for his career.

The marathon has always been part of the modern Olympics Games, but in the last quarter of the twentieth century, marathon and middle distance running became quite popular in cities and communities across the United States and around the world. Initially, Finns, followed by Swedes and Australians, dominated these competitions, but in the last forty years runners from Africa, particularly Kenya and Ethiopia, became most prominent. The success of African runners has dispelled the myth that black athletes lack the drive and perseverance to compete effectively at long and middle distances.

Coaches often play significant roles in an athletes' success. Some of the more influential track and field coaches were Cleve Abbott, Nell Jackson, Dr. LeRoy Walker, Ed Temple, and Stan Wright. Abbott coached at Tuskegee for twenty years, guiding his teams to fourteen national outdoor titles. He coached Olympians Alice Coachman, Mildred McDaniel, and Nell Jackson. Following her career as an athlete, Jackson coached at Tuskegee, Illinois State, Illinois, and Michigan State. She coached the women's Olympic team in 1956 (becoming the first African American to coach a U.S. Olympic team) and again in 1972. Dr. Walker, long-time track coach and later chancellor at North Carolina Central University, was the first African American to coach a men's Olympic track and field squad, in 1976. He held administrative posts in the AAU and the Athletics Congress (forerunner of USATF) and served as president of the U.S. Olympic Committee. Temple, in his long career coaching the Tennessee State Tigerbelles, developed Wilma Rudolph, Mae Faggs, Wyomia Tyus, Edith McGuire, and Madeline Manning-Mims. His athletes won thirty-four national team titles and twenty-three Olympic medals, thirteen of which were gold. He coached the U.S. women's team at the Olympics and the Pan American Games twice. Stan Wright coached at Texas Southern, Western Illinois, and California State University at Sacramento. He was an assistant coacha for the 1968 and 1972 Olympic teams, and served the U.S. Olympic Committee and the Athletics Congress in various capacities.

Track and field was the earliest sporting venue in which African Americans could demonstrate their physical talent and athletic prowess. On the track, in the jumping pit, or inside throwing rings, they competed on equal footing with their opponents. Here they were evaluated by the stopwatch and measuring tape, not the color of their skin. Unfortunately, what solace they found in track and field did not transcend its boundaries to reach mainstream society. Frustrated, repudiated, and exploited, African-American athletes used the only vehicle they had—the megaphone of sport—to express the sentiment of their people, as they did at Mexico City in 1968. While track and field was never intended to create social justice, indirectly it has contributed to that goal.

J. Thomas Jable

See also: Civil Rights; Olympic Games; Racial Theories; Women.

FURTHER READING
Bale, John. "Track and Field, Running and Hurdling." In *Encyclopedia of World Sport, from Ancient Times to the Present*, vol. III, edited by D. Levinson and K. Christensen. Santa Barbara: ABC Clio, 1996, 1056–62.
Tricard, Louise Mead. *American Women's Track and Field, A History, 1895 through 1980*. Jefferson, NC: McFarland, 1996.
USA Track and Field (www.usatf.org).

Emlen TUNNELL

Born March 29, 1925, Bryn Mawr, Pennsylvania
Died July 22, 1975, Pleasantville, New York
Football player

A graduate of Radnor, PA, High School, Tunnell attended the University of Toledo before graduating from the University of Iowa in 1948. He is best known as one of the first African Americans to reintegrate the National Football League (NFL) as a player and coach. His fourteen-year NFL playing career began with the New York Giants in 1948 and ended with the Green Bay Packers in 1961.

Tunnell did not have a significant college athletic career, because of injuries. He played parts of seasons at the University of Toledo and the University of Iowa, sandwiched around a tour of duty in the U.S. Coast Guard. Undrafted by any team, he had to talk the Giants into giving him a tryout.

Tunnell made the team and became the first African American to play for the Giants. He was an immediate success as a defensive back and kick returner. In eleven seasons he helped lead the Giants to a conference championship in 1958 and an NFL championship in 1956. Tunnell was named to the All-Pro team in 1951, 1952, 1955, and 1956. Tunnell left the Giants in 1959 to move with Vince Lombardi, his former defensive coach, to the Green Bay Packers. The Packers won a division championship in 1960 and an NFL championship in 1961.

The following year, Tunnell rejoined the Giants as the NFL's first African American assistant coach. In 1967 he was the first African American, and first defensive specialist, elected to the Pro Football Hall of Fame.

C. Robert Barnett

FURTHER READING
Carroll, Bob et al., eds. *Total Football: The Official Encyclopedia of the National Football League*. New York: HarperCollins, 1999.
Eskenazi, Gerald. *There Were Giants in Those Days*. New York: Grosset and Dunlap, 1976.
Izenberg, Jerry. *New York Giants: Seventy-Five Years*. New York: Time Life Books, 1999.
Porter, David L., ed. *The Biographical Dictionary of American Sports: Football*. Westport, CT: Greenwood Press, 1987.
Pro Football Hall of Fame. "Emlen Tunnell" (www.profootballhof.com)
Riffenburgh, Beau. *The Official NFL Encyclopedia*. New York: New American Library, 1986.

★ ★ ★

Mike TYSON

Born June 30, 1966, Brooklyn, New York
Boxer

Tyson grew up in Brooklyn, New York, with his mother and two siblings. At age twelve he was sent to a juvenile offenders school, where he met former boxer Bobby Stewart. Stewart rewarded Tyson's academic improvements with boxing lessons. During this time, Tyson was introduced to

Heavyweight boxer Mike Tyson talking with reporters following a training session in preparation for his upcoming fight against Bruce Seldon at the MGM Grand Garden Arena in Las Vegas. *(AP/Wide World Photos)*

Constantine "Cus" D'Amato, the legendary trainer. D'Amato took custody of Tyson and began training him at a small gym in Catskill, New York. After the death of Tyson's mother, D'Amato became Tyson's legal guardian and boxing manager.

Tyson had a short but impressive amateur career—he was the 1984 National Golden Gloves heavyweight champion. Tyson turned professional in 1985 after losing in the U.S. Olympic tournament. He won his first professional fight with a first-round knockout; he was to score first-round knockouts against eleven of his first fifteen professional opponents. In 1986, Tyson became the youngest heavyweight champion, by defeating Trevor Berbick with a second-round knockout. In 1987, he earned the undisputed heavyweight championship title, which he held until 1990, when James "Buster" Douglas handed him his first loss as a professional. In 1992 Tyson was convicted of rape. In 1995, after serving his prison term, he mounted a comeback for the heavyweight championship. He regained the World Boxing Association and World Boxing Council titles in 1996. He lost the championship to Evander Holyfield later that year. Tyson gained infamy by biting Holyfield's ear in a 1997 rematch.

Clay E. Harshaw

See also: Boxing.

FURTHER READING

Ashe, Arthur R., Jr. *A Hard Road to Glory: A History of the African-American Athlete Since 1946.* New York: Warner Books, 1988.

Myler, Patrick. *A Century of Boxing Greats: Inside the Ring with the Hundred Best Boxers.* New York: Robson/Parkwest, 1998.

Porter, David L., ed. *Biographical Dictionary of American Sports: 1989–1992 Supplement for Baseball, Football, Basketball, and Other Sports.* Westport, CT: Greenwood Press, 1992.

Sugden, John. *Boxing and Society: An International Analysis.* Manchester, UK: Manchester University Press, 1996.

★ ★ ★

Wyomia TYUS

Born August 29, 1945, Griffin, Georgia
Sprinter

The youngest of four children, Tyus was raised in a highly competitive atmosphere, with three sports-minded elder brothers. Her father (Willy) was a dairy farmer, and her mother (Maria) was a laundress.

In high school Tyus was a standout performer in basketball and in track and field. In 1962 she won the 100-yard dash at the Amateur Athletic Union Championship in Los Angeles, California. In the fall of 1963 she enrolled at Tennessee State University and became a member of Coach Ed Temple's celebrated Tigerbelles.

At the 1964 Tokyo Olympics the nineteen-year-old Tyus was the unheralded member of the U.S. women's sprint trio. She had never beaten Edith McGuire—also a Tennessee Tigerbelle and a U.S. Olympian—in either high school or college. At Tokyo, however, Tyus had an electrifying start and won by a wide margin. In the 4 x 100-meter relay (42.8 seconds), she earned a silver medal. Her Mexico 100-meter run of eleven seconds set a world record. She won a total of eight National AAU titles, five of them outdoors. In 1969 Tyus married Art Simberg, a representative for Puma, a German sport equipment manufacturer, and joined the ranks of the ill-fated Professional International Track Association. Despite her success—she was undefeated over sixty yards—the circuit folded, and her financial returns were meager.

The mother of two children (Simone and Tyus), Tyus was elected to the National Track and Field Hall of Fame in 1980, the Women's Sports Foundation: International Sports Hall of Fame in 1981, and the U.S.

Tennessee State's Wyomia Tyus breaks the tape in capturing the 100-yard dash at the 1963 National A.A.U. Women's Track and Field meet in Dayton, Ohio. *(AP/Wide World Photos)*

Olympic Hall of Fame in 1985. In her post-track career she is a motivational speaker.

Scott A.G.M. Crawford

See also: Ed Temple; Track and Field.

FURTHER READING

Kirsch, George B. "Wyomia Tyus." In *Encyclopedia of Ethnicity and Sports in the United States*, edited by George Kirsch, Othello Harris, and Claire E. Nolte. Westport, CT: Greenwood Press, 2000.

Layden, Joe. *Women in Sports*. Santa Monica, CA: General, 1997.

Oglesby, Carole A., et al., eds. *Encyclopedia of Women and Sports in America*. Phoenix, AZ: Oryx, 1998.

Porter, David L., ed. *African American Sports Greats: A Biographical Dictionary*. Westport, CT: Greenwood Press, 1995.

Sherrow, Victoria. *Encyclopedia of Women and Sports*. Santa Barbara, CA: ABC-CLIO, 1996.

UNITED GOLFERS ASSOCIATION

Founded in 1926, the United Golfers Association (UGA) was the first national organization for African-American golfers. Known as the United States Colored Golfers Association until 1929, the UGA sponsored a yearly National Open tournament for black golfers, who were denied entrance into events sponsored by such all-white organizations as the amateur United States Golf Association (USGA) and the Professional Golfers Association (PGA). The UGA nurtured and supported African-American golfers during the Jim Crow era until the white golfing establishment finally welcomed black athletes in the 1950s and 1960s.

The UGA's birth in the mid-1920s united disparate supporters of the African-American game. Dr. George Grant, of Washington, DC, the organization's first president, and Robert Hawkins, who built Mapledale Country Club in Stow, Massachusetts, the site of the inaugural championship and one of the first black-owned courses in the country, were two of the UGA's important early leaders.

The association's championship, which awarded men's and women's titles, quickly proved successful and became African-American golf's marquee event, attracting the best black players from around the country. Pioneering golfers like Robert "Pat" Ball from Chicago and Howard Wheeler from Los Angeles became celebrities in the black community for repeatedly winning the UGA championship in the 1930s and 1940s.

Increasingly ignored by white golfers, African Americans built parallel structures of their own, hosting numerous UGA-sponsored tournaments at municipal golf courses across the country. In 1938, the UGA began publication of the magazine *United Golfer* to chronicle and champion the accomplishments of its members.

From 1942 to 1945, the UGA suspended its championship tournament, but a new generation of golfers came to dominate the organization after the war. Between 1949 and 1959, Ted Rhodes and Charlie Sifford combined to win every UGA National Open title. The success of black golfers, however, brought increasing pressure on golf's white establishment to end its segregationist stance. Finally, in 1961, the PGA rescinded its infamous "Caucasian clause," eliminating one of the last formal barriers to black competition.

As African Americans became more welcome on white golf courses and in country clubs around the nation, the UGA struggled to survive; the organization hosted its final National Open championship in 1976. Nevertheless, the UGA had provided a much-needed sanctuary in which black golfers could hone their skills while they struggled to overcome white America's segregationist policies.

Gregory Bond

See also: Golf.

FURTHER READING
Ashe, Arthur R., Jr. *A Hard Road to Glory: A History of the African-American Athlete, 1919–1945*. New York: Amistad, 1988.
Dawkins, Marvin P., and Graham Kinloch. *African-American Golfers During the Jim Crow Era*. Westport, CT: Praeger, 2000.
Kennedy, John H. *A Course of Their Own: A History of African American Golfers*. Kansas City, MO: Stark Books, 2000.
Robinson, Lenwood, Jr. *Skins and Grins: The Plight of the Black American Golfer*. Chicago: Chicago Spectrum Press, 1997.
Sinnette, Calvin H. *Forbidden Fairways: African-*

Americans and the Game of Golf. Chelsea, MI: Sleeping Bear Press, 1998.

★ ★ ★

Wes UNSELD

Born March 14, 1946, Louisville, Kentucky
Basketball player, coach, and executive

Wes Unseld's father, Charles Unseld, worked two jobs, as a construction worker and an oiler for International Harvester. He had been a prizefighter and played basketball with the Indianapolis Clowns (predecessors of the Harlem Globetrotters). A graduate of Seneca High School and the University of Louisville, Wes Unseld has spent his career as a professional basketball player and coach of the Baltimore/Washington Bullets, and executive vice president and general manager of the Washington Wizards, as the Bullets are now known.

In high school, Unseld was a four-year letter winner and an All-State (1963, 1964), All-Conference (1963, 1964, 1965), All-District (1963, 1964, 1965), and All-Regional selection (1963, 1964). He was selected number two in the 1968 NBA draft by the Baltimore Bullets. With the Bullets he ranked seventh on the league's all-time rebounding list; is one of a handful of players to have tallied at least 10,000 points and 10,000 rebounds for a career; and played 984 games for the Bullets, more than any other player in franchise history. His total of 13,769 boards tops the franchise career list, and his 3,822 assists is a Bullets record. He was the league's MVP and Rookie of the Year in 1968–1969, and a five-time NBA All-Star (1969, 1971–1973, 1975). He captained the Baltimore and Washington Bullets to four NBA finals appearances in the 1970s and to a championship in 1977–1978.

After retiring in 1980, Unseld moved into the front office as executive vice president of the Bullets (now Wizards) and later became executive president of the organization, primarily planning for and selling the proposed MCI Center. Unseld has been with the Bullets/Wizards for twenty-eight years. He coached the team for seven seasons in the late 1980s and early 1990s.

Away from basketball, Unseld has been involved in elementary education. He provided the financial backing for his wife to open a private elementary school near the city, which serves 175 children from preschool through the fifth grades. In 1975, Unseld received the NBA's first J. Walter Kennedy Citizenship Award for his contributions to the community. He was elected to the Basketball Hall of Fame in 1987 and in 1996 was named to the NBA Fiftieth Anniversary All-Time Team. Unseld has been head of Capital Center Charities, a volunteer at Kernan Hospital, and a member of the board of trustees, Mt. St. Mary's College.

Doris R. Corbett

FURTHER READING
Harris, Merv. *The Lonely Heroes: Professional Basketball's Great Centers*. New York: Viking Press, 1975.
———, ed. *On Court with the Superstars of the NBA*. New York: Viking Press, 1973.
National Basketball Association (www.nba.com).
New York Times, December 21, 1994; November 12, 1995.
Washington Wizards (www.washingtonwizards.com).

★ ★ ★

Gene UPSHAW

Born August 15, 1945, Robstown, Texas
Football player and executive

Gene Upshaw's mother, Cora, was a domestic, and his father, Eugene, Sr., worked for a local oil company. As a youngster,

Upshaw and his three younger brothers picked cotton to earn money and contribute to the family coffers. He excelled in academics and as a pitcher on the baseball team at Robstown High School. After graduation from high school he enrolled at nearby Texas A & M University. Upshaw tried out for the football team in hopes of winning an athletic scholarship to pay his tuition. By his senior year he had grown to six feet, five inches, weighed 265 pounds, and had garnered national acclaim as an offensive lineman.

The Oakland Raiders drafted Upshaw in the first round in 1967, and he started as an offensive guard for the team until his retirement in 1982. Upshaw played in ten AFC title games, three Super Bowls, and six Pro Bowls. Deemed a master lead-blocker on the sweep and "one of the best linemen to ever play" the game, he was selected AFC Lineman of the Year in 1973, 1974, and 1977 and NFL Lineman of the Year in 1977. Upshaw was inducted into the Professional Football Hall of Fame in 1987. His accomplishments off the field helped change professional football and the role of the athlete. From 1970 to 1976 he served as union representative for the Raiders' players and as president and executive director of the National Football League Players' Association since 1980. He was at the forefront of the players' strike in 1982. In addition, Upshaw was elected to the Executive Council of the AFL-CIO in 1985; he was one of the chief architects of the 1993 agreement between NFL players and owners that ushered in the era of limited free agency and the multimillion-dollar contract in pro football. Included among his many accolades for distinguished community service and labor leadership is the Byron "Whizzer" White Humanitarian Award in 1980 and the A. Philip Randolph Award in 1982.

Donald Spivey and Logan Bailey-Perkins

FURTHER READING
Hall of Fame Raiders, Oakland Raiders Publicity Office, Oakland, CA, 2001.
Pro Football Hall of Fame—Enshrinees, Professional Football Hall of Fame, Canton, OH, 1987.

VOLLEYBALL

The 1977 women's volleyball team at Tuskegee Institute (now Tuskegee University) became the first predominately black college volleyball team to win an AIAW-sanctioned state title in 1977, defeating the University of Montevallo. In the 1980s dominant women's black volleyball teams also came out of Howard University and St. Augustine. Three black members of the 1984 Olympic squad earned silver medals by defeating China. Flo Hyman (top hitter at the 1981 World Cup Tournament), Rita Crockett (named All-World in 1982 and member of the defunct 1980 Olympic team), and Rose Magers trained under Coach Ariel Selinger.

Hyman was an All-American volleyball player at the University of Houston from 1974 through 1976. At six feet, five inches, she left school in 1976 to concentrate on playing for the U.S. national team. She helped lead the team to a silver medal in 1984, the highest finish ever for an American women's national team. She was voted best hitter at the World Cup Games in Tokyo in 1981 and became the first American woman to be named to the All-World Cup team. Her coach, Arie Selinger, called her "a leader on the court," adding, "If Flo plays well, the team follows." In 1986, Hyman was playing professionally in Japan when she collapsed on the bench and died of Marfan's syndrome, a congenital defect of the aorta. Since 1987, the Women's Sports Foundation has presented an annual Flo Hyman Award to the woman athlete who, in the course of her career, has exemplified Hyman's "dignity, spirit and commitment to excellence."

Rose Magers, Hyman's teammate, attended the University of Houston, earning such awards as Most Improved, Best Spiker, and Most Valuable Player in the conference. Besides being a member of the 1984 silver medal-winning Olympic volleyball team (the highest-finishing women's team in U.S. history) she played nine years in Japan (1984–1993) as a professional player/coach. During this time she was three-time MVP, six-time best spiker, one-time best blocker and six-time post point-maker in the league. Before accepting the head coaching position at Martin Methodist College, she coached at Lee High School in Huntsville for four years. She compiled a record of 10–50 and was ranked in the top ten in the state. In her first year at Martin Methodist College, she was voted the 1996 TransSouth Conference Coach of the Year.

Rose Magers-Powell has founded Rocket City Volleyball Club (RCVC). Under her guidance, RCVC has won approximately twenty regional tournaments, five district championships, and four regional championships; she has sent five teams to the national tournament. During the summer Rose conducts camps all over the United States. She also coaches and assists in the Junior Olympic Program at the Olympic Center in Colorado Springs, Colorado.

A star of the 1988 Seoul Games was Prikeba (Keba) Phipps, who was also instrumental in the Women's World Championship of 2002. In those games, the U.S. team beat Germany 3–0 (28–26, 25–20, 27–25), duration 1:22, on September 8, 2002, extending its winning streak to eight matches and qualifying for the quarterfinals. Phipps had fifteen points, making her the best scorer of the match. The United States made it to the finals for the first time in a major world tournament since the 1984 Los Angeles Olympic Games. In the finals the United States competed against Italy, but without Phipps, who had scored twenty points against Russia. She had suffered an eye injury during training the day before, and the decision had been made not to play her. "It was the right decision, but naturally she was missed," explained her coach Toshiaki Yoshida.

As these black role models and mentors continue to emerge on the volleyball scene, so will new talent. Volleyball continues to grow as a sport and the future looks bright for black participants.

Brenda P. Wiggins

FURTHER READING
Ashe, Arthur R., Jr. *A Hard Road to Glory: A History of the African-American Athlete Since 1946*. Vol. 3. New York: Amistad, 1993.
Hickok Sports. 2003. "Hyman, 'Flo' (Flora)" (www.hickoksports.com/biograph/hymanflo.shtml).
Women's World Championship 2002 Press Information. 2002 (www.fivb.ch/EN/Volleyball/Competitions/WorldChampionships/women/2002/Press/match078.asp).

WAKE-ROBIN GOLF CLUB

The Wake-Robin Golf Club was the first organization consisting of African-American women golfers. Established in 1937 in Washington, DC, and still in existence today, the club has sponsored annual tournaments, organized a junior golf program, and served as an inspiration to African-American women golfers across the country. At least four of its members have been elected to the United Golfers Association Hall of Fame, and the club's membership has steadily risen. Like other parallel institutions in the African-American community, the club has been a source of great pride, provided a refuge for blacks in a sometimes hostile racial environment, and served as a symbol of possibility and achievement.

David K. Wiggins

See also: Golf.

FURTHER READING
Dawkins, Marvin P., and Graham Kinloch. *African American Golfers During the Jim Crow Era*. Westport, CT: Greenwood Press, 2000.
McDaniel, Pete. *Uneven Lies: The Heroic Story of African Americans in Golf*. Greenwich, CT: American Golfer, 2000.
Sinnette, Calvin H. *Forbidden Fairways: African Americans and the Game of Golf*. Chelsea, MI: Sleeping Bear, 1998.

★ ★ ★

Boxer Joe Walcott smiling for the cameras at his Hamden, New Jersey training quarters prior to his 1947 heavyweight title fight against Joe Louis. *(Sports Archive)*

Joe WALCOTT

Born January 31, 1914, Merchantville, New Jersey
Died February 25, 1994, Camden, New Jersey
Boxer

Walcott, born Arnold Raymond Cream, took the ring name of his boxing idol, Joe

Walcott, a welterweight champion from Barbados. "Jersey" Joe turned pro in 1930, at the age of sixteen. Because the results of his early fights were never recorded, it is impossible to determine his overall record. Nevertheless, Walcott achieved boxing fame as, at thirty-seven, the oldest man to win the heavyweight championship with a seventh-round knockout of Ezzard Charles on July 18, 1951.

Walcott's knockout of Charles stands as a testament to talent and sheer determination. During his early days, he had been a club fighter of no distinction. In 1944, Walcott's career was at a standstill. Married with a wife and six children and little means of supporting them, Walcott returned to the ring with a vengeance in 1945. The wins came his way, including two out of three over future light-heavyweight champion Joey Maxim.

His most noteworthy fights came against Joe Louis in 1947, Charles in 1951, and Rocky Marciano in 1952, all heavyweight title fights. He knocked Louis down twice but lost a split decision. He became the champion with his win over Charles, but he lost the title in a thirteenth-round knockout by Marciano. Regarded as an artist in the ring, Walcott was ahead on points when the younger, stronger Marciano caught him with a right.

Following his retirement, Walcott became a Camden County sheriff and, in the early 1980s, chairman of the New Jersey State Athletic Commission. His chairmanship ended when he was charged with taking bribes from undercover FBI agents. He was inducted into the International Boxing Hall of Fame in 1990.

Dennis Gildea

See also: Boxing; Charles Ezzard.

FURTHER READING
Matthews, Wallace. "Sports Notes." *Newsday*, February 27, 1994, 18.
Mead, Chris. *Champion: Joe Louis, Black Hero in White America*. New York: Penguin Books, 1985.
Mee, Bob. "Obituary: Jersey Joe Walcott." *London Independent*, February 28, 1994.
Rodda, John. "Craftsman of the Ring." *London Guardian*, March 1, 1994.

★ ★ ★

Herschel WALKER

Born March 3, 1962, Wrightsville, Georgia
Football player

Following a brilliant career at the University of Georgia, Walker became the second-leading rusher in professional football (USFL and NFL) history.

One of seven children of Willis and Christine Walker, a seamstress, Herschel played football at Johnson County High School, where he rushed for over three thousand yards as a senior. At the University of Georgia, the six-foot one-inch, 222-pound running back amassed over 5,000 yards rushing, a NCAA record for three seasons. He led the Bulldogs to three straight conference championships and the 1980 National Championship, setting eleven NCAA records. He was named All-American in 1980–1982 and College Football Player of the Year during his junior year, when he won the Heisman Trophy.

Walker left school early (1983) and became the first "bonus baby" to sign a contract with the New Jersey Generals of the new United States Football League, subsequently amassing more than 7,000 total yards over three seasons. He returned to Georgia in the off-season to complete a degree in criminal justice in 1984. When the USFL suspended operations in 1986, Walker signed with the NFL Dallas Cowboys, who had drafted him in 1985. He played in Pro Bowls during the 1987 and 1988 seasons. Although popular with Dallas fans, he was traded in 1989. He then played with several NFL clubs over the next decade: the Minnesota Vikings (until 1992), Philadelphia Eagles (until 1995), and New York Giants (until 1996). At age thirty-six, Herschel returned to the Cowboys but was used sparingly. He finished his pro career with over 18,000 all-purpose yards. Walker was inducted into the College Hall of Fame in 1999. In retirement, he took up bobsledding and finished seventh in the two-man sled in the 1988 Calgary Winter Olympics. Walker enjoyed a short stint as a country music singer in 1997.

Walker lives in the Dallas area with his wife Cindy and their son, Christian. He manufactures his own sport drink and is spokesman for a beverage company. He works with children, is active in the Arthritis Association's "Joints in Motion Program," and plays in celebrity golf tournaments for charity.

Steven J. Overman

FURTHER READING

Benaugh, Jim. *Sports Great Herschel Walker.* Berkeley Heights, NJ: Enslow, 1990.
Coyne, Tom. "Herschel Walker Leads List of Inductees." *Detroit News* (www.detnews.com), August 11, 2000.
Grossman, Gerald H. "The Great Herschel Walker." *Encore* 10 (January 1982): 46–47.
Prugh, Jeff. *The Herschel Walker Story: From the Georgia Backwoods to the Heisman Trophy to the Pros.* New York: Random House, 1983.
Sporting News (www.sportingnews.com/nfl/players).

★ ★ ★

Leroy WALKER

Born June 14, 1918, Atlanta, Georgia
Track and field coach, sports administrator

He was born the youngest of thirteen children to Mary and Willie Walker. His father, a railroad worker, died when Leroy was a young boy. Soon he moved to New York City to live with an older brother; his mother, however, remained the dominant influence in his life. A good student and athlete, he accepted an athletic scholarship in 1936 to Benedict College in Columbia, South Carolina. He received a master's degree in physical education in 1941 and in 1957 earned a Ph.D. degree from New York University. He married Katherine McDowell in 1938, and together they raised three children. She died unexpectedly in 1978.

Walker's professional career began in 1941 at Benedict College as chairman of the Department of Physical Education and coach of basketball, football, and track and field. From 1942 to 1945 he held similar posts at Bishop College and Prairie View Agricultural and Mechanical College, both in Texas. In 1945 he began a forty-one-year association with North Carolina College (now North Carolina Central University) in Durham. For several years he served as chairman of the physical education department and coached basketball, football, and track and field. From 1974 to 1983 he served as vice chancellor for university relations and as chancellor from 1983 until his retirement in 1986.

It was through track that he established his athletic coaching and administration legacy. A number of his athletes competed in the Olympic Games beginning in 1956. Walker served as a coach or consultant for several foreign Olympic teams and in 1976 was the first African American to serve as U.S. men's head coach. From 1973 through the 1990s he held a number of significant administrative posts in track and field, education, and the Olympic movement. He was the first African American to serve as president of the American Alliance for Health, Physical Education, Recreation, and Dance, in 1977–1978, and as president of the U.S. Olympic Committee, 1992–1996. He holds honorary doctorates from sixteen colleges and universities as well as numerous awards in athletics and higher education.

Richard A. Swanson

See also: Track and Field.

FURTHER READING
Gaddy, Charles. *An Olympic Journey: The Saga of an American Hero—LeRoy T. Walker.* Glendale, CA: Griffin, 1998.
Smith, Jessie Carney. *Notable Black American Men.* Detroit: Gale, 1999.
Who's Who Among African Americans, 1996–97. Detroit: Gale, 1996.

★ ★ ★

Mel WALKER

Born April 27, 1914, Toledo, Ohio
High jumper

Walker attended Libbey High School in Toledo, Ohio. While at Libbey he won a state championship in the high jump. Upon graduation he entered Ohio State University (OSU) and became a close friend and teammate of Jesse Owens. Walker shared the 1936 NCAA title in the high jump with his OSU teammate Dave Albritton. At the 1936 Olympic Trials, a drainage ditch obstructed Walker's unique approach to the high jump pit. His altered approach proved unsuccessful, and he did not qualify. In 1937, Walker set the world record with a mark of 6 feet 10¼ inches on his third attempt in Malmö, Sweden. In 1938, he again shared a title with Albritton at the AAU championships. During his collegiate career, Walker won three Big Ten events, won or tied for first in five AAU outdoor championships, and won or tied for first in three AAU indoor championships.

For his outstanding athletic achievements at OSU, Walker was awarded the Golden Shoe Award in 1936. He was inducted into the OSU Athletic Hall of Fame in 1981 and the Ohio Track and Field Hall of Fame in 1987.

Clay E. Harshaw

FURTHER READING
Ashe, Arthur R., Jr. *A Hard Road to Glory: A History of the African-American Athlete, 1919–1945.* New York: Warner Books, 1988.
Baker, William J. *Jesse Owens: An American Life.* New York: Free Press. 1986.
Lawson, G. *World Record Breakers in Track and Field Athletics.* Champaign, IL: Human Kinetics, 1997.
Ohio Association of Track and Cross Country Coaches. "Hall of Fame" (www.oatccc.com).
Pollard, James. *Ohio State Athletics: 1879–1959.* Columbus: Ohio State University Athletic Department, 1959.
"Walker, Melvin Eugene" (www.weltrekordler.de/hj08statistik.htm).

★ ★ ★

Moses Fleetwood WALKER

Born October 7, 1857, Mt. Pleasant, Ohio
Died May 11, 1924, Steubenville, Ohio
Baseball player

Moses Walker was one of seven children born to Moses W. and Caroline O'Hara Walker. His father was a cooper (barrel maker) and later became a relatively affluent physician and, finally, a Methodist Episcopal minister. His mother was a homemaker. "Fleet," as he was called in his home, graduated from Steubenville High School and enrolled in Oberlin College's preparatory program for one year before matriculating in 1878 at the college, where he remained for three years. He briefly attended the University of Michigan in 1882 and 1883. Walker played professional baseball from 1883 through mid-1889. He would go on to be a postal employee, inventor, and entrepreneur.

At Oberlin College Walker played on the

In 1884 Moses Fleetwood Walker made history by playing with the Toledo Club of the American Association to become the first African American in Major League Baseball. Following his career in baseball, Walker would become a successful businessman and write a book *Our Home Colony*, in which he encouraged his fellow African Americans to leave the United States. (National Baseball Hall of Fame Library, Cooperstown, NY)

first varsity baseball team in 1881. The next two years he and his brother, Weldy, played for the University of Michigan but left prior to completing their degrees.

Walker played his first full season of professional baseball in 1883 for Toledo, in the Northwestern League. Toledo moved into the American Association in 1884, and Walker thus became the first African-American major league player. A talented barehanded catcher, he faced racism from some teammates, opponents, and umpires on the field and endured racial prejudice from opposing fans and at dining and lodging establishments. His baseball career ended with stints in Cleveland (Western League, 1885–1886), Newark (1887), and Syracuse (1888–1889), both in the International League. He was the last black player in that league until Jackie Robinson in 1946.

Richard A. Swanson

See also: Baseball; Civil Rights.

FURTHER READING
Carney Smith, Jessie. *Notable Black American Men*. Detroit: Gale, 1999.
Peterson, Robert. *Only the Ball Was White*. Englewood Cliffs, NJ: Prentice Hall, 1970.
Ribowsky, Mark. *A Complete History of the Negro Leagues: 1884–1955*. Secaucus, NJ: Carol, 1997.
Zang, David W. *Fleet Walker's Divided Heart*. Lincoln: University of Nebraska Press, 1995.

★ ★ ★

Charlie WARD

Born October 12, 1970, Thomasville, Georgia
Basketball player

Ward, a Heisman trophy winner in football, is one of the most versatile athletes in recent times. With opportunities in three professional sports, he chose a career in the National Basketball Association.

One of seven children of Charles, Sr., a high school teacher and coach, and Willard, a librarian, young Charlie suffered from a rare bone condition but recovered to excel in football, baseball, and basketball at Thomas County Central High School.

Following a season at Tallahassee Community College, Ward entered Florida State University in 1990. He played basketball and was named the Metro Conference's top point guard. He was "redshirted" for the 1990 football season before becoming the first African-American quarterback at FSU his senior year and leading the Seminoles to their first national championship and an Orange Bowl victory. Ward won several awards, including the 1993 Heisman Trophy. He earned a degree in therapeutic recreation in 1994.

Ward passed up opportunities to play professional baseball and football, instead signing with the NBA's New York Knicks, who had drafted him in the first round. He joined the Knicks for the 1994 season. The following season the six-foot, two-inch Ward appeared in sixty-plus games as a backup point guard. In 1997 he moved into the starting lineup for all eighty-two games. He was out three months with a fractured finger and knee injury during the 2000–2001 season. After undergoing arthroscopic surgery, he returned to the court. Ward routinely ranked high in assists in the NBA. He became known for his high-contact brand of basketball and his often-confrontational style off the court. In 1999 he criticized the league for allowing women sportswriters in locker rooms. His religious proselytizing would include remarks perceived as anti-Semitic, for which he later apologized.

Ward spends a great deal of time working with young African Americans in such organizations as the Police Athletic League and hosts basketball camps for inner-city children. He relaxes by playing in charity golf and tennis tournaments. He resides in Stamford, Connecticut with his wife, an attorney.

Steven J. Overman

FURTHER READING
Lupica, Mike. "Eyes on the Prize." *Esquire*, March 1994, 6.
Morrison, Alec. "A Winner Either Way." *Sports Illustrated* (sportsillustrated.cnn.com), October 22, 2000.
Murphy, Austin. "Twice Blessed." *Sports Illustrated*, October 5, 1992, 32ff.
NBA.com (www.nba.com).
Reilly, Rick. "A Gentleman and a Scholar." *Sports Illustrated*, December 27, 1993, 28ff.

Paul WARFIELD

Born November 28, 1942, Warren, Ohio
Football player

Born to Lena Dryden and Amelia Bell, Paul Warfield was a talented multisport athlete at Warren G. Harding High School in Warren, Ohio, and at Ohio State University. He would achieve enduring fame in the 1960s and 1970s as a pass receiver in the National Football League and briefly in the World Football League.

As a college athlete at Ohio State, Warfield earned All-American honors as a halfback, playing both offense and defense. He also excelled in track and field, competing as a broad jumper, hurdler, and sprinter. Drafted by the Cleveland Browns in 1964, he played wide receiver as a rookie on the Browns' 1964 championship team, catching fifty-two passes for 920 yards. Sidelined by a broken collar bone in 1965, he led the Browns in total pass yardage for the next four years. He played in two more NFL championship games for the Browns and was All-Pro for three of his five active years in Cleveland.

Traded to the Miami Dolphins in 1970, Warfield played on three Super Bowl teams, including the Dolphins' remarkable 1972 team, which compiled a perfect 17–0 record. In his five seasons with the Dolphins he enjoyed remarkably productive seasons, snaring 156 passes for 3,355 yards and thirty-three touchdowns. Following the 1974 season, the five-foot eleven-inch, 205-pound receiver played briefly for the Memphis Southmen in the ill-fated World Football League. He returned to Cleveland in 1976 and played there for two more seasons.

Warfield played in four Pro Bowls in his eleven healthy NFL seasons and was elected to the Pro Football Hall of Fame in 1983. He set an NFL record of 20.1 yards per catch on 427 pass receptions. With 9.6 speed over 100 yards, Warfield was a constant threat for breakaway receptions; if he had played in a modern spread formation, his statistics might have been even more formidable.

John S. Watterson

FURTHER READING
Clary, Jack. *Cleveland Browns*. New York: Macmillan, 1973.
Eckhouse, Morris. *Day by Day in the Cleveland Browns History*. New York: Leisure Press, 1984.
Neff, David S., et al., eds. *The Football Encyclopedia*. 2d ed. New York: St. Martin's Press, 1994.
Porter, David L., ed. *Biographical Dictionary of American Sports: Football*. Westport, CT: Greenwood Press, 1987.
Sporting News. "TSN Presents: Football's 100 Greatest Players" (www.sportingnews.com/nflc/100/60html).

★ ★ ★

Chester WASHINGTON

Born April 13, 1902, Pittsburgh, Pennsylvania
Died August 31, 1983, Inglewood, California
Newspaperman

Washington used his rapid typing ability to advance in journalism. After winning a typing contest at age fifteen, he became a legal secretary and copyboy for *Pittsburgh Courier* founder Robert L. Vann. He later graduated from Virginia Union College and rejoined the *Courier*. There, he served as a reporter, city editor, sports editor, corporate secretary, and West Coast Bureau chief. He selected athletes for the *Courier*'s black college All-American football team. He served as a secretary for heavyweight boxer Joe Louis and later ghostwrote his autobiography.

Washington later became the first black editorial employee of the *Los Angeles Mirror-News*, which was owned by the *Los Angeles Times*'s publisher, the Times-Mirror Company. While at the *Mirror-News*, he interviewed Fidel Castro in Havana and covered major court cases. He also became editor of the *Los Angeles Sentinel* and the owner of the Wave Community Newspapers. Wave became the nation's largest black-owned newspaper chain and was once listed on *Black Enterprise* magazine's list of the top 100 black-owned businesses.

Washington was known for his pleasant disposition and community activities. He served as chairman of the Los Angeles County Parks and Recreation Commission and worked on the board of the California Museum of Science and Industry. He received an honorary doctorate from Virginia Union, the Greater Los Angeles Press Club's best editorial award, and the National Newspaper Publishers Association's award for general excellence. A golf course in Los Angeles was named for him.

Michael Marsh

FURTHER READING
Buni, Andrew. *Robert L. Vann of the Pittsburgh Courier*. Pittsburgh: University of Pittsburgh Press, 1974.
Hernandez, Marita. "Pioneer Black Journalist Dies." *Los Angeles Times*, September 1, 1983.
McCormick, Shelton. "Wave's Chester Washington Eulogized." *Los Angeles Sentinel*, September 15, 1983.
Reisler, Jim. *Black Writers/Black Baseball: An Anthology of Articles from Black Sportswriters Who Covered the Negro Leagues*. Jefferson, NC: McFarland, 1993.

★ ★ ★

Gene WASHINGTON

Born November 23, 1944, LaPorte, Texas
Football player

Gene Washington was the son of Henry and Alberta Washington. At George Washington Carver High School in Baytown, Texas, Washington participated in baseball, basketball, football, and track and field. In

1964, he matriculated at Michigan State University (MSU). Washington was a fine hurdler while at MSU. He lettered in indoor and outdoor track and field in 1965, 1966, and 1967. He was co-captain of the track and field teams during his last two seasons. Nonetheless, Washington's most notable sports accomplishments at MSU would take place on the football field. Among other honors, the six-foot three-inch, 216-pound wide receiver was selected as an All-American in 1965 and 1966. Washington earned a B.S. degree in physical education and social science in 1967 and a master's degree in student personnel administration in 1972. In 1992, Washington was inducted into the MSU Athletic Hall of Fame.

In the 1967 National Football League draft, Washington was the first-round choice of the Minnesota Vikings. His career with the Vikings lasted through the 1972 season. Washington was a member of the Vikings team that played against the Kansas City Chiefs in Super Bowl IV. He was selected to the NFL's Pro Bowl in 1969 and 1970. Washington's playing career was cut short by a foot injury while he was a Denver Bronco in 1973. In 1970, Washington married Claudith Goudeau, a 1970 MSU graduate. They have three daughters, Lisa, Gina, and Maya.

Deane A. Lamont

FURTHER READING

Henderson, Ashyia N., ed. *Who's Who Among African Americans.* Detroit: Gale Group, 2000.

Porter, David L., ed. *Biographical Dictionary of American Sports: 1992–1995 Supplement for Baseball, Football, Basketball and Other Sports.* Westport, CT: Greenwood Press, 1995.

Who's Who in America, 2001. New Providence, NJ: Marquis Who's Who, 2001.

Kenny WASHINGTON

Born August 31, 1918, Los Angeles, California
Died June 24, 1971, Los Angeles, California
Football player

A graduate of Lincoln High School in Los Angeles, Kenny Washington entered UCLA, where he lettered in baseball, football, track, and boxing. He starred in football from 1937 to 1939 as a runner, passer, and punter. In 1938, he led the Pacific Coast League in scoring and was chosen for the All-Conference team. Washington led UCLA to a number-seven national ranking the following year. He finished the 1939 season with five UCLA records to his name, including the all-time rushing title. Washington led the nation in total offense in 1939 and earned several honors, including selection to the All-American team. He was also named the Southern California Athlete of the Year, and *Liberty* magazine judged him to be football's Back of the Year.

Upon graduation in 1940, Washington became a Los Angeles police officer and continued to play football for the Hollywood Bears (1940–1941, 1945) and the San Francisco Clippers (1944). He led the Pacific Coast Pro Football League in rushing, passing, and scoring before being chosen, along with UCLA teammate Woody Strode, to reintegrate the National Football League as a member of the Los Angeles Rams in 1946. Washington led the NFL in rushing average in 1947 but retired after the 1948 season to become a business executive and civic leader.

In addition to being named to the All-Time Pacific Coast Conference team, Kenny Washington was the first UCLA player ever chosen to the National Football Foundation College Football Hall of Fame.

Gerald R. Gems

See also: Woody Strode.

FURTHER READING

Ashe, Arthur R., Jr. *A Hard Road to Glory: Football.* New York: Amistad Press, 1988.

Kirsch, George, Othello Harris, and Claire B. Nolte, eds. *Encyclopedia of Ethnicity and Sports in the United States.* Westport, CT: Greenwood Press, 2000.

Maher, Tod, and Bob Gill, eds. *The Pro Football Encyclopedia.* New York: Macmillan, 1997.

Porter, David L., ed. *Biographical Dictionary of American Sports: Football.* Westport, CT: Greenwood Press, 1987.

★ ★ ★

Ora WASHINGTON

Born January 16, 1899, Philadelphia, Pennsylvania
Died May 1971, Philadelphia, Pennsylvania
Tennis player, basketball player

Ora Washington is considered one of the greatest female athletes of the twentieth century. Her accomplishments in basketball and tennis spanned the decades of the 1920s, 1930s, and 1940s.

Washington's entrance into sport occurred as a way to lessen the grief over the death of her sister. In 1924 Washington won her first national tennis championship, at Baltimore's Druid Hill Park. In addition to several state and regional tennis victories, Washington was the American Tennis Association's national champion from 1929 to 1935 and again in 1937. Segregationist policies and attitudes became evident when Washington challenged white tennis champion Helen Wills Moody, who declined all invitations for a match.

Washington's basketball accomplishments were impressive as well. In the 1920s she captained the Germantown, PA, YWCA Hornets, frequently leading all scorers with more than half of the team's total points. In the early 1930s she joined the *Philadelphia Tribune* squad and throughout the decade the team traveled to numerous states throughout the South and the Midwest. By the end of the 1934 season the team had won ninety-seven out of 109 games played against some of the best black colleges as well as community teams, both white and black.

Yet to be fully recognized, Washington's legacy as a working-class African-American woman is a very important one. Her outstanding athletic achievements over three decades are a testament to her perseverance and dedication. Following her athletic career Washington remained in Germantown, where she played a prominent role in teaching tennis to young boys and girls.

Rita Liberti

See also: Tennis.

FURTHER READING

Ashe, Arthur R., Jr. *A Hard Road To Glory: A History of the African-American Athlete, 1919–1945.* New York: Warner Books, 1988.

"Bennett Meets Eastern Squad." *Greensboro Record,* March 9, 1934.

"Girl Net Star Is Floor Hash." *Philadelphia Tribune,* March 28, 1931.

Young, A.S. "Doc." *Negro Firsts in Sports.* Chicago: Johnson, 1963.

★ ★ ★

Quincy WATTS

Born June 19, 1970, Detroit, Michigan
Sprinter

Quincy Watts is the son of Rufus Watts and Allitah Hunt Watts. At age four, he moved with his mother to Los Angeles, where he began competing in age-group track meets. He began training with renowned sprint coach John Smith while at Taft High School in Woodland Hills, California. He was California state high school champion in the 100 meters in 1987 and at 200 meters in both 1986 and 1987. He enrolled at the University of Southern California in 1988 and began concentrating on the 400 meters. Quickly moving to world class at that distance, he helped the United States win a silver medal at the 1991 World Championships, with a relay leg of 43.4 seconds, one of the fastest relay legs ever to that time.

Watts graduated from USC in 1992, winning the NCAA 400 meters in his senior year. At the 1992 Olympic Trials he finished third, although he lowered his personal best to 43.97 in the semifinals of that meet. At the 1992 Barcelona Olympic Games he won his semifinal heat in 43.71 to set a new Olympic record. He bettered that in the final, winning the gold medal in 43.50, the second-fastest time ever. Watts added a second gold medal as a member of the 4 x 400-meter relay team. Although Watts competed for several years after the 1992 Olympics, he never again reached those peaks. Difficulty with injuries and problems with weight gain eventually ended his track career.

Adam R. Hornbuckle

FURTHER READING
Hendershott, Jon. "The Man Called 'Q.'" *Track and Field News* 46 (March-April 1992): 52–54.
Johnson, Dave. "Another WR for Us." *Track and Field News* 45 (October 1992): 37.
Laney, Ruth. "Watts Nabs a Pair of Golds." *Track and Field News* 45 (October 1992): 19.

★ ★ ★

WEIGHTLIFTING AND BODYBUILDING

Although organized weightlifting and bodybuilding competitions extend back to the turn of the twentieth century, involvement of African Americans did not begin until the 1930s. Their participation was limited at first to Olympic weightlifting (press, snatch, and clean and jerk), but the success of West Indian blacks provided encouragement to their American counterparts to enter physique contests. Critical breakthroughs coinciding with the civil rights movement occurred in the 1960s. By the end of the century, African Americans had become a dominant force in the bodybuilding world.

The first notable figure was John Terry of New York City, who, under the guidance of Englishman Charles Ramsey and Bob Hoffman of York, Pennsylvania, won the national championships from 1938 to 1941 as a featherweight. He also set an unofficial world record of 535 pounds in the deadlift and was on the U.S. Olympic team in 1936. Far surpassing Terry, however, was John Davis of Brooklyn, who in 1938 won the world light-heavyweight title in Vienna at age seventeen and broke two world records in the process. After World War II he set many more records as a heavyweight and won five more world championships and Olympic gold medals in 1948 (London) and 1952 (Helsinki). Davis was the first black to win an Olympic weightlifting title and the only American of his race to become both an Olympic and world champion. Though often overshadowed by Davis, the achievements of Jim Bradford were hardly insignificant. He won silver medals at the 1952 Helsinki and 1960 Rome Olympics and four world championships (1951, 1954, 1955, and 1959), garnering valuable team points for the United States.

That few significant black bodybuilders had emerged by this time may be attributed to the relative lack of physique competitions before 1939 and the perception that subjective standards of judging would discriminate against blacks. Indeed Davis, who possessed a fine build, stated that he would never enter a Mr. America contest sponsored by the Amateur Athletic

Union because "a negro cannot win." Still, in 1941 he was the first African American to appear on the cover of a major bodybuilding magazine. A demonstration of Davis's prophecy was provided by Melvin Wells of Buffalo, whose size and muscularity, especially in the arms and upper back, seemed unparalleled. Yet Wells could win only the Most Muscular Man award at Mr. America contests in 1949 and 1950. Though never outspoken, he strongly suspected racial prejudice as the reason for his not winning the overall title. Likewise George Paine of New York (1953 and 1954) and Arthur Harris of Atlanta (1956 and 1959), though possessing superlative physiques, had to settle for Most Muscular Man titles. However much racial prejudice may have been a factor in these decisions, however, other criteria, such as symmetry, presentation, character, and athleticism, were collectively more important than sheer muscularity in the selection of a Mr. America.

Meanwhile, Caribbean men of color, such as Paine and Enrico Tomas, were winning Mr. Universe titles in London and inspiring greater numbers of African Americans to enter competitions, thereby challenging the nonphysical standards that were applied to both Mr. and Miss America contests in the 1950s. It was Harold Poole, an exceptionally developed strength athlete from Indianapolis, who rebelled against the AAU establishment. Named Most Muscular Man twice but failing to win the Mr. America title after four tries, Poole rudely walked off the stage at the 1963 event. Two weeks later he smashed his second-place trophy to bits at the Teenage Mr. America contest. Similarly when Cuban-born Sergio Oliva of Chicago, later dubbed "the Myth," could fare no better than two Most Muscular awards in 1965 and 1966, he suspected racism. "The A.A.U. guys who don't know the Civil War is over, say [1966 Mr. America Bob] Gajda is the winner when everybody in the house knew it was me." Not surprisingly, Poole and Oliva soon defected to the International Federation of Bodybuilders contests of rival promoter Joe Weider, where they won a variety of national and international titles.

Chris Dickerson, a New Yorker who exhibited a gentlemanly demeanor along with striking muscularity and symmetry, became the first African American to win the AAU Mr. America contest in 1970. An equally well-balanced James Morris of Los Angeles won it in 1973 and thereafter, coinciding with changes in judging criteria, blacks became frequent winners until the contest's demise in 1999. Meanwhile professional bodybuilding, largely under the aegis of the Weider organization and inspired by the Arnold Schwarzenegger revolution, took off during the 1970s. As the Mr. Olympia contest displaced the Mr. America contest in prestige, well-endowed blacks quickly came to the fore, led by Oliva, who won the former title three times. Then Lee Haney, who possessed matchless physique and posing artistry, won the Mr. Olympia a record eight times between 1984 and 1991. Called the "Atlanta Assassin," he was "unmatched," observed a report of his 1984 victory. "Just standing in the lineup of twenty Pros, Lee stood out like Woody Allen at a bodybuilding convention." By the late 1990s African Americans had become the most dynamic element in world bodybuilding, featuring the likes of Shawn Ray, Flex Wheeler, and Ronnie Coleman. In monthly worldwide rankings conducted by *Muscle Mag International* (1999–2001), it was not unusual for most of the top five places to be occupied by American blacks, a far cry from the days of Melvin Wells. Also, the success of Carla Dunlap of New Jersey in capturing the Ms. Olympia title in 1983, followed by six-time winner Lenda Murray of Detroit (1990–1995), inspired other women of color to take up bodybuilding and win major contests.

Quite different, however, was the experience of African Americans in weightlifting or its sister sport powerlifting, formed in the 1960s. Weighing less than 131 pounds, Lamar Gant of Flint, Michigan, was world champion more times (thirteen) than any power lifter in history, and middleweight Oscar Chaplin III of Savannah, Georgia, became the first American to win a world title in Olympic lifting in over three decades when he won the junior world championships in 2000. But presence of American blacks has not been particularly notable in either of these strength sports. Rather, it was in the subjective and aesthetic medium of bodybuilding, coincident with the civil rights movement of the 1960s, that African Americans became a dominant force.

John D. Fair

See also: John Davis; Olympic Games.

FURTHER READING
Kiiha, Osmo. "John Henry Davis, Jr." *Iron Master* 11 (April 1993): 6–35.
Wayne, Rick. *The Bodymen*. St. Lucia, West Indies: Star, 1978.
———. *Muscle Wars: The Behind the Scenes Story of Competitive Bodybuilding*. New York: St. Martin's, 1985.
Webster, David. *Barbells + Beefcake: An Illustrated History of Bodybuilding*. Irvine, Ayrshire, Scotland: Coasbyprint, 1979.

Reginald WEIR

Born September 30, 1911, New York, New York
Died August 22, 1987, New York, New York
Tennis player

Weir, who was to become an outstanding tennis player, first honed his talents at the age of ten on the public courts in Harlem. A star player at Dewitt Clinton High School, Weir went on to City College of New York, where he distinguished himself as a student and captained the tennis team for three consecutive years. In 1929 Weir attempted, along with another African-American player, Gerald Norman, Jr., to enter the all-white United States Lawn Tennis Association (USLTA) junior indoor championships at the Seventh Regiment Armory in New York City. Although their applications were denied, the effort by Weir and Norman to enter the tournament was significant in that it would be the first time the NAACP lobbied to desegregate tennis.

In 1931 Weir captured his first men's singles title of the American Tennis Association (ATA), the all-black tennis organization that paralleled the USLTA. He would win the tournament again in 1932, 1933, 1937, and 1942. In 1948 Weir made history by becoming the first African American to play in a USLTA-sponsored tournament. Weir made history again four years later when he and doubles partner George Stewart became the first African-American men to compete in the national tournament at Forest Hills. This followed by just two years Althea Gibson's participation in the tournament.

Weir's life outside of tennis was equally successful. A holder of an M.D. degree from New York University, he practiced family medicine from 1935 until about two years prior to his death in 1987.

David K. Wiggins

See also: Tennis.

FURTHER READING
Ashe, Arthur R., Jr. *A Hard Road To Glory: A History of the African-American Athlete*. New York: Amistad, 1993.
Smith, Jessie Carney. *Black Firsts: 2,000 Years of Extraordinary Achievement*. Detroit: Visible Ink Press, 1994.

★ ★ ★

Willie WELLS

Born August 10, 1905, Austin, Texas
Died January 22, 1989, Austin, Texas
Baseball player

Called the "Shakespeare of Shortstops," he was the first shortstop in baseball history to combine dazzling fielding with home-run power. Wells set a single-season Negro league record with twenty-seven homers in eighty-eight games for the St. Louis Stars in 1926. A scrappy, intelligent player, Wells had a prolific career in Latin America, where Mexican League fans dubbed him "El Diablo"; the opposition would always say, "Don't hit it to shortstop because The Devil is playing out there." He batted .320 over seven Cuban Winter League seasons, winning two home-run titles and two Most Valuable Player awards.

As player-manager of the Newark Eagles in the 1940s, he became known as an extraordinary leader and teacher, and several of his young players later became stars in the majors, including Larry Doby, Monte Irvin, and Don Newcombe. He established a lifetime batting average of .358 (in games for which there are confirmed records), and he often took the Negro National League batting title (hitting .403 in 1930). Wells's hot bat and aggressive play made him a frequent bean-ball target; he became a pioneer in his use of batting helmets. His fielding talents earned him eight nominations to the East-West All-Star Game, a remarkable feat considering that Wells had played nine of his finest seasons before the inaugural All-Star Game in 1933. In the early 1950s, Wells became the player-manager of the Winnipeg Buffaloes. He returned to the United States in 1954 as manager of the Birmingham Black Barons. *Total Baseball* lists Wells as one of the 400 greatest baseball players of all time. In 1999, members of the Society for Baseball Research chose him, in a tie with Norman "Turkey" Stearnes and Martin Dihigo, as the eighth-greatest Negro league player. The National Baseball Hall of Fame Committee on Baseball Veterans elected Wells to the Hall of Fame in 1997.

Larry S. Bonura

FURTHER READING
"40 Greatest Negro League Figures by SABR." *Baseball Almanac* (www.baseball-almanac.com/legendary/lisabr40.shtml).
Holway, John B., and Bob Carroll. "The 400 Greatest." *Baseball Almanac* (www.baseball-almanac.com/legendary/li400gr.shtml).
Holway, John. *Voices from the Great Black Baseball Leagues*. Rev. ed. New York: Da Capo, 1992.
National Baseball Hall of Fame (www.baseballhalloffame.org/hofers_and_honorees/hofer_bios/wells_willie.htm).
Riley, James A. *Dandy, Day and the Devil*. Cocoa, FL: TK, 1987.
Shatzkin, Mike, ed. *The Ballplayers: Baseball's Ultimate Biographical Reference*. New York: Arbor House, 1990.
"Wells, Willie." *The Handbook of Texas Online* (www.tsha.utexas.edu/handbook/online/articles/view/WW/fwe72.html).
"Willie Wells: The Devil From Texas." *Negro League Baseball* (www.negroleaguebaseball.com/1999/October/willie_well.html).

★ ★ ★

Charlie WEST

Born January 25, 1899, Washington, Pennsylvania
Died December 5, 1979, Washington, DC
Football player, medical doctor

The son of William B. West, a grocery store owner, and Hannah Thomas West, a public school teacher, Charlie West was one of the outstanding all-around athletes in early twentieth-century America. He first garnered attention on the playing fields in high school, being selected All-Western Pennsylvania in football, track, and baseball. Following graduation from high school, West attended Washington and Jefferson College, where he continued to distinguish himself athletically. He captained the schools track and field team his senior year and captured the pentathlon at the prestigious Penn Relays in both 1923 and 1924. He was also a halfback on Washington and Jefferson's football team, being selected as honorable mention to Walter Camp's All-American team in each of his four seasons and starring on the school's 1922 Rose Bowl squad, which held the powerful University of California to a scoreless tie.

West, unfortunately, was not immune from the racial prejudice experienced by other African Americans. In 1923 Washington and Lee College, which just seven years earlier had demanded that Rutgers bench Paul Robeson, similarly refused to play against Washington and Jefferson unless West was held out of the contest. In sharp contrast to Rutgers, which had acquiesced in the Robeson case, Washington and Jefferson refused to keep West out of the contest, and the game was never played.

West traveled with the U.S. team to Paris for the 1924 Olympic Games following his graduation from Washington and Jefferson. For some unknown reason, however, he never participated in the games. He also signed a contract with the Akron professional football team but opted instead to pursue the study of medicine at Howard University. He paid his way through Howard by coaching the football team. After taking his degree, he practiced medicine in Alexandria, Virginia, specializing in the treatment of tuberculosis.

David K. Wiggins

FURTHER READING
Ashe, Arthur R., Jr. *A Hard Road to Glory: A History of the African-American Athlete, 1919–1945*. New York: Warner Books, 1988.

Charlie West, the great all-around athlete from Washington and Jefferson College, in 1934 while the head football coach at Howard University. Typical of many other prominent African American student-athletes, West did some coaching to help pay for post-graduate studies. *(Moorland-Spingarn Research Center/Howard University Archives)*

Davis, Arthur P. *From the Dark Tower*. Washington, DC: Howard University Press, 1981.

North, E. Lee. *Battling The Indians, Panthers, and Nittany Lions: The Story of Washington & Jefferson College's First Century of Football, 1890–1990*. Canton, OH: Daring, 1991.

Tynen, Jim. "Charlie West: Black Quarterback Won Admiration On, Off Football Field." *Pittsburgh Press*, January 10, 1988.

★ ★ ★

Howard WHEELER

Born April 8, 1911, Atlanta, Georgia
Died April 25, 1968, Philadelphia, Pennsylvania
Golfer

Howard Wheeler entered the world of golf as a caddie in Atlanta, having completed only elementary school. He carried clubs for Robert Tyre "Bobby" Jones at Brookhaven Country Club and eventually rose to caddie master at the East Lake Golf Club before joining the black professional circuit as a touring professional.

Wheeler possessed a tall, lean frame and skillfully used it to become one of the longest hitters of the golf ball. He claimed his first tournament victory in the 1931 Atlanta Open. Two years later, Wheeler won his first United Golf Association (UGA) national championship. In his long career, Wheeler added five more UGA national titles; he won for the second time in 1938, then captured three in a row from 1946 to 1948, and finally won again in 1958. In the midst of those national title victories, Wheeler also collected his share of minor events, such as the 1951 Joe Louis Invitational. Wheeler's career peaked in the late 1940s, when he rivaled Ted Rhodes as the country's top African-American golfer. Unlike Ted Rhodes, Bill Spiller, or Charlie Sifford, however, it seems that Wheeler never made any serious effort to challenge the policies of the Professional Golfers Association's tour, instead remaining content to shine as arguably the brightest star in black professional golf in the early post-World War II period.

Stephen R. Lowe

See also: Golf; Charlie Sifford; United Golfers Association.

FURTHER READING
Kennedy, John H. *A Course of Their Own: A History of African American Golfers*. Kansas City, MO: Andrews McMeel, 2000.
McDaniel, Pete. *Uneven Lies: The Heroic Story of African Americans in Golf*. Greenwich, CT: American Golfer, 2000.
Sinnette, Calvin. *Forbidden Fairways: African Americans and the Game of Golf*. Chelsea, MI: Sleeping Bear, 1998.

★ ★ ★

Bill WHITE

Born January 28, 1934, Lakewood, Florida
Baseball player and executive

Bill White was the only child of a sharecropper family, but he grew up in Warren, Ohio, where his father worked in the steel mills and his mother clerked for the air force. White played thirteen seasons in baseball's major leagues, earned acclaim as an announcer with the New York Yankees, and in 1989 was named president of the National League.

White's goal was to become a doctor. He attended Hiram College, where he also played baseball and football. After graduating in 1953, White signed a baseball contract with the New York Giants, hoping to earn enough money to put him through medical school.

However, his baseball career soon took precedence. White's professional debut was with Danville, Virginia, where he was the only black player in the Carolina

St. Louis Cardinal first baseman Bill White watches his grand-slam leave Busch Stadium in a 1960 game against the Philadelphia Phillies. (AP/Wide World Photos)

Rizzuto as part of the New York Yankees broadcast team and handled CBS-Radio national broadcasts. The popular Rizzuto-White team worked together for eighteen seasons. White left broadcasting in 1989 to accept the position of National League president. Shattering major league baseball's abysmal racial hiring practices, White became the highest-ranking black executive of a professional sports league. After a successful tenure as league president, White retired in 1994.

Ron Briley

FURTHER READING
Bill White file. National Baseball Hall of Fame Museum and Library. Cooperstown, New York.
Randolph, Laura B. "Bill White: National League President." *Ebony,* August 1992, 52–54.
Smith, Claire. "National League President Bill White: Baseball's Angry Man." *New York Time Magazine,* October 13, 1991, 28–31, 53–56.

League. Surviving the racial taunts in Danville, White worked his way up the Giants farm system, playing for Sioux City, Dallas, and Minneapolis, before joining the Giants in 1956, hitting twenty-two home runs in his rookie campaign. After missing most of the 1957 and 1958 seasons for military service, White was traded to the St. Louis Cardinals.

In seven seasons with the Cardinals, White became a fixture at first base, winning seven consecutive Gold Gloves and playing an instrumental role in the Cardinals' 1964 world championship. In October 1965, White was traded to the Philadelphia Phillies. In 1969, after three years in Philadelphia, White was reacquired by the Cardinals, for whom he served primarily as a pinch hitter.

Retiring after the 1969 season, White remained in St. Louis, where he did a weekly radio sports show and broadcasted games with Harry Carey. In 1971, he joined Phil

★ ★ ★

Jo Jo WHITE

Born November 16, 1946, St. Louis, Missouri
Basketball player

The youngest son of the Reverend George and Elizabeth White, Jo Jo White is best known as a college and professional basketball player. White is also an Olympic gold medalist, a former coach, and a sports agent.

White played basketball at McKinley High School in St. Louis for two years, receiving All-State honors both years. After graduating from high school in 1965, he attended the University of Kansas, where his basketball career was astounding. He was selected as an All-American in 1968 and 1969, named All-Big Eight Conference three years, and selected League MVP in

1968. During his collegiate career, White represented the United States on the gold-medal teams in the 1966 University Games, the 1967 Pan American Games, and the 1968 Olympic Games.

White graduated from the University of Kansas in 1969. He served six months in the U.S. Marine Corps before joining the Boston Celtics as the team's first-round draft pick. Although he missed one-quarter of his first professional season, White earned a position on the 1970 NBA All-Rookie Team. During his ten seasons with the Celtics, he played on two championship teams and in seven NBA All-Star Games. He was selected the MVP of the 1976 NBA playoffs. The Celtics retired his uniform in 1982.

White returned to the University of Kansas in 1981 as part of the basketball coaching staff. After two seasons, he left to become the owner of his sports agency, where he represented young basketball players. At the age of forty-one, he attempted a comeback with the Topeka (Kansas) Sizzlers of the Continental Basketball Association. He played one season with the team. Part of his reason for the comeback was to assist younger players in becoming professionals.

Clay E. Harshaw

FURTHER READING
Ashe, Arthur R., Jr. *A Hard Road to Glory: A History of the African-American Athlete Since 1946*. New York: Warner Books, 1988.
Page, James A. *Black Olympian Medalists*. Englewood, CO: Libraries Unlimited, 1991.
Porter, David L., ed. *Biographical Dictionary of American Sports: Basketball and Other Indoor Sports*. New York: Greenwood Press, 1987.
Rhoden, William. "Jo Jo White Makes a Return at 41 with a Helping Hand as His Goal." *New York Times*, November 18, 1987.

★   ★   ★

Reggie WHITE

Born December 19, 1961, Chattanooga, Tennessee
Football player

Reggie White, the son of Thelma and Charles White, graduated from Howard High School in Chattanooga, Tennessee, and the University of Tennessee with a bachelor of arts degree in human services. White would spend his career as a professional football player, a pastor, and a philanthropist.

Following an All-American senior year at Tennessee, White was drafted by the Memphis Showboats of the United States Football League (USFL). The USFL folded in 1983, and White was selected by the Philadelphia Eagles as a first-round draft pick in the NFL's supplemental draft of USFL players in 1984. White remained with the Philadelphia Eagles for nine seasons before joining the Green Bay Packers in 1993. White became the first man to play defensive end in twelve consecutive Pro Bowl games. He was selected to be a member of the NFL's seventy-fifth anniversary All-Time team, establishing White as one of the greatest defensive ends to ever play the game. He played in 166 consecutive games, one of the longest streaks in NFL history. White holds the NFL all-time record for sacks, with 197.5 throughout his NFL career. He was named Rookie of the Year in 1986, Pro Bowl MVP in 1987, and defensive player of the year in 1991. In 1997, White became the NFL's all-time sack leader with his 176th sack and helped lead the Green Bay Packers to a Super Bowl victory.

White's off-field accomplishments have been well documented. An ordained minister, he is the co-pastor of the City Church of East Knoxville, Tennessee; he is also president of Big Doggie Records, which releases a wide array of gospel albums. White built Hope Place, a shelter for unwed mothers, and founded the Alpha Omega Ministry.

Doris R. Corbett

FURTHER READING
Bigelow, Barbara C. *Contemporary Black Biography*. Detroit: Gale Research, 1994.
A Closer Look (www.acloserlook.com/9612acl/sponsor/inthetrenches.html).
Mark, Kibibi, V. *The African American Encyclopedia*. Tarrytown, NY: Marshall Cavendish, 1999.
Packers.com (www.packers.com/team/players/white_reggie/index.html).
White, Reggie. *In the Trenches the Autobiography*. New York: Nelson Thomas, 1999.

★ ★ ★

Sherman WHITE

Born December 16, 1928, Philadelphia, Pennsylvania
Basketball player

Because he was one of the players involved in a 1951 college basketball scandal, White's superb play while at Long Island University (LIU) has been virtually ignored by sport historians. During the 1949–1950 and 1950–1951 seasons, White and other players at LIU did business with gamblers; he ultimately was sentenced to a year in jail. Until March 1998, White was reticent to speak about his involvement in the scandals, but then he broke his silence by granting an interview with Dave Anderson of the *New York Times*. White contended in the article that the Home Box Office documentary *City Dump* did not reveal the whole story about the 1951 scandal.

White had been named Player of the Year by the *Sporting News* in 1951; when arrested he was only seventy-seven points away from setting an all-time collegiate scoring record and was the nation's leading scorer, with a 27.7-point average. The New York Knicks were slated to select White as their number-one choice, which would have considerably strengthened a good team that already had such players as Harry Gallatin, Dick McGuire, Carl Braun, and Sweetwater Clifton. After his rejection by the NBA, White played on weekends for Wilkes-Barre and Hazelton in the Eastern League for nine years. Thereafter, before he retired, he was a respected coach for youngsters of the Newark YMCA and East Orange, NJ, playgrounds.

Albert J. Figone

FURTHER READING
Anderson, Dave. "When Sherman White Threw It All Away." *New York Times*, March 27, 1998, 1, 9.
Cohen, Stanley. *The Game They Played*. New York: Farrar, Straus and Giroux, 1977.
Figone, Albert J. "Gambling and College Basketball: The Scandal of 1951." *Journal of Sport History* 16 (Spring 1989): 32–53.
Rosen, Stanley. *Scandals of 51: How the Gamblers Almost Killed Basketball*. New York: Holt, Rinehart, and Winston, 1977.
White, Sherman. "The Basketball Fix Wrecked My Life." *Sport*, July 1951, 14–15, 76–77.

★ ★ ★

Sol WHITE

Born June 12, 1868, Bellaire, Ohio
Died 1955, New York, New York
Baseball player, coach, and executive

An athlete, a coach, a team executive, and an author, Sol White lived all aspects of the early African-American baseball experience. White's playing career, which lasted more than twenty years near the turn of the twentieth century, took him across the country to all-black leagues, integrated teams in organized baseball, African-American teams in white leagues, and finally to all-black barnstorming teams. As his athletic career came to an end, White helped to organize one of the best all-black teams in the country, and, more importantly, in 1907 he penned the first history of African-American baseball.

White's professional career began in 1887 with the Pittsburgh Keystones of the short-lived National Colored League (NCL), the first attempt at a nationwide league of black baseball teams. After the NCL folded, the hard-hitting infielder played several years in integrated minor leagues, including stints with biracial teams in Wheeling, West Virginia, in 1887 and in Fort Wayne, Indiana, in 1895. Between these two engagements he played for all-black teams in otherwise white minor leagues from 1889 to 1891.

After organized baseball drew the color line for good in the 1890s, black athletes were forced onto segregated barnstorming teams, and White played for several of the nineteenth century's best, including the Cuban Giants, the New York Big Gorhams, the Cuban X-Giants, and the Page Fence Giants. In 1902, White teamed with H. Walter Schlichter, the white sports editor of the *Philadelphia Item*, to found the Philadelphia Giants. For the next eight years, with White as the manager, the Giants were one of the most successful black teams in the country.

While with the Philadelphia Giants, White, who had attended Wilberforce University in the 1890s, authored *Sol White's History of Colored Base Ball*, the first work devoted to documenting the story of the African-American baseball experience. This slim volume preserved the memory of early black pioneers for future generations of scholars.

Around 1910, White went into a long period of semiretirement, punctuated by brief engagements as a sportswriter for the *Cleveland Advocate* in 1919 and as the secretary of the Negro National League's Columbus Buckeyes in the 1920s. For the last twenty years of his life White lived in Harlem, where he was a popular interview for the black press. He died in the 1950s with little notice; his exact date of death and location of his gravesite are unknown.

Gregory Bond

FURTHER READING
Malloy, Jerry. "The Strange Career of Sol White, Black Baseball's First Historian." *Nine* 4 (Spring 1996): 217–36.
McKinney, G.B. "Negro Professional Baseball Players in the Upper South in the Gilded Age." *Journal of Sport History* 3 (Winter 1976): 273–80.
White, Sol. *Sol White's History of Colored Base Ball, with Other Documents on the Early Black Game, 1886–1936*, edited by Jerry Malloy. Lincoln: University of Nebraska Press, 1995.

★ ★ ★

Willye WHITE

Born January 1, 1939, Money, Mississippi
Long jumper

Born to sharecroppers Willie and Johnnie White, Willye White was raised by her maternal grandparents. She graduated from Tennessee State University and received a public health administration degree from Chicago State University. Her professional career is in administration.

White joined the Tigerbelles track and field team of Tennessee State University at age sixteen and set a division record in the broad-jump (18 feet 6 inches) at her first national AAU meet. She subsequently competed in the 1956 Olympics and won a silver medal in the long jump (19 feet 11¾ inches). She competed in the Olympics from 1956 to 1972, medaling once more with a silver in the 400-meter relay (1964). During her career, White was on thirty-nine international teams, including four Pan American teams, and was the first woman to represent the United States in five Olympics. She won two Olympic medals, twelve national titles, and advanced the national long-jump record seven times. White was the first recipient of the Pierre de Coubertin International Fair Play Trophy and was inducted into the Black Sports, U.S. Track and Field, and International Women's Sports Halls of Fame.

After retiring from competition in 1972, White was a member of the President's Commission on Olympic Sports and consulted for the U.S. Olympic Job Opportunity Program. She is currently the director of health and fitness for the Chicago Department of Public Health. She commits her time to the WE CARE Role Model Program and other programs with the Police Department and the Board of Education.

Debra A. Henderson

FURTHER READING

Davis, Michael D. *Black American Women in Olympic Track and Field.* Jefferson, NC: McFarland, 1992.

Layden, Joe. *Women in Sports.* Santa Monica, CA: General Publishing Group, 1997.

National Fitness Leaders Association. "Willye White" (wellness.uwsp.edu).

Page, James A. *Black Olympian Medalists.* Englewood, CO: Libraries Unlimited, 1991.

USA Track and Field. "Willye White" (www.usaft.org).

★ ★ ★

Mal WHITFIELD

Born October 11, 1924, Bay City, Texas
Runner

A three-time Olympic gold medalist, Mal Whitfield established himself as one of the great middle-distance runners of his era. He was a sergeant in the U.S. Air Force when he attended Ohio State University, where he won the collegiate 800 meters in 1948 and 1949. At the London Olympic Games in 1948, Whitefield won the 800-meters and took the bronze in the 400-meters. He added a gold in the 4 x 400-meter relay. Four years later in Helsinki, Whitefield repeated his gold in the 800-meters and garnered the silver medal in the 400-meters. Between 1948 and 1954, he lost only three of sixty-nine 800-meter and 880-yard runs and set five world records. In 1955, Whitfield was the first black recipient of the Sullivan Award for the nation's premier amateur athlete.

Whitfield narrowly missed making his third Olympic team in 1956, but he had many other career highlights. Competitive in all distances from 200 meters to the mile, "Marvelous Mal" won the 1954 Sullivan Award, set six world records, and won eight National AAU titles. He later served the U.S. Department of State in Africa. He was inducted into the U.S. Olympic Hall of Fame in 1988.

Richard D. Loosbrock

FURTHER READING

Amateur Athletic Foundation of Los Angeles (www.aafla.org/SportsLibrary/Olympika/Olympika_1993/olympika0201d.pdf).

Ashe, Arthur R., Jr. *A Hard Road to Glory: A History of the African-American Athlete Since 1946.* New York: Warner Books, 1988.

"Diplomat in Short Pants: Mal Whitfield." *Sports Illustrated*, February 7, 1955, 12–15.

USA Track and Field (www.usatf.org/athletes/hof/whitfield.shtml).

Wenn, Stephen R., and Jeffrey P. Wenn. "Muhammad Ali and the Convergence of Olympic Sport and U.S. Diplomacy in 1980: A Reassessment from Behind the Scenes of the U.S. State Department." *Olympika: International Journal of Olympic Studies* 2 (1993): 45–66.

Whitefield, Mal. "Let's Boycott the Olympics." *Ebony*, March 1964, 95–96.

★ ★ ★

Sydney WICKS

Born September 19, 1949, Los Angeles, California
Basketball player

Wicks was a versatile athlete at Hamilton High School in Los Angeles, CA, participating in track, baseball, and basketball. He gained All-City and All-American prep school basketball honors in 1967. While attending Santa Monica City College in California, he was the Most Valuable Player in the Metropolitan Conference in basketball. At the University of California at Los Angeles (UCLA), Wicks, a sociology major, was selected for *Look* magazine's All-American team, the All-Pacific Eight Conference team, and the Helms Athletic foundation Co-Player of the Year in 1970 (with Pete Maravich of Louisiana State University) and in 1971 (with Austin Carr of Notre Dame). He was a member of three National Collegiate Athletic Association (NCAA) championship teams.

The Portland Trailblazers of the National Basketball Association (NBA) drafted him in 1971, and he became the NBA's Rookie of the Year for 1971–1972. Wicks played a decade in the NBA—with Portland 1971–1976, the Boston Celtics 1976–1978, and San Diego 1978–1981. He averaged 16.8 points per game for his professional career. He participated in four NBA All-Star Games while with Portland. He was elected to the UCLA Athletic Hall of Fame in 1985.

John R. Schleppi

FURTHER READING
Boston Traveler, April 20, 1972.
Hubbard, Jan, ed. *The Official NBA Encyclopedia*. 3d ed. New York: Doubleday, 2000.
UCLA Basketball Guide, 1970–1971, 34–35.

Archie WILLIAMS

Born May 1, 1915, Oakland, California
Sprinter

Archie Williams is the son of Wadsworth and Lillian Wall Williams. He ran track at University High in Oakland and then enrolled at San Mateo Junior College, prior to transferring to the University of California at Berkeley. Until 1936 Archie Williams was virtually unknown in major track circles, but he made astounding progress in the Olympic year. After running 47.4 seconds for 440 yards in April, he clocked 46.8 in May and then, in a heat of the NCAA Championships in June, he set a world 400-meter world record of 46.1 seconds. Although he finished only third at the 1936 AAU Championships, Williams won the U.S. Olympic Trials at 400 meters in 46.6. At the Berlin Olympics he beat Britain's Godfrey Brown by inches to win the gold medal. Shortly after the Olympics, at a meet in Sweden, Williams injured his leg. He continued to compete in track sporadically until 1939 but never again reached his form of 1936.

Williams graduated from the University of California at Berkeley in 1939 with a degree in engineering but planned on becoming a pilot. During World War II he was an instructor at the Tuskegee Institute training program for black pilots. He later served in the U.S. Air Force, flying bombers before retiring in 1964 as a lieutenant colonel. While in the military he earned degrees in aeronautical engineering and meteorology. He later became a computer technology teacher in Marin County, California.

Bill Mallon

See also: Track and Field.

FURTHER READING
Carlson, Lewis H., and John J. Fogarty. *Tales of Gold: An Oral History of the Summer Olympic Games Told by America's Gold Medal Winners.* Chicago: Contemporary Books, 1987.
Wallechinsky, David. *The Complete Book of the Olympics.* New York: Viking, 1984.

★ ★ ★

Doug WILLIAMS

Born August 9, 1955, Zachary, Louisiana
Football player and coach

Williams attended Cheneyville High School in Zachary, Louisiana, from 1971 to 1974 and starred in football, basketball, and baseball. His athletic prowess earned him a scholarship to Grambling State College, where he quarterbacked the Tigers football team from 1974 to 1977 under the tutelage of legendary coach Eddie Robinson. Williams accomplished many firsts, among them: first player from a black college selected to the Associated Press's first-team All-American squad (1977); and first quarterback from a black college to be picked in the first round of the NFL draft (1978). In just his second year in professional football he quarterbacked the Tampa Bay Buccaneers to the 1979 NFC championship game.

Williams signed with the Oklahoma Outlaws of the fledgling United States Football League in 1984 and led the team to first place. The following year, however, when the USFL folded, he was picked by the Washington Redskins. Two years later, on January 31, 1988, he became the first African American to quarterback a team to victory in the Super Bowl, setting records for most yards passing (340), most passing yards in a quarter (240), most touchdown passes (four), and the longest completion (eighty yards). His performance earned him MVP honors. Due to recurring knee problems, Williams retired from professional football in 1989 and took a job coaching at Northeast High School in his hometown of Zachary, Louisiana. From there he moved on to coaching stints at the U.S. Naval Academy and the World Football League, and as a scout for the Jacksonville Jaguars of the NFL. In 1997, he returned to his alma mater to take up the mantle from retiring coach Eddie Robinson. Williams guided the Tigers to a 7–4 record in his second year at the helm. In 1999 the team compiled a 10–2 record and won the Southwestern Athletic Association football championship.

Donald Spivey and Logan Bailey-Perkins

See also: Eddie Robinson.

FURTHER READING
Smith, Jesse Carney. *Black Firsts: 2,000 Years of Extraordinary Achievement.* Detroit: Visible Ink Press, 1994.
Williams, Doug, with Bruce Hunter. *Quarterblack: Shattering the NFL Myth.* Chicago: Bonus Books, 1990.

★ ★ ★

Ike WILLIAMS

Born August 2, 1923, Brunswick, Georgia
Died September 5, 1994, Los Angeles, California
Boxer

Probably more than any other American boxer, Ike Williams had a career that was both brilliant and besmirched. He was the lightweight champion from 1945 to 1951, but in order to attain success in the ring, he was forced to sign a contract with mobster Blinky Palermo, who, along with Frankie Carbo, exerted unchallenged control over boxing in the mid-1940s and 1950s. In 1960, he testified to the Kefauver Anti-Crime Committee in the U.S. Senate that in two of his championship defenses, he received just $25,000 of the $65,000 he was supposed to earn.

Williams turned pro in 1940 and earned recognition as a contender in 1944, when he beat Sammy Angott. A year later, he knocked out Juan Zurita in Mexico City to earn the National Boxing Association title. In 1947, he knocked out Bob Montgomery to become the undisputed lightweight champion. A vicious body puncher, he became famous for his willingness to fight above his weight division, tangling with the likes of Tippy Larkin, Kid Gavilan (three times), Joe Miceli (three times), and Johnny Bratton (two times). Overall, Williams compiled a 125–24–5 record with sixty knockouts. He was inducted into the International Boxing Hall of Fame in 1990. Before winning the title in 1945, Williams was blacklisted by the Boxing Managers Guild. In order to get fights, he was forced to sign a managerial contract with Palermo. While title defenses against Enrique Bolanos, Jesse Flores, and Beau jack were legitimate bouts, Williams later testified that he was offered bribes to throw his second fight against Carter and the second fight against Gavilan. Although he said he refused the bribes, he lost both fights. The loss to Carter in 1951 stripped him of his championship.

Dennis Gildea

See also: Boxing.

FURTHER READING
Coughlan, Robert. "How the 113C Runs Boxing." *Sports Illustrated*, January 17, 1955, 11–13, 47–50.
———. "A Nationwide Look at Boxing's Straw Bosses." *Sports Illustrated*, January 31, 1955, 18–19, 49–53.
International Boxing Hall of Fame. "Ike Williams" (www.ibhof.com).

Joseph "Smokey" WILLIAMS

Born April 6, 1886, Seguin, Texas
Died March 12, 1946, New York, New York
Baseball player

The son of an African-American father and a mother of mixed African-American and Native American ancestry (the dates of his birth and death are in dispute), this six-foot four-inch, 200-pound, hard-throwing right-hander dominated early twentieth-century black baseball. For almost thirty years, Williams dazzled fans and players with a blinding fastball that earned him the nicknames "Cyclone" and "Smokey Joe."

Playing from 1905 to 1932, he is said to have pitched dozens of no-hitters, many of them against amateur teams but some against the likes of the New York Giants. In 1914, he earned forty-one wins against only three losses. In 1917, Williams struck out twenty batters and pitched a no-hitter against the National League champion Giants, though he lost the game, 1–0, on an error. On August 7, 1930, at age forty-four, he struck out twenty-seven Kansas City Monarchs in a 1–0, twelve-inning, night-game victory. Williams outdueled the great Walter Johnson and Grover Cleveland Alexander, as he reeled off a 20–7 record in exhibitions against white major-league competition. In a 1952 poll of former black sportswriters and players, Williams beat Satchel Paige, 20–10, for the distinction of the greatest pitcher in Negro league baseball history. *Total Baseball* lists Williams as one of the 400 greatest baseball players of all time. In 1999, members of the Society for Baseball Research chose him in a tie with George "Mule" Suttles as the thirteenth greatest Negro league player. The National Baseball Hall of Fame Committee on Baseball Veterans elected Williams to the Hall of Fame in 1999.

Larry S. Bonura

FURTHER READING

Baseball Immortals (www.baseballimmortals.net/Negro_Leaguers/smokey_joe_williams.htm).

Black Baseball's Negro Baseball Leagues (www.blackbaseball.com/players/williams.htm).

Caplan, Jeff. "Honored at Last: Baseball Hall of Fame to Induct One of Negro Leagues' Best." *Fort Worth Star-Telegram*(www.star-telegram.com/news/doc/1047/1:99NOLAN1/1:99NOLAN1071999.html).

"40 Greatest Negro League Figures by SABR." *Baseball Almanac* (www.baseball-almanac.com/legendary/lisabr40.shtml).

Holway, John B. *Smokey Joe and the Cannonball*. Washington, DC: Capital Press, 1983.

Holway, John B., and Bob Carroll. "The 400 Greatest." *Baseball Almanac* (www.baseball-almanac.com/legendary/li400gr.shtml).

Lester, Larry. "Smokey and the Bandit." *National Pastime* (1994), 18–20.

National Baseball Hall of Fame (www.baseballhalloffame.org/hofers_and_honorees/hofer_bios/williams_joe.htm).

Peterson, Robert. *Only the Ball Was White*. Englewood Cliffs, NJ: Prentice Hall, 1970.

Rogosin, Donn. *Invisible Men: Life in Baseball's Negro Leagues*. New York: Atheneum, 1983.

"Williams, Joe," *The Handbook of Texas Online* (www.tsha.utexas.edu/handbook/online/articles/view/WW/fwiuj.html).

★ ★ ★

Serena WILLIAMS

Born September 26, 1981, Saginaw, Michigan
Tennis player

Serena Williams is the daughter of Richard, a part-owner of a security business, and Oracene, a nurse, and the fifth of the Williams sisters. Coached by her father, Serena Williams played in her first tournament while only four years old and during the next five years won forty-fix of forty-nine tournaments she entered. Her early prowess enabled her to succeed her sister, Venus, as the number-one player in the under-twelve age group in Southern California before ending her participation in junior events.

Serena Williams holding up the winning trophy next to her sister Venus after capturing the 2002 U.S. Open Tennis Tournament. *(AP/Wide World Photos)*

Following coaching by Rick Macci at his tennis academy in Florida, Williams made her professional debut in 1995. The five-foot, eleven-inch Williams has a compact, muscular frame that enhances her powerful, all-around game, and she displays brash confidence, athleticism, and charisma. At the age of eighteen she captured her first Grand Slam event, winning the 1999 U.S. Women's Singles Championship, thus becoming the first African American since Althea Gibson to win this event. Williams won with her sister Venus the U.S. Women's Doubles Championship in 1999, the All-England Ladies' Doubles Championship at Wimbledon in 2000, and the gold medal in doubles in the Sydney Olympic Games in 2000.

Williams, who lives in Palm Beach Gardens, Florida, continues to play on the tennis circuit, enjoying her $12 million endorsement contract with Puma and her success on the court.

Angela Lumpkin

See also: Tennis; Venus Williams.

FURTHER READING

Chappell, Kevin. "Richard Williams: Venus and Serena's Father Whips the Pros and Makes His Family No. 1 in Tennis." *Ebony*, June 2000, 92–98.

Peyser, Marc, and Allison Samuels. "Venus and Serena Against the World." *Newsweek*, August 24, 1998, 44–48.

Phelps, Shirelle, ed. *Contemporary Black Biography*. Detroit: Gale, 1999.

Price, Scott L. "Father Knew Best: With Her Galvanizing Win at the U.S. Open, Serena Williams Proved Dad Right—He Predicted that She, Not Older Sister Venus, Would Be the Better Player—but May Have Created Family Tension." *Sports Illustrated*, September 20, 1999, 38–43.

Price, Scott L. "For the Ages." *Sports Illustrated*, July 7, 2000, 36–44.

★ ★ ★

Venus WILLIAMS

Born June 17, 1980, Los Angeles, California
Tennis Player

The daughter of Richard, a part-owner of a security business, and Oracene, a nurse, Venus Williams was the fourth of five sisters. Coached initially by her father, Williams developed her powerful game on the public courts of Compton, California. This tennis prodigy displayed her aptitude for winning early, capturing the Southern California under-twelve championship by age ten, the last age-group tennis competition her father permitted her to enter. Rick Macci helped mold her game in six-hour-per-day/six-day-per-week practices after the family moved to Florida. She turned pro in October of 1994 and entered her first major tennis championship in 1997.

The six-foot, two-inch Williams has delivered serves as fast as 127 miles per hour. Her athleticism, aggression, and extreme confidence on the court intimidate many opponents. Her first win in a Grand Slam event occurred in 2000, when she became the first African American since Althea Gibson to win the All-England Ladies' Singles Championship at Wimbledon. With her sister and best friend Serena, Williams also won the Ladies Doubles Championship at Wimbledon in 2000. Also in 2000, Williams won gold medals in singles and doubles (with Serena) in the Sydney Olympic Games. In the historic contest with Serena for the United States Tennis Association Women's Singles Championship in 2001, Williams handily demonstrated her dominance on the court to earn the $850,000 paycheck. Her $12 million endorsement contract with Reebok helped finance her new home in Palm Beach Gardens, Florida, where she lives when not playing on the tennis circuit.

Angela Lumpkin

See also: Tennis; Serena Williams.

FURTHER READING

Chappell, Kevin. "Richard Williams: Venus and Serena's Father Whips the Pros and Makes His Family No. 1 in Tennis." *Ebony*, June 2000, 92–98.

Jenkins, Sally, "Venus Rising: At 14, Fledgling Pro Venus Williams Has It All—Talent, Charisma and a Tennis Dad." *Sports Illustrated*, November 14, 1994, 30–32.

Montville, Leigh. "Slice Girls." *Sports Illustrated*, February 2, 1998, 66–69.

Peyser, Marc, and Allison Samuels. "Venus and Serena Against the World." *Newsweek*, August 24, 1998, 44–48.

Phelps, Shirelle, ed. *Contemporary Black Biography*. Detroit: Gale, 1998.

★ ★ ★

Bill WILLIS

Born October 5, 1921, Columbus, Ohio
Football player

Bill Willis was the son of Clement and Willana Willis. Sadly, his father died when

Willis was only four, and he was raised by his grandfather and mother. At Columbus East High School he thought he was destined to be successful in track. However, his forte was football, and as a senior he earned Honorable Mention All-State honors.

Willis entered Ohio State University in 1941 and the following year, as a sophomore, starred on a Buckeye team that went 9–1, won the 1942 Western (Big Ten) Conference championship, and was ranked number one by the Associated Press. Two years later, in 1944, Willis was named to both the United Press and *Look* All-American teams. He was also the first black player in the starting lineup for the Annual College All-Star Game (1944).

In 1945, Willis and Marion Motley became the first African Americans to sign with the Cleveland Browns of the new professional league known as the All-America Football Conference (AAFC). Willis had a distinguished career in professional football. In 1950, the Browns moved to the NFL and won the league championship; Willis was named their MVP. Willis was also named to the first three Pro Bowls. In his post-athletic career, he was an assistant commissioner of recreation for Cleveland, deputy director of correctional services, and then director of youth services.

He married Odessa Porter in 1947, and they had three sons, William, Jr., Clement, and Dan. Willis, who retired in 1983, was inducted into the Pro Football Hall of Fame in 1977.

Scott A.G.M. Crawford

FURTHER READING
Ashe, Arthur R., Jr. *A Hard Road to Glory.* New York: Amistad, 1988.
Hickok, Ralph. *A Who's Who of American Sports Champions.* Boston: Houghton Mifflin, 1995.
Porter, David L., ed. *African-American Sports Greats: A Biographical Dictionary.* Westport, CT: Greenwood Press, 1995.
Smith, Thomas G. "Outside the Pale: The Exclusion of Blacks from the National Football League, 1934–1946." *Journal of Sport History* 15 (Winter 1988): 255–81.
Watterson, John Sayle. *College Football.* Baltimore: Johns Hopkins University Press, 2000.

★ ★ ★

Harry WILLS

Born May 15, 1889, New Orleans, Louisiana
Died December 21, 1956, New York, New York
Boxer

In 103 career fights, Harry Wills, the "Brown Panther of New Orleans," lost just eight times, but he will remain most famous for losing his chance at the heavyweight championship. Throughout Jack Dempsey's reign, Wills was the number-one-ranked contender, but racism and the long shadow cast by Jack Johnson prevented him from getting a title shot. In 1922, 1924, and again in 1925, a Dempsey-Wills fight seemed imminent. Wills and Dempsey actually signed to meet each other, but for a variety of reasons the bout never came off. Many powerful white Americans did not want another Johnson as champion. Wills received $50,000 for the cancellation, but it was Luis Angel Firpo and then Gene Tunney who got cracks at Dempsey.

A powerful man who stood six feet, four inches and weighed 220 pounds, Wills defeated some of the better white heavyweights, including Willie Meehan in 1914. On Dempsey's way to the top, he lost twice to Meehan and drew with him once. Wills also faced the top black heavyweights of the era. He fought Sam Langford twenty-two times, compiling a 6–2 record with fourteen no-decisions. He also beat Sam McVey three times and battled Joe Jeannette to two no-decisions.

Deprived of his shot at Dempsey, he saw

his career go into decline. A month after Tunney took the title from Dempsey, Wills met Jack Sharkey in Brooklyn and was disqualified on a foul in the thirteenth round. A year later, a younger Paolino Uzcudun knocked him out in the last significant bout Wills fought. He was inducted into the International Boxing Hall of Fame in 1992.

Dennis Gildea

See also: Boxing.

FURTHER READING
International Boxing Hall of Fame. "Harry Wills" (www.ibhof.com).
Kahn, Roger. *A Flame of Pure Fire: Jack Dempsey and the Roaring Twenties.* New York: Harcourt Brace, 1999.
Roberts, Randy. *Jack Dempsey: The Manassa Mauler.* Baton Rouge: Louisiana State University Press, 1979.

★ ★ ★

Los Angeles Dodgers infielder and base stealing king Maury Wills posing for the cameras in 1971 at spring training in Vero Beach, Florida. *(AP/Wide World Photos)*

Maury WILLS

Born October 2, 1932, Washington, DC
Baseball player and manager

Maury Wills was one of thirteen children; his father (Guy) was a machinist and a minister, and his mother (Mabel) was an elevator operator. He attended Cardozo High School in Washington and became a professional baseball player, broadcaster, and manager. He reintroduced the stolen base as an important offensive weapon and became the third African American, following Frank Robinson and Larry Doby, to manage a major league team.

Despite his speed, Wills languished in the minor leagues for eight seasons before manager Bobby Bragan suggested he become a switch-hitter. His batting improved, and by the end of the 1959 season he was in the majors, playing shortstop for the Los Angeles Dodgers. He combined his speed with base-running savvy to steal fifty bases in 1960, more than any National League player had stolen since Max Carey's fifty-one in 1923. Two years later, he stole 104 bases, breaking the major league record Ty Cobb had set in 1915.

Wills led the National League in stolen bases for six straight years, but more importantly, his special talent caused all teams to refashion their offenses to incorporate the running game. The Dodgers added fine pitching to Wills's speed to win pennants in 1959, 1963, 1965, and 1966.

After retiring in 1972, Wills was a television commentator, manager in the winter leagues, and minor league instructor for the Dodgers. He managed the Seattle Mariners for parts of the 1980 and 1981 seasons, compiling a record of 26–56.

Steven P. Gietschier

FURTHER READING

Broeg, Bob. "Wills Triggered a New Steal Era." *Sporting News*, October 15, 1977, 8.
Furlong, Bill. "Behind the Scenes in the Maury Wills Record Race." *Sport*, October, 1962, 57–62.
Koppett, Leonard. "Wills Prompted Running Revolution." *Sporting News,*" August 30, 1980, 17.
Wills, Maury, as told to Steve Gardner. *It Pays to Steal*. Englewood Cliffs, NJ: Prentice Hall, 1963.
Wills, Maury, with Don Freeman. *How to Steal a Pennant*. New York: G.P. Putnam, 1976.

★ ★ ★

Rollo WILSON

Born Franklin, Pennsylvania
Died January 12, 1956, Philadelphia, Pennsylvania
Sportswriter, boxing promoter, league president

Rollo Wilson graduated from Temple University, where he gained high honors, and the University of Pittsburgh, where he earned a pharmacy degree. During World War I, he served in the medical corps. Afterward, he became a respected sports journalist. Wilson was also to become a promoter and sports official.

Wilson joined the *Pittsburgh Courier* in 1926, when the *Pittsburgh American* folded. He also covered events for the *Philadelphia American* and the *Philadelphia Tribune*. Acknowledged by his peers as the "dean" of black sportswriters, he combined a deep knowledge of facts with a lively writing style. Unlike many other black sportswriters of his time, he did not focus on racial controversies. Instead, he wrote about issues within the Negro leagues, often using strong language. He was known for covering baseball in the Philadelphia area, Joe Louis fights, and the Penn Relays.

He was also an inspector and deputy commissioner for the Pennsylvania Athletic Commission, a fight manager and promoter, and president of the Negro National League. For two years, he also was a reporter for the *Franklin Evening News*.

Wilson suffered a heart attack outside Connie Mack Stadium after covering a football game between the Pittsburgh Steelers and Philadelphia Eagles and passed away at the age of sixty-five. After his death, the *Courier* declared that Wilson had probably known more major sports figures than any other reporter.

Michael Marsh

FURTHER READING

Buni, Andrew. *Robert L. Vann of the Pittsburgh Courier*. Pittsburgh: University of Pittsburgh Press, 1974.
Reisler, Jim. *Black Writers/Black Baseball: An Anthology of Articles from Black Sportswriters Who Covered the Negro Leagues*. Jefferson, NC: McFarland, 1993.
"W. Rollo Wilson Dies in Philly." *Pittsburgh Courier*, November 17, 1956.

★ ★ ★

Dave WINFIELD

Born October 3, 1951, St. Paul, Minnesota
Baseball player

Dave Winfield was one of two sons born to Frank and Arline Winfield. An outstanding athlete in both basketball and baseball, Winfield opted for the latter, where he was to achieve fame and fortune with lucrative free-agent contracts and, in 2001, induction into the Baseball Hall of Fame.

His parents separated when he was three, and Winfield, along with his older brother, was raised by his mother and grandmother. At St. Paul Central High School, he earned varsity letters in baseball and football. Following high school graduation in 1969, Winfield was drafted by the Baltimore Orioles, but he accepted an athletic scholarship at the University of Minnesota, where he played both baseball and basketball. In 1973, he was selected the year contract with the New York Yankees worth approximately $25 million dollars. Although Winfield achieved considerable success in a Yankee uniform, he often quarreled with team owner George Steinbrenner.

In 1990, the Yankees traded Winfield to the California Angels. Again testing the free-agent market, in December 1991 Winfield signed with the Toronto Blue Jays, playing a leading role in the franchise's 1992 world championship. Winfield spent the 1993 and 1994 baseball seasons in Minnesota before closing out his career in 1995 with the Cleveland Indians.

During his twenty-two major league seasons, Winfield batted .285, slugged 465 home runs, stole 223 bases, and accumulated 3,110 hits. Since his baseball career, Winfield has devoted considerable time to the David M. Winfield Foundation for underprivileged children.

Ron Briley

FURTHER READING

Dave Winfield file. National Baseball Hall of Fame Museum and Library, Cooperstown, New York.
"Slugger Dave Winfield Continues to Shine On and Off the Field." *Jet*, September 27, 1993, 48.
Swift, E.M. "Yanked About by the Boss." *Sports Illustrated*, April 11, 1988, 36–39.
Winfield, Dave, and Tom Parker. *Winfield: A Player's Life*. New York: W.W. Norton, 1988.

New York Yankees outfielder Dave Winfield rounding third base after hitting a home run in a 1982 game against the Baltimore Orioles at Yankee Stadium. *(AP/Wide World Photos)*

Most Valuable Player in the College World Series.

Leaving the University of Minnesota a few credits short of graduation in 1973, Winfield was drafted by four professional teams in three sports, but he elected to cast his lot with baseball and the San Diego Padres, with whom he played in the outfield for eight seasons. During his last four years with the Padres, he averaged .292, twenty-six home runs, and ninety-nine runs batted in.

Despairing of the Padres becoming a contender, Winfield opted for free agency, signing in December 1980 a lucrative ten-

★ ★ ★

Jimmy WINKFIELD

Born April 12, 1883, Chilesburg, Kentucky
Died March 23, 1974, Maisons-Laffitte, France
Jockey

Jimmy Winkfield was the last great black jockey to race in America. As one of only four jockeys to win back-to-back Kentucky Derbies, he was also the last African American to win the Derby in the twentieth century. Throughout his thirty-two-year career, Winkfield rode about 2,600 winning races in America and Europe.

In the spring of 1897 Winkfield started work as a stable hand, progressing to jockey the next year. In 1900 he finished third in the Kentucky Derby and ranked third among jockeys at the New Orleans Fairgrounds. At Chicago's Harlem track that August, white riders, jealous of successful black jockeys, crowded Winkfield and his horse into a fence, injuring both.

Winkfield won Kentucky Derbies in 1901 and 1902, ranking fourteenth nationally among jockeys, but the next year he failed to win his third straight Derby. Later in 1903, Winkfield reneged on a riding contract; the enraged trainer threatened to have him banned from racing. He accepted an offer to ride in Russia and forged a successful and profitable European career, winning the 1904 Russian National Riding Championship. Turmoil following the Russian Revolution forced Winkfield to flee the country in April 1919; he resumed riding in France in 1920, retiring in 1930.

He bought a small estate in Maisons-Laffitte and became a trainer. When the Nazis invaded France he brought his wife and two children to Aiken, South Carolina, where he worked with racehorses until returning to France in 1953. He last visited America for surgery in 1960 and to attend the 1961 Kentucky Derby.

Susan Hamburger

See also: Horse Racing.

FURTHER READING
Gates, Henry Louis, Jr., and Cornell West. *The African-American Century: How Black Americans Have Shaped Our Country*. New York: Free Press, 2000.
Hotaling, Edward. *The Great Black Jockeys: The Lives and Times of the Men Who Dominated America's First National Sport*. Rocklin, CA: Forum, 1999.
New York Times, March 25, 1974.
"The Saga of Jimmy Winkfield." *Ebony*, June 1974, 64–70.

★ ★ ★

Kellen WINSLOW

Born November 5, 1957, St. Louis, Missouri
Football player

A graduate of East St. Louis High School (Illinois), Winslow was drafted in the first round (thirteenth overall) into the National Football League (NFL) by the San Diego Charges in 1979, out of the University of Missouri.

The San Diego Chargers had traded up to acquire Winslow with their first-round pick. He was considered the final weapon the Chargers needed to gain "aerial supremacy" in the NFL.

Winslow, however, had an average first season, one that was hampered by injuries. He missed two weeks of training camp with a torn hamstring and then broke his leg weeks into the season. He had only twenty-five catches and two touchdowns when his first year as a pro ended after seven contests. Having much to prove to himself and his teammates, Winslow had a stellar, league-leading second season in 1980, his best year as a pro. He led the NFL in receptions with eighty-nine, thirty more than the next-best tight end. He gained 1,290 yards with nine touchdowns and averaged 14.5 yards per reception. He was considered too fast for linebackers to cover and generally found himself checked by defensive backs. A big tight end, Winslow broke tackles with relative ease. He was hard to bring down by any single player; it usually took several players to bring him to the ground. "When you think about Winslow, you think Superman," said Miami Dolphins head coach Don Shula in a press conference in 1982. The superlatives about Winslow were numerous. He was once said to have defied the "All Pro" classification—he was "All Universe."

Winslow ended his injury-plagued but stellar NFL career in 1987, as the premier tight end of his era. Winslow played in five Pro Bowls, had a career record 541 receptions for 6,741 yards, scored forty-five touchdowns, and averaged 12.5 yards per reception. He was elected into the NFL Hall of Fame in 1995.

Gary A. Sailes

FURTHER READING
Ashe, Arthur R., Jr. *A Hard Road To Glory: A History of the African-American Athlete Since 1946.* New York: Amistad, 1993.
JPJ Net (www.jpj.net/mikeg/playerpercent20profiles/winslow.htm).
Pro Football Hall of Fame (www.profootballhof.com/players/enshrinees/kwinslow.cfm).
Shropshire, Kenneth L. *In Black and White: Race and Sports in America.* New York: New York University Press, 1996.

★ ★ ★

WOMEN

African-American women have been involved in various aspects of sport since very early in the history of the United States. The evidence is clear from slave narratives, travel accounts, plantation diaries, and other published testimony that African-American women participated in informal games and organized competitive recreational activities with other slave children and white children on both small farms and larger plantations in the antebellum South. Generally free from the hard work and toil required of their mothers and fathers, slave girls had time to roam the fields and woods of their own plantation, engage in dances, and participate in numerous games and physically challenging competitive activities. Although less is known about the smaller number of free African-American women of the pre-Civil War period, they also must have participated to some extent in sport-related activities.

African-American women continued their involvement in sport throughout the latter half of the nineteenth century. Although at a disadvantage because of this country's deep-seated gender and racial stereotypes, African-American women exercised, engaged in an assortment of recreations and popular pastimes, and participated in sport both within and outside of educational institutions. The scant information indicates that upper-class African-American women in particular visited "watering holes," engaged in gymnastics, bicycled, golfed, rode horses, and played croquet and tennis.

The early part of the twentieth century saw an increasing number of African-American women participating in sport. The growth of popular sport, the playground movement, the rise of consumer culture, and the northward migration of southern blacks all combined to produce an atmosphere conducive to the participation of African-American women in athletics and highly competitive sport. In addition, the African-American community seemed receptive, and in some cases encouraging, to women engaging in sport than the white community was to white women. While white women avoided sport because of its masculine image, African-American women tested their physical skills and exhibited their competitive spirit in basketball, softball, track and field, and a host of other popular sports. Why it was more acceptable for African-American women to participate in sport than for their white counterparts is a difficult question to answer with any certainty, but it probably stemmed, according to Susan Cahn, from the fact that "African-American women did not tie femininity to a specific, limited set of activities and attributes defined as separate and opposite from masculinity." This left African-American women free to pursue careers in sport and a host of other activities without the constant fear of being branded mannish or unfeminine.

Perhaps the most famous group of African-American women athletes during the early twentieth century was the track and field team at Tuskegee Institute. Organized in 1929, it dominated the sport during the 1930s and 1940s, winning all but one AAU outdoor championship between 1937 and 1948. Lula Hymes, Leila Perry, and especially Alice Coachman were three of the many women track and field performers from Tuskegee Institute who realized national recognition for their athletic exploits.

Succeeding Tuskegee Institute as the next great power in women's track and field was Tennessee State University. Coached by the great Edward Temple, the Tigerbelles dominated women's track and field during the 1950s and 1960s. The most famous Tigerbelle of all was Wilma Rudolph, the beautiful sprinter who garnered international acclaim for capturing three gold medals in the 1960 Rome Olympics. Nicknamed the "black gazelle" by the American press, Rudolph realized hero status in the African-American community; her exploits were recounted in black newspapers, periodicals, and popular magazines.

Coinciding with the outstanding exploits of Wilma Rudolph and her Tennessee State teammates were the great performances of tennis pioneer Althea Gibson. A native of Harlem and mentored by tennis legend Dr. William Johnson, Gibson startled the world in 1957 and 1958 by capturing both the Wimbledon and U.S. Open championships. Her triumphs in two of tennis's most prestigious championships brought her worldwide fame and immediate hero status in the African-American community. Although never wanting to be a race leader or symbol of justice in the mold of Jackie Robinson, Gibson, by her exploits on the tennis courts, served as a needed example of achievement for African Americans and helped open doors for other black women in sport and the larger American society.

The status of African-American women athletes in the post-Gibson era has been mixed. The passage of Title IX and other legislation has been of enormous benefit to African-American women athletes, just as it has been to white women athletes. The last three decades have seen an increasing number of African-American women athletes distinguish themselves in sport at all levels of competition. Unfortunately, they are disproportionately represented in only a few sports, most notably basketball and track and field. A number of societal factors have resulted in the funneling of the bulk of African-American women athletes into these two sports and conversely an underrepresentation in such sports as golf, tennis, and swimming.

The disproportionate representation on the playing fields, however, pales in comparison to the status of African-American women in coaching and upper-level administrative positions within sport. Other than Anita De Frantz (the only African American on the International Olympic Committee) and a smattering of coaches and athletic officials at the high school, college, and professional levels, African-American women are almost nonexistent within positions of power in sport. This is an indication that racism still pervades what is commonly considered one of America's most democratic institutions.

David K. Wiggins

See also: Ed Temple.

FURTHER READING

Brooks, Dana, and Ronald Althouse. *Racism in College Athletics: The African American Experience*. Morgantown, WV: Fitness Information Technology, 2000.

Cahn, Susan. *Coming on Strong: Gender and Sexuality in Twentieth-Century Women's Sports*. New York: Free Press, 1994.

Festle, Mary Jo. *Playing Nice: Politics and Apologies in Women's Sports*. New York: Columbia University Press, 1996.

Guttmann, Allen. *Women's Sports: A History*. New York: Columbia University Press, 1991.

Stockard, Bessie. "The Black Female Athlete: Past and Present." *Crisis* 90 (May 1983): 16–18.

Vertinsky, Patricia, and Gwendolyn Captain. "More Myth than History: American Culture and Representations of the Black Female's Athletic Ability." *Journal of Sport History* 25 (Fall 1998): 532–61.

★ ★ ★

Lynette WOODARD

Born August 12, 1959, Wichita, Kansas
Basketball player

Lynette Woodard is the daughter of Lugene, a firefighter, and Dorothy. As a fourteen-year-old freshman at Wichita's North High School, Woodard played on the junior varsity team and a year later led her school team to its first-ever state title. At the state championship Woodard was spotted by University of Kansas coach Marian Washington, who recognized in Woodard a precocious talent. Not surprisingly, Woodard was recruited as a Lady Jayhawk in 1978.

At Kansas, the five-foot, eleven-inch Woodard was the epitome of versatility. She ball-handled like a guard, was tall and strong enough to play as a power forward, and dominated the statistic sheets in terms of rebounding *and* scoring. In the years 1978–1981 she was an annual recipient of a Kodak All-American award. Her senior year saw her set a women's collegiate basketball record of 3,649 points. In 1984, she captained the U.S. women's team to a gold medal in the Los Angeles Olympic Games. The following year she was inducted into the Women's Sport Foundation's Hall of Fame.

In 1995 Lynette Woodard made history by becoming the first woman to play for the famed Harlem Globetrotters. (AP/Wide World Photos)

Her most celebrated accomplishment took place, however, in 1985, when she became the first woman to play for the Harlem Globetrotters. While some saw Woodard's role on the Globetrotters as a form of exploitation or manipulation (capitalizing upon the promotional and publicity value of a handsome and athletic female to bolster dropping spectator figures), Woodard found her two-year stint with the touring team both educational and enjoyable.

From 1989 to 1993 she played professional basketball in Italy and Japan. Subsequently, she worked for the Kansas Missouri School District and then was vice president of MAGNA Securities Corporation, a unique brokerage firm in that it was owned and operated by women of color. In 1997 Woodard joined the Cleveland Rockers organization in the fledgling Women's National Basketball League.

Scott A.G.M. Crawford

FURTHER READING
Kirsch, George, Othello Harris, and Claire E. Nolte, eds. *Encyclopedia of Ethnicity and Sports in the United States*. Westport, CT: Greenwood Press, 2000.
Layden, Joe. *Women in Sports*. Santa Monica, CA: General Publishing Group, 1997.
Sherrow, Victoria. *Encyclopedia of Women and Sports*. Santa Barbara, CA: ABC-CLIO, 1996.

★ ★ ★

John WOODRUFF

Born July 5, 1915, Connellsville, Pennsylvania
Runner

John Woodruff is the grandson of slaves; his father, Silas, worked for the H.C. Frick Coke Company, and his mother, Sarah, did laundry for wealthy families. Woodruff graduated from Connellsville High School, earned an undergraduate degree in sociology from the University of Pittsburgh in 1939, and earned a master's from New York University in 1941.

In 1935 Woodruff broke the national high school record for the mile. In his first year at the University of Pittsburgh, Woodruff qualified for the 1936 Olympic games in the 880-meter race. Woodruff came from back in the pack to win the gold medal in the race. In his remaining three years at the University of Pittsburgh Woodruff won several races, including three national championships in the half-mile. In 1944 he set the American record at 800 meters with a time of 1:48.6. Woodruff's performance, along with those of Jesse Owens and other African-American athletes at the 1936 Olympics in Berlin, upset Adolf Hitler's intended display of Aryan supremacy.

Following his athletic career Woodruff served in the U.S. military during World War II and the Korean War. He later worked in New York City with the Children's Aid Society and the Department of Welfare, served as recreation director for the Police Athletic League, and taught in the public schools.

The John Woodruff 5-K Run and Walk in Connellsville was established in his honor. Woodruff was inducted into the USA Track and Field Hall of Fame in 1978.

Rita Liberti

See also: Track and Field.

FURTHER READING
Connellsville Area Historical Society (www.fay-west.com/connellsville/historic/woodruff/shtml).
Ehrbar, Tommy. "Hitting His Stride." *Pitt Magazine* 1 (June 1996): 30–31.
Henderson, Edwin B. *The Negro in Sports*. Washington, DC: Associated Publishers, 1939.
Mandell, Richard D. *The Nazi Olympics*. New York: Macmillan, 1971.
USA Track and Field (www.usatf.org).

★ ★ ★

Eldrick "Tiger" WOODS

Born December 30, 1975, Cypress, California
Golfer

Golf great "Tiger" (born Eldrick T.) Woods is the son of Earl Woods, a retired lieutenant colonel in the U.S. Army. Although Woods is usually identified as African American, his father is of African, American Indian, and Chinese ancestry, and his mother, Kultida Punsawad Woods, is Thai,

"Tiger" Woods celebrating with his classic pumping of the fist after making an eagle putt on the 18th green in the 2000 Mercedes Championships in Kapalua, Hawaii. The putt forced a playoff with Ernie Els, which Woods won on the second hole. (AP/Wide World Photos)

Chinese, and Caucasian. After completing high school, Woods attended Stanford University for two years before joining the professional golf tour in August 1996.

By the time Woods turned professional, he had compiled one of the finest amateur golf records ever. In addition to junior events, Woods won the U.S. Amateur in 1994, 1995, and 1996, becoming the first golfer in history to win that title in three consecutive years. He won his first professional tournament, the Las Vegas Invitational, just weeks after joining the PGA Tour. In 1997, Woods won his first major tournament, the Masters. While continuing to collect minor tournament titles, in 1999 Woods won his second major event, the PGA Championship. In 2000–2001, Woods had one of the greatest competitive golf seasons in history, becoming the first player to win four straight major titles (U.S. Open, British Open, PGA Championships in 2000, and the Masters in 2001), completing the career Grand Slam and winning twelve tournaments overall. By early 2001, the twenty-five-year-old Woods had won twenty-seven professional events. In the process, Woods signed multimillion-dollar endorsement contracts, making him one of the wealthiest and arguably the most recognized athlete in the world.

Although it is too early to evaluate Woods's historical significance, it is safe to conclude that he is by far the most successful minority athlete in golf and that he will be considered among the greatest competitive golfers of all time. Woods should also be mentioned with the likes of Walter Hagen, Byron Nelson, and Arnold Palmer—men who contributed to golf by popularizing it and broadening its appeal. Finally, whereas Lee Elder's place in history was established when he became the first minority golfer to compete in the Masters Tournament, in 1975, Tiger Woods will always be remembered as the first minority golfer to win that coveted title.

Stephen R. Lowe

See also: Golf.

FURTHER READING
Rosaforte, Tim. *Raising the Bar: The Championship Years of Tiger Woods*. New York: St. Martin's Press, 2000.
———. *Tiger Woods: The Makings of a Champion*. New York: St. Martin's Press, 1997.

Strege, John. *Tiger: A Biography of Tiger Woods.* New York: Broadway Books, 1997.

Woods, Earl, with Pete McDaniel. *Training a Tiger.* New York: HarperCollins, 1997.

★ ★ ★

James WORTHY

Born February 27, 1961, Gastonia, North Carolina
Basketball player

The son of Ervin and Gladys Worthy, James Worthy grew up in Gastonia, graduating from Ashbrook High School in 1979. From 1979 until 1982 Worthy attended the University of North Carolina (UNC). A broken ankle ended his freshman season after only fourteen games. The following season, however, Worthy was named second-team All-ACC and helped UNC to a second-place finish in the NCAA Tournament. In 1982 Worthy, now a first-team All-ACC and UPI All-America selection, averaged 15.6 points per game and led the Tar Heels to a 63–62 victory over Georgetown in the NCAA title game. He scored twenty-eight points in the championship game and was voted Final Four Most Valuable Player. Worthy left UNC after his junior year, with 1,219 career points.

The Los Angeles Lakers made Worthy the first pick of the 1982 NBA draft. He helped the Lakers win NBA titles in 1985, 1987, and 1988. A model of consistency, the six-foot, nine-inch Worthy featured a rare blend of speed and power. He was named to the NBA All-Star teams of 1986–1992. Nicknamed "Big Game James," Worthy excelled in important contests. He scored thirty-six points against Detroit in the seventh game of the 1988 finals and was selected NBA Finals Most Valuable Player. Worthy was named third-team All-NBA in 1990 and 1991.

Worthy retired following the 1994 season. He had scored 16,320 points in the NBA, averaging 17.6 per game—21.1 points per game in the postseason. In 1997 Worthy was named one of the top fifty players in NBA history.

Jim L. Sumner

FURTHER READING

Morris, Ron. *ACC Basketball: An Illustrated History.* Chapel Hill, NC: Four Corners Press, 1988.

Rapoport, Ron. "One on One with James Worthy." *Sport*, May 1991, 15–16.

Smith, Ron, Ira Winderman, and Mary Schmidt Boyer, eds. *Complete Encyclopedia of Basketball.* New York: Carlton Books, 2001.

Springer, Steve. *The Los Angeles Times Encyclopedia of the Lakers.* Los Angeles: Los Angeles Times, 1998.

★ ★ ★

WRESTLING

Wrestling has not been one of the most popular sports among African Americans. The popularity of other sports, limited funding, opposition to interracial matches, and other factors have limited the involvement of African Americans in wrestling. There have been, however, a select number of African Americans who have achieved success in wrestling in predominantly white universities, historically black colleges and universities, the armed forces, and local clubs.

Perhaps the most notable of these wrestlers were those who competed for predominantly white universities and captured various titles at the NCAA or NAIA championships and in Olympic, AAU, and Pan-American Games competition. These would include such outstanding grapplers as Robert Douglas of Oklahoma State University, Lee Kemp of the University of Wisconsin, Darryl Burley of Lehigh University, Kenny Monday of

Oklahoma State University, Nate Carr of Iowa State University, Jimmy Jackson of Oklahoma State University, and Ron Simmons of Florida State University. Of these men it is probably Douglas who has had the most profound and long-lasting influence on the sport. A Big Eight champion in 1965 at the 147-pound division and captain of the 1968 Olympic team, Douglas became the first African-American wrestling coach at a major white institution (Arizona State) and was an assistant coach of the 1984 U.S. Olympic team. Douglas's record as both competitor and coach resulted in his election to the National Wrestling Hall of Fame in 1987.

David K. Wiggins

FURTHER READING
Ashe, Arthur R., Jr. *A Hard Road to Glory*. New York: Amistad, 1993.
"Negro Wrestlers." *Ebony* 17 (May 1962): 43–44.

Andrew S. "Doc" YOUNG

Born October 29, 1919, Danbrooke, Virginia
Died September 6, 1996, Los Angeles, California
Journalist

After graduating from Hampton Institute in 1941, Young began his journalism career as a sportswriter and editor for the *Cleveland Call and Post*. In 1949, Young became the sports editor for the largest black newspaper in the western United States, the *Los Angeles Sentinel*. During the same period, Young was the West Coast editor for the *Chicago Defender*. Later, he moved to Chicago and worked six years as the *Defender*'s associate editor.

Young remained closely affiliated with the *Los Angeles Sentinel*, serving as its longtime executive editor. A prolific writer, he published hundreds of magazine articles and syndicated columns in numerous newspapers. Young was sports editor for *Jet*, *Ebony*, and *Hue* magazines and worked as a publicist for several movies. He published several notable sports books, including *Negro Firsts in Sports*, *Great Negro Baseball Stars*, *Black Athletes in the New Golden Age of Sports*, and *Sonny Liston: The Champ Nobody Wanted*.

Young was a member of the Baseball Writers Association and influential leader in pressuring major league baseball to open an African-American wing inside its Hall of Fame. Later in his career, Young became heavily involved in Republican politics, working for the gubernatorial campaign of Nelson Rockefeller in 1964 and the presidential campaigns of Richard Nixon in 1968 and Gerald Ford in 1976. Young was a longtime member of the National Association for the Advancement of Colored People (NAACP) and the Los Angeles Urban League.

Tracey M. Salisbury

Andrew S. "Doc" Young, the prolific sportswriter of the *Chicago Defender* who spent much of his career charting the history of the African-American experience in sport. (Sports Archive)

FURTHER READING
Ashe, Arthur R., Jr. *A Hard Road to Glory: A History of the African-American Athlete*. New York: Warner Books, 1988.
Kirsch, George B., Othello Harris, and Claire E. Nolte, eds., *Encyclopedia of Ethnicity and Sports in the United States*. Westport, CT: Greenwood Press, 2000.
Los Angeles Times, September 13, 1996.

★ ★ ★

Buddy YOUNG

Born January 5, 1926, Chicago, Illinois
Died September 4, 1983, Terrell, Texas
Football player

The son of a Pullman porter, Claude Young, and his wife Lillian, Buddy Young first attended Englewood High School in Chicago, where he was told that he was too small, at five feet, four inches, for football. Upon transferring to Phillips High School, Young starred in football and track. In 1943, he led the Chicago league in scoring; 80,000 spectators thronged to Soldier Field to witness the city championship game against the Catholic League opponent.

At the University of Illinois in 1944, Young tied Red Grange's freshman scoring record with thirteen touchdowns. He also tied the world record for the sixty-yard dash and led Illinois to the national track championship. He spent 1945 in the merchant marine, playing football at a California naval base, and marrying Geraldine Young. He returned to Illinois in 1946; that year its football team claimed the Western Conference (Big Ten) championship and routed UCLA in the Rose Bowl. The following year he led Illinois in rushing and total offense and set the school record for the longest run from scrimmage. Young was also selected the Most Valuable Player in the College All-Star Game and won All-American honors.

He started his pro football career in 1947 with the New York Yankees of the All-American Football Conference, subsequently playing with Brooklyn, New York, Dallas, and Baltimore of the National Football League. He led the league (1949, AAFC; 1951, 1952, NFL) in punt returns and kickoff returns (1952, NFL) and set the Baltimore record for the longest kickoff return. The Colts retired his jersey number; he served the team as a scout from 1956 to 1963 before becoming the NFL director of player relations until his death in a car accident.

Gerald R. Gems

FURTHER READING
Ashe, Arthur R., Jr. *A Hard Road To Glory: Football.* New York: Amistad Press, 1988.

Chicago Tribune, September 6, 1983.
LaBlanc, Michael L., ed. *Professional Sports Team Histories.* Detroit: Gale Research, 1994.
Maher, Tod, and Bob Gill, eds. *The Pro Football Encyclopedia.* New York: Macmillan, 1997.
Porter, David L., ed. *Biographical Dictionary of American Sports: Football.* Westport, CT: Greenwood Press, 1987.

★ ★ ★

Fay YOUNG

Born October 2, 1884, Williamsport, Pennsylvania
Died October 27, 1957, Chicago, Illinois
Journalist

Young attended Medford High School in Massachusetts and South Division High School in Chicago. He started freelancing for the *Chicago Defender* in 1912 while he worked as a dining car waiter for the Northwestern Railroad. Three years later, the paper made him a paid staff member. Except for his three years as the managing editor of the *Kansas City Call,* he spent his entire career with the *Defender.* There, he was a reporter, city editor, sports editor, and managing editor.

Young was the first full-time black sportswriter in the country and the first to cover black college sports. He also developed the first sports section in a black newspaper, while he was sports editor of the *Defender.* A booster of black athletes, Young was one of the first black sportswriters to protest organized baseball's ban on black players. He also attended the founding meeting of the Negro National League and served as its official scorer-statistician. In addition he was secretary and director of publicity for the Negro American League, a broadcaster on WSBC-AM, and a timekeeper for boxing matches.

Although some perceived him as gruff, Young earned recognition for activities away from the office. A horticulturist, stockbreeder, and philanthropist, he was also interested in the education of black youths; after he helped Tennessee A & I State University establish its poultry plant, the school named it after him.

Michael Marsh

See also: Sportswriters.

FURTHER READING
Cowans, Russ. "Fabulous 'Fay': Defender's Frank Young Had Long Well-Rounded and Colorful Career." *Chicago Defender*, November 9, 1957.
Ebony, October 1970, 56–58, 60–62, 64.
Orodenker, Richard, ed. *Dictionary of Literary Biography: American Sportswriters and Writers on Sport*. Vol. 241. Farmington Hills, MI: Bruccoli Clark Layman, 2001.
Reisler, Jim. *Black Writers/Black Baseball: An Anthology of Articles from Black Sportswriters Who Covered the Negro Leagues*. Jefferson, NC: McFarland, 1993.

★ ★ ★

Paul "Tank" YOUNGER

Born June 25, 1928, Grambling, Louisiana
Football player

Younger earned his nickname at Grambling College, where he matriculated in 1945. Initially considered a lineman, Coach Eddie Robinson recognized the rapid acceleration that propelled Younger's six-foot three-inch, 225-pound frame and transformed him into a running back; he soon began running over would-be tacklers. Younger led the nation in scoring as a freshman, with twenty-five touchdowns. In 1948, the *Pittsburgh Courier* named him to its All-American team, and he finished his collegiate tenure with a national record of sixty career touchdowns.

The Los Angeles Rams signed Younger as a free agent in 1949. He enjoyed a ten-year career in the National Football League, with the Rams (1949–1957) and Pittsburgh Steelers (1958), as a running back and linebacker. As the first African American from a historically black college to play in the NFL, Younger put stereotypical and racist assumptions about talent and coaching into question. He won selection to the All-NFL team as a linebacker in 1951, was third in the league in rushing in 1954, and garnered Pro Bowl selection five times. Younger was the first African American to play in the league's All-Star contest and its first black assistant general manager, in 1975.

Gerald R. Gems

FURTHER READING
Ashe, Arthur R., Jr. *A Hard Road to Glory: Football*. New York: Amistad Press, 1988.
LaBlanc, Michael L. ed. *Professional Sports Team Histories*. Detroit: Gale Research, 1994.
Maher, Tod, and Bob Gill, eds. *The Pro Football Encyclopedia*. New York: Macmillan, 1997.

CHRONOLOGY

1777

Bill Richmond, born a free black in Staten Island, New York, travels to England, where he becomes a successful boxer, tavern owner, and mentor to Tom Molineaux.

1810

Tom Molineaux, reputedly a former slave from Virginia, fights the first of his two championship bouts against Tom Crib in England.

1866

The Pythian Baseball Club is founded in Philadelphia.

1872

Bud Fowler becomes the first black professional baseball player, on a team from New Castle, Pennsylvania.

1875

Jockey Oliver Lewis captures the first Kentucky Derby.

1879

Frank Hart competes in the Sir Astley belt pedestrian race in New York's Madison Square Garden.

1884

Moses Fleetwood Walker becomes the first African American in major league baseball by playing with Toledo in the American Association.

Jockey Isaac Murphy wins his first of three Kentucky Derbies.

1885

The Cuban Giants, often considered the first black professional baseball team, are organized.

1890

George Dixon captures the world bantamweight title by defeating Nunc Wallace.

1892

Biddle University (now Johnson C. Smith) defeats Livingston College in a Thanksgiving Day football game.

William Henry Lewis of Harvard is selected for the first time as a center on Walter Camp's All-American football team.

1894

The League of American Wheelmen inserts a whites-only clause in its constitution.

1896

John Shippen plays in his first of five U.S. Open golf championships.

Marshall "Major" Taylor wins his first professional bicycle race, in New York's Madison Square Garden.

1904

George Poage becomes first African American to represent the United States in the Olympic Games.

Jockey Jimmy Winkfield travels to Russia and wins that country's National Riding Championship.

Charles Follis signs a professional football contract with the Shelby Athletic Association.

1905

Sol White documents the beginnings of black baseball in his *Sol White's History of Colored Base Ball*.

1908

John Baxter Taylor, the outstanding quarter-miler from the University of Pennsylvania, captures a gold medal as a member of the 4 x 400-meter relay team at the Olympic Games in London.

CHRONOLOGY

1910

Jack Johnson defeats former heavyweight champion Jim Jeffries in Reno, Nevada.

1912

The Central Intercollegiate Athletic Association (CIAA) is founded.

1916

Fritz Pollard of Brown University plays in the Rose Bowl, against Washington State.

American Tennis Association (ATA) is founded in Washington, DC.

1919

Howard and Lincoln (Pennsylvania) Universities begin their annual Thanksgiving Day football game.

1920

Rube Foster organizes the Negro National League (NNL).

Paul Robeson, the great scholar-athlete from Rutgers University, signs to play professional football for the Fritz Pollard-coached Akron Pros.

1921

Shady Rest Golf and Country Club, the first of its kind in the African-American community, is organized in Scotch Plains, New Jersey.

1923

Bob Douglas establishes the New York Renaissance Five basketball team in Harlem.

1925

The United Golfers Association (UGA) is founded.

1927

The Harlem Globetrotters are founded in Chicago by Abe Saperstein.

1929

Tuskegee Institute organizes a women's track and field team.

1930

Josh Gibson, often referred to as the "black Babe Ruth," begins his outstanding fifteen-year career in Negro League Baseball by joining the Homestead Grays.

1932

Eddie Tolan captures both the 100 and 200-meter dashes at the Olympic Games in Los Angeles.

1933

Gus Greenlee organizes Negro League Baseball's East-West All-Star game.

1934

The National Football League (NFL), after years of integrated play, once again has no African-American players on its teams' rosters.

1936

Jesse Owens captures four gold medals in the Olympic Games in Berlin.

The New York Pioneer Track Club for Harlem men and boys is founded by Robert Douglas, William Culbreath, and Joseph J. Yancey.

1937

The Negro American League (NAL) is founded.

1938

Joe Louis defeats Max Schmeling in a first-round knockout.

1939

Edwin Bancroft Henderson writes the first book on the history of African-American athletes, *The Negro in Sports*.

1946

Woody Strode and Kenny Washington reintegrate the NFL by signing with the Los Angeles Rams.

1947

Jackie Robinson reintegrates major league baseball by joining the Brooklyn Dodgers.

Larry Doby becomes the first African American to play in the American League by signing with the Cleveland Indians.

1948

Alice Coachman captures a gold medal in the high jump at the Olympic Games in London.

John Davis wins his first of two gold medals in the heavyweight division at the Olympic Games in London.

Don Barksdale captains the U.S. gold medal-winning Olympic basketball team.

Sam Lacy is admitted to the Baseball Writers Association.

1949

The American Bowling Congress (ABC) is founded.

1950

Arthur Dorrington begins his professional career with Atlantic City of the Eastern Hockey League.

Earl Lloyd, former West Virginia State College star, integrates the National Basketball Association (NBA) by playing with the Washington Capitols.

1951

Willie Mays begins his major league baseball career with the New York Giants (San Francisco Giants after 1957).

Sherman White of Long Island University is sentenced to a year in jail for his involvement in college basketball scandals.

Joe Louis retires from boxing for the final time after failed comeback attempts.

1954

Mal Whitfield becomes first African American to win the James E. Sullivan Award as the best amateur athlete in the United States.

1955

Indianapolis's Crispus Attucks High School, led by the great Oscar Robertson, wins the first of its back-to-back Indiana state basketball championships.

1957

Althea Gibson wins the singles title at both the U.S. Open and Wimbledon tennis championships.

1958

Willie O'Ree becomes the first black player in the National Hockey League by signing with the Boston Bruins.

Syracuse University's Jim Brown wins the Jim Thorpe Award as college football's outstanding running back.

1959

The Boston Red Sox become the last team in major league baseball to integrate by signing Pumpsie Green.

1960

Wilma Rudolph wins three gold medals at the Olympic Games in Rome.

Floyd Patterson regains boxing's heavyweight title by knocking out Sweden's Ingemar Johansson.

1961

The Caucasian-only clause in the Professional Golfer's Association Constitution is eliminated.

John McLendon becomes head coach of the Cleveland Pipers of the American Basketball Association.

Ernie Davis, an outstanding running back from Syracuse University, wins the Heisman Trophy.

1962

The Washington Redskins become the last team in the NFL to integrate when they sign the Cleveland Browns' Bobby Mitchell.

Basketball's Wilt Chamberlain scores 100 points against the New York Knickerbockers.

1964

Cassius Clay (later Muhammad Ali) captures the heavyweight championship by defeating Sonny Liston in Miami, Florida.

1965

Jerry Levias integrates the Southwest Conference by signing a football scholarship with Southern Methodist University.

American Football League's East-West All-Star game is moved from New Orleans after black players threaten a boycott because of the city's racial segregation.

1966

Texas Western University's basketball team, with five black starters, defeats the University of Kentucky in College Park, Maryland.

CHRONOLOGY

Bill Russell becomes player-coach of the Boston Celtics.

Emmett Ashford becomes the first African-American umpire in major league baseball.

1967

Renee Powell becomes first African-American woman on the ladies' Professional Golf Association (PGA) tour.

Harry Edwards leads a boycott of the San Jose State and University of Texas at El Paso football game and the New York Athletic Club's 100th anniversary track and field meet at Madison Square Garden.

The New York Athletic Commission strips Muhammad Ali of his heavyweight championship after his refusal to be inducted into the army.

1968

Tommie Smith and John Carlos raise black-gloved fists in protest on the victory stand at the Mexico City Olympic Games.

Arthur Ashe wins the singles title at the U.S. Lawn Tennis Association Championships at Forest Hills, New York.

Bob Beamon breaks the world long-jump record at the Mexico City Olympic Games with a leap of twenty-nine feet, two and a half inches.

1969

Curt Flood challenges the reserve clause by refusing to accept a trade to the Philadelphia Phillies.

Fourteen black football players from the University of Wyoming are kicked off the team after wearing black armbands in a game against Brigham Young to protest Mormon racial policies.

1970

Bodybuilder Chris Dickerson becomes the first black Mr. America.

1971

Satchel Paige is elected to the Baseball Hall of Fame.

Kareem Abdul-Jabbar of the Milwaukee Bucks is the NBA top scorer and most valuable player.

1972

Wayne Embry is appointed general manager of the Milwaukee Bucks.

1973

George Foreman captures the heavyweight championship over Joe Frazier in Kingston, Jamaica.

O.J. Simpson of the Buffalo Bills breaks a National Football League's single-season record by rushing for 2,003 yards.

1974

The Don King–orchestrated world heavyweight championship fight between Muhammad Ali and George Foreman is staged in Kinshasa, Zaire, in Africa.

Hank Aaron breaks Babe Ruth's record of 714 home runs.

1975

Lee Elder becomes first African American to play in the Masters Golf Tournament.

Frank Robinson becomes major league baseball's first African-American manager.

Archie Griffin of Ohio State becomes the first player to win the Heisman Trophy twice.

1976

Bill Lucas is named director of player personnel of the Atlanta Braves.

1977

Walter Payton of the Chicago Bears rushes for a single-game record of 275 yards.

Reggie Jackson of the New York Yankees hits three home runs in one game and five total in the World Series against the Los Angeles Dodgers.

1979

Willie Jeffries becomes head football coach at Wichita State University.

Magic Johnson leads the Michigan State University basketball team to the National Collegiate Athletic Association (NCAA) championship.

CHRONOLOGY

1981

James Frank, president of Lincoln (Missouri) University, becomes the first African-American president of the NCAA.

1982

John Chaney is hired as basketball coach at Temple University.

1984

Lynette Woodard becomes a member of the Harlem Globetrotters.

Carl Lewis duplicates Jesse Owens's four Berlin gold medal-winning performances at the Los Angeles Olympic Games.

1986

Anita De Frantz, president of the Amateur Athletic Foundation, is named as a representative to the International Olympic Committee (IOC).

Mike Tyson becomes the World Boxing Council (WBC) heavyweight champion.

1987

Sugar Ray Leonard defeats Marvelous Marvin Hagler in a controversial split decision for the WBC middleweight championship.

1988

The Black Coaches Association (BCA) is founded by seventeen Division I basketball coaches.

Jackie Joyner-Kersee wins a gold medal in the heptathlon at the Olympic Games in Seoul, Korea.

Quarterback Doug Williams leads the Washington Redskins to a Super Bowl championship over the Denver Broncos.

1989

Bill White is named president of major league baseball's National League.

1991

Ricky Henderson breaks major league baseball's base-stealing record.

Willie T. Ribbs becomes first African American to qualify for the Indianapolis 500.

1992

The Black Women in Sports Foundation is organized in Philadelphia.

The Rainbow Coalition for Fairness in Athletics is established.

Dominique Dawes and Elizabeth Okino compete on the U.S. gymnastic team at the Olympic Games in Barcelona, Spain.

1993

Mannie Jackson becomes the first African American to own the Harlem Globetrotters.

1995

Hoop Dreams, an award-winning film documenting the quest for basketball fame of black players from Chicago, is released.

1996

ESPN names Michael Jordan "Sportsman of the Century."

1997

Tiger Woods captures his first Masters golf tournament.

Eddie Robinson retires as football coach at Grambling after amassing 408 victories.

2000

Serena and Venus Williams win the gold medal in women's doubles at the Olympic Games in Sydney, Australia.

2001

Barry Bonds of the San Francisco Giants breaks Mark McGwire's single-season home-run record.

Lisa Leslie leads the Los Angeles Sparks to the Women's National Basketball Association (WNBA) championship.

2002

Emmett Smith of the Dallas Cowboys breaks Walter Payton's all-time NFL rushing record.

BIBLIOGRAPHY

Aaron, Hank, with Lonnie Wheeler. *I Had a Hammer: The Hank Aaron Story.* New York: HarperCollins, 1991.

Abdul-Jabbar, Kareem, and Peter Knobler. *Giant Steps: The Autobiography of Kareem Abdul-Jabbar.* New York: Bantam, 1983.

Abrahams, Roger D. *Singing the Master: The Emergence of African American Culture in the Plantation South.* New York: Pantheon Books, 1992.

Ali, Muhammad, with Richard Durham. *The Greatest: My Own Story.* New York: Random House, 1975.

Allen, Maury. *Jackie Robinson: A Life Remembered.* New York: Franklin Watts, 1987.

Andrews, David. "The Fact(s) of Michael Jordan's Blackness: Excavating a Floating Racial Signifier." *Sociology of Sport Journal* 13 (1996): 125–58.

———, ed. "Deconstructing Michael Jordan: Reconstructing Postindustrial America." *Sociology of Sport Journal* 13 (1996).

Ashe, Arthur R., Jr. *A Hard Road to Glory: A History of the African-American Athlete.* 3 vols. New York: Ballantine, 1976.

Ashe, Arthur, and Arnold Rampersad. *Days of Grace: A Memoir.* New York: Alfred A. Knopf, 1993.

Astor, Gerald. *And a Credit to His Race: The Hard Life and Times of Joseph Louis Barrow.* New York: Saturday Review Press, 1974.

Axthelm, Pete. *The City Game.* New York: Harper and Row, 1970.

Azevedo, Mario, and Jeffrey T. Sammons. "Contributions in Science, Business Film, and Sports." In *Africana Studies: A Survey of Africa and the African Diaspora*, edited by Mario Azevedo, 353–60. Durham, NC: Carolina Academic Press, 1993.

Bacote, Clarence A. *The Story of Atlanta University: A Century of Service, 1865–1965.* Atlanta: Atlanta University Press, 1969.

Bak, Richard. *Joe Louis: The Great Black Hope.* New York: Taylor, 1996.

Baker, William J. *Jesse Owens: An American Life.* New York: Free Press, 1986.

———. *Sports in the Western World.* Urbana: University of Illinois Press, 1988.

Ball, Donald. "Ascription and Position: A Comparative Analysis of 'Stacking' in Professional Football." *Canadian Review of Sociology and Anthropology* 10 (May 1973): 97–113.

Banker, Stephen. *Black Diamonds: An Oral History of Negro League Baseball.* Princeton, NJ: Visual Education Corporation, 1989.

Bankes, James. *The Pittsburgh Crawfords: The Lives and Times of Black Baseball's Most Exciting Team!* Dubuque, IA: Win. C. Brown, 1991.

Barrow, Joe Louis, Jr., and Barbara Munder. *Joe Louis: 50 Years an American Hero.* New York: McGraw–Hill, 1988.

Bass, Amy. *Not the Triumph but the Struggle: The 1968 Olympics and the Making of the Black Athlete.* Minneapolis: University of Minnesota Press, 2002.

Bederman, Gail. *Manliness and Civilization: A Cultural History of Gender and Race in the United States, 1880–1917.* Chicago: University of Chicago Press, 1995.

Behee, John. *Hail to the Victors! Black Athletes at the University of Michigan.* Ann Arbor, MI: Swink–Tuttle Press, 1974.

Bennett, Bruce L. "Bibliography on the Negro in Sports." *Journal of Health, Physical Education, and Recreation* 41 (September 1970): 77–78.

———. "Supplemental Selected Annotated Bibliography on the Negro in Sports." *Journal of Health, Physical Education, and Recreation* 41 (September 1970): 71.

Bennett, Lerone, Jr. *Before the Mayflower: A History of Black America.* Chicago: Johnson, 1982.

Berkow, Ira. *The Dusable Panthers: The Greatest, Blackest, Saddest Team from the Meanest Street in Chicago.* New York: Atheneum, 1978.

BIBLIOGRAPHY

Berry, Bonnie, and Earl Smith. "Race, Sport, and Crime: The Misrepresentation of African Americans in Team Sports and Crime." *Sociology of Sport Journal* 17 (2000): 171–97.

Berryman, Jack W. "Early Black Leadership in Collegiate Football: Massachusetts as a Pioneer." *Historical Journal of Massachusetts* 9 (June 1981): 17–28.

Birrell, Susan. "Women of Color, Critical Autobiography, and Sport." In *Sport, Men, and the Gender Order: Critical Feminist Perspectives*, edited by Michael A. Messner and Donald F. Sabo, 185–99. Champaign, IL: Human Kinetics, 1990.

Birrell, Susan, and Cheryl Cole, eds. *Women, Sport, and Culture*. Champaign, IL: Human Kinetics, 1993.

Bontemps, Arna. *Famous Negro Athletes*. New York: Dodd, Mead, 1964.

Brailsford, Dennis. *Bareknuckles: A Social History of Prizefighting*. Cambridge, MA: Lutterworth Press, 1988.

Brashler, William. *Josh Gibson: A Life in the Negro Leagues*. New York: Harper and Row, 1978.

Brawley, Benjamin. *History of Morehouse College*. Atlanta: Morehouse College, 1917.

Brooks, Dana D., and Ronald C. Althouse. *The African American Athlete Resource Directory*. Morgantown, WV: Fitness Information Technology, 1996.

———. "African American Head Coaches and Administrators: Progress But . . . ?" In *Racism in College Athletics: The African American Athlete's Experience*, edited by Dana D. Brooks and Ronald C. Althouse, 101–42. Morgantown, WV: Fitness Information Technology, 2000.

———, eds. *Racism in College Athletics: The African American Athlete's Experience*. Morgantown, WV: Fitness Information Technology, 2000.

Broome, Richard. "The Australian Reaction to Jack Johnson, Black Pugilist, 1907–09." In *Sports in History: The Making of Modern Sporting History*, edited by Richard Cashman and Michael McKerman, 343–63. St. Lucia, Australia: University of Queensland Press, 1979.

Brown, Jim. *Off My Chest*. New York: Doubleday, 1964.

Brown, Jim, with Steve Delsohn. *Out of Bounds*. New York: Kensington, 1989.

Brown, Roscoe C., Jr. "A Commentary on Racial Myths and the Black Athlete." In *Social Problems in Athletics*, edited by Daniel M. Landers, 168–73. Urbana: University of Illinois Press, 1976.

Bruce, Janet. *The Kansas City Monarchs: Champions of Black Baseball*. Lawrence: University Press of Kansas, 1985.

Bryant, Howard. *Shut Out: A Story of Race and Baseball in Boston*. New York: Routledge, 2002.

Cahn, Susan. *Coming on Strong: Gender and Sexuality in Twentieth-Century Women's Sport*. New York: Free Press, 1994.

Capeci, Dominic J., Jr., and Martha Wilkerson, "Multifarious Hero: Joe Louis, American Society, and Race Relations During World Crisis, 1935–1945." *Journal of Sport History* 10 (Winter 1983): 5–25.

Captain, Gwendolyn. "Enter Ladies and Gentlemen of Color: Gender, Sport, and the Ideal of African American Manhood and Womanhood During the Late Nineteenth and Early Twentieth Centuries." *Journal of Sport History* 18 (Spring 1991): 81–102.

Carroll, John M. *Fritz Pollard: Pioneer in Racial Advancement*. Urbana: University of Illinois Press, 1992.

Cashmore, Ernest. *Black Sportsmen*. London: Routledge and Kegan Paul, 1982.

Chadwick, Bruce. *When the Game Was Black and White: The Illustrated History of Baseball's Negro Leagues*. New York: Abberville Press, 1992.

Chalk, Ocania. *Black College Sport*. New York: Dodd, Mead, 1976.

———. *Pioneers of Black Sport: The Early Days of the Black Professional Athlete in Baseball, Basketball, Boxing, and Football*. New York: Dodd, Mead, 1975.

Chambers, Ted. *The History of Athletics and Physical Education at Howard University*. Washington, DC: Vantage, 1986.

Coakley, Jay J. *Sport in Society: Issues and Controversies*. 5th ed. St. Louis: Times Mirror/Mosby, 1994.

Cone, Carl B. "The Molineaux–Cribb Fight, 1810: Wuz Tom Molineaux Robbed?" *Journal of Sport History* 9 (Winter 1982): 83–91.

Creeden, Pamela J., ed. *Women, Media and Sport: Challenging Gender Values*. Thousand Oaks, CA: Sage, 1994.

Davies, Richard O. *America's Obsession: Sports and Society Since 1945*. New York: Harcourt Brace, 1994.

Davis, Jack E. "Baseball's Reluctant Challenge: Desegregating Major League Spring Training Sites, 1961–1964." *Journal of Sport History* 19 (Summer 1992): 144–62.

Davis, John P. "The Negro in American Sports." In *The American Negro Reference Book*, edited by John P. Davis, 775–825. Englewood Cliffs, NJ: Prentice Hall, 1966.

Davis, Laurel R. "The Articulation of Difference: White Preoccupation with the Question of Racially Linked Genetic Differences Among Athletes." *Sociology of Sport Journal* 7 (1990): 179–87.

Davis, Lenwood G. *Joe Louis: A Bibliography of Articles, Books, Pamphlets, Records, and Archival Material*. Westport, CT: Greenwood Press, 1983.

Davis, Lenwood G., and Belinda Daniels, comps. *Black Athletes in the United States: A Bibliography of Books, Articles, Autobiographies, and Biographies on Professional Black Athletes, 1800–1981*. Westport, CT: Greenwood Press, 1983.

Davis, Michael D. *Black American Women in Olympic Track and Field: A Complete Illustrated Reference*. Jefferson, NC: McFarland, 1992.

Davis, O.K. *Grambling's Gridiron Glory: Eddie Robinson and the Tigers Success Story*. Rustin, LA: M & M Printing, 1983.

Davis, Timothy. "African American Student–Athletes: Marginalizing the NCAA Regulatory Structure." *Marquette Sports Law Journal* 6 (Spring 1996): 199–227.

———. "The Myth of the Superspade: The Persistence of Racism in College Athletics." *Fordham Urban Law Journal* 22 (November 3, 1995): 615–98.

Dawkins, Marvin P., and Graham C. Kinloch. *African American Golfers During the Jim Crow Era*. Westport, CT: Greenwood, 2000.

Dixon, Phil, and Patrick J. Hannigan. *The Negro Baseball Leagues: A Photographic Essay*. Matotuck, NY: Ameon, 1992.

Dorinson, Joseph, and Joram Warmund, eds. *Jackie Robinson: Race, Sports, and the American Dream*. Armonk, NY: M.E. Sharpe, 1998.

Dyreson, Mark. "American Ideas About Race and Olympic Races from the 1890s to the 1950s: Shattering Myths or Reinforcing Scientific Racism?" *Journal of Sport History* 28 (Summer 2001): 173–216.

Dyson, Michael Eric. "Be Like Mike? Michael Jordan and the Pedagogy of Desire." In *Reflecting Black: African American Cultural Criticism*, edited by Michael Eric Dyson, 64–75. Minneapolis: University of Minnesota Press, 1993.

Early, Gerald. *The Culture of Bruising: Essays on Prizefighting, Literature, and Modern American Culture*. New York: Ecco Press, 1994.

———. *The Muhammad Ali Reader*. New York: Ecco Press, 1998.

———. *Tuxedo Junction: Essays on American Culture*. New York: Ecco Press, 1989.

Edmonds, Anthony O. *Joe Louis*. Grand Rapids, MI: William B. Eerdmans, 1973.

———. "Second Louis–Schmeling Fight: Sport, Symbol, and Culture." *Journal of Popular Culture* 7 (Summer 1973): 42–50.

Edwards, Harry. *The Revolt of the Black Athlete*. New York: Free Press, 1970.

———. *Sociology of Sport*. Homewood, IL: Dorsey Press, 1973.

Eisen, George, and David K. Wiggins, eds. *Ethnicity and Sport in North American History and Culture*. Westport, CT: Praeger, 1995.

Eitzen, D. Stanley, and George H. Sage. *Sociology of North American Sport*. Dubuque, Iowa: Brown and Benchmark, 1993.

Entine, John. *Taboo: Why Black Athletes Dominate Sports and Why We Are Afraid to Talk About It*. New York: Public Affairs Press, 2000.

Farr, Finis. *Black Champion: The Life and Times of Jack Johnson*. London: Macmillan, 1964.

Fitzpatrick, Frank. *And the Walls Came Tumbling Down: Kentucky, Texas Western, and the Game That Changed American Sports*. New York: Simon & Schuster, 1999.

BIBLIOGRAPHY

Fleischer, Nat. *Black Dynamite: The Story of the Negro in the Prize Ring from 1782 to 1938.* New York: Ring Magazine, 1947.

Fletcher, Marvin E. "The Black Soldier Athlete in the United States Army, 1890–1916." *Canadian Journal of History of Sport and Physical Education* 3 (December 1971): 16–26.

Fox, Stephen. *Big Leagues: Professional Baseball, Football, and Basketball in National Memory.* New York: William Morrow, 1994.

Franklin, John Hope, and Alfred A. Moss, Jr. *From Slavery to Freedom: A History of African Americans.* 8th ed. New York: Alfred A. Knopf, 2000.

Gaddy, Charles. *An Olympic Journey: The Saga of an American Hero: Leroy T. Walker.* Glendale, CA: Griffin, 1998.

Gems, Gerald R. "Blocked Shot: The Development of Basketball in the African American Community of Chicago." *Journal of Sport History* 22 (Summer 1995): 135–48.

———. "Shooting Stars: The Rise and Fall of Blacks in Professional Football." *Professional Football Research Association Annual Bulletin* (1988): 1–16.

George, Nelson. *Elevating the Game: Black Men and Basketball.* New York: HarperCollins, 1992.

Gerber, Ellen, et al. *The American Woman in Sport.* Reading, MA: Addison–Wesley, 1974.

Gerlach, Larry R. "Baseball's Other 'Great Experiment': Eddie Klep and the Integration of the Negro Leagues." *Journal of Sport History* 25 (Fall 1998): 453–81.

Gibson, Althea. *I Always Wanted to Be Somebody.* New York: Harper and Brothers, 1958.

Gilmore, Al–Tony. *Bad Nigger: The National Impact of Jack Johnson.* New York: Kennikat, 1975.

———. "The Myth, Legend and Folklore of Joe Louis: The Impressions of Sport on Society." *South Atlantic Quarterly* 82 (Summer 1983): 256–68.

Gissendanner, Cindy Himes. "African American Women and Competitive Sport, 1920–1960." In *Women, Sport and Culture,* edited by Susan Birrell and Cheryl Cole, 81–92. Champaign, IL: Human Kinetics, 1993.

———. "African American Women Olympians: The Impact of Race, Gender, and Class Ideologies, 1932–1968." *Research Quarterly for Exercise and Sport* 67 (June 1996): 172–82.

Goodman, Michael H. "The Moor vs. Black Diamond." *Virginia Cavalcade* 29 (Spring 1980): 164–73.

Gorn, Elliott J. *The Manly Art: Bare–Knuckle Prize Fighting in America.* Ithaca, NY: Cornell University Press, 1994.

———, ed. *Muhammad Ali: The People's Champ.* Urbana: University of Illinois Press, 1995.

Gorn, Elliott J., and Warren Goldstein. *A Brief History of American Sports.* New York: Hill and Wang, 1993.

Grundman, Adolph. "Image of Intercollegiate Sports and the Civil Rights Movement: A Historian's View." *Arena Review* 3 (October 1979): 17–24.

Grundy, Pamela. "From Amazons to Glamazons: The Rise and Fall of North Carolina Women's Basketball, 1920–1960." *The Journal of American History* 87 (June 2000): 112–46.

Guttmann, Allen. *A Whole New Ball Game: An Interpretation of American Sports.* Chapel Hill: University of North Carolina Press, 1988.

Harris, Francis C. "Paul Robeson: An Athlete's Legacy." In *Paul Robeson: Artist and Citizen,* edited by Jeffrey C. Stewart, 35–48. New Brunswick, NJ: Rutgers University Press and the Paul Robeson Cultural Center, 1998.

Hartmann, Douglas. "Rethinking the Relationships Between Sport and Race in American Culture: Golden Ghettos and Contested Terrain." *Sociology of Sport Journal* 17 (2000): 229–53.

Hauser, Thomas. *The Black Lights: Inside the World of Professional Boxing.* New York: McGrawHill, 1986.

———. *Muhammad Ali: His Life and Times.* New York: Simon & Schuster, 1991.

Henderson, Edwin B. *The Black Athlete: Emergence and Arrival.* New York: Publishers Company, 1968.

———. *The Negro in Sports.* Washington, DC: Associated Publishers, 1939, 1949.

———. "Physical Education and Athletics Among Negroes." In *Proceedings of the Big Ten Symposium on the History of Physical Ed-*

ucation and Sport, edited by Bruce L. Bennett, 67–83. Chicago: Athletic Institute, 1972.

Henry, Grant. "A Bibliography Concerning Negroes in Physical Education, Athletics, and Related Fields." *Journal of Health Physical Education, and Recreation* 44 (May 1973): 65–70.

Hine, Darlene Clark, William C. Hine, and Stanley Harrold. *The African American Odyssey*. 2 vols. Englewood Cliffs, NJ: Prentice Hall, 2000.

Hoberman, John. *Darwin's Athletes: How Sport Has Damaged Black America and Preserved the Myth of Race*. Boston: Houghton Mifflin, 1997.

Holway, John. *Blackball Stars: Negro League Pioneers*. Westport, CT: Meckler, 1988.

———. *Voices from the Great Negro Baseball Leagues*. New York: Dodd, Mead, 1975.

Hoose, Philip M. *Necessities: Racial Barriers in American Sports*. New York: Random House, 1989.

Horton, James Oliver, and Lois E. Horton. *Hard Road to Freedom: The Story of African America*. New Brunswick, NJ: Rutgers University Press, 2001.

Hotaling, Edward. *The Great Black Jockeys: The Lives and Times of the Men Who Dominated America's First National Sport*. Rocklin, CA: Primo, 1999.

Hurd, Michael. *Black College Football, 1892–1992: One Hundred Years of History, Education, and Pride*. Virginia Beach, VA: Donnin, 1998.

Jable, J. Thomas. "Sport in Philadelphia's African American Community, 1865–1900." In *Ethnicity and Sport in North American History and Culture*, edited by George Eisen and David K. Wiggins, 157–76. Westport, CT: Greenwood Press, 1994.

Janis, Laura. "Annotated Bibliography on Minority Women in Athletics." *Sociology of Sport Journal* 2 (September 1985): 266–74.

Jarvie, Grant, ed. *Sport, Racism and Ethnicity*. London: Falmer Press, 1991.

Jiobu, Robert. "Racial Inequality in a Public Arena: The Case of Professional Baseball." *Social Forces* 67 (1988): 524–34.

Johnson, Jack A. *Jack Johnson Is a Dandy: An Autobiography*. New York: Chelsea House, 1969.

Johnson, Rafer, with Philip Goldberg. *The Best That I Can Be: An Autobiography*. New York: Random House, 1998.

Jones, Greg, et al. "A Log–linear Analysis of Stacking in College Football." *Social Science Quarterly* (March 1987): 70–83.

Jones, Wally, and Jim Washington. *Black Champions Challenge American Sports*. New York: David McKay, 1972.

Jones, William H. *Recreation and Amusement Among Negroes in Washington*. Westport, CT: Negro Universities Press, 1970.

Jordan, Larry E. "Black Markets and Future Superstars: An Instrumental Approach to Opportunity in Sport Forms." *Journal of Black Studies* 11 (March 1981): 289–306.

Kahn, Lawrence M. "Discrimination in Professional Sports: A Survey of the Literature." *Industrial and Labor Relations Review* 44 (April 1991): 395–418.

Kaye, Andrew. "'Battle Blind': Atlanta's Taste for Black Boxing in the Early Twentieth Century." *Journal of Sport History* 28 (Summer 2001): 217–32.

Kelley, Robin D.G., and Earl Lewis, eds. *To Make Our World Anew: A History of African Americans*. New York: Oxford University Press, 2000.

Kennedy, John H. *A Course of Their Own: A History of African American Golfers*. Kansas City, MO: Andrews McMeel, 2000.

Keown, Tim. *Skyline: One Season, One Team, One City*. New York: McMillan, 1994.

Kimball, Richard Ian. "Beyond the Great Experiment: Integrated Baseball Comes to Indianapolis." *Journal of Sport History* 26 (Spring 1999): 142–62.

King, Wilma. *Stolen Childhood: Slave Youth in Nineteenth–Century America*. Bloomington: Indiana University Press, 1995.

Lacy, Sam, with Moses J. Newsom. *Fighting for Fairness: The Life Story of Hall of Fame Sportwriter Sam Lacy*. Centreville, MD: Tidewater, 1998.

Lamb, Chris. "I Never Want to Take Another Trip like This One: Jackie Robinson's Journey to Integrate Baseball." *Journal of Sport History* 24 (Summer 1997): 177–91.

Lanctot, Neil. *Fair Dealing and Clean Playing: The Hilldale Club and the Development of Black Professional Baseball, 1910–1932. Jefferson, NC: McFarland, 1994.

Lansbury, Jennifer H. "'The Tuskegee Flash' and 'the Slender Harlem Stroker': Black Women Athletes on the Margin." *Journal of Sport History* 28 (Summer 2001): 233–52.

Lapchick, Richard. *Broken Promises: Racism in American Sports*. New York: St. Martin's Press, 1984.

———. *Five Minutes to Midnight: Race and Sport in the 1990's*. Lanham, MD: Madison Books, 1991.

———. *The Politics of Race and International Sport: The Case of South Africa*. Westport, CT: Greenwood Press, 1975.

Lavoie, Mark. "The Economic Hypothesis of Positional Segregation: Some Further Comments." *Sociology of Sport Journal* 6 (1989): 163–66.

Lawson, Hal A. "Physical Education and Sport in the Black Community: The Hidden Perspective." *Journal of Negro Education* 48 (Spring 1979): 187–95.

Lee, George L. *Interesting Athletes: Black American Sports Heroes*. New York: Ballantine, 1976.

LeFlore, James. "Athleticism Among American Blacks." In *Social Approaches to Sport*, edited by Robert M. Pankin, 104–21. Toronto: Associated University Presses, 1982.

Leonard, Wilbert M., II. "Salaries and Race/Ethnicity in Major League Baseball: The Pitching Component." *Sociology of Sport Journal* 6 (1989): 152–62.

———. *A Sociological Perspective of Sport*. New York: MacMillan, 1993.

———. "Stacking in College Basketball: A Neglected Analysis." *Sociology of Sport Journal* 4(1987): 403–9.

Levine, Lawrence W. *Black Culture and Black Consciousness: Afro-American Folk Thought from Slavery to Freedom*. New York: Oxford University Press, 1977.

Liberti, Rita. "'We Were Ladies, We Just Played Basketball Like Boys': African American Womanhood and Competitive Basketball at Bennett College, 1928–1942." *Journal of Sport History* 26 (Fall 1999): 567–84.

Lipsyte, Robert, and Peter Levine. *Idols of the Game: A Sporting History of the American Century*. Atlanta: Turning, 1995.

Logan, Rayford. *Howard University: The First Hundred Years, 1867–1967*. New York: New York University Press, 1969.

Lomax, Michael E. "Black Baseball's First Rivalry: The Cuban Giants versus the Gorhams of New York and the Birth of the Colored Championship." *Sport History Review* 28 (November 1997): 134–45.

———. "Black Entrepreneurship in the National Pastime: The Rise of Semiprofessional Baseball in Black Chicago, 1890–1915." *Journal of Sport History* 25 (Spring 1998): 43–64.

Louis, Joe, with Edna and Art Rust, Jr. *Joe Louis: My Life*. New York: Harcourt Brace Jovanovich, 1978.

Lowenfish, Lee. "Sport, Race, and the Baseball Business: The Jackie Robinson Story Revisited." *Arena Review* 2 (Spring 1978): 2–16.

Loy, John, and Joseph McElvoque. "Racial Segregation in American Sport." *International Review of Sport Sociology* 5 (1970): 5–23.

Lucas, John A., and Ronald A. Smith. *Saga of American Sport*. Philadelphia: Lea and Febiger, 1978.

MacDonald, William W. "The Black Athlete in American Sports." In *Sports in Modern America*, edited by William J. Baker and John M. Carroll, 88–98. St. Louis: River City, 1981.

Magriel, Paul. "Tom Molineaux." *Phylon* 12 (December 1951): 329–36.

Majors, Richard. "Cool Pose: Black Masculinity and Sports." In *Sport, Men, and the Gender Order: Critical Feminist Perspectives*, edited by Michael A. Messner and Donald F. Sabo, 109–14. Champaign, IL: Human Kinetics, 1990.

Marable, Manning. "Black Athletes in White Men's Games, 1880–1920." *Maryland Historian* 4 (Fall 1973): 143–49.

Marcello, Ronald E. "The Integration of Intercollegiate Athletics in Texas: North Texas State College as a Test Case, 1956." *Journal of Sport History* 14 (Winter 1987): 286–316.

Martin, Charles H. "Integrating New Year's Day: The Racial Politics of College Bowl Games in the American South." *Journal of Sport History* 24 (Fall 1997): 358–77.

———. "Jim Crow in the Gymnasium: The Integration of College Basketball in the American South." *International Journal of the History of Sport* 10 (April 1993): 68–86.

———. "Racial Change and Big-Time College Football in Georgia: The Age of Segregation, 1892–1957." *Georgia Historical Quarterly* 80 (1996): 532–62.

Mathewson, Alfred Dennis. "Black Women, Gender Equity and the Function at the Junction." *Marquette Sports Law Journal* 6 (Spring 1996): 239–66.

Matthews, Vincent, with Neil Amdur. *My Race Be Won*. New York: Charterhouse, 1974.

Mazuri, Ali A. "Boxer Muhammad Ali and Soldier Idi Amin as International Political Symbols: The Bioeconomics of Sports and War." *Comparative Studies in Society and History* 19 (April 1977): 189–215.

McDaniel, Pete. *Uneven Lies: The Heroic Story of African-Americans in Golf*. Greenwich, CT: American Golfer, 2000.

McKinney, G.B. "Negro Professional Baseball Players in the Upper South in the Gilded Age." *Journal of Sport History* 3 (Winter 1976): 273–80.

McPherson, Barry D. "Minority Group Involvement in Sport: The Black Athlete." *Exercise and Sport Science Reviews* 2 (1974): 71–101.

Mead, Chris. *Champion: Joe Louis, Black Hero in White America*. New York: Scribner's, 1985.

Mergen, Bernard. *Play and Playthings: A Reference Guide*. Westport, CT: Greenwood Press, 1982.

Messner, Michael A., and Donald F. Sabo, eds. *Sport, Men, and the Gender Order: Critical Feminist Perspectives*. Champaign, IL: Human Kinetics, 1990.

Miller, Patrick B. "The Anatomy of Scientific Racism: Racialist Responses to Black Athletic Achievement." *Journal of Sport History* 25 (Spring 1998): 119–51.

———. "Harvard and the Color Line: The Case of Lucien Alexis." In *Sports in Massachusetts: Historical Essays*, edited by Ronald Story, 137–58. Westfield, MA: Institute for Massachusetts Studies, 1991.

———. "Slouching Toward A New Expediency: College Football and the Color Line During the Depression Decade." *American Studies* 40 (Fall 1999): 5–30.

———. "'To Bring the Race Along Rapidly': Sport, Student Culture, and Educational Mission at Historically Black Colleges During the Interwar Years." *History of Education Quarterly* 35 (Summer 1995): 111–33.

Moore, Joseph T. *Pride Against Prejudice: The Biography of Larry Doby*. Westport, CT: Greenwood Press, 1988.

Nathan, Daniel A. "Sugar Ray Robinson, the Sweet Science, and the Politics of Meaning." *Journal of Sport History* 26 (Spring 1999): 163–74.

Norwood, Stephen H. "The Making of an Athlete: An Interview with Joe Washington." *Journal of Sport History* 27 (Spring 2000): 91–145.

Noverr, Douglas A., and Lawrence E. Ziewacz. *The Games They Played: Sports in American History, 1865–1980*. Chicago: Nelson-Hall, 1988.

Olsen, Jack. *The Black Athlete: A Shameful Story*. New York: Time–Life Books, 1968.

Orr, Jack. *The Black Athlete: His Story in American History*. New York: Lion Books, 1969.

Owens, Jesse, with Paul Neimark. *Blackthink: My Life as Black Man and White Man*. New York: William Morrow, 1970.

Paino, Troy D. "Hoosiers in a Different Light: Forces of Change vs. the Power of Nostalgia." *Journal of Sport History* 28 (Spring 2001): 63–80.

Palmer, Colin A. *Passageways: An Interpretive History of Black America*. 2 vols. New York: Harcourt Brace, 1998.

Paul, Joan, et al. "The Arrival and Ascendence of Black Athletes in the Southeastern Conference, 1966–1980." *Phylon* 45 (December 1984): 284–97.

Pennington, Richard. *Breaking the Ice: The Racial Integration of Southwest Conference Football*. Jefferson, NC: McFarland, 1987.

Peterson, Robert W. *Cages to Jump Shots: Pro Basketball's Early Years*. New York: Oxford University Press, 1990.

———. *Only the Ball Was White*. Englewood Cliffs, NJ: Prentice Hall, 1970.

Pierce, Richard B. "More than a Game: The Political Meaning of High School Basketball in Indianapolis." *Journal of Urban History* 27 (November 2000): 3–23.

Porter, David L., ed. *African American Sports Greats: A Biographical Dictionary*. Westport, CT: Greenwood Press, 1995.

Rader, Benjamin G. *American Sports: From the Age of Folk Games to the Age of Spectators*. Englewood Cliffs, NJ: Prentice Hall, 1983.

Rampersad, Arnold. *Jackie Robinson: A Biography*. New York: Alfred A. Knopf, 1997.

Rayle, Susan J. "The New York Renaissance Professional Black Basketball Team, 1923–1950." Ph.D. diss., Pennsylvania State University, 1996.

Reisler, Jim. *Black Writers/Black Baseball: An Anthology of Articles from Black Sportswriters Who Covered the Negro Leagues*. Jefferson, NC: McFarland, 1994.

Remnick, David. *King of the World: Muhammad Ali and the Rise of a Hero*. New York: Random House, 1998.

Ribowsky, Mark. *A Complete History of the Negro Leagues, 1884 to 1955*. New York: Birch Lane Press, 1995.

———. *Don't Look Back: Satchel Paige in the Shadows of Baseball*. New York: Simon & Schuster, 1994.

———. *The Power and the Darkness: The Life of Josh Gibson in the Shadows of the Game*. New York: Simon & Schuster, 1996.

Richardson, Joe. *A History of Fisk University, 1865–1946*. University: University of Alabama Press, 1980.

Ritchie, Andrew. *Major Taylor: The Extraordinary Career of a Champion Bicycle Racer*. San Francisco: Bicycle Books, 1988.

Roberts, Randy. *But They Can't Beat Us! Oscar Robertson's Crispus Attucks Tigers*. Champaign, IL: Sports, 1999.

———. "Galveston's Jack Johnson: Flourishing in the Dark." *Southwestern Historical Quarterly* 82 (July 1983): 37–56.

———. "Heavyweight Champion Jack Johnson: His Omaha Image, a Public Reaction Study." *Nebraska History* 57 (Summer 1976): 226–41.

———. *Papa Jack: Jack Johnson and the Era of White Hopes*. New York: Free Press, 1983.

Roberts, Randy, and James Olson. *Winning Is the Only Thing: Sports in America Since 1945*. Baltimore: Johns Hopkins University Press, 1989.

Robinson, Jackie, with Alfred Duckett. *I Never Had It Made*. New York: Putnam, 1972.

Rogosin, Donn. *Invisible Men: Life in Baseball's Negro Leagues*. New York: Athenaeum, 1987.

Ross, Charles K. *Outside the Lines: African Americans and the Integration of the National Football League*. New York: New York University Press, 1999.

Ruck, Rob. *Sandlot Seasons: Sport in Black Pittsburgh*. Urbana: University of Illinois Press, 1987.

———. "Soaring Above the Sandlots: The Garfield Eagles." *Pennsylvania Heritage* 8 (Summer 1982): 13–18.

Rudman, William S. "The Sport Mystique in Black Culture." *Sociology of Sport Journal* 3 (1986): 305–19.

Russell, Bill, as told to William McSweeney. *Go Up for Glory*. New York: Conrad-McCann, 1966.

Russell, Bill, and Taylor Branch. *Second Wind: The Memoirs of an Opinionated Man*. New York: Random House, 1974.

Rust, Art, and Edna Rust. *Art Rust's Illustrated History of the Black Athlete*. Garden City, NY: Doubleday, 1985.

Sailes, Gary. *African Americans in Sport*. New Brunswick, NJ: Transaction, 1998.

Salzberg, Charles. *From Set Shot to Slam Dunk: The Glory Days of Basketball in the Words of Those Who Played It*. New York: E.P. Dutton, 1987.

Sammons, Jeffrey T. *Beyond the Ring: The Role of Boxing in American Society*. Urbana: University of Illinois Press, 1988.

———. "Boxing as a Reflection of Society: The Southern Reaction to Joe Louis." *Journal of Popular Culture* 16 (Spring 1983): 23–33.

———. "'Race' and Sport: A Critical Historical Examination." *Journal of Sport History* 21 (Fall 1994): 203–98.

Sellers, Robert. "African American Student–Athletes: Opportunity or Exploitation?" In *Racism in College Athletics: The African American Athlete's Experience*, edited by Dana D. Brooks and Ronald C. Althouse, 143–74. Morgantown, WV: Fitness Information Technology, 2000.

Shropshire, Kenneth L. *In Black and White: Race and Sports in America*. New York: New York University Press, 1996.

Sifford, Charlie, with James Gallo. *Just Let Me Play: The Story of Charlie Sifford, the First Black PGA Golfer*. Latham, NY: British American, 1992.

Simons, William. "Jackie Robinson and the American Mind: Journalistic Perceptions of the Reintegration of Baseball." *Journal of Sport History* 12 (Spring 1985): 39–64.

Sinnette, Calvin H. *Forbidden Fairways: African Americans and the Game of Golf*. Chelsea, MI: Sleeping Bear Press, 1998.

Skully, Gerald. "Economic Discrimination in Professional Sports." *Law and Contemporary Problems* 39 (Winter–Spring 1973): 67–84.

———. "Merit 01' Boy Networks and the Black-Bottomed Pyramid." *Hastings Law Journal* 47 (January 1996): 455–72.

Sloan–Green, Tina, et al. *Black Women in Sport*. Reston, VA: AAHPERD, 1981.

Smith, Ronald A. "The Paul Robeson–Jackie Robinson Saga and a Political Collision." *Journal of Sport History* 6 (Summer 1979): 5–27.

Smith, Thomas G. "Civil Rights on the Gridiron: The Kennedy Administration and the Desegregation of the Washington Redskins." *Journal of Sport History* 14 (Summer 1987): 189–208.

———. "Outside the Pale: The Exclusion of Blacks from the National Football League, 1934–1946." *Journal of Sport History* 15 (Winter 1988): 255–81.

Smith, Yvonne. "Women of Color in Society and Sport." *Quest* 44 (Summer 1992): 228–50.

Spivey, Donald. "Black Consciousness and Olympic Protest Movements, 1964–1980." In *Sport in America: New Historical Perspectives*, edited by Donald Spivey, 239–59. Westport, CT: Greenwood Press, 1985.

———. "End Jim Crow in Sports: The Protest at New York University, 1940–1941." *Journal of Sport History* 15 (Winter 1988): 282–303.

———. "Sport, Protest, and Consciousness: The Black Athlete in Big–Time Intercollegiate Sports, 1941–1968." *Phylon* 44 (June 1983): 116–25.

Spivey, Donald, and Tom Jones. "Intercollegiate Athletic Servitude: A Case Study of the Black Illinois Student Athletes, 1931–1967." *Social Science Quarterly* 55 (March 1975): 939–47.

Strode, Woody, and Sam Young. *Goal Dust: The Warm and Candid Memoirs of a Pioneer Black Athlete and Actor*. New York: Madison Books, 1990.

Taylor, Marshall Major. *The Fastest Bicycle Rider in the World*. Battleboro, VT: Green-Stephen Press, 1971.

Telander, Rick. *Heaven Is a Playground*. Lincoln: University of Nebraska Press, 1995.

Thompson, Richard. *Race and Sport*. London: Oxford University Press, 1964.

Torres, Jose. *Sting Like a Bee: The Muhammad Ali Story*. New York: Abelard–Schuman, 1971.

Tygiel, Jules. *Baseball's Great Experiment: Jackie Robinson and His Legacy*. New York: Oxford University Press, 1983.

———, ed. *The Jackie Robinson Reader: Perspectives on an American Hero*. New York: Penguin Dutton, 1997.

Van Deburg, William. *A New Day in Babylon: The Black Power Movement and American Culture, 1965–1975*. Chicago: University of Chicago Press, 1992.

Vertinsky, Patricia, and Gwendolyn Captain. "More Myth than History: American Culture and Representations of the Black Female's Athletic Ability." *Journal of Sport History* 25 (Fall 1998): 532–61.

Wacquant, Loic. "The Social Logic of Boxing in Black Chicago: Toward a Sociology of Pugilism." *Sociology of Sport Journal* 9 (1992): 221–54.

Walker, Chet, with Chris Messenger. *Long Time Coming: A Black Athlete's Coming-of-Age in America*. New York: Grove Press, 1995.

Watkins, Ralph. "Recreation, Leisure and Charity in the Afro–American Community of Buffalo, New York: 1920–1925." *Afro–Americans in New York Life and History* 6 (July 1982): 7–15.

Weaver, Bill L. "The Black Press and the Assault on Professional Baseball's Color Line, October 1945–April 1947." *Phylon* 40 (Winter 1979): 303–17.

White, G. Edward. *Creating the National Pastime:*

BIBLIOGRAPHY

Baseball Transforms Itself, 1903–1953. Princeton, NJ: Princeton University Press, 1996.

Wiggins, David K. "Critical Events Affecting Racism in Athletics." In *Racism in College Athletics: The African American Athlete's Experience*, edited by Dana D. Brooks and Ronald C. Althouse, 23–49. Morgantown, WV: Fitness Information Technology, 1993.

———. "From Plantation to Playing Field: Historical Writings on the Black Athlete in American Sport." *Research Quarterly for Exercise and Sport* 57 (June 1986): 101–16.

———. The Future of College Athletics Is at Stake: Black Athletes and Racial Turmoil on Three Predominantly White University Campuses, 1968-1972." *Journal of Sport History* 15 (Winter 1988): 304–33.

———. *Glory Bound: Black Athletes in a White America*. Syracuse, NY: Syracuse University Press, 1997.

———. "Great Speed but Little Stamina: The Historical Debate over Black Athletic Superiority." *Journal of Sport History* 16 (Summer 1989): 158–85.

———. "Issac Murphy: Black Hero in Nineteenth-Century American Sport, 1861–1896." *Canadian Journal of History of Sport and Physical Education* 10 (May 1979): 15–32.

———. "The Play of Slave Children in the Plantation Communities of the Old South, 1820–1860." *Journal of Sport History* 7 (Summer 1980): 21–39.

———. "Prized Performers, but Frequently Overlooked Students: The Involvement of Black Athletes in Intercollegiate Sports on Predominantly White University Campuses, 1890-1972." *Research Quarterly for Exercise and Sport* 62 (June 1991): 164–77.

———. "Sport and Popular Pastimes: The Shadow of the Slavequarter." *Canadian Journal of History of Sport and Physical Education* 11 (May 1980): 61–88.

———. "Wendell Smith, the *Pittsburgh Courier–Journal* and the Campaign to Include Blacks in Organized Baseball, 1933–1945." *Journal of Sport History* 10 (Summer 1983): 5–29.

———. "The Year of Awakening: Black Athletes, Racial Unrest, and the Civil Rights Movement of 1968." *International Journal of the History of Sport* 9 (August 1992): 188–208.

Wiggins, William H. "Boxing's Sambo Twins: Racial Stereotypes in Jack Johnson and Joe Louis Newspaper Cartoons, 1908 to 1938." *Journal of Sport History* 15 (Winter 1988): 242–54.

———. "Jack Johnson as Bad Nigger: The Folklore of His Life." *Black Scholar* 2 (January 1971): 4–19.

Williams, Linda. "Sportswomen in Black and White: Sports History from an Afro-American Perspective." In *Women, Media and Sport: Challenging Gender Values*, edited by Pamela J. Creeden, 45–66. Thousand Oaks, CA: Sage, 1994.

Winters, Manque. *Professional Sports: The Community College Connection*. Inglewood, CA: Winnor Press, 1982.

Woolfolk, George. *Prairie View: A Study in Public Conscience, 1878–1946*. New York: Pageant Press, 1962.

Young, Alexander, Jr. "The Boston Tarbaby." *Nova Scotia Historical Quarterly* 4 (September 1974): 277–93.

———. "Joe Louis, Symbol." Ph.D. diss., University of Maryland, 1968.

Young, Andrew S. "Doc." *Great Negro Baseball Stars and How They Made the Major Leagues*. New York: A.S. Barnes, 1953.

———. *Negro Firsts in Sports*. Chicago: Johnson, 1963.

Zang, David W. "Calvin Hill Interview." *Journal of Sport History* 15 (Winter 1988): 334–55.

———. *Fleet Walker's Divided Heart: The Life of Baseball's First Black Major Leaguer*. Lincoln: University of Nebraska Press, 1995.

Zuckerman, Jerome, et al. "The Black Athlete in Post–bellum 19th Century." *Physical Educator* 29 (October 1972): 142–46.

GENERAL INDEX

Aaron, Hank, **1:**1–2; **2:**229, 230
AAU. *See* Amateur Athletic Union
Abbott, Cleveland, **1:**2; **2:**231, 373
Abdul-Jabbar, Kareem (Lew Alcindor), **1:**3–4, 26, 35, 40, 102, 142; **2:**297, 303–4
Above the Rim (film), **1:**102
Adams, Lucinda, **1:**4–5
Adderley, Herb, **1:**5
African American Tennis Association, **2:**335
Agents, **1:**6–7
   Nehemiah, Renaldo, **2:**256
Air Up There, The (film), **1:**102
Albritton, David, **1:**7–8; **2:**372, 386
Alcindor, Lew. *See* Abdul-Jabbar, Kareem
Alexander, Alpha, **1:**35
Alexander, Grover Cleveland, **2:**405
Alexis, Lucien, Jr., **1:**199
Ali, Muhammad (Cassius Clay), **1:**8–9, 16, 17, 45–46, 69, 91, 95, 100, 109, 110, 112, 158, 167, 197, 213–14; **2:**241, 260, 266, 277, 312, 343
All-Americans (college basketball)
   Bellamy, Walter, **1:**32–33
   Bing, Dave, **1:**33
   Boozer, Bob, **1:**39–40
   Cooper, Chuck, **1:**75
   Dantley, Adrian, **1:**77–78
   Dukes, Walter, **1:**89
   Ewing, Patrick, **1:**97–98
   Ford, Phil, **1:**108
   Jackson, Mannie, **1:**173
   Jordan, Michael, **1:**190–91
   Leslie, Lisa, **1:**207–8
   Manning, Danny, **2:**224
   Monroe, Earl, **2:**239–40
   Murphy, Calvin, **2:**246
   O'Neal, Shaquille, **2:**268–69
   Russell, Cazzie, **2:**319–20
   Sampson, Ralph, **2:**321
   Scott, Charlie, **2:**324
   Stallworth, Dave, **2:**346
   Thompson, David, **2:**367–68
   Thompson, John, **2:**368–69
   White, Jo Jo, **2:**398–99
   Woodward, Lynette, **2:**415–16
   Worthy, James, **2:**418
All-Americans (college football)
   Adderley, Herb, **1:**5
   Bass, Dick, **1:**26–27
   Campbell, Earl, **1:**58–59
   Carter, Cris, **1:**62–63
   Davis, Ernie, **1:**78–79

All-Americans (college football) *(continued)*
   Dickerson, Eric, **1:**83–84
   Drew, Charles, **1:**87–88
   Eller, Carl, **1:**94–95
   Greene, Joe, **1:**128–29
   Holland, Jerome Brud, **1:**157
   Hurt, Eddie, **1:**162
   LeVias, Jerry, **1:**208–9
   Lewis, William Henry, **1:**211–12
   Little, Floyd, **1:**214
   Lott, Ronnie, **1:**216
   Marshall, Bob, **2:**225–26
   Marshall, Jim, **2:**226
   Matson, Ollie, **2:**227
   Newsome, Ozzie, **2:**259
   Parker, Jim, **2:**276
   Perkins, Don, **2:**281
   Pollard, Fritz, **2:**283–84
   Reed, Dwight, **2:**296
   Renfro, Mel, **2:**297–98
   Rice, Jerry, **2:**301
   Robeson, Paul, **2:**304–5
   Rodgers, Johnny, **2:**313–14
   Rogers, George, **2:**315–16
   Rozier, Mike, **2:**316
   Sanders, Deion, **2:**322
   Sayers, Gale, **2:**323
   Simmons, Ozzie, **2:**330
   Simpson, O. J., **2:**331
   Smith, Bruce, **2:**335–36
   Smith, "Bubba," **2:**336–37
   Smith, Emmitt, **2:**337–38
   Swann, Lynn, **2:**352–53
   Tatum, Jack, **2:**357–58
   Taylor, Lawrence, **2:**360–61
   Walker, Herschel, **2:**384–85
   Warfield, Paul, **2:**388–89
   Washington, Gene, **2:**389–90
   West, Charlie, **2:**396
   White, Reggie, **2:**399–400
   Willis, Bill, **2:**407–8
   Young, Buddy, **2:**422
Allen, Hank, **1:**159–60
Allen, Marcus, **1:**9–10
Allen, Ray, **1:**102
Amateur Athletic Union (AAU), **2:**371, 392–94
Amateur Fencers League of America, **1:**99
Ambers, Lou, **1:**11–12
American Bowling Congress, **1:**42, 69; **2:**252
American Football League, **1:**107
American Negro League, **2:**253

GENERAL INDEX

American Tennis Association (ATA), **1:**10, 118, 120–21; **2:**363–64, 391, 394
Amsterdam News (newspaper), **2:**345
Anderson, Dave, **2:**400
Anderson, Elmer, **1:**167
Anderson, Raymond, **1:**7
Angott, Sammy, **2:**405
Antuofermo, Vito, **1:**137
Any Given Sunday (film), **1:**101
Apartheid, **1:**69, 92
Archibald, Nate, **1:**11
Arguello, Alexis, **1:**46
Arledge, Roone, **1:**107
Armstrong, Henry, **1:**11–12, 45, 100
Armstrong Manual Training School, **1:**168
Armstrong, Sherman, **2:**300
Ashe, Arthur, Jr., **1:**12–13, 16, 17, 102, 153; **2:**291, 363, 364
Ashford, Emmett, **1:**13–14
Ashford, Evelyn, **1:**15; **2:**265, 372
Associated Negro Press, **1:**54
Association football, **1:**105
Association Tennis Club of Washington, **1:**10
Atkins, W. E., **1:**63
Atlanta Daily World (newspaper), **2:**303
Atlanta University, **1:**150
Auerbach, Red, **2:**247, 318
Autobiographies, **1:**15–17, 104

Babilonia, Tai, **2:**267
Bach, Joe, **2:**296
Baillet-Latour, Henri de, **2:**265
Baird, Tom, **2:**252
Baker, Buck, **2:**325
Baker, Dusty, **1:**72
Baker, William J., **1:**153
Baldwin, Jerry, **1:**72
Ball, Robert "Pat," **2:**377
Ball, Walter, **1:**138
Balls, Iolanda, **2:**231
Baltimore Afro-American (newspaper), **1:**41, 200; **2:**303, 345
Bankhead, Sam, **1:**32
Banks, Ernie, **1:**19; **2:**270
Barco, J. W., **1:**63
Barker, Violet, **1:**99
Barkley, Charles, **1:**19–20; **2:**266
Barkley, Iran, **1:**144
Barksdale, Don, **1:**20–21, 25; **2:**266
Barnett, Dick, **2:**297
Barney, Lem, **1:**167
Barron, Allan P., **1:**35
Bartholomew, Joseph, **1:**124
Basilio, Carmen, **1:**45
Bass, Dick, **1:**26–27
Baton twirling, **2:**246
Baylor, Don, **1:**27, 72
Baylor, Elgin, **1:**28, 148; **2:**297
Beamon, Bob, **1:**28–29, 42; **2:**372
Beer, Klaus, **1:**42

Behee, John, **1:**154
Beliveau, Jean, **1:**165
Bell, Bill, **1:**29–30
Bell, Bobby, **1:**30–31
Bell, James "Cool Papa," **1:**22, 31–32, 129; **2:**254
Bell, "Puggy," **1:**24
Bellamy, Walter, **1:**32–33, 39
Bench, Johnny, **2:**243
Benitez, Wilfred, **1:**206
Berbick, Trevor, **2:**375
Berra, Yogi, **1:**58
Bikila, Abebe, **2:**265
Bing, Dave, **1:**33
Bird, Larry, **1:**184
Birrell, Susan, **1:**156
Black Athlete, The: Emergence and Arrival (Henderson), **1:**145, 153
Black Bill, **1:**176
Black Coaches Association (BCA), **1:**33–34; **2:**293, 302
Black Entertainment Television, **1:**183
Black Newspaper Publishers Association, **1:**69
Black Sports (magazine), **1:**35
Black Women in Sports Foundation, **1:**35
Black World Championship Rodeo, **1:**36; **2:**313
Blair, George E., **1:**36
Blount, Mel, **1:**36–37; **2:**261
Body and Soul (film), **1:**100
Body and Soul (film, remake), **1:**100
Bolanos, Enrique, **2:**405
Bolden, Edward, **1:**37–38, 91
Bonds, Barry, **1:**38–39, 146
Bonds, Bobby, **1:**38
Bontemp, Arna, **1:**153
Boozer, Bob, **1:**39–40
Borican, John, **1:**40
Bostic, Joseph, **1:**22, 41; **2:**345
Boston, Ralph, **1:**41–42; **2:**372
Boswell, Sonny, **1:**24
Bowie State University, **1:**63
Boxing Hall of Fame
    Armstrong, Henry, **1:**11–12
    Foster, Bob, **1:**110
    Frazier, Joe, **1:**112
    Jeannette, Joe, **1:**176
    King, Don, **1:**196–97
    Moore, Archie, **2:**241–42
    Patterson, Floyd, **2:**276–77
    See also International Boxing Hall of Fame
Boycotts and protests
    against Brigham Young University, **1:**29
    college football in 1960s, **1:**107
    Harry Edwards and, **1:**91–92
    historians on, **1:**155
    Moscow Olympics (1980), **1:**81–82
    against National Negro League, **1:**76
    1965 AFL All-Star Game, **1:**31
    1929 NYU-Georgia basketball game, **1:**68
    Olympic black-power protest (Mexico City, 1968), **1:**17, 29, 60, 69–70, 97; **2:**265, 266, 340, 372
Brackman, Harold, **1:**154

GENERAL INDEX

Braddock, James, **1:**44, 210, 217
Bradford, Jim, **2:**392
Bradley, Bill, **2:**297
Bragan, Bobby, **2:**409
Branham, George, **1:**42
Bratton, Johnny, **2:**405
Braun, Carl, **2:**400
Brian's Song (film), **1:**101
Bright, John, **1:**105; **2:**251
Brisco-Hooks, Valerie, **1:**46–48; **2:**372
Brock, Louis, **1:**48; **2:**270
Brodie, John, **2:**273
Brokaw, Tom, **2:**291
Broughton, Jack, **1:**43
Brown, Delmar, **1:**60
Brown, Dewey, **1:**124
Brown, Godfrey, **2:**403
Brown, Jim, **1:**16, 49–50, 101, 195, 199, 214; **2:**237
Brown, Joe, **1:**45
Brown, Larry, **1:**50–51
Brown, Mary K., **1:**6
Brown, Panama Al, **1:**44
Brown, Paul, **2:**237, 246
Brown, Roger, **1:**51
Brown, "Rookie," **1:**204
Brown, Roosevelt, **1:**52
Brown, Tim, **1:**101
Brown, Walter, **1:**75
Brown, Walter S., **1:**203
Bruce, Janet, **1:**154
Brumel, Valery, **2:**367
Brundage, Avery, **1:**69, 91
Bryant, Bear, **2:**307
Bryant, Kobe, **1:**52–53
Bullock, Matthew, **1:**53–54, 128
Bunce, Steven, **1:**176
Bunche, Ralph, **1:**24
Burley, Daniel, **1:**54; **2:**345
Burley, Darryl, **2:**418
Burns, Isaac. *See* Murphy, Isaac
Burns, Tommy, **1:**44, 178
Burrell, Chris, **1:**160
Burrell, Lewis, **1:**160
Burrell, Louis, Jr., **1:**160
Burrell, Stanley (M. C. Hammer), **1:**160
Burwell, Bryan, **2:**345
Butler, Sol, **1:**55
Buxton, Angela, **1:**121
Byrd, Larry, **1:**180

Caan, James, **1:**101
Caddies (golf), **1:**123–24
Cahn, Susan, **1:**156; **2:**413–14
Calhoun, Lee, **1:**57
Callahan, Clay, **1:**174
Callis, J. J., **1:**203
Camacho, Hector, **1:**207
Camp, Walter, **1:**106
Campanella, Roy, **1:**16, 57–58, 101; **2:**219
Campbell, Earl, **1:**58–59

Campbell, Milt, **1:**59; **2:**372
Campos, Manuel, **2:**251
Capricorn One (film), **1:**101
Captain, Gwendolyn, **1:**156
Carbo, Frankie, **1:**213; **2:**404
Carey, Harry, **2:**398
Carey, Max, **2:**409
Carlos, John, **1:**29, 60, 70, 97; **2:**265, 266, 340, 372
Carmichael, Harold, **1:**61
Carnegie, Herb, **1:**165
Carnegie, Ossie, **1:**165
Caroline, J. C., **1:**61–62
Carpentier, Georges, **1:**176
Carr, Austin, **2:**403
Carr, Nate, **2:**419
Carroll, John, **1:**154
Carter, Butch, **1:**62–63, 72
Carter, Cris, **1:**62–63
Carter, Jack, **2:**238
Carter, Jimmy, **1:**74; **2:**267
Carter, Mike, **1:**134
Carter, Rubin "Hurricane," **1:**100
Casey, Bernie, **1:**101
Castro, Fidel, **2:**389
Catto, Octavius, **2:**287–88
CBS (Columbia Broadcasting System), **2:**291
Center for the Study of Sport and Society, **2:**291, 293
Central Intercollegiate Athletic Association (CIAA), **1:**24, 63–64, 151; **2:**233, 234
Cepeda, Orlando, **2:**230
Chalk, Ocania, **1:**153
Chamberlain, Wilt, **1:**16, 25, 64–65, 102, 120, 138, 148, 205; **2:**297
Chandler, Happy, **2:**303
Chaney, John, **1:**65–66, 71
Channels, Isadore, **2:**363
Chaplin, Oscar, III, **2:**394
Charity, Ron, **1:**12
Charles, Ezzard, **1:**45, 66, 217; **2:**384
Charleston, Oscar, **1:**22, 67, 129; **2:**219, 254
Chase, Jack, **2:**241
Cheyney State College, **1:**150
Chicago Bee (newspaper), **1:**54
Chicago Defender (newspaper), **1:**54, 76, 200; **2:**345, 421, 422
Chicago Herald-American (newspaper), **2:**341
Chicago Women's Golf Club, **1:**124
City Dump (documentary), **2:**400
Civil rights, **1:**67–70
  and golf, **1:**124–25
  historians on athletes and, **1:**155
  and integration in athletics, **2:**253
  See also Boycotts and protests; Segregation and integration
Clark, Dwight, **2:**256
Clark, Nathan, **2:**354
Clark University, **1:**150
Clay, Cassius, Jr. *See* Ali, Muhammad
Cleveland Advocate (newspaper), **2:**401
Cleveland Call and Post (newspaper), **2:**421

GENERAL INDEX

Clifton, Nat "Sweetwater," **1:**25, 69, 71, 138, 214–15; **2:**400
Coaches and managers, **1:**23, 71–72
  Baylor, Don, **1:**27
  Bell, Bill, **1:**29–30
  Chaney, John, **1:**65–66, 71
  Daniels, Isabelle, **1:**77
  Embry, Wayne, **1:**95–96
  Gaines, Clarence "Bighouse," **1:**115
  Gaither, Jake, **1:**115–16
  Green Bay Packers (1999), **2:**299
  Green, Tina Sloan, **1:**199
  Hurt, Eddie, **1:**162
  Jones, K. C., **1:**187
  Kemp, Ray, **1:**195–96
  Lewis, William Henry, **1:**211–12
  McLendon, John, **2:**233–34
  Miller, Cheryl, **2:**236
  Newsome, Ozzie, **2:**259
  Nunn, William, Jr., **2:**261
  Pollard, Fritz, **2:**284
  Raveling, George, **2:**295–96
  Reed, Dwight, **2:**296
  Rhodes, Ray, **2:**298–99
  Richardson, Nolan, **2:**301–2
  Robinson, Eddie, **2:**307
  Robinson, Frank, **2:**308–9
  Russell, Bill, **2:**318–19
  segregation and integration, **2:**301–2
  Shell, Art, **2:**326–27
  Silas, Paul, **2:**329–30
  Smith, John, **2:**338–39
  Snowden, Fred, **2:**341–42
  Stringer, Vivian, **2:**350–51
  Temple, Ed, **2:**362
  Thomas, Isiah, **2:**366–67
  Thompson, John, **2:**368–69
  in track and field, **2:**373
  Tunnell, Emlen, **2:**374
  Unseld, Wes, **2:**378
  Walker, Leroy, **2:**385–86
  Williams, Doug, **2:**404
  women as, **2:**414
Coachman, Alice, **1:**72–74, 152; **2:**265, 372, 373, 414
Cobb, Ty, **1:**146; **2:**409
Cobb, William Montague, **1:**74; **2:**290
Coburn, Ruth, **1:**42
Coetzee, Gerrie, **2:**343
Coleman, Ronnie, **2:**393
College athletics, segregation and integration, **1:**68, 103, 107, 130, 142, 151, 195, 208–9; **2:**229, 328, 396
College Football Association, **1:**107
Collett, Wayne, **2:**266, 338
Color barrier. *See* Boycotts and protests; Civil rights; Segregation and integration
Colored Hockey League, **1:**165
Colored Intercollegiate Athletic Association. *See* Central Intercollegiate Athletic Association
Colored World Series. *See* Negro World Series

Comiskey, Charles, **1:**111
Conlan, Jocko, **2:**315
Connors, John, **2:**251
Cook, C. C., **1:**168
Cook, Ralph V., **1:**10, 168
Coolidge, Calvin, **2:**228
Coon, Carleton S., **2:**290
Cooney, Gerry, **1:**109, 158, 197
Cooper, Chuck, **1:**25, 69, 75, 214–15; **2:**261
Cooper, Cynthia, **2:**267
Cooper, Michael, **1:**16
Cooper, "Tarzan," **1:**24
Corbett, Jim, **1:**43, 85, 174
Corbitt, Ted, **1:**75–76
Cosby, Bill, **2:**300
Cosell, Howard, **1:**8
Court-Martial of Jackie Robinson, The (television film), **1:**101
Cousy, Bob, **2:**318
Cowans, Russ, **1:**76
Cream, Arnold Raymond. *See* Walcott, Joe
Crescent Athletic Club, **1:**168
Cribb, Tom, **1:**43; **2:**238, 302, 334
Crockett, Rita, **2:**381
Cromwell, Dean, **2:**289–90
Crutchfield, Jimmie, **1:**32
Culbreath, William, **2:**256
Cumberland, Duke, **1:**24

Daly, Bill, **1:**160
D'Amato, Cus, **1:**45, 46; **2:**276, 375
Dandridge, Ray, **1:**22
Daniels, Cheryl, **1:**42
Daniels, Isabelle, **1:**77; **2:**228
Dantley, Adrian, **1:**77–78
Davenport, Willie, **2:**267
Davies, Lynn, **1:**41
Davis, Al, **2:**326, 327
Davis, Bronco Jim, **2:**312
Davis, Bruce, **1:**99
Davis, Dwight, **1:**10
Davis, Ernie, **1:**78–79, 107, 214; **2:**237
Davis, Jack, **1:**57
Davis, John Henry, **1:**79; **2:**266, 392
Davis, Laurel R., **1:**156
Dawes, Dominique, **1:**80, 135; **2:**267
De Frantz, Anita, **1:**81–82; **2:**267, 414
De Zonie, Hank, **1:**25
DeBusschere, Dave, **2:**297
Decatur, William J., **1:**168
Dehnert, Dutch, **2:**258
Dempsey, Jack, **1:**202; **2:**408–9
Dent, Jim, **1:**125
Detroit Tribune (newspaper), **1:**76
Devers, Gail, **1:**82–83
DiBiase, Mike, **2:**241
Dickerson, Chris, **2:**393
Dickerson, Eric, **1:**83–84
Didrickson, Babe, **1:**192
Dightman, Myrtis, **2:**313

GENERAL INDEX

Dihigo, Martin, **2**:395
Dillard, Harrison, **1**:84–85; **2**:372
DiMaggio, Joe, **1**:54; **2**:286
Dirty Dozen, The (film), **1**:101
Ditka, Mike, **2**:220
Dixon, George, **1**:43, 85–86
Doby, Larry, **1**:86; **2**:219, 395, 409
Don't Look Back: The Story of Leroy "Satchel" Paige (television film), **1**:101
Dorinson, Joseph, **1**:155
Dorrington, Arthur, **1**:69, 87
Dougherty, Romeo, **2**:345
Douglas, Bob, **1**:24; **2**:257
Douglas, Buster, **1**:46; **2**:375
Douglas, Robert, **2**:256, 418
Douglass, Haley G., **1**:168
Douglass High School, **1**:168
Downing, Al, **1**:1
Drew, Charles, **1**:24, 87–88
Drew, Howard, **1**:88; **2**:371
DuBois, W. E. B., **1**:17; **2**:326
Dukes, Walter, **1**:89
Dundee, Angelo, **1**:95
Dunlap, Carla, **2**:393
Dunn, Willie, **2**:327
Duran, Roberto, **1**:46, 137, 206, 207
Durham, Diane, **1**:135
Durham, Yank, **1**:112
Dwyer, Michael F., **2**:330
Dwyer, Philip J., **2**:330
Dyreson, Mark, **1**:156; **2**:292

East-West All-Star Game, **1**:22, 129; **2**:252
East-West League, **2**:253, 254
Eastern Colored League, **1**:91; **2**:253, 254
Easton, James, **1**:81–82
Eaton, Hubert, **1**:120; **2**:363
Ebony (magazine), **1**:54; **2**:421
Edwards, Harry, **1**:60, 69, 91–92; **2**:266, 291, 340
Edwards, Teresa, **1**:92–93; **2**:267
Elder, Lee, **1**:93–94, 125; **2**:417
Elizabeth City State University, **1**:63
Eller, Carl, **1**:94–95
Ellis, Jimmy, **1**:95, 112
Embry, Wayne, **1**:95–96
Emperor Jones (film), **1**:101
Englehardt, Fred, **1**:139–40
Entine, John, **2**:292
Ervin, Anthony, **2**:267
Erving, Julius, **1**:35, 96, 102
Evans, Fred, **2**:354
Evans, Lee, **1**:97; **2**:372
Everett, Danny, **2**:339
Ewing, Patrick, **1**:97–98; **2**:369

Faggs, Mae, **1**:99; **2**:362, 373
Farrell, Charles, **2**:293
Farrington, John, **1**:116
Fayetteville State University, **1**:63
Ferenczy, Alex, **1**:49; **2**:240

Fiall, George, **1**:24
Films and television, **1**:100–102
  Abdul-Jabbar, Kareem as actor, **1**:3–4, 102
  Ali, Muhammad as actor, **1**:100
  Armstrong, Henry as actor, **1**:100
  baseball, **1**:100–101
  basketball, **1**:101–2
  boxing, **1**:100
  Brown, Jim as actor, **1**:50, 101
  Brown, Tim as actor, **1**:101
  Butler, Sol as actor, **1**:55
  Casey, Bernie as actor, **1**:101
  Chamberlain, Wilt as actor, **1**:65, 102
  Erving, Julius as actor, **1**:102
  football, **1**:101
  Frazier, Walter, Jr. as sports announcer, **1**:113
  Gault, Willie as actor, **1**:119
  Gibson, Althea as actress, **1**:121
  about golf, **1**:102
  Greene, Joe as actor, **1**:101, 129
  Grier, Rosey as actor, **1**:101, 132
  Hagler, "Marvelous" Marvin as actor, **1**:137
  Jeannette, Joe as actor, **1**:176
  Johnson, Jack as actor, **1**:179
  Jordan, Michael as actor, **1**:102
  Lee, Canada as actor, **1**:100
  Lemon, Meadowlark as actor, **1**:102
  Louis, Joe as actor, **1**:100
  Moore, Archie as actor, **1**:66; **2**:241
  Moore, Lenny as announcer, **2**:243
  Morgan, Joe as commentator, **2**:244
  Norton, Ken as actor, **1**:100
  O'Neal, Shaquille as actor, **1**:102
  Perkins, Don as sportscaster, **2**:281
  racial theories and television, **2**:291–92
  Rashad, Ahmad as sportscaster, **2**:294–95
  Robeson, Paul as actor, **2**:304
  Robinson, Jackie as actor, **1**:100–101; **2**:310
  Robinson, Sugar Ray as actor, **1**:100
  Simpson, O. J. as actor, **1**:101; **2**:331
  Smith, "Bubba" as actor, **1**:101; **2**:337
  Strode, Woody as actor, **1**:101; **2**:351
  Swann, Lynn as sports announcer, **2**:352–53
  tennis, **1**:102
  Thompson, John as commentator, **2**:369
  track and field, **1**:102
  White, Bill as announcer, **2**:398
  Williamson, Fred as actor, **1**:101
Final Exam (film), **1**:102
Finney, Arthur, **1**:167
Firpo, Luis Angel, **2**:408
Fish That Saved Pittsburgh, The (film), **1**:102
Fisk University, **1**:150, 151
Fitzgerald, Ella, **2**:326
Flippin, George, **1**:102–3
Flood, Curt, **1**:103–4
Flores, Jesse, **2**:405
Flores, Tom, **2**:326
Florida A & M University, **1**:152
Flowers, Tiger, **1**:44, 104

GENERAL INDEX

Foggs, Mae, **1:**77
Foley, Larry, **1:**174
Folley, Zora, **1:**110
Follis, Charles, **1:**105
Ford, Gerald, **2:**421
Ford, James, **1:**199
Ford, Phil, **1:**108
Foreman, George, **1:**46, 100, 109, 112, 197; **2:**241, 260, 266
Foster, Andrew "Rube." *See* Foster, Rube
Foster, Bob, **1:**46, 110
Foster, Rube, **1:**22, 91, 110–11; **2:**253, 254
Fowler, Bud, **1:**22
Foxx, Jamie, **1:**101
Franke, Nikki, **1:**35
Franklin Evening News (newspaper), **2:**410
Frazier, Charles R., **1:**63
Frazier, Hector, **1:**112
Frazier, Joe, **1:**46, 95, 109, 110, 112, 197; **2:**266
Frazier, Marvis, **1:**112
Frazier, Walter, Jr., **1:**112–13; **2:**297
Frederick, Jane, **1:**192
Freeman, Burt, **1:**99
Freeman, Henry, **1:**10
Frick, Ford, **1:**69
Fryar, Irving, **2:**316
Fuhr, Grant, **1:**166
Fulks, Joe, **1:**199
Fuller, William, **2:**238
Fullmer, Gene, **1:**45
Futch, Eddie, **2:**260

Gaines, Clarence "Bighouse," **1:**115
Gaines, Joseph. *See* Gans, Joe
Gaither, Jake, **1:**115–16, 152
Galiber, Joe, **1:**25
Galimore, Ron, **1:**134
Galimore, Willie, **1:**116, 134
Gallatin, Harry, **2:**400
Galloway, Hipple "Hippo," **1:**165
Gans, Joe, **1:**44, 104, 117
Gant, Lamar, **2:**394
Garcia, Ceferino, **1:**12
Garrett, Mike, **1:**117–18
Garrison, Zina, **1:**118; **2:**364
Garvey, Marcus, **2:**228
Gates, "Pop," **1:**24
Gatewood, Bill, **1:**31
Gault, Willie, **1:**119
Gavilan, Kid, **2:**405
Gehrig, Lou, **2:**229
Gems, Gerald R., **1:**154, 155
Gentry, Alvin, **1:**72
George, Nelson, **1:**155
George V, King of England, **2:**312
Gervin, George, **1:**119–20
Ghosts of Manila, The (Kram), **1:**112
Gibbs, Joe, **2:**239
Gibson, Althea, **1:**10, 12, 16, 69, 118, 120–21, 152; **2:**326, 363–64, 394, 406, 407, 414

Gibson, Bob, **1:**121–22
Gibson, Josh, **1:**22, 67, 122, 129, 205; **2:**219
Gill, Turner, **2:**316
Gilliam, Joe, **2:**261
Gilmore, Artis, **1:**122–23
Gissendanner, Cindy, **1:**156
Glickman, Marty, **2:**328
Goldberg, Arthur, **1:**104
Golden Gloves, **1:**44, 45
Gordon, Ed, Jr., **1:**125–26
Gordy, Fuller, **1:**42
Gore, Al, **2:**342
Gottlieb, Eddie, **1:**37
Gourdin, Ned, **1:**126–27
Graham, Otto, **1:**5; **2:**237, 246
Grambling State College, **1:**152; **2:**307
Grange, Harold "Red," **1:**6; **2:**422
Grant, Francis, **1:**124
Grant, Frank, **1:**127
Grant, George, **2:**377
Graves, William, **1:**40
Gray, Edward, **1:**127–28
Greased Lightning (film), **2:**325
Great, The (film), **1:**100
Great White Hope, The (film), **1:**100
Greb, Harry, **1:**104
Green, Leroy, **1:**110
Green, Pumpsie, **1:**22
Green, Tina Sloan, **1:**35, 199
Greene, Joe, **1:**101, 128–29
Greenlee, Gus, **1:**22, 67, 129
Greenwood, L. C., **2:**261
Greer, Hal, **1:**130
Gregory, Ann, **1:**130–31
Gregory, George, **1:**24
Gregory, George, Jr., **1:**131
Grier, Mike, **1:**166
Grier, Rosey, **1:**101, 132
Griffey, Ken, **1:**132
Griffey, Ken, Jr., **1:**132–33
Griffith, Clark, **1:**69, 205
Griffith-Joyner, Florence, **1:**133; **2:**265, 372
Grundman, Adolph, **1:**155
Gwynn, Tony, **1:**134

Hagen, Walter, **2:**417
Hagler, "Marvelous" Marvin, **1:**46, 137, 144, 207
Halas, George, **2:**307
Halliard, Wendy, **1:**35
Halls of fame. *See* Boxing Hall of Fame; International Boxing Hall of Fame; Naismith Memorial Basketball Hall of Fame; National Baseball Hall of Fame; Professional Football Hall of Fame; U.S. National Track and Field Hall of Fame
Hamilton, Bobby, **2:**300
Hammer, M. C. (Stanley Burrell), **1:**160
Hampton Institute, **1:**63, 150, 151
Haney, Lee, **2:**393
Hard Road to Glory, A (Ashe), **1:**13, 153
Harding, Ben, **1:**42

GENERAL INDEX

Harewood, Darian, **1:**102
Hargrave, H. P., **1:**63
Harlem Globetrotters, **1:**24, 25, 64, 71, 89, 121, 137–38, 143, 173, 204–5; **2:**358, 415
Harlem Magicians, **1:**75, 143
Harris, Alphonso, **1:**42
Harris, Arthur, **2:**393
Harris, Ed, **2:**345
Harris, Franco, **1:**139
Harris, James, **2:**307
Harris, Morris, **1:**176
Harris, Tom, **1:**200; **2:**277
Harrison, Miles, **1:**199
Hart, Clyde, **1:**181
Hart, Frank, **1:**139–40
Haskins, Don, **2:**301
Havemeyer, Theodore F., **2:**327
Hawkins, Connie, **1:**138, 140–41
Hawkins, Robert, **2:**377
Hawkins, Tommy, **2:**290
Haydon, Benjamin Robert, **1:**159
Hayes, Bob, **1:**141–42; **2:**372
Hayes, Elvin, **1:**142
Hayes, Wilbur, **2:**252
Haynes, Marques, **1:**138, 142–43, 205; **2:**358
Haywood, Spencer, **1:**143–44, 167
Hazzard, Walt, **1:**189
He Got Game (film), **1:**102
Hearns, Thomas, **1:**46, 137, 144, 167, 207
Heaven Is a Playground (film), **1:**102
Heisman Trophy
  Allen, Marcus, **1:**9–10
  Campbell, Earl, **1:**58–59
  Davis, Ernie, **1:**78–79
  Garrett, Mike, **1:**117–18
  Jackson, Bo, **1:**171–72
  Rodgers, Johnny, **2:**313–14
  Rogers, George, **2:**315–16
  Rozier, Mike, **2:**316
  Sanders, Barry, **2:**321
  Simpson, O. J., **2:**331
  Walker, Herschel, **2:**384–85
  Ward, Charlie, **2:**387–88
Henderson, Edwin Bancroft, **1:**23, 53–54, 128, 145, 153, 168; **2:**363
Henderson, Rickey, **1:**146
Henriquez de Zubiera, Constantin, **2:**264
Heritage Bowl, **1:**152
Hewitt-Courtourier, Naomi, **1:**135
High school athletics, segregation and integration, **1:**121
Hightower, Stephanie, **1:**146–47
Hill, Calvin, **1:**147–48
Hill, Fitz, **1:**72
Hill, Grant, **1:**148–49
Hill, Jimmy, **1:**55
Hill, Kelli, **1:**135
Hines, Jim, **1:**149; **2:**372
Historically black colleges and universities (HCBU), **1:**149–52; **2:**354

Historiography, **1:**153–56
Hitler, Adolf, **2:**265
Hoberman, John, **2:**292
Hoffman, Bob, **2:**392
Hogan, Ernest, **1:**175
Holdsclaw, Chamique, **2:**267
Holland, Jerome Brud, **1:**157
Holman, Nat, **1:**25; **2:**258
Holman, Steve, **1:**157–58
Holmes, Larry, **1:**46, 158, 197; **2:**260, 343, 344
Holmes, Talley, **1:**10; **2:**363
Holston, Isabelle. *See* Daniels, Isabelle
Holt, Johnny, **1:**24
Holtz, Lou, **2:**357
Holway, John, **1:**154
Holyfield, Evander, **1:**109; **2:**375
Homer, **2:**371
Hoop Dreams (film), **1:**102
Horse Soldiers, The (film), **1:**121
Hotaling, Ed, **2:**291
Howard, Ed, **1:**199
Howard High School, **1:**168
Howard, Kevin, **1:**207
Howard Medical School, **1:**168
Howard University, **1:**63, 150, 151, 168; **2:**354, 363
Hubbard, William Dehart, **1:**42, 151, 161; **2:**265, 371
Huckleberry Finn (film), **2:**241
Hudson, Dick, **1:**138
Hudson, Martha, **1:**161
Hue (magazine), **2:**421
Hunt, Edward E., Jr., **2:**290
Hunter, C. J., **1:**188
Hurricane (film), **1:**100
Hurt, Eddie, **1:**162
Hyman, Flo, **2:**381
Hymes, Lula Mae, **1:**162–63; **2:**414

Ice Station Zebra (film), **1:**101
Iliad (Homer), **2:**371
Indianapolis Freeman (newspaper), **1:**215
Integration. *See* Segregation and integration
Intercollegiate Athletic Association of the United States, **1:**106
International Afro-American Sports Hall of Fame Gallery, **1:**167
International Boxing Club, **1:**45
International Boxing Hall of Fame
  Flowers, Tiger, **1:**104
  Frazier, Joe, **1:**112
  Gans, Joe, **1:**117
  Hagler, "Marvelous" Marvin, **1:**137
  Leonard, Sugar Ray, **1:**207
  Lewis, John Henry, **1:**211
  Liston, Sonny, **1:**213–14
  Louis, Joe, **1:**217
  McVey, Sam, **2:**234
  Moore, Archie, **2:**241–42
  Norton, Ken, **2:**260
  Patterson, Floyd, **2:**276–77
  Robinson, Sugar Ray, **2:**311–12

GENERAL INDEX

International Boxing Hall of Fame *(continued)*
    Walcott, Joe, **2:**383–84
    Williams, Ike, **2:**405
    Wills, Harry, **2:**408–9
    See also Boxing Hall of Fame
International League of Baseball Clubs in America and Cuba, **1:**167–68
International Olympic Committee (IOC), **1:**81–82
International Tennis Hall of Fame, **1:**13
International Track Association, **1:**60; **2:**236, 339, 375
Interscholastic Athletic Association of Middle Atlantic States, **1:**168
Irish, Ned, **1:**71, 138
Irvin, Monte, **1:**169; **2:**219, 395
Isaacs, John, **1:**24; **2:**258
Islam
    Abdul-Jabbar, Kareem, **1:**3–4
    Ali, Muhammad, **1:**8–9
    Rashad, Ahmad, **2:**293–95
It's Good to Be Alive (television film), **1:**101

Jack, Beau, **1:**45; **2:**405
Jack Johnson (documentary), **1:**100, 176
Jack, "Rajo," **1:**171
Jackie Robinson Story, The (film), **1:**101; **2:**310
Jackson, Bo, **1:**171–72
Jackson, Henry. *See* Armstrong, Henry
Jackson, Inman, **1:**138
Jackson, Jesse, **2:**293
Jackson, Jimmy, **2:**419
Jackson, Levi, **1:**172
Jackson, Mannie, **1:**173
Jackson, Melody. *See* Armstrong, Henry
Jackson, Morris, **2:**353
Jackson, Nell, **2:**373
Jackson, Peter, **1:**43, 173–75; **2:**289
Jackson, Reggie, **1:**38, 175
Jackson, Rufus "Sonnyman" and "See," **2:**286
Jackson, Wayne, **1:**199
Jacobs, Mike, **1:**210
Jamaica Kid, **1:**104
James, Clyde, **2:**354
James, Craig, **1:**83
Jarvis, Mike, **1:**71
Jeannette, Joe, **1:**44, 176; **2:**234, 408
Jefferson, Bernie, **1:**176–77
Jeffries, James, **1:**100
Jeffries, Jim, **1:**44, 174, 178
Jenkins, "Fats," **1:**24
Jenner, Bruce, **2:**263
Jensen, Arthur R., **2:**291
Jesse Owens Story, The (television film), **1:**102
Jet (magazine), **1:**54; **2:**421
Jeter, Emily, **2:**353
Jockeys. *See* Horse racing
Joe Louis Story, The (film), **1:**100
Joe Palooka, Champ (film), **1:**100
Johansson, Ingemar, **1:**45; **2:**276
Johnson, Battling Jim, **1:**176
Johnson, Ben, **1:**133

Johnson, C. Howard, **1:**203
Johnson C. Smith University, **1:**63, 150, 151
Johnson, Cornelius, **1:**7, 177–78; **2:**265, 372
Johnson, Earvin "Magic." *See* Johnson, Magic
Johnson, Fred, **2:**363
Johnson, George, **1:**63
Johnson, Jack, **1:**16, 44, 100, 176, 178–79; **2:**234, 289, 408
Johnson, John Henry, **1:**179
Johnson, John Lester, **1:**176
Johnson, Judy. *See* Johnson, William "Judy"
Johnson, Magic, **1:**16, 26, 180; **2:**266
Johnson, Michael, **1:**181–82
Johnson, Oscar, **1:**10; **2:**363
Johnson Publishing Company, **1:**54
Johnson, Rafer, **1:**59, 182–83; **2:**266, 372
Johnson, Robert L., **1:**183–84
Johnson, Robert W., **1:**120
Johnson, Walter, **1:**12; **2:**363, 405
Johnson, William, **2:**414
Johnson, William "Judy," **1:**67, 129, 184
Joiner, William A., **1:**168
Jones, Barbara, **1:**161, 185–86; **2:**228
Jones, Bill, **1:**24
Jones, David "Deacon," **1:**132, 186
Jones, Doug, **1:**110
Jones, Hayes, **1:**186–87
Jones, James Earl, **1:**100, 101
Jones, K. C., **1:**187
Jones, Laura, **1:**42
Jones, Lucious, **2:**303
Jones, Marion, **1:**188
Jones, "Piano Man," **2:**241
Jones, Robert Tyre "Bobby," **2:**397
Jones, Roy, **2:**266
Jones, Sam, **1:**188–89
Jones, Uriah, **1:**99
Jones, Wali, **1:**189–90
Jones, Wally, **1:**153
Jordan, Michael, **1:**26, 102, 120, 190–91; **2:**266
Journalists. *See* Sportswriters
Joyner, Al, Jr., **1:**133, 192
Joyner-Kersee, Jackie, **1:**133, 191–93; **2:**265, 372

Kalule, Ayub, **1:**206
Kane, Martin, **2:**290–91
Kansas City Call (newspaper), **2:**422
Karolyi, Bela, **1:**135
Keep Fighting (film), **1:**100
Keith, Floyd, **1:**34
Kelly, Fred "Bud," **1:**165
Kelly, Leroy, **1:**195
Kemp, Lee, **2:**418
Kemp, Ray, **1:**107, 195–96
Kennedy, Robert F., **1:**132
Kerr, Johnny, **1:**120
Kersee, Bob, **1:**47, 133, 192
Keyes, Leroy, **1:**196
King, Don, **1:**196–97
King, Henry, **1:**160

GENERAL INDEX

King Solomon's Mines (film), **1:**101
King, William "Dolly," **1:**25, 197–98
Knight, Bob, **2:**366
Knight, David, **2:**287
Kram, Mark, **1:**112
Ku Klux Klan, **1:**25, 160
Kuhn, Bowie, **1:**103
Kuznetsov, Vasily, **1:**183

La Guardia, Fiorello, **1:**202
Labor issues
 in baseball, **1:**103–4
 in football, **2:**220, 379
Lacayo, Richard, **2:**312
Lacy, Sam, **1:**22, 199–200; **2:**345
Ladies Professional Golf Association, **1:**121
Lakes, Charles, **1:**135
Lalonde, Donny, **1:**207
Lamar, Ed, **2:**251
LaMotta, Jake, **1:**45; **2:**311–12
Lanctot, Neil, **1:**154
Landis, Kenesaw Mountain, **1:**69; **2:** 261, 304
Lane, Betty Jean, **1:**200
Lane, Dick, **1:**201
Lane, Floyd, **1:**25
Langford, Sam, **1:**44, 104, 176, 201–2; **2:**408
Lanier, Bob, **1:**202–3
Lansbury, Jennifer, **1:**156
Lapchick, Joe, **2:**258
Lapchick, Richard, **1:**155; **2:**291
Larkin, Tippy, **2:**405
Lasker, Terrence, **1:**99
Lautier, Lewis, **1:**200
League of Colored Base Ball Players, **1:**203
LeDroit Park, **1:**168
Lee, Canada, **1:**100
Lee, Jimmy, **1:**160
Lee, Spike, **1:**100
Lees, Tom, **1:**174
LeFlore, Ron, **1:**101
Lemon, Meadowlark, **1:**102, 138, 203–5
Lenglen, Suzanne, **1:**6
Leonard, Buck, **1:**205–6
Leonard, Sugar Ray, **1:**46, 137, 144, 206–7; **2:**266, 312
Leslie, Lisa, **1:**207–8
Lester, Jack, **2:**234
LeVias, Jerry, **1:**208–9
Lew, Harry "Bucky," **1:**23
Lewis, Carl, **1:**209–10; **2:**372–73
Lewis, "Country," **1:**200
Lewis, John Henry, **1:**44–45, 129, 210–11
Lewis, Oliver, **1:**211
Lewis, Steve, **2:**339
Lewis, William Henry, **1:**211–12
Lewison, Peter, **1:**99
Liberti, Rita, **1:**154
Lifeboat (film), **1:**100
Lightfoot, Charlie, **1:**165
Lilliard, Joe, **1:**107, 195, 212
Lincoln University, **1:**63, 150; **2:**296, 363

Lipscomb, Gene "Big Daddy," **1:**213
Liston, Sonny, **1:**45, 213–14; **2:**266, 277
Little, Floyd, **1:**214
Livingstone University, **1:**63, 150
Lloyd, Earl, **1:**25, 214–15
Lloyd, John Henry, **1:**215–16
Lofton, Michael, **1:**99
Lomax, Michael E., **1:**154
Lombardi, Vince, **1:**51, 201; **2:**374
Long, Bingo, **1:**101
Los Angeles Mirror-News (newspaper), **2:**389
Los Angeles Sentinel (newspaper), **2:**389, 421
Lott, Ronnie, **1:**216
Louis, Joe, **1:**16, 44, 45, 54, 66, 76, 100, 124, 167, 202,
 210–11, 217–18; **2:**261, 299, 348–49, 384, 389
Love and Basketball (film), **1:**102
Love, Nat, **2:**312
Lucas, Jerry, **1:**39
Lundy, Lamar, **1:**132
LuValle, James, **1:**218; **2:**372
Lyght, Trent, **2:**354
Lyman, Hazel, **1:**42

M. C. Hammer (Stanley Burrell), **1:**160
M Street High School, **1:**168
Macci, Rick, **2:**406, 407
MacCracken, Henry, **1:**106
Mackey, Biz, **2:**219
Mackey, John, **2:**220–21
Magers-Powell, Rose, **2:**381
Maher, Charles, **2:**290
Malcolm X, **1:**8
Malina, Robert, **2:**291
Malone, Karl, **2:**221–22
Malone, Moses, **2:**222–23
Managers. *See* Coaches and managers
Manley, Abe, **2:**223
Manley, Effa, **2:**223
Manning, Danny, **2:**224
Manning-Mims, Madeline, **2:**224–25, 362, 373
Manuel, Jerry, **1:**72
Mapledale Country Club, **2:**377
Maravich, Pete, **2:**403
Marble, Alice, **1:**121; **2:**363
Marcello, Ronald, **1:**155
Marciano, Rocky, **1:**45, 66, 217; **2:**241, 384
Marshall, Bob, **2:**225–26
Marshall, Jim, **2:**226
Marson, Mike, **1:**166
Martin, Charles, **1:**155
Martin, Clyde, **1:**125
Marvin, Lee, **1:**50
Mary, Queen of England, **2:**312–13
Mashiani, Jan, **2:**264
Mathewson, Alfred Dennis, **1:**156
Mathias, Bob, **1:**59; **2:**372
Mathis, Buster, **1:**112
Matson, Ollie, **2:**227
Matthews, Margaret, **1:**77; **2:**227–28
Matthews, Vincent, **1:**17; **2:**266

GENERAL INDEX

Matthews, William Clarence, **2:**228–29
Mattingly, R. N., **1:**168
Maxim, Joey, **2:**241, 384
May, George S., **1:**130
Mays, Willie, **1:**16, 38; **2:**229–30
McAuliffe, Jack, **1:**85
McCard, H. S., **1:**10
McCauley, Ed, **2:**318
McCovey, Willie, **2:**230
McDaniel, Jimmy, **2:**363
McDaniel, Mildred, **2:**231, 373
McDaniel, Pete, **1:**155
McElhenny, Hugh, **1:**179
McGall, Albert, **2:**289
McGee, Pam, **2:**231–32
McGowan, Alex, **2:**364–65
McGrath, H. Price, **1:**211
McGuire, Dick, **2:**400
McGuire, Edith, **2:**232–33, 362, 373, 375
McIntyre, Manny, **1:**165
McKegney, Tony, **1:**166
McLendon, John, **1:**71; **2:**233–34
McMahon, Roderick and Edward, **2:**251
McNeil, Lori, **1:**118; **2:**364
McVey, Sam, **1:**44; **2:**234, 408
Mead, Chris, **1:**153
Mee, Bob, **1:**176
Meehan, Chuck, **1:**68
Meehan, Willie, **2:**408
Meriweather, Willie, **1:**120
Metcalfe, Ralph, **1:**7; **2:**235, 289, 369–70, 371
Miceli, Joe, **2:**405
Michigan Chronicle (newspaper), **1:**76
Mid-Eastern Athletic Conference, **1:**151
Mikan, George, **1:**24, 143
Milburn, Rod, **2:**235–36
Miller, Cheryl, **2:**236, 267
Miller, John, **2:**244
Miller, Patrick B., **1:**154, 156; **2:**292
Miller, Walk, **1:**104
Minter, Alan, **1:**137
Mitchell, Bobby, **1:**79; **2:**237
Molinas, Jack, **1:**51
Molineaux, Tom, **1:**43, 45, 210; **2:**237–38, 303, 334
Monday, Kenny, **2:**418
Monday Night Football (television show), **1:**107
Monk, Art, **2:**238–39
Monplaiser, Sharon, **1:**99
Monroe, Earl, **1:**115; **2:**239–40
Monroe, Willie, **1:**137
Montgomery, Bob, **2:**405
Montgomery, Eleanor, **2:**240
Moon, Warren, **2:**240–41
Moore, Archie, **1:**45, 66, 100; **2:**241–42, 276
Moore, Bobby. *See* Rashad, Ahmad
Moore, Davey, **1:**45
Moore, Lenny, **2:**242–43
Moorer, Michael, **1:**109
Morehouse College, **1:**150
Morgan, Joe, **2:**243–44

Morgan, Marion, **2:**227
Morgan State University, **1:**151, 162; **2:**354
Morris Brown College, **1:**150
Morris, Cecil, **2:**315–16
Morris, James, **2:**393
Moses, Edwin, **2:**244, 372
Moss, Simeon, **1:**199
Most Valuable Player (American Basketball Association)
    Gilmore, Artis, **1:**123
    Haywood, Spencer, **1:**143–44
Most Valuable Player (major league baseball)
    Aaron, Hank, **1:**1
    Banks, Ernie, **1:**19
    Baylor, Don, **1:**27
    Bonds, Barry, **1:**38–39
    Campanella, Roy, **1:**57–58
    Griffey, Ken, Jr., **1:**132–33
    Henderson, Rickey, **1:**146
    Mays, Willie, **2:**229–30
    McCovey, Willie, **2:**230
    Morgan, Joe, **2:**243–44
    Newcombe, Don, **2:**258–59
    Robinson, Frank, **2:**308–9
    Robinson, Jackie, **2:**309–10
    Thomas, Frank, **2:**365
Most Valuable Player (National Basketball Association)
    Abdul-Jabbar, Kareem, **1:**3
    Johnson, Magic, **1:**180
    Jordan, Michael, **1:**190–91
    Malone, Karl, **2:**221–22
    Malone, Moses, **2:**222–23
    Olajuwon, Hakeem, **2:**263
    Reed, Willis, **2:**297
    Robertson, Oscar, **2:**303–4
    Robinson, David, **2:**306
    Unseld, Wes, **2:**378
Most Valuable Player (National Football League)
    Allen, Marcus, **1:**9–10
    Brown, Larry, **1:**50–51
    Campbell, Earl, **1:**58–59
    Payton, Walter, **2:**278–79
    Rice, Jerry, **2:**301
Most Valuable Player (Women's National Basketball Association)
    Leslie, Lisa, **1:**207–8
Motley, Marion, **2:**245–46
Motown Records, **1:**42
Mr. America, **2:**392–93
Mr. Olympia, **2:**393
Mr. T, **1:**100
Ms. Olympia, **2:**393
Mugabi, John, **1:**137
Muhammad, Eddie Mustaffa, **2:**344
Munger, George, **2:**361
Murphy, Calvin, **2:**246–47
Murphy, Isaac, **1:**68, 159; **2:**247–48, 289
Murray, Bob, **2:**354
Murray, Eddie, **2:**248

Murray, Jim, **1:**204
Murray, Lenda, **2:**394
Murray, Rich, **2:**248
Myer, Billy, **1:**85
Myers, Dave, **1:**68

NAACP. *See* National Association for the Advancement of Colored People
Naismith, James, **1:**71; **2:**233
Naismith Memorial Basketball Hall of Fame
   Abdul-Jabbar, Kareem, **1:**3–4
   Archibald, Nate, **1:**11
   Baylor, Elgin, **1:**28
   Bellamy, Walter, **1:**32–33
   Chamberlain, Wilt, **1:**64–65
   Chaney, John, **1:**65–66
   Frazier, Walter, Jr., **1:**112–13
   Gaines, Clarence "Bighouse," **1:**115
   Gervin, George, **1:**119–20
   Greer, Hal, **1:**130
   Hawkins, Connie, **1:**140–41
   Haynes, Marques, **1:**142–43
   Johnson, Magic, **1:**180
   Jones, K. C., **1:**187
   Jones, Sam, **1:**188–89
   Lanier, Bob, **1:**202–3
   Malone, Moses, **2:**222–23
   McLendon, John, **2:**233–34
   Monroe, Earl, **2:**239–40
   New York Renaissance Five, **1:**24
   Robertson, Oscar, **2:**303–4
   Russell, Bill, **2:**318
   Thompson, David, **2:**367–68
   Unseld, Wes, **2:**378
Naked Gun (film), **1:**101
Nathaniel, Clifton. *See* Clifton, Nat "Sweetwater"
National Association for the Advancement of Colored People (NAACP), **1:**68, 74, 145, 197; **2:**261, 394
National Association of Colored Base Ball Clubs of the United States and Cuba, **2:**251
National Association of Colored Professional Base Ball Clubs, **1:**168; **2:**255
National Association of Intercollegiate Athletics (NAIA), **2:**233–34
National Baseball Hall of Fame
   Aaron, Hank, **1:**2
   Banks, Ernie, **1:**19
   Bell, James "Cool Papa," **1:**31–32
   Brock, Louis, **1:**48
   Campanella, Roy, **1:**57–58
   Charleston, Oscar, **1:**67
   Doby, Larry, **1:**86
   Foster, Rube, **1:**110–11
   Gibson, Bob, **1:**121–22
   Gibson, Josh, **1:**122
   Irvin, Monte, **1:**169
   Jackson, Reggie, **1:**175
   Johnson, William "Judy," **1:**184
   Lacy, Sam, **1:**200
   Leonard, Buck, **1:**205–6

National Baseball Hall of Fame (*continued*)
   Lloyd, John Henry, **1:**215–16
   Mays, Willie, **2:**229–30
   McCovey, Willie, **2:**230
   Morgan, Joe, **2:**243
   Paige, Satchel, **2:**275
   Puckett, Kirby, **2:**286–87
   Robinson, Frank, **2:**308–9
   Robinson, Jackie, **2:**309–10
   Smith, Wendell, **2:**341
   Stargell, Willie, **2:**346–47
   Stearnes, Norman "Turkey," **2:**347
   Wells, Willie, **2:**395
   Williams, Joseph "Smokey," **2:**405
   Winfield, Dave, **2:**410–11
National Bowling Association, **1:**42; **2:**252
National Collegiate Athletic Association (NCAA)
   AAU and, **2:**371
   African-American coaches in, **1:**71–72
   beginning of, **1:**106
   Black Coaches Association and, **1:**34
   Central Intercollegiate Athletic Association and, **1:**63
   football and television contracts, **1:**107
   and historically black colleges and universities, **1:**151; **2:**234
   minority hiring in, **2:**293
National Colored League, **2:**401
National Football League, **1:**105, 106–7
National Junior Tennis League, **2:**364
National Negro Bowling Association. *See* National Bowling Association
National Track and Field Hall of Fame
   Albritton, David, **1:**7
   Beamon, Bob, **1:**29
   Borican, John, **1:**40
   Boston, Ralph, **1:**41–42
   Calhoun, Lee, **1:**57
   Campbell, Milt, **1:**59
   Dillard, Harrison, **1:**84–85
   Evans, Lee, **1:**97
   Johnson, Rafer, **1:**182–83
   Manning-Mims, Madeline, **2:**224–25
   McGuire, Edith, **2:**233
   Metcalfe, Ralph, **2:**235
   Milburn, Rod, **2:**236
   Owens, Jesse, **2:**271–72
   Temple, Ed, **2:**362
   Tolan, Eddie, **2:**370
   Tyus, Wyomia, **2:**375
   Woodruff, John, **2:**416
NBC (National Broadcasting Company), **1:**107; **2:**291–92, 295
NCAA. *See* National Collegiate Athletic Association
Negro American League, **1:**22; **2:**252–53, 255
Negro in Sports, The (Henderson), **1:**145, 153
Negro League Baseball Museum, **2:**253
Negro leagues, **1:**110–11, 153–54; **2:**275, 347, 348–49
   See also individual leagues; Negro League Baseball Museum

GENERAL INDEX

Negro National League, **1:**22, 37, 41, 54, 67, 91, 111, 129, 169; **2:**223, 252, 253, 254, 255, 261, 422
Negro Southern Intercollegiate Athletic Conference, **1:**151
Negro Southern League, **2:**253, 254, 255
Negro World Series, **1:**38
Nehemiah, Renaldo, **2:**256
Nelson, "Battling," **1:**117
Nelson, Ben, **1:**40
Nelson, Byron, **2:**417
New York Age (newspaper), **1:**54
New York Amsterdam News (newspaper), **1:**41, 54
New York Herald (newspaper), **1:**159
New York Olympic Club. *See* New York Pioneer Club
New York People's Voice (newspaper), **1:**41
New York Pioneer Club, **1:**76; **2:**256–57
New York Renaissance Five, **1:**24; **2:**257–58, 328
Newcombe, Don, **2:**219, 258–59, 395
Newell, Pete, **1:**39
Newsome, Ozzie, **2:**259
Nicklaus, Jack, **1:**93–94
Nike, **1:**20, 191; **2:**355
Nixon, Richard, **2:**421
Norfolk, Kid, **1:**104
Norman, Gerald, Jr., **2:**394
Norman, Peter, **2:**340
Norris, James, **1:**217
Norris, Terry, **1:**207
North Carolina Central University, **1:**63
Norton, Gerald, Jr., **2:**363
Norton, Ken, **1:**100, 158, 197; **2:**260
Norwood, Stephen, **1:**154
Nunn, William, Jr., **2:**260–61
Nunn, William, Sr., **2:**261

Oberlin Athletic Club, **1:**168
O'Brien, Dan, **2:**263
Okino, Betty, **1:**135
Olajuwon, Hakeem, **2:**263–64, 321
Oldfield, Barney, **1:**171
O'Leary, Daniel, **1:**139–40
Olin, Bob, **1:**210
Oliva, Sergio, **2:**393
Olsen, Merlin, **1:**132
Olympia (film), **1:**102
Olympic Games, **2:**264–67
　AAU and, **2:**371
　Adams, Lucinda, **1:**4
　African-American reporters at, **1:**76
　Africans in, **2:**265, 373
　Albritton, David, **1:**7
　Ali, Muhammad, **1:**8–9; **2:**266
　Ashford, Evelyn, **1:**15
　Barkley, Charles, **1:**20
　Barksdale, Don, **1:**20–21
　basketball, **2:**266
　Beamon, Bob, **1:**28–29
　Bellamy, Walter, **1:**32–33
　Berlin Games (1936), **1:**102

Olympic Games *(continued)*
　black-power protests (Mexico City, 1968), **1:**17, 29, 60, 69–70, 91–92, 97; **2:**265, 266, 340, 372
　Boozer, Bob, **1:**39–40
　Boston, Ralph, **1:**41–42
　boxing, **2:**266
　Brisco-Hooks, Valerie, **1:**46–48
　Butler, Sol, **1:**55
　Calhoun, Lee, **1:**57
　Campbell, Milt, **1:**59
　Carlos, John, **1:**60, 70, 97; **2:**265, 266, 372
　Coachman, Alice, **1:**72–74
　Collett, Wayne, **2:**266
　Corbitt, Ted, **1:**75–76
　Daniels, Isabelle, **1:**77
　Dantley, Adrian, **1:**77–78
　Davis, John Henry, **1:**79
　Dawes, Dominique, **1:**80
　De Frantz, Anita, **1:**81–82; **2:**267
　Devers, Gail, **1:**82–83
　Dillard, Harrison, **1:**84–85
　Drew, Howard, **1:**88
　Edwards, Teresa, **1:**92–93
　Evans, Lee, **1:**97
　Faggs, Mae, **1:**99
　Ford, Phil, **1:**108
　Foreman, George, **1:**109
　Frazier, Joe, **1:**112
　Gaines, Clarence "Bighouse," **1:**115
　Garrison, Zina, **1:**118
　Gault, Willie, **1:**119
　Gordon, Ed, Jr., **1:**125–26
　Gourdin, Ned, **1:**126–27
　Griffith-Joyner, Florence, **1:**133
　gymnastics, **2:**267
　Hayes, Bob, **1:**141–42
　Haywood, Spencer, **1:**143–44
　Hightower, Stephanie, **1:**146–47
　Hill, Grant, **1:**148–49
　Hines, Jim, **1:**149
　Holman, Steve, **1:**157–58
　Hubbard, William DeHart, **1:**161
　Hudson, Martha, **1:**161
　Hurt, Eddie, **1:**162
　Johnson, Cornelius, **1:**177–78; **2:**265
　Johnson, Magic, **1:**180
　Johnson, Michael, **1:**181–82
　Johnson, Rafer, **1:**182–83; **2:**266
　Jones, Eleanor, **2:**240
　Moses, Edwin, **2:**244
　O'Brien, Dan, **2:**263
　Olajuwon, Hakeem, **2:**263–64
　Owens, Jesse, **2:**265, 271–72
　Patterson, Floyd, **2:**276–77
　Patterson, Mickey, **2:**277–78
　Pickett, Tidye, **2:**282–83
　Poage, George, **2:**283
　Pollard, Fritz, Jr., **2:**284–85
　Raveling, George, **2:**295–96
　Reed, Vivian Brown, **1:**49

Olympic Games *(continued)*
  Reynolds, Butch, **2**:298
  Robertson, Oscar, **2**:303–4
  Robinson, David, **2**:306
  Robinson, Mack, **2**:310–11
  Rudolph, Wilma, **2**:317
  Russell, Bill, **2**:318–19
  Scott, Charlie, **2**:324
  Smith, John, **2**:338–39
  Smith, Tommie, **1**:60, 70, 97; **2**:265, 266, 340, 372
  Spinks, Leon, **2**:343
  Spinks, Michael, **2**:343–44
  Stokes, Louise, **2**:348
  swimming, **2**:267
  Swoopes, Sheryl, **2**:354–55
  Taylor, John Baxter, **2**:359–60
  Temple, Ed, **2**:362
  Thomas, Debra, **2**:364–65
  Thomas, John, **2**:367
  Tolan, Eddie, **2**:369–70
  Torrence, Gwen, **2**:370
  track and field, **2**:264–66
  Tyus, Wyomia, **2**:375–76
  volleyball in, **2**:381–82
  Walker, Herschel, **2**:384–85
  Walker, Leroy, **2**:385–86
  Watts, Quincy, **2**:391–92
  weightlifting in, **2**:392
  Westbrook, Peter, **1**:99
  White, Jo Jo, **2**:398–99
  White, Willye, **2**:401–2
  Whitfield, Mal, **2**:402
  Williams, Archie, **2**:403
  Williams, Serena, **2**:406, 407
  Williams, Venus, **2**:406, 407
  winter sports, **2**:267, 364–65, 385
  Woodruff, John, **1**:7; **2**:416
  Woodward, Lynette, **2**:415–16
100 Percent Wrong Club, **2**:303
One In a Million: The Ron LeFlore Story (television film), **1**:101
O'Neal, Shaquille, **1**:102; **2**:268–69
O'Neil, Buck, **2**:269–70
O'Ree, Willie, **1**:166; **2**:270
Orr, Jack, **1**:153
Our Home Colony (Walker), **2**:387
Owens, Jesse, **1**:7, 16, 41, 74, 102; **2**:235, 265, 271–72, 277, 289, 290, 310, 371, 372, 386
Owens, R. C., **2**:272–73
Owl, The (newspaper), **1**:54

Pacino, Al, **1**:101
Paddock, Charlie, **1**:55
Paige, Satchel, **1**:16, 22, 41, 67, 101, 205; **2**:275, 315, 349, 405
Paine, George, **2**:393
Palace, Fred, **2**:315
Palermo, Blinky, **1**:213; **2**:404, 405
Palmer, Arnold, **2**:417
Pardon the Interruption (television show), **2**:345

Paris, John, **1**:166
Parker, Eugene, **1**:7
Parker, Jim, **2**:276
Parrish, Bernie, **1**:17
Patterson, Floyd, **1**:16, 45, 95, 213; **2**:241, 266, 276–77
Patterson, Inez, **2**:353
Patterson, Mickey, **2**:277–78
Paul, Joan, **1**:155
Payton, Edward, **2**:278
Payton, Walter, **2**:278–79, 337
Peacock, Eulace, **2**:289
Pearson, Drew, **2**:279–80
Peete, Calvin, **1**:125; **2**:280–81
Pele, **1**:35
Penneyman, Martha. *See* Hudson, Martha
Pennington, Richard, **1**:155
People's Voice (newspaper), **2**:345
Pep, Willie, **1**:45
Percy, Lord (British commander), **2**:302
Perenchio, Jerry, **1**:112
Perez, Tony, **2**:243
Perkins, Don, **1**:148; **2**:281
Perry, Joe, **2**:282
Perry, Leila, **2**:414
Peters, Brock, **1**:100
Peters, Roumania and Margaret, **2**:363
Peterson, Horace M., III, **2**:253
Peterson, Robert, **1**:154
Pettingill, C. H., **2**:330
Petway, Bruce, **2**:347
Phal, Louis, **1**:44
Philadelphia American (newspaper), **2**:410
Philadelphia Tribune (newspaper), **2**:345, 410
Phillips, Bum, **2**:316
Phipps, Prikeba (Keba), **2**:381–82
Piccolo, Brian, **1**:101
Pickett, Bill, **2**:312–13
Pickett, Tidye, **2**:282–83, 348
Pierce, J. W., **1**:63
Pierce, Richard, **1**:154
Pingatore, Gene, **2**:366
Pinto Jim, **2**:312
Pittsburgh American (newspaper), **2**:410
Pittsburgh Courier (newspaper), **1**:68–69, 116; **2**:260–61, 286, 303, 341, 345, 389, 410
Pittsburgh Kid (film), **1**:100
Poage, George, **1**:151; **2**:264, 283, 371
Police Academy films, **2**:337
Pollack, Syd, **2**:348–49
Pollard, Fritz, **2**:283–84, 304
Pollard, Fritz, Jr., **1**:7, 106; **2**:284–85
Poole, Harold, **2**:393
Posey, Cum, **1**:23–24; **2**:219, 285–86
Powell, Michael, **1**:29
Powels, George, **1**:103; **2**:308
Prairie View A & M, **1**:150
Predominantly white colleges and universities (PWCU), **1**:152, 154
Price, Bernie, **1**:24

GENERAL INDEX

Primer on College Football, A (Lewis), **1:**211
Professional Bowlers Association, **1:**42
Professional Football Hall of Fame
    Adderley, Herb, **1:**5
    Bell, Bobby, **1:**30–31
    Blount, Mel, **1:**36–37
    Brown, Jim, **1:**49–50
    Brown, Roosevelt, **1:**52
    Campbell, Earl, **1:**58–59
    Dickerson, Eric, **1:**83–84
    Greene, Joe, **1:**128–29
    Harris, Franco, **1:**139
    Johnson, John Henry, **1:**179
    Jones, David "Deacon," **1:**186
    Kelly, Leroy, **1:**195
    Lane, Dick, **1:**201
    Lott, Ronnie, **1:**216
    Mackey, John, **2:**220–21
    Matson, Ollie, **2:**227
    Mitchell, Bobby, **2:**237
    Moore, Lenny, **2:**243
    Motley, Marion, **2:**245–46
    Newsome, Ozzie, **2:**259
    Parker, Jim, **2:**276
    Payton, Walter, **2:**278–79
    Perry, Joe, **2:**282
    Renfro, Mel, **2:**297–98
    Sayers, Gale, **2:**323
    Shell, Art, **2:**326–27
    Simpson, O. J., **2:**331
    Singletary, Mike, **2:**332
    Swann, Lynn, **2:**352–53
    Tunnell, Emlen, **2:**374
    Upshaw, Gene, **2:**378–79
    Warfield, Paul, **2:**388–89
    Willis, Bill, **2:**407–8
    Winslow, Kellen, **2:**413
Professional Golfers Association, **1:**93, 124–25; **2:**342, 377, 397
Proposition 42 (NCAA), **2:**295
Proposition 48 (NCAA), **1:**66, 152; **2:**295
Protests. *See* Boycotts and protests
Pruett, Scott, **2:**300
Pryor, Aaron, **1:**46
Pryor, Richard, **1:**101; **2:**325
Puckett, Kirby, **2:**286–87
Purnell, J. Whipper, **2:**287
Pyle, Charles C. "Cash and Carry," **1:**6
Pythian Base Ball Club, **2:**287–88

Qawi, Dwight Muhammad, **2:**344
Quarry, Jerry, **1:**95

Racial theories, **2:**289–92
    Berlin Olympic Games and Nazi, **2:**265, 372
    Cobb on, **1:**74; **2:**290
    Louis-Schmeling fight and Nazi, **1:**217
    scholars on, **1:**156

Racism. *See* Apartheid; Boycotts and protests; Civil rights; Ku Klux Klan; Segregation and integration; Stereotypes
Radcliff, Alec, **2:**292
Radcliffe, Ted, **2:**292–93
Rainbow Coalition for Fairness in Athletics, **2:**293
Rampersad, Arnold, **1:**17, 155
Ramsey, Charles, **2:**392
Ransom, Samuel, **1:**23
Rashad, Ahmad, **2:**293–95
Raveling, George, **2:**295–96
Ray, Albert, **1:**199
Ray, Shawn, **2:**393
Reach Sporting Goods, **1:**203
Reed, Dwight, **2:**296
Reed, Vivian Brown, **1:**49
Reed, Willis, **2:**297
Reed-Smith, Andre, **2:**335
Reese, Sara Lomax, **1:**35
Remember the Titans (film), **1:**101
Remnick, David, **1:**153
Renfro, Mel, **2:**297–98
Retton, Mary Lou, **1:**135
Reynolds, Butch, **2:**298
Rhetta, B. M., **1:**10
Rhoden, William, **2:**345
Rhodes, Ray, **2:**298–99
Rhodes, Ted, **1:**125; **2:**299, 328, 342, 377, 397
Rhodesia, **1:**69
Ribbs, Willy T., **2:**300
Rice, Jerry, **1:**62; **2:**301
Richardson, Nolan, **1:**71; **2:**301–2, 369
Richmond, Bill, **1:**43; **2:**238, 302–3
Rickard, Tex, **1:**117
Rickey, Branch, **1:**69, 105; **2:**309
Ricks, "Pappy," **1:**24
Riefenstahl, Leni, **1:**102
Riskiev, Rufat, **2:**343, 344
Ritchie, Andrew, **1:**153
Rizzuto, Phil, **2:**398
Roberts, Eric, **2:**261
Roberts, Randy, **1:**153
Roberts, Ric, **2:**303
Roberts, Robin, **2:**230
Robertson, Oscar, **1:**25, 35, 39, 40; **2:**266, 303–4
Robeson, Paul, **1:**24, 101, 106, 167; **2:**304–5, 396
Robinson, Bill A. "Bojangles," **2:**370
Robinson, David, **2:**306
Robinson, Eddie, **1:**71, 152; **2:**307, 404, 423
Robinson, Frank, **2:**308–9, 409
Robinson, Jackie, **1:**16, 17, 22, 24–25, 57, 69, 100–101, 154–55, 167; **2:**243, 309–10, 311, 341, 349
Robinson, Mack, **1:**7; **2:**310–11, 372
Robinson, Sugar Ray, **1:**16, 45, 100; **2:**311–12
Rockefeller, Nelson, **2:**421
Rocky films, **1:**100
Rodgers, Johnny, **2:**313–14
Rogan, Wilbur, **2:**315
Rogers, George, **2:**315–16

Rogosin, Donn, **1:**154
Roosevelt, Franklin D., **1:**69, 126
Roosevelt, Theodore, **1:**106
Rose, Pete, **2:**243
Rosenbloom, Carroll, **2:**273
Ross, Barney, **1:**11
Roxborough, John, **1:**217
Rozelle, Pete, **1:**107
Rozier, Mike, **2:**316
Ruck, Rob, **1:**154
Rudolph, Wilma, **1:**16, 47, 49, 77, 102, 152, 161, 167; **2:**233, 265, 317, 362, 372, 373, 414
Runyan, Damon, **2:**292
Russell, Bill, **1:**16, 17, 25, 69, 96, 187; **2:**266, 318–19, 368
Russell, Cazzie, **2:**297, 319–20
Ruth, Babe, **1:**1, 6, 175; **2:**229, 230
Rutigliano, Sam, **1:**148

Saddler, Sandy, **1:**45
Saitch, "Bruiser," **1:**24
Salow, Morris, **1:**110
Salzberg, Charles, **1:**155
Sampson, Charles, **2:**313
Sampson, Ralph, **2:**321
Samuel, Tony, **1:**72
Sanders, Barry, **2:**321
Sanders, Deion, **2:**322
Sanders of the River (film), **1:**101
Sanford, G. Foster, **2:**304
Saperstein, Abe, **1:**24, 71, 138, 143; **2:**358
Sarron, Petey, **1:**11
Sayers, Gale, **1:**101; **2:**279, 323
Schiffer, Frank, **1:**105
Schlichter, H. Walter "Slick," **2:**251, 401
Schmeling, Max, **1:**44, 217
Schorling, John, **1:**110–11
Schroeder, Joyce Tanac, **1:**135
Schwartzwalder, Ben, **1:**49
Schwarzenegger, Arnold, **2:**393
Schwikert, Tasha, **1:**135
Scotch Hills Country Club. *See* Shady Rest Golf and Country Club
Scott, Charlie, **2:**324
Scott, Wendell, **2:**300, 324–25
Scott, William L., **2:**330
See-Saw Circle, **2:**361
Segregation and integration, **2:**289
  auto racing, **1:**171; **2:**325
  baseball, **1:**22–23, 69, 100–101, 154–55, 200; **2:**229, 255, 287–88, 303, 304, 309–10, 341, 387, 401, 422
  basketball, **1:**69, 75, 138, 198, 214–15; **2:**258, 318
  bodybuilding, **2:**392–94
  bowling, **1:**42, 69; **2:**252
  boxing, **1:**43–44, 85, 174, 176, 178, 202; **2:**234, 408
  coaching, **2:**301–2
  at Coachman celebration, **1:**73
  college athletics, **1:**68, 103, 107, 130, 142, 151, 195, 208–9; **2:**229, 328, 396

Segregation and integration *(continued)*
  fencing, **1:**99
  football, **1:**107, 195, 212; **2:**237, 328, 330, 351, 374, 390
  golf, **1:**123–25, 130–31; **2:**299, 342
  Henderson and, **1:**145
  high school athletics, **1:**121
  historians on, **1:**154–55
  hockey, **1:**69, 165–66
  horse racing, **1:**159–60
  McLendon's efforts at integration, **2:**233–34
  Nunn and *Pittsburgh Courier*, **2:**261
  rodeo, **2:**312–13
  sportswriters and, **2:**344–45
  swimming, **2:**353–54
  tennis, **1:**10, 69; **2:**363–64, 391, 394
  track and field, **1:**76; **2:**256–57
Selke, Frank, **1:**165
Sepia (magazine), **1:**54
Sergeant Joe Louis on Tour (film), **1:**100
Shady Rest Golf and Country Club, **1:**124; **2:**325–26
Shanahan, Mike, **2:**326
Sharkey, Jack, **2:**409
Sharman, Bill, **1:**187; **2:**318
Shavers, Ernie, **1:**158
Shavlakadze, Robert, **2:**367
Shaw University, **1:**63, 150, 151
Sheffield, John, **1:**199
Shell, Art, **2:**326–27
Shell, Donnie, **2:**261
Shelton, Bryan, **2:**364
Shippen, John, Jr., **1:**124; **2:**326, 327
Shockley, William B., **2:**291
Showboat (film), **1:**101
Shriver, Pam, **1:**118
Shula, Don, **2:**412
Sidat-Singh, Wilmeth, **1:**24; **2:**327–28
Sifford, Charlie, **1:**125; **2:**328–29, 377, 397
Silas, Paul, **1:**72; **2:**329–30
Silhouettes (newsletter), **2:**253
Silva, Chris, **2:**354
Simmons, Ozzie, **2:**330
Simmons, Ron, **2:**419
Simms, Willie, **2:**330–31
Simons, William, **1:**155
Simpson, O. J., **1:**101, 147; **2:**331
Sims, Billy, **2:**321
Singletary, Mike, **2:**332
Sinnette, Calvin, **1:**155
Sirhan, Sirhan, **1:**132
Skelly, Jack, **1:**43, 85
Slaight, Allan, **2:**367
Slater, "Duke," **2:**332–33
Slaughter, Fred, **1:**6–7
Slavery, **2:**333–34
Slavin, Frank, **1:**174
Sloan, Ted, **2:**331
Slocum, Hilton, **1:**24
Slowe, Lucy Diggs, **2:**334–35, 363

GENERAL INDEX

Smith, Bruce, **2:**335–36
Smith, "Bubba," **1:**101; **2:**336–37
Smith, C. Lamont, **1:**7
Smith, Calvin, **1:**149
Smith, Charles. *See* Smith, "Bubba"
Smith, Emmitt, **2:**337–38
Smith, John, **2:**338–39, 391
Smith, Marshall, **2:**290
Smith, Ozzie, **2:**339
Smith, Ronald, **1:**155
Smith, Thomas, **1:**155
Smith, Tommie, **1:**29, 60, 70, 97; **2:**265, 266, 340, 372
Smith, Walker, Jr. *See* Robinson, Sugar Ray
Smith, "Wee Willie," **1:**24
Smith, Wendell, **1:**22, 69, 76; **2:**261, 341, 345
Smith, Will, **1:**100
Smith, Yvonne, **1:**156
Smythe, Conn, **1:**165
Snowden, Fred, **2:**341–42
Snyder, Jimmy "The Greek," **2:**291
Sol White's History of Colored Base Ball, **2:**401
Soldier's Story, A (film), **1:**101
Soria, Sixto, **2:**343, 344
Soul Train (television show), **2:**278–79
South Africa, **1:**69, 92
Southern Negro League. *See* Negro Southern League
Southwestern Athletic Conference, **1:**151
Southwestern Colored Cowboys Association, **2:**312–13
Sowell, Rick, **1:**199
Space Jam (film), **1:**102
Speedy, Walter, **1:**124
Spelman College, **1:**151
Spiller, Bill, **2:**328, 342, 397
Spinks, Leon, **1:**46, 158; **2:**260, 343
Spinks, Michael, **1:**46, 158; **2:**343–44
Spirit of the Times (newspaper), **1:**159
Spirit of Youth (film), **1:**100
Spivey, Donald, **1:**154, 155
Sports Illustrated (magazine), **1:**59; **2:**290–91
Sports Illustrated Women/Sport (magazine), **2:**355
Sportswriters, **2:**344–45
  Bostic, Joseph, **1:**41; **2:**345
  Cowans, Russ, **1:**76
  Lacy, Sam, **1:**199–200; **2:**345
  Nunn, William, Jr., **2:**260–61
  Nunn, William, Sr., **2:**261
  Roberts, Ric, **2:**303
  Smith, Wendell, **2:**341, 345
  Washington, Chester, **2:**389
  Wilson, Rollo, **2:**410
  Young, Andrew S. "Doc," **2:**421
  Young, Fay (Frank A.), **2:**422–23
Square Joe (film), **1:**176
St. Augustine's College, **1:**63
St. Julien, Marlon, **1:**160
St. Paul's College, **1:**63
Stadler, Joseph, **2:**264, 283
Stagg, Amos Alonzo, **2:**307
Stallone, Sylvester, **1:**100

Stallworth, Dave, **2:**346
Stallworth, John, **2:**261
Stanley, Marianne, **2:**236
Stargell, Willie, **2:**346–47
Starr, Bart, **1:**5, 201
Stearnes, Norman "Turkey," **2:**347, 395
Steinbrenner, George, **2:**411
Stent, Sophronia Pierce, **1:**99
Stereotypes
  in basketball films, **1:**102
  about black quarterbacks, **2:**241
  in boxing films, **1:**100
Stewart, Bobby, **2:**374
Stewart, Emanuel, **1:**144
Stewart, George, **2:**394
Stingley, Darryl, **2:**358
Stokes, Louise, **2:**282, 348
Stone, Oliver, **1:**101
Stone, Toni, **2:**348–49
Stovey, George, **2:**349–50
Strickland, Bill, **1:**7
Stringer, Vivian, **1:**71; **2:**350–51
Strode, Woody, **1:**101; **2:**351, 390
Strong, Nat, **1:**167, 168; **2:**251
Sullivan, James, **1:**88
Sullivan, John L., **1:**43, 85, 174
Super Bowl
  Adderley touchdown interception in, **1:**5
  establishment of, **1:**107
  Williams as first winning African-American quarterback, **2:**404
Supreme Court
  baseball's reserve clause challenge, **1:**103–4
  football and television contracts, **1:**107
Suttles, George "Mule," **2:**405
Swann, John, **2:**354
Swann, Lynn, **2:**352–53
Swoopes, Sheryl, **2:**267, 354–55

Taggert, Tomas D., Jr., **1:**200
Taliaferro, George, **2:**357
Tanner, James M., **2:**290
Tarkanian, Jerry, **1:**120
Tatum, Jack, **2:**357–58
Tatum, Reece "Goose," **1:**138, 143, 204; **2:**358
Taw, Len, **2:**264
Taylor, Charles, **2:**359
Taylor, John Baxter, **1:**151; **2:**264–65, 289, 359–60
Taylor, Lawrence, **2:**360–61
Taylor, Marshall "Major," **1:**16, 68; **2:**289, 360–61
Television. *See* Films and television
Temple, Ed, **1:**4, 71, 77, 161; **2:**233, 362, 373, 375, 414
Temple University, **1:**35
Tennessee A & I, **1:**151
Tennessee State University, **1:**152; **2:**354, 362, 414
Terrell, Kim, **1:**42
Terry, John, **2:**392
Theismann, Joe, **2:**280
Thomas, Debra, **2:**267, 364–65

Thomas, Frank, **2:**365
Thomas, Isiah, **2:**366–67
Thomas, John, **2:**367
Thomas, Thurman, **2:**335
Thomas, Wendell, **1:**199
Thompson, David, **2:**367–68
Thompson, John, **1:**98; **2:**368–69
Thomson, John, **1:**146
Thorpe, Jim, **1:**125; **2:**284
Tick Tick Tick (film), **1:**101
Tidye Pickett, **2:**265
Tiger, Dick, **1:**110
Title IX, **2:**414
Tittle, Y. A., **2:**273
Tolan, Eddie, **1:**126; **2:**289, 369–70, 371
Tomas, Enrico, **2:**393
Tomlinson, Nikki, **1:**99
Torrence, Gwen, **2:**370
Towering Inferno, The (film), **1:**101
Traveling All-Stars & Motor Kings (film), **1:**101
Tribune Independent (newspaper), **1:**76
Tricard, Louis Mead, **2:**362
Troye, Edward, **1:**159
Truman, Harry S., **1:**73
Tunnell, Emlen, **1:**16; **2:**374
Tunney, Gene, **1:**104; **2:**408, 409
Turner, Ted, **1:**2
Tuskegee Institute, **1:**2, 124, 150, 151, 152; **2:**363, 414
Tygiel, Jules, **1:**153, 155; **2:**345
Tyler, Dorothy, **1:**73
Tyson, Cicely, **1:**102
Tyson, Mike, **1:**46; **2:**344, 374–75
Tyus, Wyomia, **2:**362, 372, 373, 375–76

Ueberroth, Peter, **1:**92
Unitas, Johnny, **2:**243
United Golfer (magazine), **2:**377
United Golfers Association, **1:**93, 124, 131; **2:**299, 326, 328, 377, 397
United States Colored Golfers Association. *See* United Golfers Association
United States Golf Association (USGA), **1:**125, 130–31; **2:**377
United States Lawn Tennis Association (USLTA), **1:**10, 121; **2:**363, 394
United States League (Negro baseball), **1:**129
United States Tennis Association, **2:**364
Unseld, Wes, **2:**378
Upshaw, Gene, **2:**326, 378–79
U.S. Golf Association, **2:**327
USA Track and Field, **2:**371
Uzcudun, Paolino, **2:**409

Vandenberg, Wayne, **1:**28
Vann, Robert L., **2:**261, 389
Vaughn, Govoner, **1:**173
Veeck, Bill, **1:**86, 205
Venable, Charlie, **1:**42
Vertinsky, Patricia, **1:**156
Virginia State University, **1:**63, 151

Virginia Union University, **1:**63, 150
Vitale, John, **1:**213

Wake-Robin Golf Club, **1:**124; **2:**383
Walcott, "Jersey Joe," **1:**45, 66
Walcott, Joe, **2:**383–84
Waldorf, Lyn, **1:**176–77
Walker, Herschel, **2:**267, 384–85
Walker, Leroy, **2:**373, 385–86
Walker, Mel, **2:**386
Walker, Moses Fleetwood, **1:**22, 68; **2:**350, 386–87
Walker, Weldy, **2:**387
Wallace, Coley, **1:**100
Wallace, Nunc, **1:**85
Walsh, Christy, **1:**6, 16
Walsh, Stella, **1:**200
Walter, Mickey, **1:**104
Ward, Charlie, **2:**387–88
Warfield, Paul, **2:**388–89
Warmund, Joram, **1:**155
Warner, Ed, **1:**25
Warner, Pop, **2:**307
Washington, Allen, **1:**63
Washington, Benjamin, **1:**168
Washington, Booker T., **1:**2
Washington, Chester, **2:**389
Washington, Denzel, **1:**100, 101, 102
Washington, Gene, **2:**389–90
Washington, Jim, **1:**153
Washington, Kenny, **2:**351, 390
Washington, MaliVai, **2:**364
Washington, Marian, **2:**415
Washington, Ora, **2:**363, 391
Washington, Rudy, **1:**34
Washington Tribune (newspaper), **1:**200
Watkins, Fenwich, **1:**24
Watts, Bobby, **1:**137
Watts, Quincy, **2:**339, 391–92
Wave Community Newspapers, **2:**389
WCBM, **1:**41
Weathers, Carl, **1:**100, 101
Weider, Joe, **2:**393
Weir, Reginald, **2:**363, 394
Wells, Melvin, **2:**393
Wells, Willie, **2:**395
Wepner, Chuck, **1:**214
Wertz, Vic, **2:**229
West, Charlie, **2:**396
West, Jerry, **1:**39; **2:**297, 304
West, Mae, **1:**179
Westbrook, Peter, **1:**99; **2:**267
Wheeler, Flex, **2:**393
Wheeler, Howard, **1:**125; **2:**328, 377, 397
Wheeler, John N., **1:**16
When We Were Kings (documentary), **1:**100
Whitaker, Pernell, **2:**266
White, Bill, **2:**397–98
White, Charles, **1:**9–10
White, Jacob, **2:**287
White, Jo Jo, **2:**398–99

GENERAL INDEX

White Men Can't Jump (film), **1:**102
White, Morgan, **1:**135
White, Reggie, **2:**399–400
White, Sherman, **2:**400
White, Sol, **1:**168; **2:**400–401
White, Willye, **2:**228, 401–2
Whitfield, Fred, **2:**313
Whitfield, Mal, **2:**402
Wicks, Sidney, **2:**403
Wiggins, David, **1:**154, 155–56
Wilberforce University, **1:**124, 150
Wilbon, Michael, **2:**345
Wiley College, **1:**150
Wilkerson, John, **1:**118
Wilkes, Keith, **1:**102
Wilkie, Wendell, **1:**202
Wilkins, Lenny, **1:**72
Wilkinson, G. C., **1:**168
Wilkinson, J. L., **2:**252, 254
Wilkinson, John F. N., **1:**10
Willard, Jess, **1:**44, 100
William Morris Agency, **1:**6
Williams, Archie, **1:**7; **2:**372, 403
Williams, Billy Dee, **1:**101
Williams, Bobby, **1:**72
Williams, Charles H., **1:**63
Williams, Doug, **2:**307, 404
Williams, Hank, **1:**24
Williams, Henry L., **2:**225
Williams, Ike, **1:**45; **2:**404–5
Williams, Joseph "Smokey", **2:**405
Williams, Linda, **1:**156
Williams, Lucinda, **1:**161; **2:**228
Williams, Serena, **1:**102; **2:**364, 406, 407
Williams, Venus, **1:**102; **2:**364, 406, 407
Williamson, Fred, **1:**101
Willingham, Tyrone, **1:**72
Willis, Bill, **2:**246, 407–8
Willis, Willie, **1:**42
Wills, Harry, **1:**44, 176; **2:**408–9
Wills, Maury, **2:**409
Wills Moody, Helen, **2:**363, 391
Wilma (television film), **1:**102
Wilson, Clyde, **1:**42
Wilson, Rollo, **2:**410
Wilson, Tome, **2:**255
Winfield, Dave, **2:**410–11
Winkfield, Jimmy, **1:**160; **2:**411–12
Winkfield, Robert, **1:**160
Winslow, Kellen, **2:**412–13
Winston-Salem University, **1:**63
Winter, Tex, **1:**39
Witt, Katarina, **2:**267, 365
Womble, Warren, **1:**39
Women, **2:**413–14
   Adams, Lucinda, **1:**4–5
   Ashford, Evelyn, **1:**15
   biographies of, **1:**153
   Black Women in Sports Foundation, **1:**35
   Brisco-Hooks, Valerie, **1:**46–48

Women *(continued)*
   Coachman, Alice, **1:**72–74
   Daniels, Isabelle, **1:**77
   Dawes, Dominique, **1:**80
   De Frantz, Anita, **1:**81–82
   Devers, Gail, **1:**82–83
   Edwards, Teresa, **1:**92–93
   Faggs, Mae, **1:**99
   Garrison, Zina, **1:**118
   Gibson, Althea, **1:**120–21
   Green, Tina Sloan, **1:**199
   Gregory, Ann, **1:**130–31
   Hightower, Stephanie, **1:**146–47
   historians on, **1:**156
   historically black colleges and universities, **1:**152
   Hudson, Martha, **1:**161
   Hymes, Lula Mae, **1:**162–63
   Jones, Barbara, **1:**185–86
   Jones, Marion, **1:**188
   Joyner-Kersee, Jackie, **1:**191–93
   Lane, Betty Jean, **1:**200
   Leslie, Lisa, **1:**207–8
   Manley, Effa, **2:**223
   Manning-Mims, Madeline, **2:**224–25
   Matthews, Margaret, **2:**227–28
   McDaniel, Mildred, **2:**231
   McGee, Pam, **2:**231–32
   McGuire, Edith, **2:**232–33
   Miller, Cheryl, **2:**236
   Montgomery, Eleanor, **2:**240
   Patterson, Mickey, **2:**277–78
   Pickett, Tidye, **2:**282–83
   Reed, Vivian Brown, **1:**49
   Rudolph, Wilma, **2:**317
   Slowe, Lucy Diggs, **2:**334–35
   Stokes, Louise, **2:**348
   Torrence, Gwen, **2:**370
   Tyus, Wyomia, **2:**375–76
   Washington, Ora, **2:**391
   White, Willye, **2:**401–2
Women's Basketball Hall of Fame
   Stringer, Vivian, **2:**350–51
Women's International Bowling Congress, **1:**42; **2:**252
Wood, Wilbur, **1:**23
Woodard, Lynette, **2:**267
Wooden, John, **1:**3, 123, 183; **2:**258
Woodman, Joe, **1:**201
Woodruff, John, **1:**7; **2:**371–72, 416
Woods, Eldrick "Tiger," **1:**102, 125; **2:**416–17
Woodson, Carter G., **1:**153
Woodward, Lynette, **2:**415–16
World Boxing Council, **1:**46
Worthy, James, **2:**418
Wright, Archibald Lee. *See* Moore, Archie
Wright, Ernie, **2:**252
Wright, Stan, **2:**373
Wright, William H., **1:**10

Xavier University, **1:**151

Yancey, Bill, **1**:24
Yancey, Joseph J., **2**:256
Yang, C. K., **1**:183
YMCA (Young Men's Christian Associations), **1**:99
Yoshida, Toshiaki, **2**:382
Young, Andrew S. "Doc," **1**:153; **2**:421
Young, Buddy, **2**:421–22
Young, Fay (Frank A.), **1**:76; **2**:345, 422–23
Young, Kevin, **2**:339
Young, Monroe, **2**:255

Young, Whitney, **1**:144
Younger, Paul "Tank," **2**:423
YWCA (Young Women's Christian Associations), **1**:99

Zang, David W., **1**:153
Zouski, Steve, **1**:109
Zuk, Bob, **2**:347
Zurita, Juan, **2**:405

SPORTS INDEX

Auto racing, **2:**324–25
  Jack, "Rajo," **1:**171
  Ribbs, Willy T., **2:**300
  segregation and integration, **1:**171; **2:**325

Baseball, **1:**21–23
  Aaron, Hank, **1:**1–2
  American Negro League, **2:**253
  Ashford, Emmett, **1:**13–14
  Banks, Ernie, **1:**19
  Baylor, Don, **1:**27, 72
  Bell, James "Cool Papa," **1:**22, 31–32
  Bolden, Edward, **1:**37–38
  Bonds, Barry, **1:**38–39
  Brock, Louis, **1:**48
  Campanella, Roy, **1:**57–58
  Charleston, Oscar, **1:**22, 67
  coaching and managerial positions, **1:**23, 72
  Doby, Larry, **1:**86
  East-West All-Star Game, **1:**22, 129; **2:**252
  East-West League, **2:**253, 254
  Eastern Colored League, **1:**91; **2:**253, 254
  films about, **1:**100–101
  Flood, Curt, **1:**103–4
  Foster, Rube, **1:**22, 110–11
  Gibson, Bob, **1:**121–22
  Gibson, Josh, **1:**22, 122
  Grant, Frank, **1:**127
  Greenlee, Gus, **1:**22, 129
  Griffey, Ken, Jr., **1:**132–33
  Gwynn, Tony, **1:**134
  Henderson, Rickey, **1:**146
  historically black colleges and universities, **1:**150, 151–52
  Irvin, Monte, **1:**169
  Jackson, Bo, **1:**171–72
  Jackson, Reggie, **1:**175
  Johnson, William "Judy," **1:**184
  League of Colored Base Ball Players, **1:**203
  Leonard, Buck, **1:**205–6
  Lloyd, John Henry, **1:**215–16
  Mackey, Biz, **2:**219
  Manley, Effa, **2:**223
  Matthews, William Clarence, **2:**228–29
  Mays, Willie, **2:**229–30
  McCovey, Willie, **2:**230
  Morgan, Joe, **2:**243–44
  Murray, Eddie, **2:**248
  National Association of Colored Base Ball Clubs of the United States and Cuba, **2:**251
  Negro American League, **1:**22; **2:**252–53, 255

Baseball (continued)
  Negro leagues, **1:**110–11, 153–54
  Negro National League, **1:**22, 37, 41, 54, 67, 91, 111, 129, 169; **2:**223, 252, 253, 254, 255, 261, 422
  Negro Southern League, **2:**253, 254, 255
  Negro World Series, **1:**38
  O'Neil, Buck, **2:**269–70
  Paige, Satchel, **2:**275
  Posey, Cum, **2:**285–86
  Puckett, Kirby, **2:**286–87
  Radcliffe, Ted, **2:**292–93
  reserve clause challenge of Curt Flood, **1:**103–4
  Robinson, Frank, **2:**308–9
  Robinson, Jackie, **1:**17, 22, 57, 69, 100–101
  Rogan, Wilbur, **2:**315
  Sanders, Deion, **2:**322
  segregation and integration, **1:**22–23, 69, 100–101, 154–55, 200; **2:**229, 255, 287–88, 303, 304, 309–10, 341, 387, 401, 422
  Smith, Ozzie, **2:**339
  sportswriters and, **2:**345
  Stargell, Willie, **2:**346–47
  Stearnes, Norman "Turkey," **2:**347
  Stone, Toni, **2:**348–49
  Stovey, George, **2:**349–50
  Thomas, Frank, **2:**365
  Walker, Moses Fleetwood, **1:**22; **2:**386–87
  Wells, Willie, **2:**395
  White, Bill, **2:**397–98
  White, Sol, **2:**400–401
  Williams, Joseph "Smokey," **2:**405
  Wills, Maury, **2:**409
  Winfield, Dave, **2:**410–11
  See also Most Valuable Player (major league baseball); National Baseball Hall of Fame

Basketball, **1:**23–26
  Abdul-Jabbar, Kareem, **1:**3–4
  Archibald, Nate, **1:**11
  Barkley, Charles, **1:**19–20
  Barksdale, Don, **1:**20–21
  Baylor, Elgin, **1:**28
  Bellamy, Walter, **1:**32–33
  Bing, Dave, **1:**33
  Boozer, Bob, **1:**39–40
  Brown, Roger, **1:**51
  Bryant, Kobe, **1:**52–53
  Chamberlain, Wilt, **1:**64–65
  Chaney, John, **1:**65–66
  Clifton, Nat "Sweetwater," **1:**71
  coaching and managerial positions, **1:**72
  Cooper, Chuck, **1:**25, 69, 75

SPORTS INDEX

Basketball *(continued)*
   Dantley, Adrian, **1**:77–78
   Dukes, Walter, **1**:89
   Edwards, Teresa, **1**:92–93
   Embry, Wayne, **1**:95–96
   Erving, Julius, **1**:96
   Ewing, Patrick, **1**:97–98
   films about, **1**:101–2
   Ford, Phil, **1**:108
   Gaines, Clarence "Bighouse," **1**:115
   Gervin, George, **1**:119–20
   Gibson, Bob, **1**:121–22
   Gilmore, Artis, **1**:122–23
   Greer, Hal, **1**:130
   Gregory, George, Jr., **1**:131
   Harlem Globetrotters, **1**:24, 25, 64, 71, 89, 121, 137–38, 143, 173, 204–5; **2**:358, 415
   Harlem Magicians, **1**:75, 143
   Hawkins, Connie, **1**:140–41
   Hayes, Elvin, **1**:142
   Haynes, Marques, **1**:142–43
   Haywood, Spencer, **1**:143–44
   Henderson, Edwin Bancroft, **1**:23
   Hill, Grant, **1**:148–49
   historically black colleges and universities, **1**:151
   Jackson, Mannie, **1**:173
   Johnson, Magic, **1**:16, 26
   Johnson, Robert L., **1**:183–84
   Jones, K. C., **1**:187
   Jones, Sam, **1**:188–89
   Jones, Wali, **1**:189–90
   Jordan, Michael, **1**:26, 190–91
   King, William "Dolly," **1**:197–98
   Lanier, Bob, **1**:202–3
   Lemon, Meadowlark, **1**:203–5
   Leslie, Lisa, **1**:207–8
   Lloyd, Earl, **1**:214–15
   Malone, Moses, **2**:222–23
   Manning, Danny, **2**:224
   McGee, Pam, **2**:231–32
   McLendon, John, **2**:233–34
   Miller, Cheryl, **2**:236
   Monroe, Earl, **2**:239–40
   Murphy, Calvin, **2**:246–47
   New York Renaissance Five, **1**:24; **2**:257–58
   Olajuwon, Hakeem, **2**:263–64
   Olympic Games, **2**:266
   O'Neal, Shaquille, **2**:268–69
   Posey, Cum, **2**:285–86
   Raveling, George, **2**:295–96
   Reed, Willis, **2**:297
   Richardson, Nolan, **2**:301–2
   Robertson, Oscar, **2**:303–4
   Robinson, David, **2**:306
   Russell, Bill, **2**:318–19
   Russell, Cazzie, **2**:319–20
   Scott, Charlie, **2**:324
   segregation and integration, **1**:69, 75, 138, 198, 214–15; **2**:258, 318
   Sidat-Singh, Wilmeth, **2**:327–28

Basketball *(continued)*
   Silas, Paul, **2**:329–30
   slam dunk, **1**:141
   Snowden, Fred, **2**:341–42
   Stallworth, Dave, **2**:346
   Stringer, Vivian, **2**:350–51
   Swoopes, Sheryl, **2**:354–55
   Tatum, Reece "Goose," **2**:358
   Thompson, David, **2**:367–68
   Thompson, John, **2**:368–69
   Unseld, Wes, **2**:378
   Ward, Charlie, **2**:387–88
   Washington, Ora, **2**:391
   White, Jo Jo, **2**:398–99
   White, Sherman, **2**:400
   Wicks, Sidney, **2**:403
   Woodward, Lynette, **2**:415–16
   Worthy, James, **2**:418
   See also All-Americans (college basketball); Most Valuable Player (American Basketball Association); Most Valuable Player (National Basketball Association); Most Valuable Player (Women's National Basketball Association); Naismith Memorial Basketball Hall of Fame
Bobsled, **1**:119; **2**:385
Bodybuilding, **2**:392–94
Bowling, **1**:42
   National Bowling Association, **2**:252
   segregation and integration, **1**:42, 69; **2**:252
Boxing, **1**:43–46
   Ali, Muhammad, **1**:8–9, 45–46
   Armstrong, Henry, **1**:11–12, 45
   Charles, Ezzard, **1**:45, 66
   Dixon, George, **1**:43, 85–86
   Ellis, Jimmy, **1**:95
   films about, **1**:100
   Flowers, Tiger, **1**:44, 104
   Foreman, George, **1**:46, 109
   Foster, Bob, **1**:46, 110
   Frazier, Joe, **1**:46, 112
   Gans, Joe, **1**:44, 117
   Golden Gloves, **1**:44, 45
   Hagler, "Marvelous" Marvin, **1**:46, 137
   Hearns, Thomas, **1**:46, 144
   Holmes, Larry, **1**:46, 158
   Jackson, Peter, **1**:173–75
   Jeannette, Joe, **1**:176
   Johnson, Jack, **1**:44, 178–79
   King, Don, **1**:196–97
   Langford, Sam, **1**:201–2
   Leonard, Sugar Ray, **1**:46, 206–7
   Lewis, John Henry, **1**:210–11
   Liston, Sonny, **1**:45, 213–14
   Louis, Joe, **1**:44, 45, 217
   McVey, Sam, **2**:234
   Molineaux, Tom, **2**:237–38
   Moore, Archie, **1**:45; **2**:241–42
   Norton, Ken, **2**:260
   Olympic Games, **2**:266
   Patterson, Floyd, **1**:45; **2**:276–77

SPORTS INDEX

Boxing *(continued)*
    Richmond, Bill, **2:**302–3
    Robinson, Sugar Ray, **1:**45; **2:**311–12
    segregation and integration, **1:**43–44, 85, 174, 176, 178, 202; **2:**234, 408
    slavery and, **2:**334
    Spinks, Leon, **1:**46; **2:**343
    Spinks, Michael, **2:**343–44
    Tyson, Mike, **1:**46; **2:**374–75
    Walcott, Joe, **2:**383
    Williams, Ike, **2:**404–5
    Wills, Harry, **2:**408–9
    See also Boxing Hall of Fame; International Boxing Hall of Fame

Cycling, **2:**361–62

Fencing, **1:**99
Figure skating, **2:**364–65
Football, **1:**105–8
    Abbott, Cleveland, **1:**2
    Adderley, Herb, **1:**5
    Allen, Marcus, **1:**9–10
    Alley-Oop pass, **2:**273
    Bass, Dick, **1:**26–27
    Bell, Bill, **1:**29–30
    Bell, Bobby, **1:**30–31
    Blount, Mel, **1:**36–37
    Brown, Jim, **1:**49–50
    Brown, Larry, **1:**50–51
    Brown, Roosevelt, **1:**52
    Bullock, Matthew, **1:**53–54
    Campbell, Earl, **1:**58–59
    Carmichael, Harold, **1:**61
    Caroline, J. C., **1:**61–62
    Carter, Cris, **1:**62–63
    Davis, Ernie, **1:**78–79
    Dickerson, Eric, **1:**83–84
    Drew, Charles, **1:**87–88
    Eller, Carl, **1:**94–95
    films about, **1:**101
    Flippin, George, **1:**102–3
    Follis, Charles, **1:**105
    free agent compensation, **2:**273
    Gaither, Jake, **1:**115–16
    Galimore, Willie, **1:**116
    Garrett, Mike, **1:**117–18
    Gault, Willie, **1:**119
    Gray, Edward, **1:**128
    Greene, Joe, **1:**128–29
    Grier, Rosey, **1:**132
    Harris, Franco, **1:**139
    Hayes, Bob, **1:**141–42
    Hill, Calvin, **1:**147–48
    Hines, Jim, **1:**149
    historically black colleges and universities, **1:**150, 152
    Holland, Jerome Brud, **1:**157
    Jackson, Bo, **1:**171–72
    Jackson, Levi, **1:**172

Football *(continued)*
    Jefferson, Bernie, **1:**176–77
    Johnson, John Henry, **1:**179
    Jones, David "Deacon," **1:**186
    Kelly, Leroy, **1:**195
    Kemp, Ray, **1:**195–96
    Keyes, Leroy, **1:**196
    Lane, Dick, **1:**201
    LeVias, Jerry, **1:**208–9
    Lewis, William Henry, **1:**211–12
    Lipscomb, Gene "Big Daddy," **1:**213
    Little, Floyd, **1:**214
    Lott, Ronnie, **1:**216
    Mackey, John, **2:**220–21
    Marshall, Bob, **2:**225–26
    Marshall, Jim, **2:**226
    Matson, Ollie, **2:**227
    Mitchell, Bobby, **2:**237
    Monk, Art, **2:**238–39
    Moon, Warren, **2:**240–41
    Moore, Lenny, **2:**242–43
    Motley, Marion, **2:**245–46
    Nehemiah, Renaldo, **2:**256
    Newsome, Ozzie, **2:**259
    origins of, **1:**105–6
    Owens, R. C., **2:**272–73
    Parker, Jim, **2:**276
    Payton, Walter, **2:**278–79
    Pearson, Drew, **2:**279–80
    Perkins, Don, **2:**281
    Perry, Joe, **2:**282
    Pollard, Fritz, **2:**283–84
    Rashad, Ahmad, **2:**293–95
    Reed, Dwight, **2:**296
    Renfro, Mel, **2:**297–98
    reserve clause challenge of John Mackey, **2:**220
    Rhodes, Ray, **2:**298–99
    Rice, Jerry, **2:**301
    Robinson, Eddie, **2:**307
    Rodgers, Johnny, **2:**313–14
    Rozier, Mike, **2:**316
    Sanders, Barry, **2:**321
    Sanders, Deion, **2:**322
    Sayers, Gale, **1:**101; **2:**323
    segregation and integration, **1:**107, 195, 212; **2:**237, 328, 330, 351, 374, 390
    semiprofessional, **1:**106
    Shell, Art, **2:**326–27
    Sidat-Singh, Wilmeth, **2:**327–28
    Simmons, Ozzie, **2:**330
    Simpson, O. J., **2:**331
    Singletary, Mike, **2:**332
    Slater, "Duke," **2:**332–33
    Smith, Bruce, **2:**335–36
    Smith, Emmitt, **2:**337–38
    Strode, Woody, **2:**351
    Swann, Lynn, **2:**352–53
    Taliaferro, George, **2:**357
    Tatum, Jack, **2:**357–58
    Taylor, Charles, **2:**359

SPORTS INDEX

Football *(continued)*
   Taylor, Lawrence, **2:**360–61
   Tunnell, Emlen, **2:**374
   Upshaw, Gene, **2:**378–79
   Walker, Herschel, **2:**384–85
   Warfield, Paul, **2:**388–89
   Washington, Gene, **2:**389–90
   Washington, Kenny, **2:**390
   West, Charlie, **2:**396
   White, Reggie, **2:**399–400
   Williams, Doug, **2:**404
   Willis, Bill, **2:**407–8
   Winslow, Kellen, **2:**412–13
   Young, Buddy, **2:**421–22
   Younger, Paul "Tank," **2:**423
   See also All-Americans (college football); Heisman Trophy; Most Valuable Player (National Football League); Professional Football Hall of Fame; Super Bowl

Golf, **1:**123–25
   caddies, **1:**93, 123–24
   Elder, Lee, **1:**93–94
   films about, **1:**102
   Gregory, Ann, **1:**130–31
   Mapledale Country Club, **2:**377
   Peete, Calvin, **2:**280–81
   Rhodes, Ted, **2:**299
   segregation and integration, **1:**123–25, 130–31; **2:**299, 342
   Shady Rest Golf and Country Club, **1:**124; **2:**325–26
   Shippen, John, Jr., **1:**124; **2:**327
   Sifford, Charlie, **2:**328–29
   Spiller, Bill, **2:**342
   tee invention for, **1:**124
   Wake-Robin Golf Club, **1:**124, 383
   Wheeler, Howard, **2:**397
   Woods, Eldrick "Tiger," **1:**125; **2:**416–17
Gymnastics, **1:**134–35
   Dawes, Dominique, **1:**80, 135
   Olympic Games, **2:**267

Handball, **2:**263
Hockey. *See* Ice hockey
Horse racing, **1:**159–60
   American style of, **2:**331
   Lewis, Oliver, **1:**211
   Murphy, Isaac, **2:**247–48
   race result form development, **1:**211
   segregation and integration, **1:**159–60
   Simms, Willie, **2:**330–31
   slavery and, **2:**334
   Winkfield, Jimmy, **2:**411–12

Ice hockey, **1:**165–66
   Dorrington, Arthur, **1:**69, 87
   O'Ree, Willie, **2:**270
   segregation and integration, **1:**69, 165–66

Lacrosse, **1:**199

Pedestrian racing, **1:**139–40

Race car driving. *See* Auto racing
Rodeo, **1:**36; **2:**312–13
Rowing, **2:**333–34
   De Frantz, Anita, **1:**81–82
Rugby, **1:**105

Swimming, **2:**267, 353–54

Tennis, **2:**363–64
   American Tennis Association, **1:**10
   Ashe, Arthur, Jr., **1:**12–13, 16, 17, 102; **2:**363, 364
   films about, **1:**102
   Garrison, Zina, **1:**118
   Gibson, Althea, **1:**10, 12, 16, 69, 118, 120–21; **2:**363–64
   segregation and integration, **1:**10, 69; **2:**363–64, 391, 394
   Slowe, Lucy Diggs, **2:**334–35
   Washington, Ora, **2:**391
   Weir, Reginald, **2:**394
   Williams, Serena, **1:**102; **2:**406
   Williams, Venus, **1:**102; **2:**407
   See also International Tennis Hall of Fame
Track and Field, **2:**371–73
   Abbott, Cleveland, **1:**2
   Adams, Lucinda, **1:**4–5
   Albritton, David, **1:**7–8
   amateurism rules challenged by Nehemiah, **2:**256
   Ashford, Evelyn, **1:**15
   Beamon, Bob, **1:**28–29
   Borican, John, **1:**40
   Boston, Ralph, **1:**41–42
   Brisco-Hooks, Valerie, **1:**46–48
   Butler, Sol, **1:**55
   Calhoun, Lee, **1:**57
   Campbell, Milt, **1:**59
   Carlos, John, **1:**60
   coaches in, **2:**373
   Coachman, Alice, **1:**72–74
   Corbitt, Ted, **1:**75–76
   Daniels, Isabelle, **1:**77
   Devers, Gail, **1:**82–83
   Dillard, Harrison, **1:**84–85
   Drew, Howard, **1:**88
   drug-testing challenge of Butch Reynolds, **2:**298
   Faggs, Mae, **1:**99
   films about, **1:**102
   Gault, Willie, **1:**119
   Gordon, Ed, Jr., **1:**125–26
   Gourdin, Ned, **1:**126–27
   Griffith-Joyner, Florence, **1:**133
   Hayes, Bob, **1:**141–42
   Hightower, Stephanie, **1:**146–47
   Hines, Jim, **1:**149
   historically black colleges and universities, **1:**151, 152

Track and Field *(continued)*
    Holman, Steve, **1:**157–58
    Hubbard, William Dehart, **1:**161
    Hudson, Martha, **1:**161
    Hymes, Lula Mae, **1:**162–63
    Johnson, Cornelius, **1:**177–78
    Johnson, Michael, **1:**181–82
    Johnson, Rafer, **1:**182–83
    Jones, Barbara, **1:**185–86
    Jones, Hayes, **1:**186–87
    Jones, Marion, **1:**188
    Joyner-Kersee, Jackie, **1:**191–93
    Lane, Betty Jean, **1:**200
    Lewis, Carl, **1:**209–10
    LuValle, James, **1:**218
    Manning-Mims, Madeline, **2:**224–25
    Matson, Ollie, **2:**227
    Matthews, Margaret, **2:**227–28
    McDaniel, Mildred, **2:**231
    McGuire, Edith, **2:**232–33
    Metcalfe, Ralph, **2:**235
    Milburn, Rod, **2:**235–36
    Montgomery, Eleanor, **2:**240
    Moses, Edwin, **2:**244
    Nehemiah, Renaldo, **2:**256
    New York Pioneer Club, **1:**76
    O'Brien, Dan, **2:**263
    Olympic, **2:**264–66, 371–73
    Owens, Jesse, **2:**271–72
    Patterson, Mickey, **2:**277–78
    Pickett, Tidye, **2:**282–83
    Poage, George, **2:**283
    Pollard, Fritz, Jr., **2:**284–85

Track and Field *(continued)*
    Reed, Vivian Brown, **1:**49
    Reynolds, Butch, **2:**298
    Robinson, Mack, **2:**310–11
    Rudolph, Wilma, **2:**317
    segregation and integration, **1:**76; **2:**256–57
    slavery and, **2:**334
    Smith, John, **2:**338–39
    Smith, Tommie, **2:**340
    Stokes, Louise, **2:**348
    Taylor, John Baxter, **2:**359–60
    Temple, Ed, **2:**362
    Thomas, John, **2:**367
    Tolan, Eddie, **2:**369–70
    Torrence, Gwen, **2:**370
    Tyus, Wyomia, **2:**375–76
    Walker, Leroy, **2:**385–86
    Walker, Mel, **2:**386
    Watts, Quincy, **2:**391–92
    White, Willye, **2:**401–2
    Whitfield, Mal, **2:**402
    Williams, Archie, **2:**403
    Woodruff, John, **2:**416
    See also National Track and Field Hall of Fame

Ultramarathon running, **1:**75–76
    See also Pedestrian racing

Volleyball, **1:**65; **2:**381–82

Weightlifting, **2:**392, 394
    Davis, John Henry, **1:**79
Wrestling, **2:**418–19

Ref.
GV
583
.A567

2004
v.2